Approaches to Teaching Dante's *Divine Comedy*

Second Edition

Approaches to Teaching Dante's *Divine Comedy*

Second Edition

Edited by

Christopher Kleinhenz

and

Kristina Olson

Modern Language Association of America
New York   2020

MLA and the MODERN LANGUAGE ASSOCIATION are trademarks owned by
the Modern Language Association of America. For information about obtaining
permission to reprint material from MLA book publications, send your request
by mail (see address below) or e-mail (permissions@mla.org).

Library of Congress Cataloging-in-Publication Data

Names: Kleinhenz, Christopher, editor. | Olson, Kristina, editor.
Title: Approaches to teaching Dante's divine comedy / edited by Christopher
    Kleinhenz and Kristina Olson.
Description: Second edition. | New York : Modern Language Association
    of America, 2020. | Series: Approaches to teaching world literature,
    1059–1133 ; 163 | Includes bibliographical references.
Identifiers: LCCN 2019039483 (print) | LCCN 2019039484 (ebook)
ISBN 9781603294690 (cloth) | ISBN 9781603294270 (paperback)
ISBN 9781603294287 (EPUB) | ISBN 9781603294294 (Kindle)
Subjects: LCSH: Dante Alighieri, 1265–1321. Divina commedia. | Dante Alighieri,
    1265–1321—Study and teaching. | Epic poetry, Italian—Study and teaching.
Classification: LCC PQ4371 .A6 2020 (print) | LCC PQ4371 (ebook) |
    DDC 851/.1—dc23
LC record available at https://lccn.loc.gov/2019039483
LC ebook record available at https://lccn.loc.gov/2019039484

Approaches to Teaching World Literature 163
ISSN 1059-1133

Cover illustration:
Joseph Anton Koch, *L'Enfer* (*Divine Comedie*) de Dante:
Detail representant l'ecrivain. Casino Massimo, Rome, fresco.
Photo © S. Bianchetti / Bridgeman Images.

POD 2021 (first printing)

Published by The Modern Language Association of America
85 Broad Street, Suite 500, New York, New York 10004-2434
www.mla.org

*We dedicate this volume
to all teachers and students of Dante,
as well as to Marge and to Michael
for their unfailing devotion and assistance
to two lifelong students of Dante.*

CONTENTS

PREFACE

The teaching of Dante's *Divine Comedy* and Dante studies in general does not exist in a vacuum. Our current thinking about the poem has its origin some seven centuries ago in the earliest commentators and relies on the countless editions, translations, critical studies, and related materials that, over the centuries, have formed the scholarly edifice on which we now stand. In many ways we are today, to use the phrase attributed to Bernard of Chartres in the twelfth century by John of Salisbury in his *Metalogicon*, like "dwarfs perched on the shoulders of giants" (176). We look, however, both back to the wisdom and achievements of the past and forward to new acquisitions of knowledge and scientific investigations that in recent years have guided our interpretations and appreciation of Dante's text.

Given that this volume complements the 1982 edition, *Approaches to Teaching Dante's* Divine Comedy, edited by Carole Slade, we do not include references to the many valuable works mentioned in that volume, which remains a fundamental contribution to discussions of more traditionally focused Dante pedagogy. Indeed, we suggest that, for a full picture of pedagogical approaches to Dante's *Comedy*, readers should consider the essays and recommendations contained in both volumes. Thus, we provide here information on the many significant contributions and advances made over the past thirty-five years. These include the ascendance of new critical, cultural, and pedagogical trends that shape current teaching practices of Dante's *Comedy*, approaches informed by new research in material philology, cultural studies, and literary theory, as well as by the abundance of digital humanities projects that illuminate both Dante's poem and the frequent presence of it in contemporary popular culture.

T. S. Eliot famously stated, "Dante and Shakespeare divide the modern world between them; there is no third" (*Dante* 46). Though Eliot offered this comment in order to make a specific comparison between the two poets, it is a statement that can be profitably expanded to explore the status of Dante studies and pedagogy in our postmodern, or "supermodern" times.[1] As evinced by the responses to our questionnaire, Dante's poem continues to dominate our curricular times. We found the breadth and depth of Dante pedagogy to be great, with a selection of more traditional approaches alongside more innovative ones; this diversity takes place in an era when the study of the humanities, and of literature itself, is the subject of much debate and the language and literature programs that house such courses on Dante are under scrutiny. Yet, ours is also a time when we have seen—and will continue to see—a burgeoning interest in the literary and artistic *fortuna* of the *Divine Comedy* in both traditional and nontraditional forms, from the analog to the digital. As much as humanistic study can be said to be in crisis within academe, it should also be noted that courses on Dante continue to be widely taught at all levels: high school, under-graduate, and graduate.

This volume is firmly based on an interest in pedagogy and focuses on how to make Dante come alive for high school and college students through a wide range of pedagogical practices, with the many resources available for teaching Dante today. We intend also to bridge the distances between both specialist discourse in the field and more innovative and dynamic approaches to teaching informed by fields outside of Dante studies and the wide array of classrooms where Dante is taught.

Dante is for everyone, and our contributors, from a wide variety of disci-plines, offer applied perspectives on some of the most important topics related to the poem today. These essays on a variety of approaches, together with our overview of available materials, should meet the needs of the new generations studying Dante's poem. In this way we hope to provide a substantial resource for Dante pedagogy today and to encourage changes within critical and peda-gogical trends.

NOTE

[1] For the concept of supermodernity, see Augé.

Part One

MATERIALS

Overview

In the past thirty-five years we have witnessed the publication of numerous book-length critical studies and hundreds of insightful essays that represent the findings of recent research on Dante and his poem. Some of these are especially recommended to instructors looking for sound and innovative resources that will enhance their understanding of a wide range of issues as they prepare their courses. Others provide more up-to-date information about Dante's life and works, and still others open windows on new ways of interpreting the *Comedy* for the twenty-first-century classroom. In these three and a half decades some important Italian editions of the *Comedy* have appeared, as well as a plethora of mostly annotated English translations of either the entire poem or one or more canticles, a situation that has led to an embarrassment of riches for instructors. In his essay in this volume Madison Sowell addresses the considerations that instructors should make when choosing a translation for their courses. With few exceptions we have limited the publications presented in the following pages to those published after 1982 in English, when the first *Approaches* volume on the *Comedy* appeared. The "Instructor's Library" section relies in part on the observations and suggestions made by survey respondents.

Italian Editions of the *Comedy*

Most Italian and bilingual English editions of the *Comedy* present Giorgio Petrocchi's Italian text, but the editions by Federico Sanguineti and Antonio Lanza are worthwhile to consult in more specialized, philologically oriented courses where comparative analyses of different manuscript readings are de rigueur. For those courses on the *Comedy* taught in Italian, instructors would be well served to adopt one of several annotated Italian editions published in recent years. In particular, we recommend the editions by Anna Maria Chiavacci Leonardi; Umberto Bosco and Giovanni Reggio; and Nicola Fosca, all of which have extensive commentary, as well as the older but still serviceable texts edited by Natalino Sapegno; and Emilio Pasquini and Antonio Enzo Quaglio. As part of the instructor's arsenal of ancillary materials, we note the digital edition, available on DVD, that Prue Shaw has produced, *Dante Alighieri*, Commedia*: A Digital Edition*, containing full transcripts of seven manuscripts (six with images), together with Petrocchi's and F. Sanguineti's editions. Depending on the level of the course and the students' knowledge of Italian, we suggest that instructors may adopt one of several texts designed for the secondary schools of Italy, for they often feature questions and exercises aimed at promoting a better understanding of the text and, at times, offer a modern Italian paraphrase of the poem.[1]

English Translations of
the *Comedy* and the Minor Works

For those numerous courses taught in English we highly recommend dual-language editions for the facility they offer those instructors who wish to note certain aspects of the Italian text. In particular, we would note the translations with commentary by Allen Mandelbaum; Robert Hollander and Jean Hollander; and Robert Durling and Ronald L. Martinez; as well as those by Robin Kirkpatrick and Stanley Lombardo for their readability, valuable notes, and sometimes extended commentary on points of interest. We recognize the appeal that some earlier versions have for many instructors (e.g., those by Mark Musa, John D. Sinclair, Charles S. Singleton, John Ciardi, and Henry Wadsworth Longfellow). We also would note that, among the many recent translations, those by Robert Pinsky, Anthony Esolen, Clive James, and Mary Jo Bang have been used to good effect by instructors. Madison Sowell's essay on evaluating English versions of the *Comedy* discusses the various elements involved in choosing translations for a course on Dante.

Readings from Dante's minor works are also used profitably in many courses. At times, the entire *Vita nuova* is assigned and relevant sections of the *Monarchia*, the *Letter to Can Grande, Convivio*, and *De vulgari eloquentia* are incorporated to provide background material for the study of the *Comedy* or to highlight their intrinsic importance in the more general medieval context. John Took provides a fine overview of these writings in *Dante: Lyric Poet and Philosopher*. Therefore, in addition to the editions and versions of the *Comedy* noted above, we call attention to several recent English translations of Dante's minor works that are important additions to class syllabi.

The most frequently used text in classes is the *Vita nuova*, often read in its entirety, and instructors should note the debate concerning its division and presentation, even though these considerations do not affect its meaning vis-à-vis the *Comedy*.[2] Generally, earlier English translations of the *Vita Nuova*—those of Musa and Barbara Reynolds—still enjoy great popularity, although the more recent versions by Anthony Robert Mortimer and by Andrew Frisardi have received favorable comments. Dante Gabriel Rossetti's nineteenth-century version is also available in a 2002 edition.

Small but representative selections from the other minor works often find their way into course syllabi and can be important additions. For investigations of Dante's views on language and lyric poetry, readings from *De vulgari eloquentia* are very important, and two translations have recently appeared by Marianne Shapiro and Steven Botterill, respectively. Similarly, for Dante's ideas about the proper relationship between church and state, the *Monarchia* is the crucial document, and some recent translations include those by Richard Kay and by Shaw, although for classroom purposes the latter is more manageable.

The *Convivio* is important for the light it shines on the evolution of Dante's thoughts on many issues, and three translations have been produced over the past thirty-five years: those of Christopher Ryan; Richard Lansing; and Frisardi, which is the most thoroughly annotated and includes the Italian text en face. There is also great benefit in assigning readings from Dante's *Rime* to provide students with insight on his other poetic adventures, and his early lyrics have recently been edited with a commentary by Teodolinda Barolini and translated by Lansing. The *Letter to Can Grande*, long the object of controversy over its authenticity, is the subject of a book-length study by Robert Hollander (*Dante's* Epistle), and the text and translation by Paget Toynbee of all the epistles may be found on the *Princeton Dante Project* Web site.[3]

The Instructor's Library

Recommended Readings for Undergraduates

As noted above, the extensive critical literature on Dante produced over the past thirty-five years provides evidence of the abiding interest in the Florentine poet and his works. In some cases, it has served as a salutary corrective to previous scholarship and has opened up new areas of investigation. As in many areas of teaching and research, older works pertaining to Dante still provide valid and valuable insights and materials for the twenty-first-century classroom. Among these we recommend Singleton for contributions to our understanding of Dante's allegory: *Essay on the* Vita nuova, *Dante Studies 1*, *Dante Studies 2*; Erich Auerbach for the concept of figuralism: *Dante, Poet of the Secular World*, "Farinata and Cavalcante" (an essay on *Inferno* 10 in *Mimesis* 174–202), and "Figura"; Karl Vossler for a synthetic view of Dante's place in the Middle Ages in *Mediaeval Culture: An Introduction to Dante and His Times*; Joseph Anthony Mazzeo for studies on Dante's reception of various traditions: *Medieval Cultural Tradition in Dante's* Comedy, *Structure and Thought in the* Paradiso; Francis Fergusson for his powerful reading of *Purgatorio* in *Dante's Drama of the Mind*; John Freccero for his emphasis on Dante's Augustinian heritage in *Dante: The Poetics of Conversion*; and many others.[4] In the following pages we present and provide brief comments on those works published over the past three and a half decades that we view as especially important and helpful for teachers of the *Comedy* (this list is not intended to be exhaustive).

Reference and Background Works

For breadth and depth of coverage the monumental *Enciclopedia Dantesca* still stands as the ultimate resource (though now dated bibliographically) for questions on virtually every word in Dante's works. For the English-speaking world Lansing's *The Dante Encyclopedia*, reflecting more recent critical trends and providing more up-to-date bibliographical references, brings together a wealth of information on a wide variety of topics.[5] Similarly, Jay Ruud's *Critical Companion to Dante* provides an overview of Dante's works with an extended section on persons, places, and things. Zygmunt G. Barański and Lino Pertile's collaborative volume, *Dante in Context*, presents insightful essays on important topics for the study of Dante, arranged in five sections with an extensive bibliography: Politics and Society; Intellectual Traditions; Linguistics and Literary Cultures; Visual and Performative Culture; Dante: Life, Works, and Reception. Michael Caesar has compiled a rich selection of excerpts from the many commentaries on Dante spanning the years from 1314 to 1870 in *Dante: The Critical Heritage*.

In addition to the large array of bibliographical resources in the first edition, we note Enzo Esposito's magisterial four-volume *Bibliografia analitica degli scritti su Dante, 1950–1970* and Luciana Giovannetti's *Dante in America: Bibliografia 1965–1980*. The annual "American Dante Bibliography" published in *Dante Studies* since 1953 is now available in a searchable electronic format on the Dante Society of America Web site (www.dantesociety.org). In 2017, the Dante Society and the Società Dantesca Italiana began collaborating on a new, bilingual version of the International Dante Bibliography with enhanced search capabilities (dantesca.ntc.it/dnt-fo-catalog/pages/material-search.jsf).

Other publications furnish materials on a host of topics pertinent to the study of Dante—Christopher Kleinhenz's *Medieval Italy: An Encyclopedia* and the collection of primary readings relating to the age of Dante, *Medieval Italy: Texts in Translation*, edited by Katherine Jansen, Joanna Drell, and Frances Andrews. Collections of texts in English translation and critical studies on pre-Dantean visions of the afterlife include those by Eileen Gardiner, *Visions of Heaven and Hell before Dante*, and Alison Morgan, *Dante and the Medieval Other World*. Historically oriented studies on the nature and concepts of purgatory and paradise include Jacques Le Goff, *The Birth of Purgatory*; Jeffrey Burton Russell, *A History of Heaven: The Singing Silence*; and Alastair J. Minnis, *From Eden to Eternity: Creations of Paradise in the Later Middle Ages*. Studies on the history of medieval Italy—and Florence in particular—are not scarce, but these contributions are especially noteworthy: George Holmes, *Florence, Rome and the Origins of the Renaissance*; Gene A. Brucker, *Florence: The Golden Age, 1138–1737*; George W. Dameron, *Florence and Its Church in the Age of Dante*; and John M. Najemy, *A History of Florence, 1200–1575*.

Dante's Life and Works

In addition to Giuseppe Mazzotta's accounts of Dante's life appearing in *The Dante Encyclopedia*, in Rachel Jacoff's *The Cambridge Companion to Dante*, and in Gaetana Marrone's *Encyclopedia of Italian Literary Studies*,[6] several book-length studies on Dante's life and works have recently appeared: Ricardo Quinones's updated *Dante Alighieri*; Stephen Bemrose, *A New Life of Dante*; Robert Hollander, *Dante: A Life in Works*; R. W. B. Lewis, *Dante*; Peter S. Hawkins, *Dante: A Brief History*; Nick Havely, *Dante*; and Marco Santagata, *Dante: The Story of His Life*. These provide insights on various aspects of Dante's works and their *Fortleben*. Some early lives of Dante and commentaries on the *Comedy* have appeared in English: Giovanni Boccaccio's *The Life of Dante* (*Trattatello in Laude di Dante*), translated by Vincenzo Zin Bollettino, and Michael Papio's fine version of *Boccaccio's Expositions on Dante's* Comedy.

Critical Studies

Given the large number of book-length studies on Dante and the *Comedy* that have appeared over the past three and a half decades, we direct our attention primarily to those contributions in English that are important and useful for instructors in the preparation of their courses. Instructors may find it helpful to have some volumes on library reserve for student use, along with a selection of reference works. John Scott's *Understanding Dante* provides a thorough and insightful overview of the poet and his works—not just the *Comedy*—and includes mini-essays that focus on specific matters crucial to their interpretation. In *Reading Dante* (Open Yale Courses) Mazzotta recreates the classroom atmosphere, presenting his lectures on all one hundred cantos of the *Comedy* with many critical insights and associations. Similarly, Kirkpatrick, first in *Dante's Inferno: Difficulty and Dead Poetry* and more recently in *Dante: The* Divine Comedy, presents a reading of the poem with numerous critical aperçus. In much the same way, in *Reading Dante* Shaw summarizes the poet's life and the entire poem in chapters titled "Friendship," "Power," "Life," "Love," "Time," "Numbers," and "Words," as does, much less extensively, Marguerite Mills Chiarenza in *The* Divine Comedy: *Tracing God's Art*. In the late 1980s the Dante Society of America launched a major but short-lived project of book-length readings of all one hundred cantos of the *Comedy*, of which only three were published: Inferno *I* by Anthony K. Cassell; Inferno *II* by Jacoff and William A. Stephany; and Inferno *III* by Maria Picchio Simonelli.

In *Dante's Poets* Barolini presents the ancient and medieval poetic context in which Dante sought to insert himself, and in *The Undivine* Comedy she argues for a reading of the poem that privileges its narrative merits and extraordinary mimesis while not diminishing its theological message. John Kleiner, in *Mismapping the Underworld*, studies three examples of error in the *Comedy* as it relates to the concept of mimetic realism in the poem. In *Dante and the Making of a Modern Author* Albert Russell Ascoli provides a well-documented intellectual biography of the poet and the evolution of his thought over the course of his life and works. Two works—Marc Cogan, *The Design in Wax*, and Christian Moevs, *Metaphysics of Dante's* Comedy—provide excellent presentations of the philosophical and theological structure of the *Comedy*. In *The Political Vision of the Divine Comedy*, Joan Ferrante provides a meticulous account of the many manifestations of political concerns in the poem, as does Scott in his more restricted *Dante's Political Purgatory*. In *Dante as Dramatist* Franco Masciandaro studies Dante's staging of various episodes in the poem. Two studies—Hawkins, *Dante's Testaments*, and V. Stanley Benfell, *The Biblical Dante*—investigate the many ways Dante employs the Bible and biblical references in the *Comedy*. Dante and the Fathers and Doctors of the Church, as well as the religious orders in general, have been the subject of several important books, such as those by Simone Marchesi, *Dante and Augustine*; Botterill, *Dante and the Mystical Tradition*; Havely, *Dante and the Franciscans: Poverty and the Papacy in the* Commedia; and Santa Casciani, editor, *Dante and the Franciscans*. The topic of women in the Middle Ages and in Dante's *Comedy* includes Ferrante's general treatment of *Women as Image in Medieval Literature from the Twelfth Century to Dante* and studies focused on Beatrice and Dante's women in general, such as Jaroslav Pelikan, *Eternal Feminines*; Robert Pogue Harrison, *The Body of Beatrice*; Olivia Holmes, *Dante's Two Beloveds*; Vincent Moleta's edited collection *"La Gloriosa Donna de la Mente": A Commentary on the* Vita nuova; and the special issue of *Texas Studies in Language and Literature*, edited by David Wallace, titled *Beatrice Dolce Memoria, 1290–1990*. Peter Armour's two highly focused studies on important aspects of *Purgatory* deserve attention, *The Door of Purgatory* and *Dante's Griffin and the History of the World*, as do Patrick Boyde's studies on the poem as a whole, *Perception and Passion in Dante's* Comedy and *Human Vices and Human Worth in Dante's* Comedy. Some studies dealing with *Paradiso* present general overviews, including John Saly, *Dante's Paradiso: The Flowering of the Self*, and James Torrens, SJ, *Presenting* Paradise. Other works shine light on specific topics: for astral influence on human activity, see Richard Kay, *Dante's Christian Astrology*, and Alison Cornish, *Reading Dante's Stars*; on the nature of angels, see Bemrose, *Dante's Angelic Intelligences*, and Susanna Barsella, *In the Light of Angels*; for the importance of medieval numerology, see John J. Guzzardo, *Dante: Numerological Studies*; on the role of hermeneutics in the poem, see William Franke, *Dante's Interpretive Journey*; for questions regarding theology, see Vittorio Montemaggi, *Reading Dante's Commedia as Theology*, and Christine O'Connell Baur, *Dante's Hermeneutics of Salvation*; for discussions of the union of incarnational theology and dialectical thought, see Guy P. Raffa, *Divine Dialectic: Dante's Incarnational Poetry*; for the ways of knowledge and the interaction of the liberal arts, ethics, politics, and theology in the Middle Ages, see Mazzotta, *Dante's Vision and the Circle of Knowledge*. Other contributions include Dino S. Cervigni's study *Dante's Poetry of Dreams*, an examination of the poet's understanding and use of dreams; Peter Dronke's *Dante and Medieval Latin Traditions*, which addresses Dante's indebtedness to earlier Latin authors; Jeffrey T. Schnapp's *The Transfiguration of History at the Center of Dante's* Paradise, which explores the subject of Dante's "Christianization" of classical epic themes. Claire E. Honess discusses Dante's concept of citizenship in *From Florence to the Heavenly City*, and Filippa Modesto explores that of friendship in *Dante's Idea of Friendship*; Gary Cestaro considers Dante's concern for language in *Dante and the Grammar of the Nursing Body*, and Warren Ginsberg examines the interest in aesthetics in *Dante's Aesthetics of Being*. Other scholars address Dante's preoccupations with notions of body and soul: Manuele Gragnolati, *Experiencing the Afterlife: Soul and Body in Dante and Medieval Culture*, and Shapiro, *Dante and the Knot of Body and Soul*; ideas of the other: Brenda Deen Schildgen, *Dante and the Orient*; Florence and the nature of cities: Catherine Keen, *Dante and the City*; and medieval law: Justin Steinberg, *Dante and the Limits of the Law*. Two recent contributions focus on Dante and Islam: Gregory B. Stone, *Dante's Pluralism and the Islamic Philosophy of Religion*, and Jan M. Ziolkowski's edited volume, *Dante and Islam*.

Articles and Journals

There are far too many fine essays to list here, but instructors should be aware of the major journals in Dante studies and consult them frequently to find examples of the latest research. The oldest periodical is *Dante Studies*, published annually by the Dante Society of America and containing (until 2016) an annotated bibliography of North American criticism on the Florentine poet. An offshoot is the *Electronic Bulletin*, renamed *Dante Notes* as of 2016, which has three categories: scholarship, pedagogy, and student essays. For these online publications and for the searchable bibliography, please consult the society's Web site (www.dantesociety.org). For eleven years (1987–98) *Lectura Dantis Virginiana* was a twice-yearly journal, and its editor, Tibor Wlassics, also published three well-received volumes of essays on individual cantos of each canticle: *Dante's* Divine Comedy: *Introductory Readings*. These are the first—and only—complete readings of the *Comedy* produced in North America, unlike the many *Lecturae Dantis* series in Italy. A new journal has recently begun publication: *Bibliotheca Dantesca* (Scholarly Commons, University of Pennsylvania Libraries). A number of periodicals in Europe are dedicated either solely or in large part to Dante: *Studi danteschi* (Società Dantesca Italiana, Florence), *L'Alighieri* (Longo, Ravenna), *Letture classensi* (Biblioteca Classense, Ravenna), *Dante* (Fabrizio Serra, Pisa), *Le tre corone: Rivista internazionale di studi su Dante, Petrarca, Boccaccio* (Fabrizio Serra, Pisa), *Rivista di studi danteschi* (Centro Pio Rajna, Rome), *Deutsches Dante-Jahrbuch* (Deutsches Dante-Gesellschaft, Munich), *Rivista internazionale di ricerche dantesche* (Fabrizio

Serra, Pisa), and *Tenzone* (Asociación Complutense de Dantología, Madrid). Many articles and book reviews appear in other North American journals devoted to literary criticism and historical research, such as the Italian issue of *MLN* (January, Johns Hopkins University Press), *Speculum* (Medieval Academy of America), *Italica* (American Association of Teachers of Italian), and so on.

Collections of Essays

One major benefit of collections of scholarly essays is that they often assemble in one place original contributions focused on a particular topic (sometimes the proceedings of a major conference) or reprint essays that may be difficult to find or that represent classic treatments of a wide range of subjects. One especially valuable publication is Lansing's eight-volume set of reprinted essays, *Dante: The Critical Complex*, which comprises the following volumes: *Dante and Beatrice: The Poet's Life and the Invention of Poetry*; *Dante and Classical Antiquity: The Epic Tradition*; *Dante and Philosophy: Nature, the Cosmos, and the Ethical Imperative*; *Dante and Theology: The Biblical Tradition and Christian Allegory*; *Dante and History: From Florence and Rome to Heavenly Jerusalem*; *Dante and Critical Theory*; *Dante and Interpretation*; and *Dante's Afterlife: The Influence and Reception of the* Commedia. The essays in these volumes provide a vast and valuable resource for instructors. The original essays in the revised edition of Jacoff's *The Cambridge Companion to Dante* provide a fine overview of the poet's life and works as seen vis-à-vis their literary predecessors and their position in the contemporary intellectual, cultural, and historical milieu. This book could serve as a supplemental text for students. Besides the three volumes of canto-by-canto readings in the *Lectura Dantis Virginiana* (noted above), two collections of essays edited by Allen Mandelbaum, Anthony Oldcorn, and Charles Ross, *Lectura Dantis:* Inferno and *Lectura Dantis:* Purgatorio, provide insightful readings of individual cantos in the first two canticles. The recent initiative at the University of Cambridge focusing on innovative ways of reading the poem has resulted in three published volumes, one per canticle: *Vertical Readings in Dante's* Comedy, edited by George Corbett and Heather Webb.

Several essay collections represent the proceedings of major conferences, such as *Dante for the New Millennium*, edited by Barolini and H. Wayne Storey; *Dante Now: Current Trends in Dante Studies*, edited by Theodore J. Cachey, Jr.; and the five volumes produced as part of the Seminario dantesco internazionale, founded by Robert Hollander in 1994.[7] Other conferences have produced proceedings volumes, such as *The* Divine Comedy *and the Encyclopedia of Arts and Sciences*, edited by Giuseppe Di Scipio and Aldo Scaglione; *Dante: Summa Medievalis*, edited by Charles Franco and Leslie Morgan; and *Dante and the Christian Imagination*, edited by Domenico Pietropaolo. Some lecture series have also resulted in essay collections, such as the one sponsored by the Newberry Library in Chicago: *Lectura Dantis Newberryana*, edited by Paolo Cherchi and Antonio C. Mastrobuono.

Other collections have a specific focus, such as the relationship between Dante and poets of antiquity in *The Poetry of Allusion: Virgil and Ovid in Dante's Commedia*, edited by Jacoff and Schnapp; *Dante and Ovid: Essays in Intertextuality*, edited by Madison U. Sowell; *Dante and the Greeks*, edited by Ziolkowski; and *Dante e la "bella scola" della poesia*, edited by Amilcare A. Iannucci. Two volumes treat questions about Dante and unorthodox views: *Dante and Heterodoxy*, edited by Maria Luisa Ardizzone and Barolini, and *Dante and the Unorthodox*, edited by James Miller, whereas the theological aspects of the *Comedy* are explored in *Dante's Commedia: Theology as Poetry*, edited by Montemaggi and Matthew Treherne. On the subject of the commentators on the poem, see *Interpreting Dante: Essays on the Traditions of Dante Commentary*, edited by Paola Nasti and Claudia Rossignoli; for the nature of the relationship between Petrarch and Dante, see *Petrarch and Dante: Anti-Dantism, Metaphysics, Tradition*, edited by Barański and Cachey; on the place of politics, theology, and poetry in Dante's works, see *"Se mai continga . . . ": Exile, Politics and Theology in Dante*, edited by Honess and Treherne, and *Dante and Governance*, edited by John Woodhouse; on the subject of the nature of desire, see *Desire in Dante and the Middle Ages*, edited by Gragnolati, Tristan Kay, Elena Lombardi, and Francesca Southerden. *Studi americani su Dante*, edited by Gian Carlo Alessio and Robert Hollander, with an introduction to American criticism on Dante by Dante Della Terza, presents essays by American scholars in Italian translation.

At times, journals dedicate special issues or supplements to a particular topic in Dante, as did *The Italianist* on the subject of Dante and the poetic genres of comedy, tragedy, satire, and lyric in *"Libri Poetarum in Quattuor Species Dividuntur": Essays on Dante and Genre*, edited by Barański. Others contain essays on wide-ranging topics, such as Cervigni's *Dante and Modern American Criticism* and Iannucci's *Dante Today*, which includes both essays and book reviews. Some essay collections follow the same open-ended criteria, including *Dante: Contemporary Perspectives*, edited by Iannucci; in contrast, others reprint classic essays, such as *Critical Essays on Dante*, edited by Mazzotta, which presents portions from medieval and Renaissance commentators and several twentieth-century essays; and Harold Bloom's four edited volumes: *Dante, Dante's Divine Comedy, Dante Alighieri* (2003), and *Dante Alighieri* (2004), a convenient source for a number of well-known essays published from the 1950s to the 1990s.

Some Festschriften pay tribute to dantisti and often include a number of essays on the Florentine poet. For example, two of these volumes honor Charles S. Singleton: *Dante, Petrarch, Boccaccio*, edited by Aldo S. Bernardo and Anthony L. Pellegrini, and *In ricordo di Charles S. Singleton*, a special issue of *Filologia e critica*. Similar volumes recognize the contributions to Dante scholarship of John A. Scott, *"Legato con Amore in un Volume,"* edited by John J. Kinder and Diana Glenn; Robert Hollander, *Le culture di Dante*, edited by Michelangelo Picone et al.; John Freccero, *Sparks and Seeds*, edited by Dana E. Stewart and Cornish; Giuseppe Mazzotta, *Tra Amici*, edited by Walter Stephens; and Christopher Kleinhenz, *"Accessus ad Auctores,"* edited by Fabian Alfie and

Andrea Dini. Moreover, there are volumes that feature the collected essays on the Florentine poet by Dante specialists, such as Freccero, *Dante: The Poetics of Conversion*, edited by Jacoff, and *In Dante's Wake*, edited by Danielle Callegari and Melissa Swain; Barolini's *Dante and the Origins of Italian Literary Culture*; the late Michelangelo Picone, *Scritti danteschi*, edited by Lanza; Kleinhenz's *Dante intertestuale e interdisciplinare: Saggi sulla* Commedia; Winthrop Wetherbee's *The Ancient Flame: Dante and the Poets*; and Richard Kay's *Dante's Enigmas: Medieval Scholasticism and Beyond*. A recent volume commemorates the scholarship of the late Amilcare A. Iannucci: *Dantean Dialogues: Engaging with the Legacy of Amilcare Iannucci*, edited by Maggie Kilgour and Elena Lombardi.

Pedagogical Materials

After the publication of Carole Slade's *Approaches to Teaching Dante's Divine Comedy*, relatively few books—or even articles—dedicated to teaching Dante's *Comedy* have appeared. Those few have generally been very useful, however, in charting the pedagogical course. Raffa's *The Complete Danteworlds* must be seen as the printed counterpart to his Web site *Danteworlds* (danteworlds.laits .utexas.edu/), which he developed at the University of Texas, Austin. It provides instructors and students with excellent overviews and finely detailed analyses of the entire poem, complete with study questions and a host of other materials. Two special "clusters" of essays on teaching Dante have appeared in the journal *Pedagogy*.[8] One is titled "Cluster on Multidisciplinary Approaches to Teaching Dante's *Commedia*," edited by Kirilka Stavreva, and contains ten essays that examine ways of teaching the poem from a variety of disciplinary perspectives and for a wide range of student audiences. The other is called "Cluster on Teaching Dante's *Divine Comedy* Vertically," edited by Schildgen, and presents an introduction and six essays that offer examples of the benefits of reading the poem "vertically," that is, by examining parallel cantos in each canticle prospectively and retrospectively.[9]

Dante and the Visual Arts, Television, Cinema, Literature, and Music

Over the past few decades we have witnessed a great flowering of interest in Dante's appropriation of artistic imagery in his poem and in the myriad artistic images his poem has spawned, ranging from manuscript illuminations and Renaissance woodcuts to nineteenth- and twentieth-century illustrations. In addition, the variegated presence of Dante's poem in the media and as the subject of cinematographic representation is a relatively new area of interest, research, and teaching.

Four edited volumes treat recent interpretations of Dante's poem in various media: Gragnolati, Fabio Camilletti, and Fabian Lampart, *Metamorphosing*

Dante: Appropriations, Manipulations, and Rewritings in the Twentieth and Twenty-First Centuries; Antonella Braida and Luisa Calè, *Dante on View: The Reception of Dante in the Visual and Performing Arts*; Iannucci, *Dante, Cinema, and Television*; and Massimo Ciavolella and Gianluca Rizzo, *Like Doves Summoned by Desire: Dante's New Life in Twentieth-Century Literature and Cinema*. The essays in these collections analyze a range of interpretations, translations, and adaptations of the *Comedy* into static and moving images, as well as performance art, from the nineteenth to the twenty-first centuries, including analyses of works that range from the Pre-Raphaelite artists to Salvador Dalí and Peter Greenaway, as well as the African American director Spencer Williams, and many more. Two recent monographs on the appropriation of Dante in a variety of media, from literature to film and the visual arts, are *Inferno Revealed: From Dante to Dan Brown* by Deborah Parker and Mark Parker and *Palinsesti danteschi: Riscrivere la* Commedia, *da Garibaldi all'era del digitale* by Antonio Rossini.

Far more numerous are the studies of Dante's reception in a single artistic medium: painting, sculpture, literature, and film. In addition to the earlier landmark volumes (e.g., Ludwig Volkmann, *Iconografia Dantesca: The Pictorial Representations to Dante's* Divine Comedy; Peter Brieger, Millard Meiss, and Singleton, *Illuminated Manuscripts of the* Divine Comedy; and Giovanni Fallani, *Dante e la cultura figurativa medievale*), some more recent studies treat the influence of the visual arts on Dante and the afterlife of the poem in paintings, such as Cassell, *Dante's Fearful Art of Justice*; Eugene Paul Nassar, *Illustrations to Dante's* Inferno; Charles H. Taylor and Patricia Finley, *Images of the Journey in Dante's* Divine Comedy; Laura Pasquini, *Iconografie dantesche: Dalla luce del mosaico all'immagine profetica*; and C. Jean Campbell, *The Commonwealth of Nature: Art and Poetic Community in the Age of Dante*.

In addition to the essays by Aida Audeh and by Heather Webb in this volume, studies that strictly treat the early visual interpretations of the poem include John Pope-Hennessy, Paradiso: *The Illuminations to Dante's* Divine Comedy *by Giovanni di Paolo*; and Hein-Th. Schulze Altcappenberg, *Sandro Botticelli: The Drawings for Dante's* Divine Comedy. Numerous other titles attend to the modern artistic interpretation of Dante during and after the eighteenth century, analyzing works by William Blake, John Flaxman, Auguste Rodin, and Gustave Doré; these include *The Doré Illustrations for Dante's* Divine Comedy; Milton Klonsky, *Blake's Dante: The Complete Illustrations to the* Divine Comedy; Antoinette Le Normand-Romain, *Rodin: The Gates of Hell*; Flaxman's *The Illustrations for Dante's* Divine Comedy, edited by Francesca Salvadori; David Bindman, Stephen Hebron, and Michael O'Neill, *Dante Rediscovered: From Blake to Rodin*; and Eric Pyle, *William Blake's Illustrations for Dante's* Divine Comedy. A comprehensive treatment of modern artists interpreting Dante, from Renato Guttuso to Salvador Dalí, can be found in Jean-Pierre Barricelli, *Dante's Vision and the Artist: Four Modern Illustrators of the* Commedia. Two recent interpretations of Dante include the British artist Tom Phillips's *Dante's*

Inferno and the American artist Sandow Birk's three-volume set, *Dante's Inferno, Dante's Purgatorio, Dante's Paradiso*. Phillips also collaborated with Peter Greenaway for *A TV Dante* on British television.

The literary afterlife of Dante's poem in Anglophone literature has been extensively examined by Havely in his monograph *Dante's British Public: Readers and Texts, from the Fourteenth Century to the Present* and several edited volumes: *Dante's Modern Afterlife: Reception and Response from Blake to Heaney*; *Dante in the Nineteenth Century: Reception, Canonicity, Popularization*; and, with Aida Audeh, *Dante in the Long Nineteenth Century: Nationality, Identity, and Appropriation*. Two other studies on the reception of Dante in the nineteenth century are those by Braida, *Dante and the Romantics*, and Alison Milbank, *Dante and the Victorians*. Those interested in the figure of Beatrice during this period should consult *A Victorian Muse: The Afterlife of Dante's Beatrice in Nineteenth-Century Literature* by Julia Straub. Most recently, Dennis Looney has published a groundbreaking study of the African American reception of Dante in *Freedom Readers: The African American Reception of Dante Alighieri and the* Divine Comedy. Finally, the interpretation of Dante in music has been addressed by Maria Ann Roglieri in *Dante and Music: Musical Adaptations of the* Commedia *from the Sixteenth Century to the Present* and by Francesco Ciabattoni in his volume *Dante's Journey to Polyphony*.

Digital Humanities Projects and Resources

Among the numerous Web sites dedicated to Dante, the following are especially recommended for their wealth of materials and for their ease of use.

Digital Dante (Columbia University; digitaldante.columbia.edu/) features the *Comedy* in the Petrocchi edition along with the English translations of Mandelbaum and Longfellow. Each canto is accompanied by illustrations from an image gallery, readings, original commentary (the "Commento Baroliniano" by Barolini), and videos of class lectures. Additionally, it features an "Intertextual Dante" page with a focus on the relationship between Dante and other authors (such as Ovid), a wide range of images (Sandow Birk's works and images from Columbia's Rare Book and Manuscript Library), readings of the poem and of various sestinas, historical commentary, and various other works by Dante with English translations.

Dante Lab Reader (Dartmouth College; dantelab.dartmouth.edu/) is an elaboration on the earlier but ongoing *Dartmouth Dante Project* (see below) and offers a customizable digital work space for the student of Dante. The user can compare many combinations of the poem, translations, and commentaries, and up to four individual searches simultaneously on one screen. Drawing on numerous texts from seven hundred years of the commentary tradition, the *Dante Lab Reader* filters over 300,000 lines of text from the poem, the commentary, and various English-language translations.

Dartmouth Dante Project (Dartmouth College; dante.dartmouth.edu/) is an excellent resource of over seventy commentaries (in Italian, Latin, and English) to the *Comedy*, from Jacopo Alighieri (1322) to Fosca (2015), allows for rapid consultation of this rich and varied tradition and could easily be adapted to classroom exercises at various levels, depending on the language abilities of the students.

Princeton Dante Project (Princeton University; etcweb.princeton.edu/dante/index.html) features a traditional approach to the digital study of Dante's *Comedy* by featuring the poem at the center of its Web site while allowing the user to consult and search the Petrocchi text of the poem, new translations into English, the texts of all of Dante's minor works (in original Italian or Latin and in English translation), readings of the poem in the original, historical, and interpretative commentaries, and links to other Dante digital projects.

The World of Dante (University of Virginia; www.worldofdante.org/index .html), developed by Deborah Parker, offers multimedia resources to enhance one's reading of the *Comedy*. It features an encoded Italian text that allows for structured searches and analyses (People, Places, Creatures, Deities, Structures, Images, Music), Mandelbaum's English translation, interactive maps (of the poem's locations and Dante's Italy), diagrams, music (with recordings by Zephyrus, an early music vocal ensemble), a database, a time line, and a gallery of illustrations from a variety of artists.

Danteworlds (University of Texas, Austin; danteworlds.laits.utexas.edu/), developed by Guy Raffa, contains an abridged version of the commentaries on each canto from *The Complete Danteworlds: A Reader's Guide to the* Divine Comedy; a gallery of images by Vellutello, John Flaxman, Gustave Doré, and Suloni Robertson; and audio recordings of key verses in the original Italian, which are structured around the locations in Dante's afterlife vision.

Dante Today: Citings and Sightings of Dante's Works in Contemporary Culture (Bowdoin College and Stanford University; research.bowdoin.edu/dante -today/), founded by Arielle Saiber and edited by Saiber and Elizabeth Coggeshall, is a crowd-sourced repository for appearances of Dante in popular culture. Anyone can submit a "citing" of Dante in popular culture (categorized on the Web site as "Consumer Goods," "Dining and Leisure," "Music," "Performing Arts," "Places," "Visual Art and Architecture," "Written Word"), which are then selected by the editors for posting. The site provides a digital archive for these references that can serve as data for students and scholars of Dante's works and their afterlife.

Dante Society of America (www.dantesociety.org/about-society) has many useful features, including *Dante Notes* and the *American Dante Bibliography*. *Dante Notes* features current and engaging research and pedagogy projects related to Dante. Now featured on this site, the annual *American Dante Bibliography* includes all publications relating to Dante (books, articles, translations, reviews) written by North American writers or published in North America for the calendar year, as well as reviews of books from elsewhere published in the

United States and Canada. In 2017 the Dante Society of America and the Società Dantesca Italiana (SDI) signed a partnership agreement to collaborate on the production of a new, bilingual version of the *Bibliografia Dantesca Internazionale* (*BDI*; *International Dante Bibliography*), with enhanced search capabilities. This powerful bibliographical instrument also integrates the materials published in the annual *American Dante Bibliography*.

Società Dantesca Italiana (dantesca.org/cms/) features links to the *Bibliografia Dantesca Internazionale* (*International Dante Bibliography*), which it maintains. The *BDI* now includes more citations for Dante criticism published in North America. The SDI sponsors the Web site *Dante Online* (www.danteonline .it/english/home_ita.asp), which includes an ample selection of Dante's works in the original and in translation, a bibliography, and an index of manuscripts.

Divine Comedy *Image Archive* (Cornell University; divinecomedy.library .cornell.edu/index.html) is a repository of scanned images from illustrated editions of Dante's poem found in the Fiske Dante Collection, Division of Rare and Manuscript Collections, Cornell University Library. These images derive from editions of the *Divine Comedy* published from the incunabula period (ending in 1500) through the early twentieth century, and the digital collection aims to include approximately two thousand images from illustrated editions of the *Comedy* from 1487 to 1921, which are mostly engravings (woodcut, copper, or steel).

These resources have had a great and positive influence on the content and conduct of undergraduate courses on Dante in both Italian and English, for generalist and specialist audiences alike, particularly insofar as they offer images, audio recordings, commentary, online texts and databases, and complex search engines, in addition to teaching materials.

NOTES

[1] Some survey respondents indicated their profitable use of other Italian editions. Celestina Beneforti provides annotated editions of selected cantos (with parallel text in modern Italian) from all three canticles, and Cristina Savettieri and Raffaele Donnarumma present an edition of and commentary on selected cantos with a supplemental CD-ROM (*Divina commedia: Testi letterari*). Stefano Jacomuzzi presents all one hundred cantos, accompanied by a modern Italian paraphrase and a rich selection of iconographical images in color. In their edition intended for Italian secondary schools, Robert Hollander and Simone Marchesi provide the entire text of the poem with an Italian paraphrase and extensive commentary on eleven cantos in each canticle as well as introductory material and sets of exercises. Giovanni Fallani, Nicola Maggi, and Silvio Zennaro include complete annotated editions of all Dante's works.

[2] On this issue the principal critics are Michele Barbi, whose 1907 edition (and division into forty-two chapters) was considered the standard text until fairly recently; Dino S. Cervigni and Edward Vasta, who presented the text without chapter or paragraph divisions; and Guglielmo Gorni, who divides the work into thirty-one chapters.

³ All Dante's works, in Italian or Latin and in English translation, are available at *Princeton Dante Project* (etcweb.princeton.edu/dante/pdp/).

⁴ For a broad selection of earlier works on Dante, see Carole Slade's listings in the 1982 *Approaches* volume (3–31).

⁵ Singleton's revised edition (1968) of Toynbee's Dante *Dictionary* (1898) is still a good resource.

⁶ Mazzotta's main entry on Dante's life is followed by shorter pieces on *"Comedia," "Commentaries," "Convivio," "De vulgari eloquentia," "Monarchia,"* and *"Vita nuova."*

⁷ The volumes published are *International Dante Seminar*, edited by Zygmunt G. Barański; *Dante: Mito e poesia*, edited by Michelangelo Picone and Tatiana Crivelli; *Dante: Da Firenze all'aldilà*, edited by Picone; *Le culture di Dante: Studi in onore di Robert Hollander*, edited by Picone, Theodore J. Cachey, Jr., and Margherita Mesirca; and *Dante the Lyric and Ethical Poet*, edited by Barański and Martin L. McLaughlin.

⁸ Both these groups of essays had their origin in a seminar or institute funded by the National Endowment for the Humanities.

⁹ Instructors are no doubt aware that other, perhaps less nuanced, teaching aids exist, such as Angelo A. De Gennaro's *The Reader's Companion to Dante's* Divine Comedy and Joseph Gallagher's *To Hell and Back with Dante*.

Part Two

APPROACHES

Introduction:
Dante's *Comedy* in the Classroom

Christopher Kleinhenz and Kristina Olson

In addition to the inclusion of selections of Dante's *Divine Comedy* in a large number of medieval and general literature surveys, fifty courses teach the poem in its entirety, according to instructors who responded to our survey.[1] These numbers do not include statistics from a number of institutions and thus only begin to suggest the wealth of courses on or including Dante's *Comedy* taught across North America. Most of these fifty courses incorporate Dante's other works, most often the *Vita nuova* (40), but also selections from the *Letter to Can Grande* (19), the *Monarchia* (13), the *De vulgari eloquentia* (10) and the *Convivio* (8). Many instructors indicated that they try to include other disciplines—such as art history (35), music (11), and film and video (9)—in their course on the *Divine Comedy*. The study of Dante is thus one pillar of the humanities, not only for a world literature canon but also across several student populations and disciplines.

Courses Taught

Dante's *Comedy* finds its place in many types of courses (from small first- and senior-year seminars to large undergraduate lectures to graduate classes) offered by a variety of departments (Italian, comparative literature, English, art history, philosophy, history, religion) and programs (honors, humanities, study abroad). Its presence in course syllabi ranges from an entire academic year or semester to periods varying from several weeks to a few class sessions. As expected, courses devoted entirely to the *Comedy* or individual canticles form part of the advanced Italian curriculum, and the language of instruction is Italian or English, with all readings being done in the original language (prerequisites are usually two or more years of Italian). Courses solely on Dante in English usually run for one semester and are offered by various departments and programs. These classes generally have no prerequisites and satisfy general education requirements, and the *Inferno* is typically the focal point in most.[2] Often courses on Dante can be taken for dual credit when the language of instruction is English, but students earning credits toward an Italian minor or major must read the poem in the original language. This differentiation is one of several indications of student diversity in the Dante classroom. One of the canticles, usually *Inferno*, is often incorporated in world, Western, or medieval literature surveys courses, such as World Masterpieces, Great Books, Great Works of Western Literature, The Medieval World: Self and Others, Epic and Romance, Classical Traditions, and so on. Dante's *Comedy* is thus frequently taught with the works of other Italian and non-Italian authors and artists, from the medieval and Renaissance periods to the modern and postmodern ages.[3]

The *Comedy* or one or more of its canticles or selected cantos are taught as one of several texts in a wide variety of lower-level survey courses, and the time allotted to it ranges from one to four weeks. In more advanced classes on medieval literature, the *Comedy* may claim much more time, often half the semester.

Sometimes the *Comedy* is the primary text in courses (some team-taught) in humanities departments and programs other than Italian: Art History; History; English; Religious Studies; Comparative Literature; Philosophy. Team-taught courses on Dante with instructors outside of Italian or English programs, such as in Religion, Philosophy, or Mathematics, have occasionally been offered with the intention of highlighting the interdisciplinary nature of the poem. In addition to their inclusion in specialized graduate-level seminars, Dante's texts increasingly appear in Italian curricula in innovative and unconventional ways. Students encounter his works in introductions to Italian cultural studies; translation studies; Italian civilization spanning from antiquity; and even Italian cinema, where the poem's visual reception is studied.[4]

There are many instructional contexts outside the college classroom that incorporate Dante's poem. High schools, adult education programs, and extension divisions often include either the *Inferno* or the entire *Comedy* in a standalone course or as part of a world or Western literature sequence. With reasonable frequency, the *Comedy* is taught in study-abroad programs in Italy (semester or summer), with the added benefit of allowing students to see first hand the places and related sites that provide the necessary context for understanding the poem. Finally, as examined by Ron Herzman in his essay in this collection, Dante has also been studied in correctional facilities as a part of literature courses.

Cantos Taught

In light of the instructional formats described above, those teaching the *Comedy* incorporate it either in its entirety or in sections. It is common for courses on the *Inferno* to teach the entire canticle and assign all of its cantos. Many instructors teach the entire poem (all three canticles), claiming that assigning selections does an injustice to the poem and stressing the importance of the full experience for students. Several survey respondents described their experience having moved from teaching the poem in toto to assigning only individual cantos, whereas others shifted their teaching methods in the opposite direction. One respondent wrote about a shift toward teaching the whole poem over the course of a career, reflecting on the lack of intellectual rigor entailed in teaching just the *Inferno*. Another instructor explained that teaching a selection of only half the cantos in the first iteration of the course meant that students could not appreciate the poem's narrative arc. In contrast, the second version of the course covered the whole poem, improving students' grasp of the *Comedy* in its entirety.

When instructors have opted for selections from the poem, they frequently assign the entire *Inferno* as well as some cantos from *Purgatorio* and *Paradiso*, or selections from all three canticles. Some instructors teach all of *Inferno* and *Purgatorio*, with certain cantos from *Paradiso*. Choices usually depend on the theme of the course (e.g., the history of lyric poetry, emphasizing *Purgatory* 24–26), especially for nonchronological survey courses. Other instructors select cantos based on their characters, such as Francesca da Rimini, Farinata, Brunetto Latini, Ulysses, and Ugolino for the *Inferno*. Instructors who teach only the *Inferno* choose cantos that describe each sin in detail, whereas others focus on moments in the poem that portray the development of the pilgrim or on those that have a rich history in literary or artistic reception.

When teaching the *Inferno* in its entirety, instructors might choose selections from *Purgatorio* and *Paradiso* based on philosophical background (e.g., cantos that address free will) or essential plot points (e.g., cantos covering the departure of Virgil and the Beatific Vision). To compensate for the selections, instructors use the "inter-cantica" essays in the Durling-Martinez edition, or the summaries offered in other translations, such as those of Mark Musa. Other instructors deal with the gaps in the reading by providing illustrations or cosmological maps to describe the realms of the afterlife.

To provide examples of selected cantos from the entire *Comedy* we offer the following outlines given by eight respondents.

Undergraduate

Inferno 1, 5, 13, 26, 33–34; *Purgatorio* 1, 6, 22; *Paradiso* 2, 6, 27, 33. For survey courses, these representative cantos illustrate Dante's moral hierarchy, incorporate significant episodes, and offer engaging characters. Important artworks influenced by events and characters can exemplify the *Comedy*'s narrative structure.

Inferno 5, 10, 26, 33–34; *Purgatorio* 1–2, 5, 16, 30–33; *Paradiso* 3, 17, 33. Optional: *Purgatorio* 12–18 and *Paradiso* 15–17 (the Cacciaguida cantos), emphasizing medieval philosophy and theology.

Inferno 1–6, for an overview of the structure and main themes, with passages from canto 7 (on greed), canto 13 (suicide), canto 19 (simony), cantos 32–33 (Ugolino), and cantos 33–34 (to engage students and reveal fundamental aspects of Dante's worldview); *Purgatorio* 1–2 (Casella), 30 (Beatrice's arrival); *Paradiso* 3, 32. These cantos present a basic understanding of the whole work: Casella's failed embrace and Virgil's departure illuminate the importance of giving up worldly attachments in *Purgatorio*, whereas *Paradiso* 3 and 32 allow students to compare the structures of Heaven, Hell, and Purgatory.

Complete *Divine Comedy*. In courses devoted wholly to the *Comedy* (whether in English or Italian), students spend the first week and a half reading the poem on their own, accompanied by lectures on background. The remainder of the course includes careful rereading and discussion of the complete *Inferno* and selections from *Purgatorio and Paradiso* focused on various themes appropriate to the instructor's interest and expertise.

Complete *Inferno*; *Purgatorio* 1–6, 8, 10–11, 13, 16–18, 20–26, 30; *Paradiso* 1, 3, 5, 6, 9–13, 15–17, 23–26, 33. This two-semester sequence covers *Inferno* in the first semester and the selections from *Purgatorio* and *Paradiso* in the second. To overcome the challenges in teaching *Paradiso*'s language, abstraction, and philosophical and theological complexity (heightened by students' lack of knowledge about ancient or medieval history), an approach that favors themes over the linear succession of cantos can be helpful. For *Paradiso*, use Auerbach's essays and start at 33.

Complete *Divine Comedy* (in translation). This large lecture course focused on the *Divine Comedy* in English also makes use of supplemental readings from Dante's other works, including the entirety of the *Vita nuova* and *De vulgari eloquentia* and selections from *Convivio* and *Monarchia*, together with other poems.

Advanced Undergraduate and Graduate

Inferno 1, 4, 5, 10, 15, 26–27, 32–33; *Purgatorio* 1–2, 11, 26–31. These selections work well for an introductory course on medieval literature in Italian.

Complete *Inferno* and *Purgatorio*; *Paradiso* 1–6, 10–18, 24–26, 29–33. Optional: the *Vita nuova*. Suitable for a seminar at the graduate level.

Approaches and Challenges

Though it might be easily surmised without a statistical analysis, it is important to give a sense of the overwhelming diversity of approaches adopted in the Dante classroom as conveyed by the survey. As one example, in response to the question, "What do you see as the most important themes or issues to emphasize in teaching Dante's Comedy?," some ninety-five themes were proposed, ranging from Dante's concept of justice to numerology (respondents often provided more than one theme for this question). Likewise, the critical and theoretical approaches adopted were varied and distinct, including more tradi-tional methods (e.g., philology; Dante's historical and political contexts; theo-logical frameworks) and modern theory (e.g., Foucault). Many respondents cited the authors and critics in our bibliographical lists in part 1 as essential to illustrating these perspectives for their students.

The greatest challenges in the Dante classroom are the historical contexts and theological concepts unknown to many students today, for which we hope the essays in this volume will provide useful suggestions. Ignorance of key in-tertexts, such as the Bible and Virgil's *Aeneid*, poses an obstacle to the instruction of the poem. These problems are often compounded by preconceptions about Dante, the poem, and the medieval period, all of which make Dante's *Comedy* seem inaccessible, foreign, or even offensive. Sharing the sentiment of many, one respondent wrote that the greatest challenge when teaching Dante is ad-justing between the poem's social and literary contexts and its pertinence today, underlining the need to address both the historical nature of the poem and its inclusiveness. This sentiment was echoed in another response that suggested laying the groundwork for a sufficiently complex understanding of the poem's context (regional, literary, historical, religious, philosophical) is crucial even while it detracts from the course's genuine subject. There are difficulties posed by a theologized view of the poem that leads students to believe it is an ortho-dox text. One instructor noted that students must be reminded that the work is poetry, not theology, and that students should view the Christian context as a tradition that informs Dante's writing. Yet others observed that they had to grapple with Dante's nonnormative stance on doctrinal matters, because stu-dents often become preoccupied with Dante's unorthodox portrayal of Heaven and Hell. Since this was a problem for Dante's original readers as well, students can speculate on Dante's reasons for this deviation.

Other challenges include the language of poetry itself, both in the original and in translation. Many instructors lament the lack of time to engage in close readings of Dante's poem, especially for students daunted by poetry in general. The ability to appreciate the beauty of a word, a verse, or a tercet within an encyclopedic poem of stunning breadth and depth is a critical skill that instruc-tors of Dante aim to teach with varying degrees of success. Such a sentiment was expressed by one respondent, who emphasized the difficulty in helping general education students learn to identify key details within the dense poem and relate these concrete elements to the abstract structure, as well as in guid-ing them to appreciate the intellectual and emotional reactions the design of the poem produces. Difficulties with language exist in the Italian-language classroom as well, though students' gratification after learning to read Dante in his original tongue is great, as they find the process of working through the language barrier both fascinating and empowering.

The paradox of teaching Dante's text is that the many difficulties and chal-lenges presented by the poem are often those features that fascinate students.

The greatest attractions of the poem dovetail with the challenges described above: allegory, the autobiographical nature of the text, the beauty of the language, the vivid punishments, conversion narrative, ethics, how the journey of the pilgrim mirrors that of the reader, the vivid imagery of Hell, *Paradiso* itself, the relationship between Dante and Virgil, the use of the Bible, and the poem's encyclopedic nature. Finally, the poet's personality can both attract and repulse many students. One person commented that while students are fascinated with Dante's imaginative mind and ability to capture the medieval worldview and moral system in a poem that is still very much alive today, they are equally disturbed by his seemingly self-righteous and judgmental nature and by his obsessive passion for Beatrice. Yet others noted that their students can empathize with the trials that Dante underwent and the challenges posed by his material and the limits of language, and in this way they are able to forge a sort of relationship with the poet, which increases their enjoyment of the *Comedy*.

All in all, the challenges, rewards, and joy in teaching Dante's *Comedy* are certainly worth the effort, as our many respondents have told us. Their thoughts and suggestions have had a profound influence on the fundamental issues presented and discussed in this volume. We are confident that instruction in the poet's life and works will continue to thrive and that students and teachers will reap many benefits from this richly rewarding educational experience.

The Essays in This Volume

The volume is organized in four sections: "Textual Traditions, Language, and Authority"; "Society and Ethics"; "The Reception of the *Comedy*"; and "Instructional Contexts and Pedagogical Strategies." Teachers of the poem and their students face many challenges, frustrations, and attractions in their study of the *Comedy*. The first section, "Textual Traditions, Language, and Authority," addresses some traditional areas of study related to the poem while attending to recent developments within those fields and offering specific advice on how to approach this material in the classroom. Seven essays fall under the heading of "Society and Ethics," focusing on trends in literary studies that have opened up Dante scholarship in multiple ways, shedding light on the desire of modern readers to reaffirm Dante's poem as a living classic that can be profitably read from new theoretical perspectives. Six essays are dedicated to "The Reception of the *Comedy*," which examine Dante and the visual arts and media, Dante's reception in African American literature, the ways in which music influenced Dante as well as the musical adaptations of the poem and its themes in later centuries, and the poet's image and work in popular culture, including video games. In the final section, "Instructional Contexts and Pedagogical Strategies," the presentation of concrete pedagogical strategies for specific instructional contexts provide readers with essential suggestions for approaching a variety of classroom challenges.

Textual Traditions, Language, and Authority

Teachers of the poem and their students face many challenges, frustrations, and attractions in their study of the *Comedy*. The eight essays of this first section address some traditional areas of study related to the poem while attending to recent developments within those fields and offering specific advice on how to approach this material in the classroom.

Teodolinda Barolini's essay, "Dante, Teacher of His Reader," addresses how the instructor of the *Divine Comedy* must, self-evidently, contend with decisions made by the author. Less self-evident perhaps is that, whereas some of Dante's authorial decisions aid in the teaching process, others offer notable challenges. One of the brilliant idiosyncrasies of the *Divine Comedy* is Dante's idea of inverting the normative communication flow in presenting information to his reader. Significant among the challenges of teaching the *Divine Comedy* is that, by beginning his story in Hell, Dante has committed himself to the strategy of communicating information upside down—indeed, to an upside-down pedagogy.

In their essay, "Teaching the *Divine Comedy* from Its Manuscripts," H. Wayne Storey and Isabella Magni remind us that how we read the *Comedy* in print is subject to hundreds of years of critical accretion and conventions that tell us more about the culture that has prepared the edition and commentary than about Dante's own early fourteenth century. Material philology examines the *Comedy* in its historical forms to consider how the poet's own culture and subsequent cultures actually read the work, considering the literary work as a document in all its iterations, from the script and layout in which it was copied to the treatment of previous manuscripts in later copies and editions.

The *Bible* is an essential intertext for the *Comedy*, as it was for the culture of the entire Middle Ages, both regarding its presumed content—the history of the Judeo-Christian community from the creation to the apocalypse—and the styles in which it was written. Ronald L. Martinez, in his essay "Duels of Interpretation: The Bible between Dante and the Church," reminds us that the aspect of Dante hardest to impart to contemporary students is the intense, detailed specificity of its engagement with its own time and place. Martinez offers ways of teaching Dante's complex relationship to the Bible, as it serves as a source text with which Dante's poem is in frequent dialogue despite the poet's ambivalence toward the authority of Scripture.

In "Following Virgil's Lantern: Teaching Dante in the Light of Antiquity," Elsa Filosa compares specific sections of Dante's *Comedy* and classical Latin texts to identify analogies, differences, and intertextual parallels in an attempt to understand Dante's relations with his ancient sources in concrete ways. The *Comedy*, deliberately and consistently, even if sometimes with sadness, sets out to marginalize the Greco-Roman classical legacy, which also includes the learning and philosophy brought to Europe from the Islamic world by the Arabs.

Dante finds places for Averroes and Avicenna in Limbo, and also for Saladin, as a model of chivalric nobility, but he condemns Mohammed and Ali for fraud. Brenda Deen Schildgen's essay, "Dante Casts Shadows over the Legacy of the Classical Past," explores how to teach this division between cultural and political spheres that pervades the *Comedy*, examining how Dante incorporates and probes the limits of Greek and Islamic philosophy and letters, even while he condemns both spheres politically.

F. Regina Psaki's essay, "Teaching Dante, Beatrice, and Courtly Love in the *Divine Comedy*," departs from the premise that we will never reach a definitive answer on *how* the poet construed his love for Beatrice, or on how that love related to the "courtly love" tradition Dante was reinterpreting when making Beatrice the medium and mover of the pilgrim's very salvation. Rather, Psaki proposes a sequence of textual loci in the poem, each paired with an example of a courtly love song and romance, to guide students in interpreting the single cantos and reaching their own conclusions about these big questions: Who was Beatrice for Dante—for the pilgrim, the poet, the author? What does the poem suggest about courtly love?

Dante is not only a supreme vernacular poet but also one of the first theorists of the vernacular, from the genealogy of vernacular poetry in chapter 25 of the *Vita nuova* to the historical and rhetorical distinctions of the *De vulgari eloquentia*. Throughout the *Comedy*, Dante engages this vernacular tradition in a variety of ways, staging encounters with his own past poetic production and fellow poets while also testing and challenging his own theoretical principles. Because Dante highlights the importance of these relationships in the *Comedy*, most instructors will want to make students aware of this tradition and its impact on Dante's poetry. In his essay, "Dante and the Spectrum of Medieval Vernacular Poetry; or, How Giacomo and Joyce, Brunetto and Eliot, and Bertran and Pound Rhyme," Martin Eisner selects three moments from the *Inferno* that can make students aware of the larger traditions, both medieval and modern, in which Dante appears, giving them some taste of Dante's poetry in the original, along with some key modern texts by James Joyce, T. S. Eliot, and Ezra Pound.

Given the wide range of languages into which the *Comedy* has been translated, Nick Havely begins his essay, "Transnational Dantes," by noting the scope and resources for expanding the teaching of Dante transnationally. He compares the contents, objectives, and outcomes of three more recent courses—in the United Kingdom, the United States, and Switzerland—that have in various ways addressed the wider reception of Dante. The uptake and outcomes of these courses are of particular interest; hence, prominence is given to students' diverse cultural and intellectual backgrounds and to some examples of essays produced for assessment. The discussion concludes by imagining future directions in such teaching and how these could involve thinking about Dante beyond yet more borders.

Society and Ethics

Seven essays fall under the heading of "Society and Ethics," in which we focus on trends in literary studies that have opened up Dante scholarship in multiple ways, shedding light on the desire of modern readers to reaffirm Dante's poem as a living classic that can be profitably read from new theoretical perspectives.

Today's students can discover in the *Comedy* a poet and text grappling with questions central to both the history of sexuality and current polemics in queer theory: what is the relation between sexual acts and personal identity, and is the latter a strictly modern creation? Does male-male sexuality subscribe or undermine patriarchy? Is queer sex inherently antisocial? How does the queer reconfigure history and time? What place does same-sex desire have in the biological universe? Dante's text offers up challenges to normative modes of sex and gender throughout, not least in the classical myths and epic narratives that inform the poem at nearly every turn. Gary Cestaro's essay, "Sodomite, Homosexual, Queer: Teaching Dante LGBTQ," offers strategies for talking about queer sex in the Dante classroom.

Students reading the *Divine Comedy* in the twenty-first century, especially those not familiar with medieval misogyny, are often puzzled by Dante's stance on women, given the plurality of perspectives offered by the poem. To lead students to a more nuanced understanding of women and gender in the *Comedy* that moves beyond designations of feminism and misogyny, Kristina Olson's essay, "Conceptions of Women and Gender in the *Comedy*," shows how to approach questions of gender and Dante's incorporation of women and the "feminine" in different modes: in terms of historicized poetics (the relation between the fictional and the historical for women in his afterlife); political rhetoric (the creation of a historiography that alternately depends on female and male morality); and language (the significance of a maternal vernacular).

Joanna Drell's essay, "Teaching Dante's *Divine Comedy* in a History Course," suggests approaches to teaching the poem in undergraduate medieval-Renaissance history classes. By examining Dante's inclusion and reimaging of different historical figures, the poem becomes an invaluable source to understand the pivotal, often chaotic history of Italy in the thirteenth and early fourteenth centuries. Dante's masterpiece not only presents his perceptions of certain political figures and social institutions of his Italy—from the communes of the North to the kingdom of the South—but also invites students to consider what constitutes historical evidence, how and to what ends it has been shaped and reshaped.

Focusing on the poet's critical approach to the papacy, an institution both established by Christ yet also embedded in thirteenth- and early-fourteenth-century politics, George Dameron's essay, "Dante and the Papacy," demonstrates how an understanding of Dante's critique can enhance our appreciation of the poem's complex religious and moral themes. A close reading of selected cantos associated with Dante's criticism of the papacy, enriched by an understanding of contemporary factional politics, can lead the reader to a deeper understanding of the poet's own perspectives regarding the proper place of the Church in mankind's journey to God through both time and space.

In writing the *Divine Comedy* and figuring himself as a character in the work, Dante deliberately foregrounded two distinct but interrelated notions. Dante the poet not only acknowledged a profound intellectual and cultural inheritance but also asserted his willingness to adapt or rewrite tradition to invent an otherworldly realm that would compel his readers to consider in an immediate way the consequences of human decisions and actions. Dante the pilgrim dramatizes a process of individual learning, erring, and growth, coupled with passages of profound self-reflection. Sherry Roush, in her essay, "The Quest for Ethical Self-Reflection," explains projects that address these notions, showing how students develop keen understandings of the intent, action, and social-societal influences of ethical decision-making, ones that highlight the not-exclusively-Catholic values and evolving ethical dilemmas of college students today.

Considering that Dante's *Comedy* is one of the great works of literary art in the Catholic tradition, in his essay, "Teaching the Theological Dimension of Dante's *Divine Comedy*," Paul J. Contino addresses such questions as: How can Dante claim that "Love" fashioned the Inferno? What is the relation between God's grace and our freely chosen work? Is such work on our part necessary? The theological issues are existential ones for students of faith, and remain integral to the aesthetic form of the *Comedy*.

Much of the appeal of the *Comedy* to contemporary readers is that, like so many of us, Dante the pilgrim knows himself to be profoundly lost: "Midway in our life's journey, I found myself in dark woods, the right way lost" (*Inf.* 1.1–3) Even students far from the crisis of middle age, however, can find in Dante's story a version of their own condition. A quick perusal of popular culture reveals how fully the poet's "nel mezzo del cammin" (*Inf.* 1.1) has become shorthand for disorientation, addiction, frustration, clinical depression, and crisis. Readers who may have no interest in fourteenth-century Italian politics or Catholic theology have nonetheless recognized in Dante's terrifying experience of loss an image of their own malaise—and with that recognition a reason to begin the journey of reading the *Comedy*. As Peter S. Hawkins demonstrates in his essay, "Dante, Poet of Loss," a Dante course might well begin by posing the issue of the student's own "dark wood."

The Reception of the *Comedy*

Six essays are dedicated to "Approaches to the Reception of the *Comedy*," which examine Dante and the visual arts and media, Dante's specific reception in African American literature, the ways in which he was influenced by the music of his age as well as the musical adaptations of the poem and its themes in later centuries, and how the poet's image and work has found its way into popular culture, including video games.

Aida Audeh's essay, "Teaching Dante and the Visual Arts," explores how art can enrich or deepen understanding of Dante's poem in an introductory or intermediate-level course intended for undergraduate students and taught by an instructor with or without background in art history. She approaches a canto from the poem by first going through literary analysis and then bringing in artists' interpretations in pairs to facilitate comparisons and contrasts that best elucidate key aspects of Dante's text.

The habit of reading typological or allegorical relations between scenes placed one above the other at the same time that one reads storylines horizontally would have been further reinforced by Dante's viewing of major fresco programs, such as those of the Baptistery in Florence and the Arena Chapel in Padua. The pervasive use of vertical parallels between scriptural (and indeed classical and mythological) events and persons through different visual media—from mosaics and frescoes to the architecture and sculptures of churches and cathedrals—highlights, therefore, a familiar medieval exegetical practice. In "Reading Dante's *Comedy* with Giotto," Heather Webb describes her experiment to test how much the entire *Comedy* might be profitably read in this way by looking for vertical parallels.

One pedagogical problem that arises in the world-literature survey course is the need to cultivate student investment in premodern texts that may feel far removed from the current moment in which students themselves are immersed. In "Rewritings and Relevance: Teaching Gloria Naylor's *Linden Hills* alongside Dante's *Inferno*," Suzanne Manizza Roszak shows how students become more engaged and invested in the material, which they perceive as more relevant to their contemporary context, when they examine the echoes of Dante's text in contemporary African American fiction. They learn to analyze how an important African American novel adapts and reshapes a premodern European one, simultaneously drawing on and challenging the primacy of the European literary tradition.

The rich soundscape of Dante's *Comedy* provides opportunities to open a multimedia perspective on the masterwork of Italian literature. Francesco Ciabattoni, in his essay, "Teaching Dante through Music," outlines several possible approaches to teaching the *Comedy* through music. One option invites the teacher to use the sacred and secular songs mentioned in the poem to illuminate the production of the troubadours and church music, thus expanding the scope of the course. In another approach, students can learn how Dante represents music in words and how this intertext, immediately recognizable to a medieval readership, would affect the reception of the poem. In addition to these, one can explore how composers of different periods were inspired by Dante's poem.

On first encountering the *Divine Comedy*, many students find the poem unapproachable, a monolith of a past age that bears little resemblance to our fast-paced, eclectic, digital one. Incorporating particular case studies of Dante's continued presence in contemporary popular culture helps render more intelligible the ethical and psychological dimensions of the poem, allowing students to understand Dante's locally and historically specific cultural commentary by analogy with their own. "Dante's Afterlife in Popular Culture," by Elizabeth Coggeshall, addresses different methods to incorporate Dante's presence in contemporary and popular media—the many and varied Dante memes—into a traditional course on the poem.

Brandon K. Essary illustrates a way of teaching Dante's *Inferno* alongside the 2010 Electronic Arts Games video game *Dante's* Inferno in his essay, "From Poem to PlayStation 3: Teaching Dante with Video Games." In it he describes his capstone course as writing intensive, utilizing a variety of writing approaches to promote high-level critical thinking. This essay reflects on the pedagogical issue of how best to utilize video games—especially those based on historical events and/or literature—in order to teach Italian literature, history, and culture.

Instructional Contexts and Pedagogical Strategies

In the final section, "Instructional Contexts and Pedagogical Strategies," readers will find essential suggestions for how to deal with a variety of challenges confronted in today's classroom through the presentation of concrete pedagogical strategies for specific instructional contexts. Nine essays offer new perspectives on ways to approach the poem.

In his essay, "On Selecting the 'Best' Translation of Dante," Madison U. Sowell weighs the many factors—tone, rhyme, register, audience, community, and others—that help instructors select the most appropriate translation of the *Comedy* for a given course.

In "Damned Rhetoric: Teaching Dante's *Inferno* in Translation to Undergraduates," Suzanne Hagedorn discusses strategies to teach Dante's *Comedy* in translation to undergraduates in both upper- and lower-division general education or in comparative literature courses. Using in-class writing exercises that lead to small- and large-group discussions, she highlights interesting rhetorical features of the speeches Dante places into the mouths of the damned: namely, their tendency to consider and discuss only themselves, and how elements in their speeches gesture at larger Christian meanings that Dante intends his reader to grasp, even while these sinners have misunderstood or ignored them, a fatal decision that has led to their present position in Hell.

Simone Marchesi presents a set of active-learning techniques in teaching Dante's *Comedy* to undergraduate students, in particular freshmen, in his essay, "Dante's *Comedy* as First-Year Seminar: From Early Engagement to Self-Reliance." These techniques are aimed at promoting student early engagement with and critical reading of the text, as well as sustained discussion in the seminars. The goal of these techniques is to allow the instructor to withdraw as much as possible from the center of instruction, becoming instead a facilitator for independent, independently motivated, and collaborative learning.

In "Writing like Dante: Understanding the *Inferno* through Creative Writing," Nicolino Applauso proposes a new approach to teaching Dante's *Inferno* through students' own creative endeavors. By implementing creative writing, students can understand theoretical concepts in connection with literature and poetry (such as metaphors, rhymes, figures of speech, etc.) and recognize the presence of a well-defined narrative structure within the *Inferno*. The main objective is thus to empower students to put theory into practice by creating original content in English or Italian, thereby developing a deeper appreciation of Dante's *Inferno*.

Given the student mix in many Dante courses, assignments can scaffold scholarly endeavor without expectation of prior formal research beyond freshman composition to produce, by end of term, a conference paper in conversation with recently published scholarly research. In "Scaffolding Scholarly Research for a Senior-Level Course on Dante in Translation," Katherine V. Haynes demonstrates how to apply modern pedagogical scaffolding to an upper-level Dante course, using the poet's own glosses and early commentaries as well as modern research to build students' knowledge base and scholarly expertise to fulfill course requirements. The pedagogical techniques of scaffolding scholarly reading and research methodology, beginning with Dante's own writing, improves critical thinking and articulation of complex thought for all students, not just majors, and is easily measurable.

In "'Cliques in Hell': Teaching Dante to Nontraditional Students," Susan Gorman teaches several cantos of the *Inferno* in her Great Works of Western Literature class for the Clemente Course in the Humanities, which allows low-income students to earn a year of humanities credits from an affiliated college or university. In her essay, Gorman outlines how to use Dante in a lower-level course to build skills in textual analysis and participation, as well as increase confidence. Gorman also discusses the ways students defamiliarize the *Inferno* for instructors.

Jessica Levenstein teaches a high school elective on Dante's *Inferno* over eleven weeks. In "Teaching Dante to High School Seniors," Levenstein discusses how to provide students with tools to make sense of the text without overwhelming them. To accomplish these goals, she helps the class understand the poem as crafted by a human hand, informed by the poet's own struggle, grievances, and passions. She draws attention to Dante's stance as God's scribe, his effort to surpass his literary models, and his anxieties about the power of language. If students can see the poet behind the veil of medieval history, religion, and culture, they can get to the heart of the poem's concerns.

Ronald Herzman's experience teaching Dante in a maximum-security correctional facility (Attica, New York) has dramatically shaped pedagogical strategies in all his subsequent experiences teaching the *Comedy*. What was forced on him because of the unusual circumstances of Attica prison has taken on new life in other circumstances and may be helpful for others who must present a poem so vast and complex to their own students, of whatever stripe.

Among issues related to self-confidence and writing ability, Herzman had to convince the inmates to take Dante seriously as a truth teller. But these students—who really wanted to know what Dante had to say about moral improvement—also came to insights before their teacher did. In his essay, "Teaching Dante in Prison," Herzman elaborates the many challenges he faced and the strategies he adopted, many of which can help instructors in various instructional formats.

In her essay, "Beatrice in the Tag Cloud," Carol Chiodo examines the opportunities offered by two related Web technologies to writing-intensive literature courses. When used thoughtfully, the blog and the tag cloud are valuable tools for teaching Dante's *Divine Comedy*. They provide an impetus for classroom discussion, an occasion for immediate formative assessment, substantive scaffolding for thesis development and argument analysis, and a constructive space for collaborative editing and peer review. In its role as an asynchronous online venue for discussion, the blog extends and enhances classroom discussion, creating a space for intellectual digression and creativity as well as ongoing instruction. The tag cloud, in turn, functions as an iterative index of the collective interests and challenges of the students in their reading and writing. Attentive course design and planning allow these technologies to play an integral role in deepening students' engagement with Dante's work, honing their critical writing skills in an online environment while leveraging the benefits of collaborative work.

NOTES

[1] Our respondents include faculty members at some eighty-five colleges and universities (as well as one community college and one high school) who teach in a variety of departments: forty-three in languages and literature departments; twenty-nine in English and comparative literature; and ten in other humanities-related fields.

[2] Some titles of courses devoted entirely to the Florentine poet are Dante and His World; Journey of (Self) Discovery: Dante's *Comedy*; To Hell and Back: Dante's Archetypal Journey, and so on.

[3] The authors may include Aquinas, Aristotle, Augustine, Jane Austen, Mary Jo Bang, Samuel Beckett, the Bible, Sandow Birk, William Blake, Giovanni Boccaccio, Jorge Luis Borges, Sandro Botticelli, Guido Cavalcanti, Miguel Cervantes, Geoffrey Chaucer, Clive James, Fabrizio De Andrè, Charles Dickens, Fyodor Dostoyevsky, Frederick Douglass, W. E. B. Du Bois, T. S. Eliot, Desiderius Erasmus, Robert Frost, Giacomino da Verona, Giotto di Bondone, Seamus Heaney, Homer, Jean de Meun, Brunetto Latini, Primo Levi, Lucan, Martin Luther, Marie de France, Herman Melville, Thomas Merton, Michelangelo, John Milton, Eugenio Montale, Toni Morrison, Ovid, Blaise Pascal, Giovanni Pascoli, Alan Paton, Francis Petrarch, Plato, Ezra Pound, Robert Pinsky, J. K. Rowling, Roberto Saviano, William Shakespeare, Statius, Alfred Tennyson, Virgil, Derek Walcott, Eli Wiesel, Wolfram von Eschenbach, William Wordsworth, and many more.

[4] Classes with titles such as Gendering the Canon: Women, Authorship, and Voice in the Italian Trecento; Courtly Love, Marriage, and Adultery; Redefining the Cosmos; and Dante on the Screen: The *Divine Comedy* in Popular Culture and Media are examples of how Dante is taught at the advanced levels in the Italian-language classroom.

Dante, Teacher of His Reader

Teodolinda Barolini

The author of the *Divine Comedy* is in many ways the teacher of his reader. The *Comedy* famously boasts addresses to the reader, apostrophes that issue authorial instructions for reading. In this essay I look at Dante's authorial pedagogy in the hope that today's teachers of the *Divine Comedy* may benefit from a brief consideration of how the *Comedy*'s author approaches his self-appointed task as teacher. We must always contend with decisions made by the author, but it may be useful to parse these decisions, noting that some facilitate the teaching process while others impede it. In the latter circumstances the presence of a teacher (or at least a commentator, a teacher through the medium of writing) is critical to the experience of reading the *Comedy*. When Dante has Francesca da Rimini say "Caina attende chi a vita ci spense" ("Caina waits for him who took our life"; *Inf.* 5.107), he effectively builds in the need for commentators who will tell readers that "Caina" is the zone of lower Hell reserved for traitors of family.[1] The earliest readers of *Inferno* 5 could conceivably have had the classical erudition to know who Minos, Dido, and the other classical figures in the canto are, and could have known of Francesca and her scandal and murder, but no reader could have known what *Caina* is, since it is part of the textual world Dante invents.

As an overarching principle, it will become apparent that in the *Divine Comedy* authorial pedagogy reflects the poet's commitment to realistic representation, to mimesis: Dante's pedagogical approach goes hand in hand with his representational strategies.

In the category of authorial choices that aid the reader (and therefore the reader's teacher), I place Dante's careful coordination at the outset of his poem of formal containers (the canto) with geographic-ideological containers (the circle of Hell and the sin punished within it). Thus, in the beginning of *Inferno* there is a one-to-one correspondence between canto and geographic section of Hell: one canto is devoted to one infernal place. In practice, *Inferno* 3 treats the vestibule of Hell (the area that houses the neutrals, the neither-good-nor-bad), *Inferno* 4 deals with the first circle of Hell (Limbo), *Inferno* 5 explores the second circle of Hell (lust), *Inferno* 6 presents the third circle of Hell (gluttony), and *Inferno* 7 handles the fourth circle of Hell (avarice and prodigality). This tight alignment of formal with geographic delimiters loosens in the latter part of *Inferno* 7, where the descent to the fifth circle occurs—for the first time—before the canto's end, so that the fifth circle, devoted to anger, no longer aligns with the boundaries of a canto. The practice of strict alignment adopted for the first six cantos is a teaching strategy, in that it allows readers (along with "Dante," the protagonist of the *Divine Comedy*) to grasp more readily the contours of the new world to which they are being introduced. These contours become more fluid, more narratologically interesting, and more difficult to keep in mind, as readers leave the circle of avarice and prodigality and enter the circle of anger.

With respect to the structure of Hell, Dante chooses to withhold and delay basic information. The explanation for Hell's moral structure is offered only in *Inferno* 11, where we learn that Dante's Hell is based on Aristotle's *Nicomachean Ethics*. This information means that the reader who has inferred from circles 2 through 5 of Dante's Hell that its arrangement is based on the seven deadly vices is mistaken, despite traversing the circles of lust, gluttony, avarice, and anger. Dante's pedagogy therefore involves surprise: withholding information allows for the staging of the pilgrim's confusion about the nature of the sins that precede the city of Dis and Virgil's sharp rebuke, in which he tells the pilgrim to turn to "la tua Etica" ("your *Ethics*"; *Inf.* 11.80) for better comprehension. The teacher of *Inferno* has to decide whether to disclose early on that the apparent logic of the seven deadly vices is only apparent, or to allow the poet his surprise in *Inferno* 11. I try to follow the poet, allowing suspense about the structure of Hell to build, while giving information that makes the buildup to the revelation of *Inferno* 11 more visible: Dante has already deviated from the template of the seven deadly vices by pairing prodigality with avarice in circle four. By introducing prodigality as equal and opposite to avarice in *Inferno* 7, the poet constructs an Aristotelian template based on the idea of a virtuous mean flanked by vicious extremes (here liberality between avarice and prodigality), a template that differs profoundly from the Christian.

We see a similar use of familiarizing techniques followed by greater narrative *variatio* and fluidity in *Purgatorio*, where Dante treats the first terrace of Mount Purgatory, the terrace of pride, as a formal teaching tool. He divides his major narrative building blocks by canto, thus making them discrete and recognizable: the biblical and classical examples of humility, the virtue that corresponds to the vice being purged, are allocated to *Purgatorio* 10; the encounters with purging prideful souls are assigned to *Purgatorio* 11; the biblical and classical examples of the vice being purged, followed by the components that consistently signal departure from a terrace (the encounter with an angel who removes a *P* from Dante's brow and the recitation of a beatitude), are allotted to *Purgatorio* 12. As we progress in *Purgatorio*, these narrative elements, common to each of the seven terraces as liturgical elements are common to a Mass, will not again be so neatly and usefully segregated. A narrative feature that aligns with the beginning of a terrace (the examples of the virtue) may be at the end of a canto (e.g., the examples of meekness in *Purgatorio* 15), whereas a narrative feature that aligns with the end of a terrace (the encounter with the angel) may be situated toward a canto's beginning (e.g., the angel in *Purgatorio* 17).

Dante's implied message to the reader suggests that we take the layout of the first terrace as a reference point: we should get our bearings here, he seems to tell us, where the purgatorial terrace is parsed by the canto delimiters in such a way as to render its narrative elements and their sequential unfolding extremely clear. We need to hold on to that reference point as we navigate the subsequent six terraces, where the same liturgically repetitive narrative building blocks are artfully, and at times confusingly, arranged. Indeed, the decoupling of the narrative elements of the terraces from the boundaries of the cantos is artful in its creation of confusion: the reader experiences the kind of ordered timelessness that is the product of a liturgical experience.

The naive-voyager paradigm is fundamental to the authorial pedagogy of the *Divine Comedy*: I refer to Dante's use of himself as a naive voyager whose learning curve offers a handy and intuitive model for the reader. The "pilgrim" (as the first-person protagonist is often called by Dante critics) voices insecurities and receives lessons and sometimes even rebukes from his teachers. Most of all, the pilgrim learns. Thus, Dante protagonist faints on the floor of Hell after listening to Francesca da Rimini's tale of love and death in *Inferno* 5, but he does not weep one tear after listening to the agonizing story of death by starvation recounted by Ugolino della Gherardesca in *Inferno* 33. Listening to Ugolino is of course an experience that occurs many cantos later than the experience of listening to Francesca. The author in this way uses textual time to signal the learning experience of the pilgrim: between *Inferno* 5 and *Inferno* 33 Dante naive voyager has learned enough about Hell to inure him from feeling sympathy for Ugolino, despite the latter's graphic use of his children's deaths to elicit his interlocutor's pity. In the language of Hell, Dante naive voyager has learned to absorb that, in Hell, "[q]ui vive la pietà quand'è ben morta" ("[h]ere pity lives when it is truly dead"; *Inf.* 20.28).

Although Dante gives us the information that in Hell "pity lives when it is truly dead," we lack the cognitive scaffolding to process and understand it, for one of the brilliant idiosyncrasies of the *Divine Comedy* is Dante's idea of inverting the normative communication flow in presenting information to his reader. By beginning his story in Hell, Dante has committed himself to the strategy of communicating information in an upside-down manner. The upside-down pedagogy that governs the experience of reading *Inferno* is a precise cor-relative to Dante's geography of Hell, an inverted cone that burrows into the earth. As the travelers climb out of Hell on Lucifer's body, they cross the center of gravity and experience the righting of that which had been upside down ("sottosopra"): "ov' è la ghiaccia? e questi com'è fitto / sì sottosopra?" ("Where is the ice? And how is he so placed / upside down?"; *Inf.* 34.103–04). Morality mirrors geography: the idea that pity cannot exist in Hell is expressed in such a way as to emphasize conceptual inversion, the lexicon creating a standoff—pity "lives" when it is "dead"—as a way of signaling the necessary conceptual adap-tation to a place where morality is upside down.

Dante challenges the readers of the *Divine Comedy* (and their teachers) by transmitting eschatological information first about Hell, and in a context, the *Inferno*, that does not so much explicate as dramatize. The result is that the reader first receives conceptual categories in incomplete form, at times in in-verted form, as with pity living when it dies. Primary among the conceptual categories allowed to remain unexplicated in this way is justice, which is pre-sented in *Inferno* with no explicit appeal to the idea that grounds the concept of the justice of Hell and makes it comprehensible: free will. The idea of free will must be supplied by the teacher—or not: it is possible to adopt a teaching strat-egy of minimal interference with the author's information flow, although the result is to pass over many excellent teaching opportunities.

In the case of free will, such a teaching opportunity is the statement on the gate of Hell that "Giustizia mosse il mio alto fattore" ("Justice moved my high maker"; *Inf.* 3.4). How was the maker of Hell moved by justice? The idea that God is just in creating Hell relies on the concept of free will, which Dante obscures throughout *Inferno*: just as his lexicon heightens rather than allevi-ates the conceptual hurdle regarding "[q]ui vive la pietà quand'è ben morta" (*Inf.* 20.28; "[h]ere pity lives when it is truly dead"), so the poet makes lexical choices that abet the reader's belief that Hell is a punishment imposed from without—for instance in the term "vendetta" ("vengeance") applied to the punishments of Hell in a phrase like "vendetta di Dio" ("God's vengeance"; *Inf.* 14.16). In this way Dante complicates the teacher's task of communicating that Hell is a freely chosen condition. In *Inferno* Dante repeatedly dramatizes that the souls in Hell were endowed with free will and freely chose their destinies, having them act out the very behaviors that led them to Hell in the first place, but he never clarifies the intellectual basis for why this is so, and therefore how it can be that "Here pity lives when it is truly dead" (*Inf.* 20.28). That lesson will come later.

The principle whereby information is presented in upside-down form in *In-ferno* can be applied to many conceptual categories, but the overarching point to keep in mind is that as a principle it puts readers in a continuous cognitive deficit, always challenging them to work for understanding. For instance, the idea of the Two and One that is Christ is first presented in the *Divine Comedy* through the revolting metamorphosis of man and serpent fused into one "perverse image" that is "two and no one": "due e nessun l'imagine perversa / parea" ("two and no one the perverse image appeared"; *Inf.* 25.77–78). The ontological nonbeing of this "perverse image," the fact that it is "né due né uno" ("neither two nor one"; *Inf.* 25.69), is a perfect perversion of the fundamental Christian mystery of the Incarnation, whereby Christ is simultaneously two and one, God and man.

We can also consider the figure of the Greek hero Ulysses from the perspective of the *Inferno*'s upside-down pedagogy. Dante gives to his Ulysses an Adamic function, meaning that in Dante's very idiosyncratic and personal mythography Ulysses inhabits a moral space analogous to that of Adam in the Christian tradition: Ulysses is a signifier of what Dante's own Adam calls "il trapassar del segno" ("the trespass of the limit"; *Par.* 26.117). We meet Dante's Adam only in *Paradiso* 26, where Adam names another emblem of trespass: Nembrot (Nimrod), traditionally identified as the builder of the Tower of Babel whom we encounter in *Inferno* 31, signifies linguistic trespass and fall and is the only Dantean sinner, other than Ulysses, whom Dante names in each canticle of the *Comedy*. (Another avatar of Ulyssean trespass named in each canticle is the mythological "failed flyer" Phaeton, but he is not an actual sinner in *Inferno*.) By the time we reach *Paradiso* 26, this strange constellation—Ulysses, Nembrot, Adam—makes sense to us.

But certainly Dante, a Christian author, leads his readers on a counterintuitive course to the understanding they eventually attain. It would have been far simpler to have presented Adam himself, rather than Ulysses, as the signifier of Adamic trespass. But in the *Comedy* we work backward, starting in Hell, and thus a meeting with Adam would have been hard to arrange. Again, we see that Dante avoids telling in favor of showing: he wants to stage an encounter, not explain Adam. Nevertheless, the principle of backward reading is not sufficient to account for Ulysses as Dante's avatar of Adam, since Nembrot alone could have fulfilled that function more straightforwardly, confronting one biblical character with another. The remarkable choice of a classical hero for the personification of Adamic trespass is the fruit of a personal mythography, saturated in early humanism and classical antiquity, which creates a yet steeper learning curve for the reader. Complicatedly, we arrive at the idea of Christian trespass through Dante's personal and original reimagining of the Greek hero.

Ultimately, however, for all its conceptual inversions and idiosyncrasies, Hell is a much simpler realm to grasp—and to teach—than Paradise, a state of being that requires us to think in paradoxes: Paradise exists in no place, "perché non è in loco e non s'impola" ("because it is not in space and it has no poles"; *Par.* 22.67), and in no time, but rather "in sua etternità di tempo fore" ("in His eternity outside of time"; *Par.* 29.16). In building readers slowly to where they can tackle the rigors, at once lexical and conceptual, of *Paradiso*, Dante's pedagogic praxis is linear and follows the arrow of time from simpler to harder, from *Inferno* to *Paradiso*.

The teacher of *Paradiso* has a model in the poet, but a severe one: this is a poet who at the beginning of *Paradiso* 2 says to stop reading. There could be no greater challenge to the compact between author and reader than the address in *Paradiso* 2, where Dante—perhaps the only great poet to instruct readers not to keep reading his greatest work—tells readers to desist from sailing behind his ship onto the watery deep lest they get lost. Knowing well that the path ahead will offer few of those blandishments of realism that readers crave (or better: of *the types of realism* that readers crave), Dante begins *Paradiso* 2 with this stern warning:

> O voi che siete in piccioletta barca,
> desiderosi d'ascoltar, seguiti
> dietro al mio legno che cantando varca,
>   tornate a riveder li vostri liti:
> non vi mettete in pelago, ché forse,
> perdendo me, rimarreste smarriti.
>
> O you who are within your little bark,
> eager to listen, following behind
> my ship that, singing, crosses to deep seas,
>   turn back to see your shores again: do not
> attempt to sail the seas I sail; you may,
> by losing sight of me, be left astray.
>   (*Par.* 2.1–6)

One reason we might get lost, sailing into the third canticle, is that it offers little for the reader to hold onto. There are few ports to shield from the perils of the open ocean: from reality unleavened by realism. For *Paradiso*, the part of the *Comedy* that most meditates on reality, on being, is experienced by readers as the least realistic.

Although Dante commands an unparalleled ability to conjure ideas through metaphoric language, for instance "lo gran mar dell'essere" ("great sea of being") of *Paradiso* 1.113, when readers respond to *Paradiso* as the least realistic of the three canticles, they are not wrong. They are reacting to the lack of those specific modalities of realism by which they are most entertained in the etymological sense of "held": *Paradiso* enlists fewer of those modalities of realism that pleasantly hold a reader's attention. Dante is always attempting to be realistic, but realism about the ontological ground of being—about *essere*—is not as entertaining as the realism of place and character so vivid earlier in the poem. Dante's authorial struggle to conjure Paradise is matched by the reader's struggle to hold onto a reality that is less tangible and retainable. And yet the author is still engaged in trying to teach his reader how best to deal with the more arduous learning experience of *Paradiso*.

Let us consider the different modalities of realism we find deployed in the *Comedy*. Dante's realism regarding place generated an immediate pictorial tradition devoted to illustrating the landscapes described by the poet: both those of the afterworld and those evoked by the souls as they recount their lives on earth. Realism of place is also reflected in the degree to which Dante's description of Purgatory for centuries inspired conceptions of the second realm, including Thomas Merton's 1948 religious autobiography *The Seven Story Mountain*. Purgatory was a relatively recent idea in Dante's time, compared with hell or paradise. As a result, Dante's realist *inventio* (including the idea of Purgatory as a mountain, Dante's own contribution to the cultural imaginary) exerted significant influence on later religious thought.

Realism in the delineation of character—the telling details by which a character is revealed—is also in greater supply in the first two canticles, and especially in the *Inferno*, where a verb in the *passato remoto* ("past absolute tense") can cause the consternation and pathos of the pilgrim's dialogue with Cavalcante de' Cavalcanti (*Inf.* 10.68). Delineation of character is present as long as Virgil is present in the poem, for in him Dante has created a character who draws readers to love him as the pilgrim does. Dante does not delineate Beatrice as a character, in the way that he does Virgil—purposely. He does not allow a character to cohere in his depiction of Beatrice, but instead disrupts any coherent delineation with contradictory signifiers: one moment she is described in eroticized lyric language, then as an admiral on a ship, then as a stern mother, and so on, always oscillating so as to disrupt cohesive character development. In this way Dante creates a "pixelated" Beatrice, the gateway to the transcendent, which is not simplifiable, comfortable, consoling, or necessarily likeable.

So how does realism function in the *Paradiso*? The social realism and the realism of place that is so strong in other parts of the *Comedy* is now miniaturized. Realism of place is present in the numerous geographic periphrases that dot *Paradiso* while social realism is mainly relegated to similes. Many similes in the *Paradiso* are little miniatures of the daily life now so distant, seen as though through a telescope. In the *Paradiso* these similes based on human social intercourse are frequently destabilizing and counterintuitive with respect to the reality of Paradise they are illuminating. For instance, to describe the movement of the souls of the heaven of the sun, who are all male, Dante compares them to ladies who pause while dancing, as they wait for a new melody to begin (*Par.* 10.79–81). An even more detailed and incongruous vignette of human society (and of women in society) is offered by the simile that describes the arrival of Saint John, who joins his comrades Saints Peter and James as though he were a maiden rising up to join the other dancers at a wedding, not through any fault of excess eagerness but as a way of honoring the bride (*Par.* 25.103–08).

The nonminiaturized realism found in *Paradiso* is much more abstract, as befits the philosophical nature of the enterprise. Perhaps we could call this a *conceptual realism*, one that struggles to represent ideas rather than people, places, or things. Dante's attempt to be faithful to reality, in other words, takes him to the mimesis of ideas: the notion that all the souls of Paradise are together in the Empyrean but displayed through the various heavens as a cognitive aid for the pilgrim (and the reader), the idea of creation in a big bang, the idea of an alternate universe. These concepts create representational challenges for the poet that simultaneously function within the naive-voyager narrative structure of the *Comedy* as pedagogic problems. Thus, at the beginning of *Paradiso* 13 Dante gives the reader a task of visualization that is in effect a lesson in how to apply conceptual or geometric realism: how to make realistic the nonrealistic (which is, of course, not the same as the nonreal).

To visualize the twenty-four souls dancing around the pilgrim at the beginning of *Paradiso* 13, the reader must imagine stars: first, fifteen stars of the first magnitude, followed by the seven stars of Ursa Major, followed by the two brightest stars of Ursa Minor, thus reaching twenty-four stars. Three times Dante orders the reader to imagine—"imagini"—and to do the work of holding the image in the mind. This is the work of making the real become realistic, therefore more "com-prehensible" (i.e., "hold-on-to-able"):

> Imagini, chi bene intender cupe
> quel ch'i' or vidi—e ritegna l'image,
> mentre ch'io dico, come ferma rupe—,
>   quindici stelle che 'n diverse plage
> lo ciel avvivan di tanto sereno
> che soperchia de l'aere ogne compage;
>   imagini quel carro a cu' il seno
> basta del nostro cielo e notte e giorno,
> sì ch'al volger del temo non vien meno;
>   imagini la bocca di quel corno
> che si comincia in punta de lo stelo
> a cui la prima rota va dintorno.

> Let him imagine, who would rightly seize
> what I saw now—and let him while I speak
> retain that image like a steadfast rock—
>   in heaven's different parts, those fifteen stars
> that quicken heaven with such radiance
> as to undo the air's opacities;
>   let him imagine, too, that Wain which stays
> within our heaven's bosom night and day,
> so that its turning never leaves our sight;
>   let him imagine those two stars that form
> the mouth of that Horn which begins atop
> the axle round which the first wheel revolves.
>   (*Par.* 13.1–12)

In the above passage the reader is commanded to do the work of the imagination, the work of giving plasticity and reality to what Dante saw, with three imperatives ("imagini") and a series of precise mental instructions, in effect the rules of a visualizing exercise, a method of self-entertainment: the reader must hold onto the first image as though to a firm rock, while Dante on his side of the collaboration proceeds to unfold the second image and then the third. If readers can hold the sequential images in mind, they then can create the composite image, still but a shadow of what Dante saw (*Par.* 13.19–20).

Despite the admonition of *Paradiso* 2, where the poet commands to desist from following his ship, the *Comedy*'s pedagogical impulse is still our lifeline in *Paradiso*. Confronted with the challenge of writing the ineffable, the poet meditates frequently on writing and representation, and also thereby on teaching and learning. In the spirit of the pedagogic principle stated in *Paradiso* 5, whereby "non fa scïenza, / sanza lo ritenere, avere inteso" ("He who hears, / but does not hold what he has heard, learns nothing"; 41–42), the author of *Paradiso* offers "study guides" like the one at the beginning of *Paradiso* 13, seeking to help the reader retain and therefore learn.

In each realm of the afterlife Dante devises different pedagogical protocols to challenge and aid the reader, making teachers not only of the pilgrim's guides, especially Virgil, "dolce pedagogo" ("sweet pedagogue"; *Purg.* 12.3), and Beatrice, "dolce guida e cara" ("sweet guide and dear"; *Par.* 23.34), but also of himself, the poet. These protocols are imbued with affect, as teaching always is (thus the adjective "sweet" above). For all that affect can cause us to hold onto the wrong idea, undermining our ability to learn when "l'affetto l'intelletto lega" ("affect binds the intellect"; *Par.* 13.120), it is also the basic motor that drives writer and reader, teacher and learner. In the address to the reader of *Paradiso* 5, Dante references the anguished desire that would overcome us if his narration were now to cease: "Pensa, lettor, se quel che qui s'inizia / non procedesse, come tu avresti / di più savere angosciosa carizia" ("Consider, reader, what your misery / and need to know still more would be if, at / this point, what I began did not go on"; *Par.* 5.109–11). Desire, for Dante, is the essential ingredient of learning.

NOTE

[1] The texts of the *Comedy* follow Petrocchi's edition and Mandelbaum's translation.

Teaching the *Divine Comedy* from Its Manuscripts

H. Wayne Storey and Isabella Magni

If you wish to stop a dinner conversation, tell your companions you teach medieval manuscripts. The same might be said even for a proposal to a college curriculum committee to suggest a course on a medieval work based on one of its original codices. And yet, even after those first years in graduate school, the idea that Dante's *Comedy* is solely that object neatly laid out in erudite and often hefty volumes in which three (or fewer!) of Dante's verses are dwarfed by a page of notes and commentary seemed as strange as a former colleague explaining he taught Italian film using only slides. The material on which Dante conceived his *Comedy* represents a dynamic medium: parchment. The printed page is no match for parchment's multiple and profound strata, which often reveal diverse cultural perspectives, including those of copyist, rubricator, illustrator, and subsequent owners and readers of the book.

The first principle for students to consider is also the primary tenet of material philology: every reproduction of a work like the *Divine Comedy* potentially divulges as much about the culture reproducing and transmitting the copy as it does about the text itself. But why would we turn to copies of the *Comedy* if we want to teach the work itself? As with most medieval literary works, we do not have the original in the author's own hand. This simple fact forces us to consider a second key principle closely linked to the first: cultural accretions adhere to the centuries of copies and printings of the *Divine Comedy*, and thus to our interpretations of this Western literary icon.

But what is an accretion? This usually geological term describes the layering of deposits of sediment or other natural materials on a rocky surface. Literary texts studied from their manuscript and even their print sources require that we treat them the way a geologist or an archeologist would approach an ancient site, working backward and carefully through layers of interpretative deposits, recording and then gently dusting away later accretions to reveal, where possible, a text and interpretations closer to the author's original.

Against that author's original we must also weigh the relation between the author's innovation and what we could call the publishing mechanisms of his own culture. Dante's invention of the linking features inherent in the rhyme scheme of his terza rima required a response in the scribal culture of the first half of the fourteenth century that Giancarlo Savino has conjectured was in part a reflection of Dante's own usage: two columns of transcription with one verse per line running down the left- and then the right-hand column of the page in a chancery, or semicursive, hand as opposed to the old and staid gothic minuscule hand popular for formal, scholastic texts in Latin as well as works in the vernacular copied in the late Due- and early Trecento. Unlike the formula for Italian lyric poetry that was read across the manuscript page (as we find in MSS Vatican Latino 3793 and Laurenziano Rediano 9), this two-column presentation by which readers followed the text down the left column and then moved to the right would have easily been suggested by deluxe copies of troubadour lyrics in Old Provençal copied in northern Italy in the late thirteenth and early fourteenth centuries (such as MSS Vatican Latino 5232 and Riccardiano 2909). One of the earliest copies of the *Comedy*, from 1337, MS Milano Trivulziano 1080, follows this Old Provençal model for Dante's epic verses. Copied by one of Florence's finest professional scribes, Francesco di ser Nardo da Barberino, this manuscript serves virtually as a luxury template for many manuscripts of the *Comedy* in the fourteenth century before the monumentalization of Dante's work in fifteenth-century copies and early printed books.

One of the first exercises undergraduate and graduate students perform in classes on the *Comedy* is to analyze the systems apparent in reproductions of Trivulziano 1080 and similar manuscripts. Rather than guiding their discoveries, I ask them what they see and in what order, and how they prioritize what they see on this *charta* (c.; manuscript page or folio) or on others. Often the undergraduates are less culturally confined, more adventuresome and thus more prone to discoveries that allow us to see in more ancient copies greater and more engaging interpretative avenues and new lights in which to read Dante's *Comedy*.

Invariably the first thing that strikes the eye is the decoration: the figures, the gold leaf that seems to backlight the sails of the little vessel of Dante's intellect and Virgil's guidance (*Purg.* 1.1–2), and eventually the overall framing effect of the decoration for this and all the opening cantos of each canticle. Students eventually come to understand the limits of any direct interpretative values between illumination and text through a careful reading of Jonathan J. G. Alexander's *Medieval Illuminators* and H. Wayne Storey's essay "The Missing Picture in the Text," both of which demonstrate the programmatic nature of illumination, the instructions to illuminators about the illustration's content, and its execution, which is usually isolated from the interpretative processes of constructing the book itself. One of the earliest extant manuscripts of the work, MS Trivulziano 1080, however, reveals standard applications of a tradition that belonged uniquely to the *Comedy*. Especially in the historiated initial *P* of *Purgatorio*'s opening line ("Per correr miglior acqua alça le vele"; "To course across more kindly waters now / my talent's little vessel lifts her sails"; *Purg.* 1.1–2) students instantly engage the canticle's—and the *Comedy*'s—predominant metaphor: the little ship of the poet's poetic and intellectual skill (repeated in *Paradiso* 2).[1] The visual metaphor is so powerful that it quickly enters the *Comedy*'s illumination program as a standard feature that will continue into the age of some printed books as woodcuts (fig. 1).

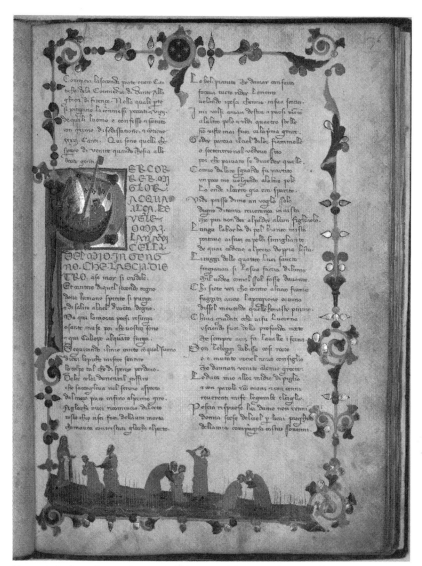

Figure 1. Archivio Storico Civico e Biblioteca Trivulziana, Milan, Trivulziano MS 1080, c. 36r.
© Comune di Milano. All rights reserved. Reprinted with the kind permission of the Biblioteca
Trivulziana.

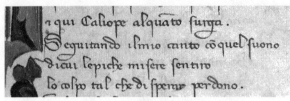

Figure 2. Trivulziano MS 1080, c. 36r. Detail: *Purgatorio* 1.9–10. The text in question reads, "[et] qui Caliope alqua(n)to surga. / Seguitando ilmio canto co(n) quel suono" ("and may Calliope rise somewhat here, / accompanying my singing with that music").

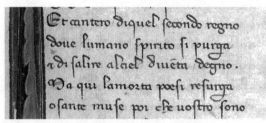

Figure 3. Trivulziano MS 1080, c. 36r. Detail: *Purgatorio* 1.7–8. The text in question reads, "(et) di salire alciel diu(e)nta degno. / Ma qui la morta poesi resurga" ("becoming worthy of ascent to Heaven. / But here, may the poem rise again from Hell's dead realm").

In addition to the technical skills developed by reading Francesco's ancient hand and learning simple forms of abbreviation, students begin to acclimate to the same uses that fourteenth-century copyists had to adapt in order to represent Dante's innovative terza rima rhyme scheme, in which, after most of the first three lines of canto 1's incipit, or opening, the terzina structure dominates the syntax and punctuation. As students learn to distinguish between lowercase and majuscule and identify medieval punctuation, they see, for example, that the brief pause between lines 9 and 10 are treated the same as the full stop at the close of verse 6 and the new "sentence" that begins line 7: a period (*punctus*) followed by a capital *S*, and a period and a capital *M* (figs. 2 and 3).

With additional scrutiny, they note subtle changes in layout even on the front (*recto*) of the canto's initial *charta* (folio). The left justification of the left column is altered in the right to accommodate what becomes (and must have already been) the reiteration of each terzina's first verse, whose initial the copyist placed to the left of the left justification—in what was known as the "little column"— for verses 2 and 3 of every terzina. In an age when verses were not numbered, these prosodic and visual markers gave readers quicker access to the terzina structure and helped them find individual terzinas. And once students recognize the absence of quotation marks and question marks, they begin to consider the interpretative and performative nature of reading itself in the Middle Ages, as we discover in Cato's direct speech to Virgil and Dante (fig. 4) and in Virgil's response introduced by the rhetorical formula of the *verbum dicendi* to denote direct address, again without punctuation (fig. 5).

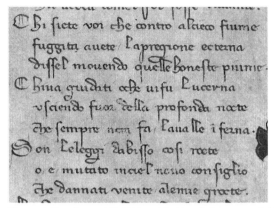

Figure 4. Trivulziano MS 1080, c. 36r. Detail: *Purgatorio* 1.40–48.

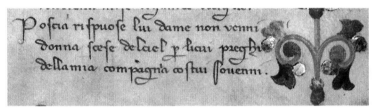

Figure 5. Trivulziano MS 1080, c. 36r. Detail: *Purgatorio* 1.52–54. The text reads, "Poscia rispuose lui[:] Da me non venni[;] / donna scese del ciel[,] p(er) li cui preghi / della mia compagn<i>a costui sovenni" ("I do not come through my own self. / There was a lady sent from Heaven; / her pleas led me to help and guide this man").

Additionally students learn about how copyists had to prepare carefully the "pages" (*chartae*) before they ever put quill to parchment by assessing the number of verses per column (thirty-six) multiplied by two columns per side to calculate both the number of pieces of parchment they would need to complete a canto (or an entire canticle) and where the canto introductions (in red) and the historiated initials should appear on the parchment in order to leave appropriate space for the rubricator and illuminator to do their work.

While investigating material sources, students learn about the process of constructing the medieval book and Dante's *Comedy* in particular. Perhaps ironically MS Budapest Italicus 1 is an effective teaching tool in demonstrating the cultural and historical dynamics at work in the stages of building a copy of Dante's masterpiece precisely because of its unique "flaws." Comparing a modern edition of the *Comedy* to any of the cantos in MS Italicus 1, students soon realize that, though it is a deluxe copy, it is an incomplete witness: Italicus 1 is missing large sections of normally interlocking terzinas throughout the three canticles. Most omissions seem part of a plan to skip sections of the work, perhaps considered of little interest by the copyist or the patron: descriptions, digressions, and the movement of the two travelers, Dante and—for two canticles—Virgil. Italicus 1 holds great interest also for its illustrations, painted by a refined artist who left the work unfinished. Asking open questions—such as, What are the characteristics of this codex? How do the images relate to the text? How are the canticles materially separated? How are images distributed among the parts of the work?—illustrates how Italicus 1 reflects the mid-fourteenth-century culture of the Veneto area and highlights the sorts of things that would have interested an aristocratic reader from around Venice. Answering these questions in groups, students ultimately assemble a composite picture of the visible issues that constitute the material construction of Dante's *Comedy*. But if most medieval manuscripts are produced with a reader or patron in mind, what does this copy tell us about who was reading the manuscript, or at least paying for its production? One of the first characteristics that stands out about Italicus 1 is that the miniatures end abruptly at the close of the fifth fascicle, or gathering of leaves (c. 36v). Many things could interrupt work on a manuscript, but it was often a lack of money that brought the project to a halt. In the case of Italicus 1, the unfinished manuscript gives us insights into the *Comedy*'s popularity. Either the scribe or a compiler left microscopic instructions to the illustrator, usually in the spaces reserved for the illuminations, indicating what or who the miniature should contain. These precious visible details, together with the careful organization of the single *charta*, with its forty-seven transcriptional lines, and the building of the book fascicle-by-fascicle, testify to a copy that was produced by between two and six different professionals—one to four copyists or compilers, an artist and possibly a rubricator—working in a strict order: the parchment was prepared and ruled, the copyist transcribed the texts, and only after each fascicle was completed were the pages sent to the rubricator and artist.

The dynamic construction of MS Italicus 1, with its incompleteness, its occasional flaws, and its meticulous planning (where to place the images, which terzinas to delete, etc.) is also visible at the level of a single *charta*. In small groups students carefully analyze the visual and textual components of *charta* 30v, containing a portion of *Purgatory* 2 and the beginning of *Purgatory* 3, together with an image that opens the page in the top left column. Carefully focusing on what they see on the *charta*, students collaboratively investigate the indexicality of the manuscript, its texts, its unfinished state (the initial and introductory *titulus* of *Purgatory* 3 are missing), and the unique correlation between the illumination and the instructions previously left for the illustrator, still clearly visible just to the right of the bottom right corner (fig. 6).

Although the instructions left for the artist reveal linguistically the origins of this codex as the Veneto, they also demonstrate how disparities commonly occurred between what was planned and what the illustrator subsequently painted. The instruction to paint "[o]meni nudi [. . .]uti bia(n)ci" ("naked men [. . .] all white") seems to refer to *Purgatory* 2.49–54, transcribed on the recto of the previous *charta*, but the artist later decides to portray Casella as he ap-

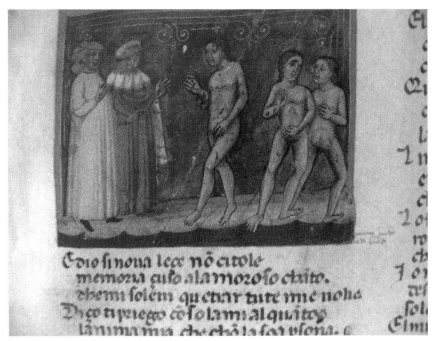

Figure 6. Eötvös Loránd University Library and Archive, Budapest, MS Italicus 1, c. 30v. Detail: *Purgatorio* 2. Reprinted with the kind permission of the University Library, Budapest, Hungary.

proaches Dante and Virgil, referring in this case to verses 76–117. Comparing this early illustration from *Purgatory* with those of the *Inferno* in Italicus 1 we see immediately why the instruction indicates the color white: the illustrations in the *Inferno*, from the cowardly "che visser sanza 'nfamia e sanza lodo" ("who lived without disgrace and without praise"; *Inf.* 3.36) to Bertran de Born (*Inf.* 28) and the three traitors in the mouths of Lucifer (*Inf.* 34), depict the damned as red. Only Virgil and the noble ancient souls of Limbo are spared the infernal color of damnation. Thus, within the context of the codex itself, the completed images and instructions reveal a narrative continuum in the reception and transmission of Dante's text and testify to a unitary program of visual and moral order and purpose that aligns with other medieval representations of the damned in European art. This simple revelation often connects students with research projects that go far beyond Dante's manuscript culture.

Always within the context of the culture in which Dante produced his *Comedy*, we must keep in mind the utility of manuscripts as precious witnesses of cultural orientations of the society in which they are produced. Though written in the Italian of his times, in one unique moment in *Purgatory* 26 Dante turns to the prestigious vernacular practiced by Old Provençal poets to pay homage to the "miglior fabbro del parlar materno" ("greatest artisan of the mother tongue";

Figure 7. Biblioteca Medicea Laurenziana, Florence, Pluteo MS 41.42, c. 78r. Detail: glossary of Old Occitan and vernacular Italian. All rights reserved. Reprinted with the kind permission of Ministero per i Beni e le Attività Culturali.

Purg. 26.117): Arnaut Daniel (fl. c. 1180–1205). Whereas Dante's masterful crafting of the mostly masculine rhymes of Old Provençal (*deman, cantan, denan, folor, valor, dolor* [lines 140, 142, 144, 143, 145, 147]) suggests his knowledge of Arnaut's language, did Dante's copyists know it as well? Evidence would suggest not. This is the lesson of a manuscript produced in Tuscany, possibly in Dante's lifetime, Laurenziano Pluteo 41.42, an Old Occitan primer and anthology. Produced in the early fourteenth century, Laurenziano 41.42 is a pivotal artifact that links three linguistic and literary cultures (vernacular Italian, Old Occitan [or Provençal], and Latin), including the Old Provençal primer *Donatz*, poems, biographies of the poets, and two glossaries (one in Occitan and Latin and one in Occitan and Italian [fig. 7]).

The glossaries and primer suggest that already in the early Trecento, Old Provençal was not a tool that Italian copyists automatically had at their disposal, but rather was already considered a foreign language and literary experience, even though a fair number of early Italian poets wrote in Old Provençal. Understanding works and cultural artifacts in the historical and geographical contexts revealed in manuscripts allows us a richer and more immediate connection to some aspects of Dante's world that printed editions cannot be expected to convey. We are mindful that, while often modifying the way the text itself is subsequently interpreted and edited, later manuscript copies of Dante's *Comedy* bear cultural and historical information mostly on the culture that receives and reproduces the *Comedy*, the patron who requests a copy of the work, and the book's production as artifact.

Thus, the interpretative accretions grow as the disseminating cultures reproduce Dante's *Comedy*, building on or altering the text of the previous generation. With the growing popularity of commentaries, sixteenth-century printers especially, in competition to sell their editions, reflected the changing interests of their readers. From 1472 to 1502, two distinct kinds of reader found their editions in the rich commentary of Cristoforo Landino (1481, 1484, 1487, 1490, 1491, 1493 and 1497, all in Venice), and in simple but elegant editions without textual commentary printed in Foligno (1472), Mantua (1474), and Venice (Wendelin of Speier, 1477; Aldus Manutius, 1502). The 1502 Aldine edition, *Le terze rime di*

Dante, boasted the scholarly editing of Pietro Bembo, together with Aldus Manutius's italic type, and would for almost two hundred years become the standard text of Dante's *Comedy*. In 1512 in Venice, Bernardino Stagnino, a member of the Giolito de' Ferrari da Trino family of printers, merged the two traditions by printing Bembo's text with Landino's commentary. By then the interests and needs of readers, and publishers' responses to them, focused on different information, structures, and apparatus than we saw in early Dante manuscripts.

Bernardino Stagnino's 1512 edition fuses Bembo's text from the Aldine 1502 edition, the woodcuts from Bernardinus Benalius and Matteo Capcasa's 1491 Venetian edition (reprinted in 1493 by Matteo di Codeca da Parma), and Landino's commentary. But in this fusion Stagnino alters key perspectives on Dante's masterpiece. As students usually quickly note, in the opening image of *Purgatory* 1 he shifts readers' attention from Dante's guiding metaphor illustrated in many fourteenth-century manuscripts to Landino's humanist orientation to the figural representations (below) of Cato (*Catone*), Virgil (*V*), and Dante (*D*), flanked by the new arrivals to Purgatory and the four stars of the Southern Hemisphere (*Purg.* 1.23). Landino's initial commentary to the opening of *Purgatorio* 1 situates Dante's second canticle—devoted to a region of the afterlife institutionalized by the church only in the 1270s—within the classical tradition: "Well instructed and erudite in the art of poetics, our author—in imitation of Virgil, Ovid, and Statius and of other heroic Latin authors—divides his second canticle into three parts" (Stagnino, c. 195r). Only at the bottom of the page in the commentary's fine print do we see the iconic subject, Dante and Virgil in the little ship of Dante's poetic skill and wisdom that opened the canto for most of the fourteenth century's manuscript culture, described simply as an "ornamento rhetorico" ("rhetorical device"). It is a passage that a subsequent reader underscored and noted in the margin (fig. 8).

The very next page of Stagnino's edition reiterates the importance of Landino's erudite commentary while continuing the visual features that marked the right column in MS Trivulziano 1080, right down to the slight separation of the initial of each terzina (*M* and *S* in verses 7 and 10) in its own "little column." The additional punctuation and the majuscules, now extended to each verse, are innovations of Bembo's cultural standards that both interpret and monumentalize Dante's epic (fig. 9).

Yet, in the same period, the popularity of the simpler textual presentation of the Aldine editions of the *Comedy* is demonstrated in Paganino Paganini and Alessandro Paganini's 1527–33 edition, which offers a stark contrast to readers. The guide letter *P* that was to be covered by a painted initial by the owner of the book represents the sole embellishment that would have accompanied Paganini's essential reprinting of Manutius's 1515 edition with its famous diagrams of "Dante col sito, et forma dell'Inferno" ("Dante with the placement and shape of the Inferno"; Bembo, *Dante*). This new visual modeling of the geography and mileage of hell will become a cultural feature central to sixteenth-century editions.

CANTO   PRIMO   195
CANTICA SECVNDA DEL DIVINO POETA
DANTHE ALIGHIERI.

Ene instituto & erudito nellarte poetica el nro auttore questa sua seco da cantica ad imitatione di Virgilio:Douidio:di Statio: degli altri heroici latini diuide in tre parti: propositione:inuocatioe:e narratione. Ma le due primo ch so no ppofitione e inuocatione vegono in luogho di proemio.Et pche e proprio officio del.phemio fare che lau ditore diueti apto e idoneo ad vdire facilmete questo pfeguiremo fe ce lo faremo beniuolo atteto e docile. Capta adiuq beniuoletia dalla ma teri.pmettedo che catera del pur gatorio cofa optima a gli animi hu mani:pche e folo mezo pel qle pof fono puenire alla cognitione diuia nella qle pfiste el fomo bene. Capta anchora beniuoletia della sua pso na dimostrado che saffatica in fcri uere qllo che alla generatione mor tale fia no folo vtile ma necessario. Preterea fa lauditore attento della gradezza della materia. Impeche co soma attetione vdiamo le cose che sono o gradi o inustiate:e maxie se sono apptinetito ad vniuersal:o e noi i pticulare: o a noftri pgiuti e amici.Ne mediocremete moue at tentione pel modo del parlare.Im

*ER correr miglior ac-
qua alza le vele
Homai la nauicella del
mi'ngegno;
Che lascia retr'a se mar
fi crudele:
Et cantero di quel feco
do regno;
Oue l'humano spirito fi purga,
Et de falir al ciel diuenta degno.*

peroche vfando traslatione e non proprij vocabuli accrescie veguita e auttorita a le cose come veggiamo in Virg.e i molti altri poeti cosi greci come latini-Ne folamete e poetitma gli ora tori exornano elloro stile co qsto colore:la cui forza pocho disotto dimostraremo.Vltiamente fa lauditore docile:cioe apto a itedere qllo di che fi debba trattare.Il che adiue ogni volta che in brieue pole pponiamo e expoiamo:Diche dipoi i tutta lopa fi trattera:coe q pmettedo trat tare del purgatorio-Ma intedi lettore: ch beche distiftamete altra cosa fia beniuoletia:altra attetioe:e altra docilita.Nietedimeno luno aiuta a pfeguire l altro. Impoche chi diueta beni uolo fi fa atteto. Et chi fta atteto audire el pncipio facilmete diueta docile. Et fpesse volte in vna medesima pola facqsta lo scrittore beniuoletia attetione e docilita:coe in qsto vfo.Et can tero di qlfcdo regno:doue l'huano spirito fi purga. Impoche tale ppofitioe pche e vtile fa be niuoletia:pche e cofa granda fa attetione:poiche expone qllo di che vuole narrare fa docilita. PER CORRER miglior acqua: E la fnia che l ingegno fuo finalza p dir miglior materia che qlla che ha detto infino a qui.Ma tale fnia pnucia no p pprie parole:ma p traflatione.Et accioche meglio dimostriamo qsto ornameto rhetorico:diciamo che tutte fe pole:le gli vfia mo fono o pprie o traflate-Proprie pole fono qlle le gli trouo o lufoto la ragioe p exprimere la cofa fuggetta a tale pole:come quado dice Nel tepo che Iunone era crucciata. Impoche tepo e era e Iunone e crucciata fono pole.pprie di qlle cose che el poeta vuole exprimere:ma qfte p-

aa iii

Figure 8. Bernardino Stagnino, *Opere del divino poeta Danthe*, 1512, c. 195r. *Purgatorio* 1.1–6 with Landino's commentary. Private collection. Reprinted with permission.

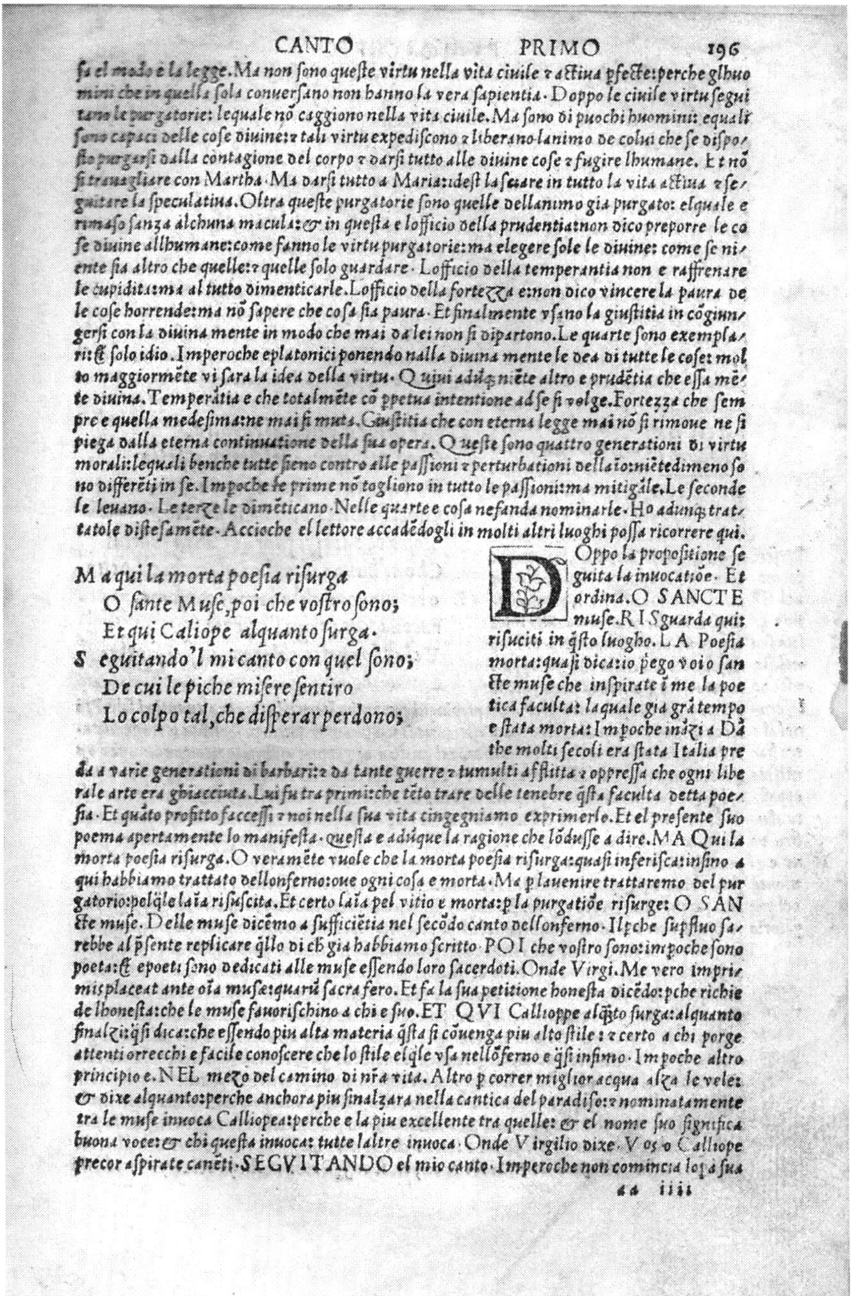
CANTO PRIMO 196

sa el modo e la legge. Ma non sono queste virtu nella vita ciuile z actiua pfecte: perche glhuomini che in quella sola conuersano non hanno la vera sapientia. Doppo le ciuile virtu seguitano le purgatorie: lequale nō caggiono nella vita ciuile. Ma sono di puochi huomini: equali sono capaci delle cose diuine: z tali virtu expediscono z liberano lanimo de colui che se dispone purgarsi dalla contagione del corpo z darsi tutto alle diuine cose z fugire lhumane. Et nō si trauagliare con Martha. Ma darsi tutto a Maria: idest lasciare in tutto la vita actiua z seguitare la speculatiua. Oltra queste purgatorie sono quelle dellanimo gia purgato: elquale e rimaso sanza alchuna macula: & in questa e lofficio della prudentia: non dico preporre le cose diuine allhumane: come fanno le virtu purgatorie: ma elegere sole le diuine: come se niente sia altro che quelle: z quelle solo guardare. Lofficio della temperantia non e raffrenare le cupidita: ma al tutto dimenticarle. Lofficio della fortezza e: non dico vincere la paura de le cose horrende: ma nō sapere che cosa sia paura. Et finalmente vsano la giustitia in cōgiungersi con la diuina mente in modo che mai da lei non si dipartono. Le quarte sono exemplari: et solo idio. Imperoche e platonici ponendo nalla diuina mente le dea di tutte le cose: molto maggiormēte vi sara la idea della virtu. Quiui adūque niēte altro e prudētia che essa mēte diuina. Temperātia e che totalmēte cō ppetua intentione ad se si volge. Fortezza che sempre e quella medesima: ne mai si muta. Giustitia che con eterna legge mai nō si rimoue ne si piega dalla eterna continuatione della sua opera. Queste sono quattro generationi di virtu morali: lequali benche tutte sieno contro alle passioni z perturbationi della aīo: niētedimeno sono differēti in se. Impoche le prime nō togliono in tutto le passioni: ma mitigāle. Le seconde le leuano. Le terze le dimēticano. Nelle quarte e cosa nefanda nominarle. Ho adunq; trattatole distesamēte. Accioche el lettore accadēdogli in molti altri luoghi possa ricorrere qui.

Ma qui la morta poesia risurga
O sante Muse, poi che vostro sono;
Et qui Caliope alquanto surga.
Seguitando'l mi canto con quel sono;
De cui le piche misere sentiro
Lo colpo tal, che disperar perdono;

DOppo la propositione seguita la inuocatiōe. Et ordina. O SANCTE muse. RISguarda qui: risuciti in q̄sto luogho. LA Poesia morta: quasi dicario pego voi o sancte muse che inspirate ī me la poetica faculta: laquale gia grā tempo e stata morta: Impoche ināzi a Dāthe molti secoli era stata Italia preda a varie generationi di barbari: z da tante guerre z tumulti afflitta z oppressa che ogni liberale arte era ghiacciuta. Lui fu tra primi: che tētō trare delle tenebre q̄sta faculta detta poesia. Et quāto profitto facessi z noi nella sua vita cingegniamo exprimerlo. Et el presente suo poema apertamente lo manifesta. questa e adūque la ragione che lōdusse a dire. MA Qui la morta poesia risurga. O veramēte vuole che la morta poesia risurga: quasi inferisca: insino a qui habbiamo trattato dellonferno: oue ogni cosa e morta. Ma p lauenire trattaremo del purgatorio: pelq̄le laīa risuscita. Et certo laīa pel vitio e morta: p la purgatiōe risurge: O SANcte muse. Delle muse dicēmo a sufficiētia nel secōdo canto dellonferno. Ilpche superfluo sarebbe al p̄sente replicare q̄llo di chē gia habbiamo scritto. POI che vostro sono: impoche sono poeta: et e poeti sono dedicati alle muse essendo loro sacerdoti. Onde Virgi. Me vero imprimis placeat ante oīa musæ: quarū sacra fero. Et fa la sua petitione honesta dicēdo: pche richiede lhonesta: che le muse fauorischino a chi e suo. ET QVI Calliope alq̄to surga: alquanto finalzi: q̄si dica: che essendo piu alta materia q̄sta si cōuenga piu alto stile: z certo a chi porge attenti orrecchi e facile conoscere che lo stile elq̄le vsa nellōferno e q̄si infimo. Impoche altro principio e. NEL mezo del camino di nr̄a vita. Altro p correr miglior acqua alza le vele: & dixe alquanto: perche anchora piu sinalzara nella cantica del paradiso: z nominatamente tra le muse innoca Calliopea: perche e la piu excellente tra quelle: & el nome suo significa buona voce: & chi questa inuoca: tutte laltre inuoca. Onde Virgilio dixe. Vos o Calliope precor aspirate canēti. SEGVITANDO el mio canto. Imperoche non comincia lopa sua

aa iiii

Figure 9. Stagnino, *Opere del divino poeta Danthe*, 1512, c. 196r. *Purgatorio* 1.7–12 with Landino's commentary. Private collection. Reprinted with permission.

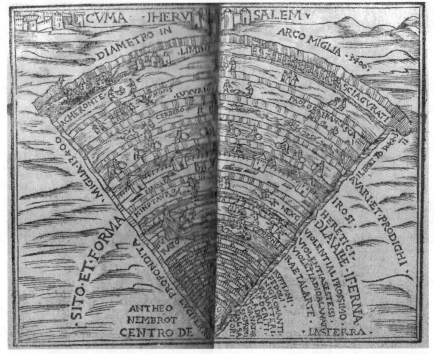

Figure 10. Paganino Paganini and Alessandro Paganini, *Dante col sito, et forma dell'Inferno*, 1527–33. Geography of Hell. Private collection. Reprinted with permission.

The interpretative renderings of Dante's narrative visualized in manuscript illuminations and woodcut inserts in early printed editions have been replaced by a concern for geographic precision (the exact dimensions of hell in miles, its location vis-à-vis Jerusalem and Cuma) and system (the placement of sins and souls) (fig. 10).

Even in later-sixteenth-century manuscripts, such as the famous Laurentian Library codex Mediceo Palatino 75, penned by the Italian poet-scholar Luigi Alamanni, we find a growing cultural tendency not only to dissect and categorize the system of sins, sinners, and hellish landscape (see especially his elaborate outline of "Peccatori dell'Inferno di Dante, e loro Luoghi, e Pene" ["Sinners in Dante's Hell, their places and punishments"] on c. 2r of the manuscript) but also to represent it in ever greater detail and with greater precision, as we find in the drawings of Jan van der Straet, called Stradanus or Giovanni Stradano (1523–1605), known especially for his illustration of Amerigo Vespucci's discovery of America (1587–89) in the collection of the Metropolitan Museum of Art.

Working in small groups, students examine and trace these interpretative accretions across handwritten and printed texts, comparing and contrasting editions, noting where one disseminating culture continues interpretations added by a preceding generation and where they abandon them. The students are assigned the task of producing cumulative definitions of the "interpretative interests and goals" of various historical periods and of key interpreters, from Dante's early commentators and illustrators to early pivotal figures such as Cristoforo Landino, Alessandro Vellutello, Pietro Bembo, Lodovico Dolce, and Pompeo Venturi.

But to what ends do students conduct these kinds of research and examinations of primary sources? In each instance they must go beyond the superficial history that aligns dates and places to discover firsthand and tangibly the complex and sometimes contradictory itineraries of cultural knowledge, not just about Dante but also about the cultural contexts that led various cultures to interpret Dante in diverse lights and with very different goals. For example, the complex responses to Dante outlined by scholars include Nick Havely's discussion of Dante in anti-papal sixteenth- and seventeenth-century England (*Dante's British Public*), Beatrice Arduini's exploration of the revisionist views of Dante in the philosophically Ficinian literary culture at the court of Lorenzo de' Medici ("Assigning" and "Il ruolo"), and Jelena Todorović's examination of the early print cultures of Florence and Venice under the influence of Counter-Reformist censure and the revision even of major authors such as Dante and Giovanni Boccaccio. In each case, Dante becomes a virtual pretext for political, moral, and philosophical agendas that attempted to change the interpretation of Dante in the most obvious ways. But often, some of those changes accrete to Dante's texts, sometimes in ways we don't notice until we begin to dust carefully, like archeologists, the layers of interpretative decades.

There are numerous secondary tools at students' disposal: among the most useful are Marisa Boschi Rotiroti's *Codicologia trecentesca della* Commedia and Sandro Bertelli's *La* Commedia *all'antica*. But even the most neutral and informative studies require a methodological orientation to apply them. Works such as Rudolf Hirsch's 1967 *Printing, Selling and Reading, 1450–1550*, Storey's "Method, History, and Theory in Material Philology" and the previously cited *Medieval Illuminators and Their Methods of Work* (Alexander) offer practical case studies that help define the practice of material philology. Each methodological guide demonstrates two principles: first, that every witness of a work—whether in manuscript or print—reflects as much the interpretative constructs of the period and disseminating culture as it does the work itself, and second, that the revelation of interpretations that Dante's work has accrued are often the result of interpretative accretions that we can discover only by valuing and examining the cultural layers that constitute the individual witnesses.

Equally useful has been the recent digitization of manuscripts collected in archives and libraries around the world. Many of these high-quality digitization projects have made it possible, or at least easier, to introduce students to medieval texts in their different cultural and historical contexts. The unprecedented access to high-resolution images of early manuscripts and print editions, now widely available on the Web, has drastically increased the potential for students to access primary materials and compare and contrast the different cultural contexts that produced and reproduced Dante's texts. Although it is certainly ideal that students have access to at least one physical example of an early copy of the *Comedy* (let us hope in the special collections of their campus libraries), we certainly know that this kind of access is not readily available in some cases. Nonetheless, new digital archives and editions can partially obviate the potential absence of such experience, giving virtual access to witnesses located hundreds if not thousands of miles away.

The individual lessons that come from applying this material and philological method are numerous and range from the politically problematic reading of "per vicenda" ("out of necessity") for "per ammenda" ("for amends") in *Purgatorio* 20.67 to the debunking of fanciful analyses of illustrators who supposedly read the *Comedy* and interpreted its verses in their illuminations. But beyond the single study of variants, manuscript illustrations, and interpretations, applying material philology invariably brings the student into closer and more meaningful and enriching contact with the actual historical materials of literature. The lesson of touching history, of examining even fragments of manuscripts produced in the Italy of Dante and Boccaccio, or of handling editions over five centuries old—books printed and in circulation before Shakespeare was born— connects students directly to objects they normally only read about as additional details of a history that seems too distant to touch or imagine.

NOTES

Of the manuscripts cited in this essay, at the time of this volume's publication only three are available online without charge: Laurenziano Pluteo 41.42, Vatican Latino 3793, and Vatican Latino 5232 (see works-cited-list entries for URLs).

[1] Quotations from Dante's *Commedia* are taken from MS Trivulziano 1080. Translations are from Mandelbaum.

Duels of Interpretation:
The Bible between Dante and the Church

Ronald L. Martinez

Modern students come to the Bible from a wide variety of backgrounds: for a few, it is the literal word of God; for some, it is a book like any other; for many, it is a cultural document that offers an indispensable background to the religious life, the moral philosophy, and the art and literature of the twenty-one centuries now known as the Christian era. In medieval European culture the Bible was the most authoritative and well-known book of all: to cite it meant to refer to what was widely agreed to be the Truth of the Word of God in Judeo-Christian tradition. Faith communities today, especially those of the Abrahamic religions (Judaism, Christianity, and Islam), rely on foundational texts for wisdom, moral guidance, and even legal opinions. But just as biblical stories are retold today in movies, the Bible reached medieval minds in manifold ways. Those educated, like Dante, learned much of it by heart, thus making it part of their ethical identities. Though only literate elites consulted the text directly, the unlearned were exposed to the Bible because its words permeated the liturgy, and it was quoted in sermons; it was also ubiquitously visualized—we can think of Giotto's frescoed Scrovegni Chapel in Padua (1305). An oft reiterated defense of religious images by Pope Gregory the Great (540–602) held in a letter to Serenus of Marseilles that "what scripture offers to those who can read is offered by pictures to those who view them, for in those pictures the ignorant can see what they ought to follow" (Gregory the Great 874; my trans.). The contents of the Bible were also disseminated through works such as Peter the Eater's *Historia scholastica* (1178), a prose paraphrase of the Bible soon translated from Latin into vernacular languages. The Bible functioned as a collective cultural treasury of narratives (Genesis, Exodus, Numbers, Judges, the Gospels, Acts), law (Leviticus, the Pauline epistles), wisdom texts (Proverbs, Ecclesiastes, Wisdom, Ecclesiasticus), and poetry (Job, Psalms, the Song of Songs, Lamentations) that unified the community of the faithful.

The Bible as Dante's Model of Mixed Styles

Not only for these reasons but also because of its content and written style, the Bible was an essential text informing Dante's major works. The Bible recounts the history of the Judeo-Christian community from the creation to the apocalypse, which Dante recalls in a pageant representing all the biblical books in *Purgatorio* 29–30, and Augustine of Hippo (fourth to fifth century CE) influentially characterized the biblical written style as at once humble and sublime, in contrast to the rigid stylistic hierarchies of classical Greek and Latin. Dante's bold mixing of styles—which explains why he titled his work "mia comedìa" ("my comedy"), a genre traditionally tolerant of conflating higher and lower stylistic registers—would have been impossible without the example of the Vulgate Latin bible, translated out of Hebrew, Aramaic, and Greek by Saint Jerome (347–420 CE). Because the Bible identified sin with dung (Joel 1.17: "Computruerunt jumenta in stercore suo" ["the beasts have rotted in their dung"]),[1] Dante can justify using scatological language in the *Inferno* for the flatterers mired in "sterco" and "merda" ("ordure" and "shit"; *Inf.* 18.113, 116).[2] Even high in *Paradiso*, Dante has his Saint Peter compare the Rome corrupted by Boniface VIII to a "cloaca / del sangue e de la puzza" ("sewer of blood and stench"; *Paradiso* 27.25–26). Without biblical language to back them up, such anticlerical sallies would have been hard to justify; even after the increased range of idioms in modern literature pioneered by authors such as James Joyce (who was strongly influenced by Dante), such passages, which were censored by the Spanish Inquisition, might raise objections today.

Medieval Forms of the Bible

Crucial to understanding Dante's use of Scripture is that the poet's Bible was very different from the versions familiar today. Because large and valuable, Bibles were only rarely portable. Difficult and unfamiliar terms in the text required interlinear and marginal glosses, and the book's deeper meanings—its moral teachings and the hidden correspondences that Christians believed unified the Old and New Testaments—had to be pointed out. Such glossed Bibles, along with other important works such as codes of Roman law and works of classical literature like Vergil's *Aeneid*, represent a crucial phase in the history of the early modern book, and of information technologies in general (the first printed book, the Gutenberg Bible [1454 CE], looked exactly like a glossed medieval manuscript). Such Bibles also helped determine the format of manuscript editions of Dante's poem. Internet resources that offer high-resolution images of both medieval Bibles and Dante manuscripts make possible direct comparisons of the two, illustrating how Dante's poem, which had generated a commentary by 1324, only a few years after the poet's death in 1321, assumed a visual appearance similar to that of an annotated Bible.[3] Presented in this form, Dante's work gained unprecedented authority for a poem in a vernacular European language.

Dante's Biblical Voice

Instruments for Bible study, and thus an understanding of the received Bible, had made great strides in the century before Dante's maturity. The thirteenth century inherited a standardized system of dividing biblical books into chapter and verse, making the book more "searchable" by readers. Scholasticism, the method of intellectual inquiry enabled by Aristotle's rediscovered philosophical works, also revolutionized the study of the Bible: authors of individual books were viewed not merely as God's mouthpieces but as writers, opening up their language for evaluation as persuasive and motivated expression. Such "humanizing" of biblical authors is one reason Dante associates himself with several of them as an author claiming inspiration by God's word. The first line of the *Comedy*, "Nel mezzo del cammin di nostra vita" ("In the middle of the journey of our life"; *Inf.* 1.1), was spotted by Dante's commentators as an echo of the first verse of King Hezekiah's canticle, as recorded by the prophet Isaiah ("in dimidio dierum meorum vadam ad portas inferi"; "In the midst of my days I shall go to the gate of hell"; 38.10). Pleading the case of Rome abandoned by its secular rulers, Dante adopts the voice of the Lamentations of Jeremiah in *Purgatorio* 6.70–151 and again in his *Epistle* XI to the Italian cardinals (1314), urging them to elect an Italian pope who would bring the papacy back to the eternal city. Especially heavy are Dante's debts to John the evangelist, also held to be the author of Revelations (or Apocalypse), and Solomon, whose Canticle of Canticles personified is the single voice that speaks up to announce the coming of Beatrice in *Purgatorio* 30.11: "Veni, sponsa, de Libano" ("Come, o bride, from Lebanon"; compare Cant. of Cant. 4.8). The evangelist Luke also plays a large role in the *Purgatorio* as the biblical author who wrote of Jesus's infancy (see below). That Dante's pilgrim in the *Comedy* mouths as *his* first word the pleading first word of Psalm 50 ("Miserere"; "Have mercy on me") marks the poet's especially deep connection with David, biblical king of Israel and Judah and also a poet. Dante makes David the "cantor de lo Spirito Santo" ("singer of the Holy Spirit") in *Paradiso* 20.38,[4] a title Dante himself seems to have claimed (*Purg.* 24.53–54). Though it was hardly unusual for medieval writers to cite scriptural authors, Dante's appropriation of biblical authority is original and remarkably bold, as when he prefers John's account of the winged animals representing the evangelists to that of Ezekiel ("Giovanni è meco"; "John is with me"; *Purg.* 29.105).

Dante and Biblical Interpretation

The scholastic technique of inquiry, which pitted opposing views against one another to arrive at the resolution of a problem, also led to a more searching analysis of biblical meaning. Allegorical interpretation was often challenged (though rarely discarded) in the interests of the literal sense, which Thomas Aquinas redefined as the whole of an author's intention. Dante's work absorbed all these currents, for example in the *Letter to Can Grande* (*Epistle* XIII, c. 1320), where terms from scholastic biblical exegesis describe the *Commedia* as a work with literal (historical) and allegorical levels, subdivided into meanings relating to Christ or the Church, the moral life of the individual soul (tropological), and the progress of the soul toward heaven (anagogical). In Dante's case, these explanatory devices are built into his poem, so to speak: if Dante claims in the *Letter to Can Grande* that the "allegorical" meaning of his pilgrim's journey through the afterlife exemplifies the action of Exodus—the liberation of the chosen people from bondage in Egypt and their arrival in the promised land—he backs up his claim by including narrative episodes and language that remind the reader of the biblical event: Psalm 113.2, "In exitu Israel de Aegypto" ("When Israel went out of Egypt"), is recited by souls arriving in Purgatory (*Purg.* 2.46), since they have been freed of the bonds of this life. Dante's poem applies Exodus 12–20 and related texts to the imagined experience of an individual of the fourteenth century, in what would have been called a typological "fulfillment" of the Bible. Dante might have borrowed the idea of countenancing his own time in this way from thirteenth-century interpreter-prophets, such as Joachim of Fiore (1135–1202 CE; see *Par.* 12.140–41), who had seen his own historical moment as echoing and reiterating biblical events in detail.

One result of the varied presentations of the Bible, and of the need for it to be explained to contemporary readers, was that the biblical text was *mediated* by its interpreters, and thus by human agents, who almost invariably nurtured political agendas. As during the later Reformation, when Protestant and Catholic readers disagreed on the biblical bases of cultic practices (differences that persist today), divergent interpretations of the Bible could in Dante's day lead to conflict, persecution, and even war. To view the Bible as a timeless background to the poem, as if Dante were in direct dialogue with the prophets and the evangelists, is misleading and cancels out both the poem's own charged historical context and the well-informed precision of its polemical use of the Bible. Indeed, the dimension of Dante's writings hardest to impart to contemporary students, yet essential to his work's incisiveness and originality—the specificity of its engagement with its own time and place—was frequently demonstrated in debates over biblical meaning.

Medieval Ideological Disputes and the Bible

In our own moment, when the scientific consensus can clash with traditional faith-based understandings of the cosmos, nature, and morality, it is instructive to focus on how interpretations of the Bible were used (and abused) in the disputes of Dante's day, much as natural law arguments (themselves perfected in the late Middle Ages and fundamental to Thomism and much of Catholic theology) are nowadays deployed—both consciously but more often unwittingly—in debates regarding issues such as abortion, same-sex marriage, and transgender rights.

Contrasting biblical interpretations mark Dante's disputes with the papacy. In the early thirteenth century, Pope Innocent III (reigned 1198–1216 CE), bent on increasing the power and dignity of the papacy, compared the relation of papal and imperial authority to that of the sun and moon. Although the moon was one of two distinct luminaries created by God, ruling the night as the sun did the day (Genesis 1.14–17), it was clearly subordinate, since it drew its light from the sun. In the same way, Innocent claimed, the power of the emperor, even within its appointed sphere of temporal rule, was subordinate to papal authority. In his *Monarchia* (1317?), Dante replies to these claims by denying the analogy Church hierarchs drew between the relative light of the planetary sun and moon and political authority—such an analogy, Dante argued, was an example of unwarranted scriptural allegorism. Although less realistic in cosmological terms, Dante was even bolder in the *Comedy* when he had his character Marco Lombardo draw on Byzantine imperial symbolism to say, from a vantage point near the center of Purgatory (*Purg.* 16.106–12), that the world had once been rightly ruled by the *two* suns of pope and emperor: a salutary condition lost when papal power usurped that of the state, thanks in part to the so-called Donation of Constantine the Great (274–337 CE), the concession to the papacy of temporal authority over half of the Roman Empire. Although the veracity of the donation was based on documentation later proven to be forged, Dante believed it had taken place and rated it as among the most disastrous actions ever taken by a Roman emperor.

Reproaching Cardinals with the Bible: Dante's Eleventh Epistle

Dante in fact considered the entire Church hierarchy derelict because of the separation of the papacy from Rome and its transfer to Avignon between 1305 and 1309, historical events that Dante represents in the allegorical dumb show of *Purgatorio* 32.148–60. In a political epistle of 1314 to Italian cardinals in conclave to elect a new pope, Dante elaborately disparages the alienation of the papacy from Rome, basing his arguments in part on biblical and legal principles, as when introducing the story of Uzzah, son of Abinadab, from the Bible (2 Sam. 6.1–7; 1 Chron. 13.9–12).[5] In the letter (*Epistle* XI.3–5; *Dante Alighieri: Four Political Letters*), written in the difficult Latin style normal to debates between church and empire, Dante imagines that hostile clergy might criticize his meddling in ecclesiastical affairs by comparing him to Uzzah, who was struck dead by God when he dared to steady the ark of the covenant—for Dante's period a symbol of the future church—as it was being transported on a teetering oxcart, presumably because Uzzah was not authorized to do so. A century before Dante's epistle, the Uzzah-accusation had been used by Pope Innocent III to restrain young Frederick II of Hohenstaufen (reigned as Holy Roman emperor 1220–50), also perceived as interfering in affairs properly the province of the papacy. So when Dante imagines that the clergy preface its reproach of him with "Quis iste?" ("Who is this?"; *Epistle* XI.5), our poet wrongfoots them by having them use a phrase spoken by Christ's disciples in the New Testament when they wonder at his power to calm a storm on the Sea of Galilee. This rhetorical gambit aligns Dante with the former emperor and with Christ, and puts the ecclesiastics in the role of frightened, ignorant disciples ("Quis, putas, est iste, quia et ventus et mare obediunt ei?"; "Who is this, thinkest thou, that both wind and sea obey him?"; Mk. 4.40). But the rhetorical jujitsu only works if the readers involved know their Bible well, something that Dante could confidently rely upon in the case of his audience of cardinals.

Wielding Christ's Words: Inferno *and* Purgatorio

Close identification with Christ's words in the Bible also characterizes one of Dante's most powerful scenes of anti-papal invective in the poem. In *Inferno* 19, shocked by the corruption of Nicholas III (reigned 1277–80), Dante's pilgrim is so bold as to reproach the former pope and his colleagues by using Christ's words in calling the Apostles Andrew and Simon Peter: "Viemmi retro" ("Come, follow me"; Matt. 4.18), reminding the simoniac pope of the original calling to the priesthood, which his avarice has betrayed.[6] Quoting Christ's words directly to a soul in Hell for the first time in the poem, Dante marks his assumption of a more authoritative voice in his disputes with the papacy.

Given the importance of the biblical words spoken by Christ, it is significant that in *Purgatorio* Dante enlists the beatitudes, which begin Christ's Sermon on the Mount (Matt. 5–7), to articulate all seven penitential levels of the mountain of Purgatory. The penitent exercise of the souls as they depart each terrace of the mountain is ratified by a version of one of the beatitudes, spoken by an angel and adapted to the particulars of each vice purged and virtue inculcated. Since liturgical interpreters such as Durandus of Mende (1230–96) assumed that the Lord's Prayer had seven petitions and implied the seven beatitudes, the presence of the beatitudes is, in fact, inaugurated with the troped form of the Lord's Prayer (also taught by Christ during the Sermon on the Mount, Matt. 6.9–13), recited by Dante's prideful (*Purg.* 11.1–24).

Dante treats the language of the beatitudes with great freedom, rendering some in Italian, some in Latin, and some—well, it's impossible to tell, because the Italian plural *beati* is identical with the Latin instances, so that Christ's words flow, so to speak, from Latin into Italian.[7] In the course of using *beati* those seven times, Dante places the word so it receives initial, final, and medial stresses of the poet's hendecasyllabic line, so that in a sense it "fills up" his meter. Not by accident, the continuity of Dante's Italian vernacular and biblical Latin suggests the name of Beatrice, whom the pilgrim will meet at the summit of the mountain after making his way with Virgil through Hell and Purgatory. Even in the adolescent *Vita nova*, Beatrice's correlation with the beatitudes is underlined during the feverish dream in which Beatrice's death is envisioned, when the protagonist declares blessed whoever sees her ("*Beato*, anima bella, chi ti *vede*"; *Vita nova* 23.28 [Gorni]). Given that in Purgatory ecclesiastical dignities and titles vanish at death—as the former Pope Adrian V points out to Dante's pilgrim (*Purg.* 19.133–38)—it is Christ's teaching, spoken by angels, along with the words of the liturgy, spoken not by priests or monks but by the souls themselves, that represents church doctrine.

Mary's Humility and the Structure of Purgatory

References to the Virgin Mary, mostly from the first books of Luke's Gospel, also have a fundamental effect on Dante's Purgatory. The first terrace, that of Pride, the "base" for all the others, reflects Mary's *Magnificat* (Luke 1.46–55), the canticle of praise she sings shortly after the Annunciation during her visit to her cousin Elizabeth (John the Baptist's mother) and that is sung liturgically daily during the vespers office. Mary praises her God, who has "put down the mighty from their seat and hath exalted the humble" (Luke 1.52), a contrast that furnishes the pattern for Dante's celebration of lowliness in Mary, King David, and the Roman emperor Trajan (*Purg.* 10.43–93), and the execration of the proud, who are literally *put down* in being represented on the sculpted pavement of the circle, to be walked on by the penitent prideful (*Purg.* 12.25–63). Mary's words not only structure the didactic scheme of the first terrace, the pattern for all the others, they contribute to the material foundations on which all of Purgatory rests.

Writing the Bible in the Sky: Paradiso

If in *Purgatorio* we see how the Bible filters into Dante's language and into the moral architecture of his purgatorial mountain, in canto 18 of *Paradiso* Dante makes the words of a biblical book spectacularly his own. Transcribing the first line of the Book of Wisdom or *Sapientia*, which the Middle Ages attributed to Solomon, into his text in the form of "skywriting" traced by the multitudinous souls of the just (*Par.* 18.73–96), Dante transmits the imperative mood of the biblical line, "Diligite iustitiam, qui iudicatis terram" ("Love justice, ye who judge the world"), as his urgent "message" for the world and for posterity. Given Dante's view of the influence of the heavens, this command is "radiated" down to the rulers of the earth by the celestial sphere of Jupiter. Since Dante could think of the celestial spheres as like books, based on biblical verses that warranted comparisons of the writings of the Church Fathers to the heavens (e.g., Ps. 103.2, Apoc. 6.14, Isa. 34.4), and on the fact that Italian *volume* can refer to either the rotation of a sphere or to a book (compare the English word *volume*), the skywriting of Dante's sixth heavenly sphere marks the near-coincidence of the biblical message with Dante's own, and of the Bible with his poem.[8]

NOTES

[1] All biblical citations in English are to the Douay-Rheims version; all Latin citations are to the Vulgate edition (*Biblia sacra*).

[2] All citations to the three parts of the *Divine Comedy*, Italian and English, are to the Durling and Martinez edition.

[3] For example, *I manoscritti* (*Dante Online*) and *The King James Bible Virtual Exhibit: The Medieval Bible*.

[4] Dante's Italian for David as singer, "cantor," is elsewhere assigned only to Virgil (*Purg.* 22.57) and is also applied to the poet's ancestor Cacciaguida (*Par.* 18.51), who is singled out as an "artista" ("artist") among the other "cantor[i]" ("singers") of Heaven.

[5] The episode might seem obscure; however, God's harshness to Uzzah occasions endless online debates and explications of the episode, many of them well-informed.

[6] Comparisons can be drawn to Pope Francis I's current reorientation of the church toward mercy and the interests of the poor, which has been resisted both within the Roman curia and in conservative Catholic circles.

[7] College undergraduates need not fear brief contact with Dante's Bible-inspired Latin, when it appears: few books in the world are so relentlessly translated online, and many sites furnish parallel-column texts of the whole Bible in its Vulgate Latin versions and in English (the preferred translation for Dante study is the Douay-Rheims version).

[8] For further reading on this topic, see studies by Auerbach, "Figura" and *Mimesis*; Carroll; Durling, "'Mio figlio'"; Ferrante, "Bible"; Hawkins, *Dante's Testaments*; Kantorowicz; Kleinhenz, "Biblical Citation" and "Dante and the Bible"; Martinez, *Cleansing*, "Forese," and "Mourning"; Menzinger; Minnis and Scott; Smalley; Ullmann.

Following Virgil's Lantern:
Teaching Dante in the Light of Antiquity

Elsa Filosa

In the late antique period, Christian churches replaced pagan temples, the former often including, expanding, hiding, or recycling various parts and often the very structures of the latter. In much the same way, Dante's *Divine Comedy* is in constant dialogue with classical authors: recontextualizing literature from antiquity for Christian purposes.

This essay addresses advanced high school and college students who are reading the *Divine Comedy* for the first time, and it focuses in particular—but not exclusively—on Dante's *Inferno* to understand reworking classical sources in a Christian perspective. In this way, students will be able to understand the way Dante reuses and reappropriates the classical literary tradition in writing his medieval masterpiece. The essay incorporates a comparative approach to some key passages of the *Comedy* and Latin literature. I provide specific class activities to enhance the ability of students to hone their skills in the analysis of two texts through these approaches: examining the same landscape, finding similar words, comparing the use of the same characters, and contrasting the differences noted in these processes. Hence, the essay gives practical pedagogical suggestions to instructors to help students confront texts composed many centuries apart and in very different historical contexts. It also provides texts of classical literature, together with precise references and class activities, as tools for teachers and students to make comparisons, find analogies and differences, and generate discussion.

"Sixth amongst Such Minds"

From the very start of the *Inferno*, Dante the pilgrim meets his favorite writers from antiquity: first Virgil, and then "the fair school," formed by Homer, Horace, Ovid, and Lucan—in this order. Virgil comes to save Dante in the dark wood and becomes his guide: "'Miserere di me,' gridai a lui, / 'qual che tu sii, od ombra od omo certo!'" ("'Have mercy on me, whatever you are,' I cried, 'whether shade or living man!'"; *Inf.* 1.65–66).[1] It is in the answer to these first words spoken by the protagonist in the poem that the reader is introduced to Virgil: he is a shade, born in Mantua at the time of Julius Caesar emperor and lived in Rome under Augustus, and hence a pagan. Everybody recognizes him, though, because he was the poet who sang of Aeneas. The pilgrim reacts with humility ("con vergognosa fronte"; "my head bent low in shame"; *Inf.* 1.81) and excitement, as seen in the two tercets starting with "Or se' tu quel Virgilio e quella fonte" and "O de li altri poeti onore e lume" ("Are you then Virgil, the fountainhead" and "O glory and light of all other poets"; *Inf.* 1.79–84), together with a declaration of discipleship: "Tu se' lo mio maestro e 'l mio autore" ("You are my teacher and my author"; *Inf.* 1.85).

Whom would you follow to hell? Would you do it because this person is your role model, the person you want to be and whom you trust unconditionally? And why? For Dante, that person was Virgil. And after all, Virgil also had another qualification: of the ancient poets Dante knew,[2] Virgil was the one most familiar with the journey through the afterlife, since he describes it in the sixth book of the *Aeneid*, when Aeneas is led by the Cumaean Sybil to the underworld. At the same time, and probably most important, Virgil is the author who set the highest standard for Latin verse, and Dante wants to be the exemplar of vernacular verse, creating a direct lineage from the best pagan epic author to the best (and first) Christian epic author. In fact, when Dante the pilgrim wakes up on the other side of the river Acheron, Virgil states, "Or discendiam qua giù nel cieco mondo / . . . / io sarò primo, e tu sarai secondo" ("Now let us descend to the blind world / . . . / I will be first and you come after"; *Inf.* 4.13, 15). This sequential positioning—Virgil first and the pilgrim second—not only applies to the plot of the *Comedy* but also might suggest the ordering of the two authors in their description of the realm of the dead. Moreover, when the pilgrim arrives in Limbo and is welcomed by the "bella scola" ("the fair school"; *Inf.* 4.94), he shows immense respect for the abovementioned literary authorities and receives the honor of being made "sesto tra cotanto senno" ("sixth amongst such minds"; *Inf.* 4.102).

For all these reasons, Dante shows the reader at the beginning of the *Comedy* the literary authorities he finds inspiring and therefore emulates. A detailed comparison between Virgil's *Aeneid* and Dante's *Inferno* demonstrates these points.[3]

READING: *Aeneid* 6.236–751. ACTIVITY: "Brain Game: Spot the Similarities." To discuss the entrance of Dante the pilgrim and his first experience with the world of *Inferno* (cantos 3–4), the class must read *Aeneid* 6.236–751 at home. In their reading, students are also asked to spot the similarities between the two texts (*Inferno* and *Aeneid*), paying particular attention to details, scenarios, and specific words. In class students and teacher together can list similarities and differences and discuss the choices that Dante made. This exercise helps students to understand how Dante the poet reuses the same material to shape his afterworld and solicits discussion on the reasons he chose Virgil as the guide for *Inferno*. This activity can be repeated for canto 5 in finding which characters in Virgil's underworld reappear in the *Comedy* and why. Again, in cantos 8 and 9, students should attempt to determine the similarities between the city of Dis and Virgilian Tartarus. Finding common contact points between the *Inferno* and the *Aeneid*, and the way Dante reelaborates characters, landscapes, and words, is crucial for students to understand the development of the literary tradition and the changeover in context from pagan to Christian. Particularly important are the verses between *Inferno* 8.82 and *Inferno* 9.106, in which Virgil fails for the first time: alone, he cannot open the door of the city of Dis and needs help from the celestial messenger. Students should discuss the reasons for Virgil's inability (e.g., the Virgilian Aeneas never enters Tartarus).

Another passage for which a comparison with the *Aeneid* is fruitful is in *Inferno* 13: the encounter with Pier delle Vigne is modeled on *Aeneid* 3.22–48. In this context, instructors could introduce such notions as intertextuality, interdiscursivity, analogy, and reuse.

Let Lucan Fall Silent, Let Ovid Not Speak

The episode at the gate of the city of Dis changes the secure perception that students and the pilgrim have of Virgil as a guide: in this key episode, the need for divine intervention in order to continue the journey begins to undermine the authority of antiquity. From this point on, we see Virgil as both immensely authoritative and fundamentally limited. Moreover, after the entry into the city of Dis and before the Malebolge (the eighth circle), we find Dante's encounter with his old master, Brunetto Latini (canto 15), in which the pilgrim learns the difference between false earthly "immortality" and true spiritual immortality. Indeed, this is the error into which his master Brunetto has fallen and into which he himself was about to fall ("M'insegnavate come l'uom s'etterna"; "You taught me how man makes himself immortal"; *Inf.* 15.85). Dante the protagonist begins to understand how authors from antiquity, despite their greatness and their immortal fame on Earth, are not saved in their eternal life and are nothing compared to the power of God and true religion. Beginning with the entrance into Malebolge, in the second half of the *Inferno*, Dante the poet is ready to challenge and surpass his pagan models, and this occurs in several episodes.

The first instance, most surprising for readers, takes place in the fifth bolgia, where the devil Malacoda tricks Virgil the guide. Together with the episode before the gates of the city of Dis, this diminishes the credibility of Virgil, and from this time on students can perceive the growing self-awareness of Dante as both poet and pilgrim. Then, it is Lucan and Ovid's turn, in canto 25, where Dante's authorial voice exclaims: "Taccia Lucano" and "Taccia Ovidio" ("Let Lucan now fall silent" and "[l]et Ovid not speak"; *Inf.* 25.94; 25.97). With these lines, Dante challenges and surpasses Lucan and Ovid from a stylistic and literary viewpoint, which conveys that the will of God, manifest in Dante's mission, is more powerful than the vocation of the pagan poets. Finally, in canto 26, readers learn the real end of Ulysses and his final voyage, one that neither Homer nor Virgil recounted.

Throughout these episodes, students can understand how Dante at once challenges the ancient authorities and stands upon them. After reading about the Malebolge, they can discuss the personal growth of Dante as character, author, and historical figure; it is also an opportune time to talk about the composition of the *Comedy* and Dante's life.

READING: Lucan's *Pharsalia*, book 9; Ovid's *Metamorphoses* 4.563–603 and 5.572–641; summary of the *Odyssey*. ACTIVITY: "Dante versus the Classics (3–0)." "Brain Game: Spot the Similarities" can be played in class again—possibly one day for each canto (*Inf.* 24 for *Pharsalia*; *Inf.* 25 for *Metamorphoses*; *Inf.* 26 for *Odyssey*). For these exercises, the class should focus on not only finding the similarities but also understanding how Dante amplifies and continues the original source. Students should observe the way the author of the *Comedy* indulges and exaggerates horrifying details when he deals with the metamorphoses of the damned souls of the thieves. Moreover, students should brainstorm on the goals of Dante's crude realism in this case (e.g., the power of Divine Justice and the author's literary skills, which he compares to those of the ancients).

This exercise helps students to analyze the explicit challenge Dante faces with pagan literature, illustrating his desire to surpass it while making himself the epic champion in describing divine power and knowledge.

Following Virgil's Lantern

When Dante and Virgil leave hell "a riveder le stelle" ("to see again the stars"; *Inf.* 34.139), they meet another interesting pagan character: Cato, a suicide and an enemy of Caesar. As the guardian of the mountain of Purgatory, Cato committed suicide out of love for liberty (*Purg.* 1.31–108; 2.118–33). Dante's Cato retains a Christian figural dimension, because the *Comedy* presents his suicide as the self-sacrifice and choice Christ himself made when coming to life in this world to die on the cross for the salvation and freedom of human beings.[4]

Once Dante and Virgil arrive on the mountain of Purgatory, Dante the pilgrim behaves in a way that clearly shows he has reached more confidence and greater independence from Virgil, even if Virgil continues to be his moral and philosophical guide. Given discussions up to this point, it is worthwhile asking the class why. We have entered a realm completely unknown to Virgil. It would be very fruitful (and often surprising and exciting) for the class to do some research on purgatory: What is it? When was it created?[5]

In *Purgatorio* Dante the protagonist meets another important pagan author: Statius, writer of the *Thebaid* and the incomplete *Achilleid*. Statius acknowledges that the *Aeneid* was, for him, the source of his poetic inspiration (*Purg.* 21.97–98) and moral behavior (*Purg.* 22.37–45), but, above all, the reason for his conversion to Christianity. He did this by following the lantern of Virgil, who was thought to have prophesied the coming of Christ in his fourth *Eclogue* (4.5–7): "Facesti come quei che va di notte, / che porta il lume dietro e sé non giova, / ma dopo sé fa le persone dotte" ("You did what he does who travels by night, / and carries a lamp behind him, that does not help him, / but makes those who follow him wise"; *Purg.* 22.67–69). In Statius's words to Virgil, "Per te poeta fui, per te Cristiano" ("Because of you I was a poet, because of you a Christian"; *Purg.* 22.73).[6]

READING: Virgil's fourth *Eclogue*; Lucan's *Pharsalia* 3.80–91. ACTIVITY: "The Saved and Damned." After reading the fourth *Eclogue* (whose verses are also translated or paraphrased in *Purg.* 22.70–72), the class should discuss the meaning of these verses. After dividing the class in two groups, one group pretends to be Virgil, and the other Statius. Both should read the same verses from two different perspectives: a pagan one (Virgil) and a Christian one (Statius). It is important for students to understand how the same text can have many nuances according to its historical and cultural context: this might also enhance understanding of how elements of pagan culture have been transformed by and absorbed in the Christian one. Moreover, it is a good moment to clarify how, although Virgil is damned to Hell in Limbo, his writings are salvific.

The same exercise works with the character of Cato. Once divided in two groups, the class can converse about the concept of suicide from both a Stoic and a Christian prospective; the suicide of Cato versus the suicide of the damned in canto 13; republican versus imperial values. This exercise might help in understanding Dante's choice of Cato as guardian of Purgatory.

At Heaven's Door

At the top of the mountain of Purgatory, in the Earthly Paradise, Dante realizes his guide has left him. The poet models the musicality of the verses that narrate the disappearance of Virgil (*Purg.* 30.49–51) on the latter's fourth *Georgic* (lines 525–27), when Orpheus loses his wife Eurydice as he exits Hades and turns to look at her. Similarly, we should not forget that a few lines before, Dante uses Dido's line (*Aeneid* 4.23) to recognize his powerful love for Beatrice. Although Virgil is gone, Statius stays with Dante and Matelda until the very end of the second canticle, underlining that Virgil is a damned soul, whereas Statius is not, because he is a Christian poet.

In the third canticle, pagan authors no longer appear as characters, but still their texts are used. The most important example of this usage takes place in the Heaven of Mars, where Dante meets his ancestor Cacciaguida. Here, for the only time in the *Comedy*, Dante the poet establishes an explicit relationship between his own text (*Par.* 15.25–27) and the *Aeneid*: this is the point in which Aeneas meets his father Anchises, who was the very reason he went into the underworld (*Aen.* 6.684–88).

READING: Virgil's fourth *Georgic*, lines 525–27; *Aeneid* 4.23; *Aeneid* 6.684–88. ACTIVITY: "Dante's Multiple Personas." The last exercise suggested— which can also be used elsewhere in the poem—assigns to a student or the class a research project on a particular character (e.g., Dido, Orpheus, Anchises). After reading the tercets and the intertextual source aloud in class, we can open a discussion in response to the following questions: Why does Dante want to say those specific words? Why does Dante want to become that particular person? There are several answers to these questions: for example, Dante wants to become Orpheus because he was the greatest of the poets, because he should have never looked back, or because he was thought to play the lyre by the god Apollo himself. This exercise helps the students to understand more clearly the relation between two texts and their contexts and how they interact. Moreover, it helps to understand the deeply rooted myths and legends in the Christian West, and how classical texts were (and still are) part of the imaginary of poets and writers.

The exercises proposed in this essay have the goals of introducing students to various modes of textual analysis and of enhancing their ability to make strict comparisons between two texts written at a distant time in history. Therefore, these types of analysis demonstrate the benefits of learning through intertextuality and historical contextualization to deeply understand how texts are generated not in isolation, but in constant interaction with the established literary tradition—creating at times the "anxiety of influence" theorized by Harold Bloom (*Anxiety*). Dante felt deeply the greatness of classical authors, but he also felt the desire to surpass them and to become the greatest author in vernacular, the first Christian epic poet.[7]

NOTES

[1] Italian quotations and English translation are from the *Divine Comedy* edited by Robert Hollander.

[2] Homer's *Odyssey* was not available to Western Europeans at the time, so Odysseus's katabasis was not an available model. There were some Latin paraphrases, but Western Europeans could not read Ancient Greek, and there was no full translation into Latin.

[3] For passages from Virgil, see Eclogues, Georgics, Aeneid: *Books 1–6;* Aeneid: *Books 7–12*.

[4] For more on this point see Fubini; Martinez, "Cato"; and Mazzotta, "Opus."

[5] See Armour, "Purgatory"; and Le Goff's fundamental study, *The Birth of Purgatory*.

[6] It is interesting to note, as Brownlee has pointed out, that "Virgil is damned, but his text is salvific; Statius is saved, but his text seems not to have Christian salvific value (148). . . . The poetics of Dante's *Inferno* thus involve a Christian recontextualization of Statius's Thebes as the epitome and emblem of human history without Christ . . . : an endlessly repeated cycle of violence and suffering with no redemptive value or power" (150). Statius's *Thebaid* provides the intertextual source in several points in the *Inferno*, such as the episode in canto 14 of Capaneus, who is a character in *Thebaid* 10; for Count Ugolino, see *Inferno* 32.130–32 and *Thebaid* 8.739–62.

[7] For further reading, see Barański, "Magister Satiricus"; Barolini, *Dante's Poets*; Marchesi, "Boccaccio's Vernacular Classicism"; and Picone, *Scritti danteschi*.

Dante Casts Shadows
over the Legacy of the Classical Past

Brenda Deen Schildgen

As Dante ascends to the final challenge of the *Commedia*, he invokes the god of poetry, Apollo, and thus features both his indebtedness to and reverence for the Greco-Roman epic tradition (*Par.* 1.13–15). Nonetheless, in the *Commedia* the poet deliberately and consistently sets out to distinguish his own Christian poem from the Greco-Roman legacy, which also includes Arabic learning and philosophy, part of the classical legacy transmitted to Europe by way of Arab translations and commentaries on Greek texts (Southern).

In featuring the inherited learned and poetic traditions (Greco-Roman) and Arabic scholarly work in philosophy, medicine, and astronomy, Dante demonstrates how this legacy had been incorporated into medieval Latin culture (see Monneret de Villard; Southern; Rodinson). When he judges the past according to his Rome-centric politics, just as he condemns Greek political figures and Roman sowers of discord, however, he also condemns Islam as a divisive force. He distinguishes Homer the poet, whom he places in his Christian version of the Elysian Fields in Limbo, from Homer's character, Ulysses, whom he condemns to Hell for violence and fraud (*Inf.* 26). He makes similar distinctions with the legacy of Islam and specific Islamic individuals. Thus, breaking the time line (since they are all after Christ), he finds places for Averroes (1126–98 CE) and Avicenna (980–1037 CE) in Limbo (*Inf.* 4), and even includes Saladin (*Inf.* 4), the Kurdish Islamic sultan of Egypt and model of chivalric virtue,[1] who had successfully retaken Jerusalem in 1187, but condemns Mohammed and Ali (*Inf.* 28).

Here he follows the conventional belief that Islam was a schism from Christianity and adopts the tradition of condemning Mohammed as a "seminator di scandalo" ("sower of discord"; *Inf.* 28.35),[2] subjecting Islam to the same moral-theological criteria he applies to those within his own Christian cultural and political milieu. For Dante, Mohammed and Ali are schismatics, Mohammed, in his view, having splintered his "new" religion from Christianity, and Ali's actions leading to the fracture between Sunni and Shia (*Inf.* 28.30–45). In this, according to Dante's system, they parallel the strife among Guelf and Ghibelline partisans on the Italian peninsula, whom he condemns to Hell: Ugolino and Ruggieri, damned for civil chaos in Pisa (*Inf.* 33), or Cassius and Brutus, condemned to the mouths of Satan for creating civil war in Rome (*Inf.* 34). These latter contrast with Dante's decision to save the pagan Cato (*Purg.* 1–2), a suicide, who supported the Roman Republic and committed suicide to bear witness to the horror of civil discord (Hollander, "Dante's Cato").

Divided into three sections, this essay explores how to approach Dante's treatment of the classical legacy that pervades the *Commedia*, examining how

Dante incorporates and also probes the limits of Greek and Arabic philosophy and letters, even though he condemns both spheres for political schism.

Liberal Arts Education

In the classroom, before discussing how Dante represents the pagan Greco-Roman legacy alongside the studies fostered in Arabic learned environments, it is useful to lay out the basic outlines of medieval school education and how this has a bearing on teaching the *Commedia*. Dante's Limbo (*Inf.* 4) is a good place to begin because it includes many topics and authors in the medieval liberal arts curriculum, a secular program of studies indebted to ancient Greco-Roman learning and letters. In Limbo, with its "nobile castello, / sette volte cerchiato d'alte mura" ("noble castle, seven times encircled by lofty walls"; *Inf.* 4.106–07), a reference to the seven liberal arts, Dante features the canon of ancient authors whose works were the staple of the curriculum. Although primarily Roman poets (Virgil, Horace, Lucan, and Ovid), he lauds Homer as "poeta sovrano" ("sovereign poet"; *Inf.* 4.88); then, Aristotle, Plato, Socrates, Democritus, Diogenes, Anaxagoras, Thales, Empedocles, Heraclitus, and Zeno; Dioscorides, Cicero, Seneca, Euclid, Ptolemy, Hippocrates, Galen, Avicenna, and Averroes (*Inf.* 4.134–44). He also includes the fictional Orpheus and Linus, probably from Virgil's *Eclogues* (*Divine Comedy*, trans. Singleton, vol. 1, pt. 2, p. 70). Clearly in the case of some of these ancient figures, Dante's knowledge is very limited, but Euclid's *Elements* and Ptolemy's *Almagest* were studied in the *quadrivium*, to be discussed below.

Ancient Greco-Roman education provided the model for the late medieval liberal arts curriculum and gave training in the verbal arts, or trivium (grammar, rhetoric, and logic), whereas Arabic transmissions of Greek science, mathematics, and philosophy were adopted into the mathematical arts, or quadrivium (Wagner, *Seven Liberal Arts* and "Seven Liberal Arts"), all of which in poetic form are incorporated into the *Commedia*.[3] Grammar was the study of the Latin language under the tutelage of the texts of the sixth-century Priscian (*Inf.* 15.109) and fourth-century Donatus (*Par.* 12.137–38). Central to this grammar education were the Roman Golden and Silver Age poets and writers, precisely those who find themselves in Dante's Limbo (Virgil, Horace, Lucan, and the Greek Homer [through various Latin summaries], and even including Ovid, Seneca, and certainly some Cicero). Following the tenth- and twelfth-century Renaissances and increased contact with Arab Spain, and from translations from Greek through Arabic into Latin, three of the subjects of the quadrivium—astronomy, geometry, and arithmetic—brought Euclid's *Elements* (translated from Arabic by Adelard of Bath, 1150 [Shelby 204]), Archimedes's treatises (from Arabic in the twelfth century and Greek in the thirteenth [Shelby 206]), and Ptolemy's *Almagest* (from Arabic by Gerard of Cremona in the twelfth century [Kren 223–26]) into the curriculum.

Plato's *Timaeus*, through the fourth-century commentary of Chalcidius, and Aristotle's *On the Heavens*, translated from Arabic with a commentary by Averroes (Kren 237), together demonstrate the role of ancient mathematical and astronomical studies in the standard quadrivium curriculum. Dante's cosmology in the *Commedia* derives primarily from the *Almagest*, but he is also in dialogue with these other texts.

The universities in the thirteenth century witnessed the increasing importance of Aristotle's *Ethics*, *Physics*, and *Metaphysics* (the latter translated directly from Greek) to the philosophy and theology curricula at the university, especially in Paris. Averroes, "che 'l gran comento feo" ("who made the great commentary"; *Inf.* 4.144), was critical for the philosophical and theological developments of the thirteenth century when Thomas Aquinas (*Par.* 10–11, 13) endeavored to synthesize Aristotelian and Christian thought through the medium of Averroes's translations and commentary.

Dante's Limbo (*Inf.* 4), where he houses these major figures of the medieval liberal arts curriculum, is almost entirely indebted to the Latin legacy of the Greco-Roman world, and also mediated, in the case of the quadrivium, through the Arabic translations. These people of great worth, as Dante labels them, he still confines to Limbo, thus excluding them from Christian revelation and salvation. The most moving aspect of this separation in the poem occurs when Virgil, Dante pilgrim's guide, master, mother, father, fount of wisdom and poetry, having accompanied him for sixty-one cantos, tells his student, "Non aspettar mio dir più né mio cenno; / libero, dritto e sano è tuo arbitrio" ("No longer expect word or sign from me. Free, upright, and whole is your will"; *Purg.* 27.139–40). Three cantos later, when Dante sees his childhood love, Beatrice, once again, in a reprise of book 4 of the *Aeneid* that rewrites the Dido and Aeneas affair and parting, he—that is, Dante pilgrim—like Dido, knows "i segni de l'antica fiamma" ("the tokens of the ancient flame"; *Purg.* 30.48). The poem continues, "Ma Virgilio n'avea lasciati scemi / di sé" ("But Virgil had left us bereft of himself"; *Purg.* 30.49–50). In this nostalgic and ironic moment, when Beatrice replaces Virgil as the pilgrim's guide, Dante poet, while showing his indebtedness to Virgil's poetry, nonetheless, marginalizes Virgil in Limbo, casting a poignant and long shadow over the legacy of the classical past. Without Virgil, there would be no journey and no poem, but Virgil is nonetheless confined to Limbo.

The Classical Legacy and Christian Theology

Because of the recovery of Aristotle's *De anima*, and Averroes's commentary on it, profound theological controversy arose in the thirteenth century. Averroistic ideas were expounded by Siger of Brabant, a scholarly opponent of Thomas Aquinas at the University of Paris, among others. In his *Quaestiones in tertium De anima* ("Questions on the Third Part of *On the Soul*"), *De anima intellectiva*

("On the Intelligible Soul"), and *De aeternitate mundi* ("On the Eternity of the World"), for example, Siger promoted the heretical view that the soul was a separate entity, and that, like the world, it was immortal and eternal, that is, preexisting the body into which it was born (Mandonnet; van Steenberghen). These arguments attracted so much attention that a papal interdiction in 1277 forbade teaching them (Mandonnet; van Steenberghen). Thus, Dante condemns Christians associated with Averroism, like Frederick II (1194–1250), who was associated with the heavily Arabized Sicilian court, to the circle of the Epicureans (*Inf.* 10). In contrast, he praises Averroes himself, whom, as highlighted above, he puts in Limbo, while Siger of Brabant (*Par.* 10.136), who was accused of Averroism, he places in Heaven. Thus, Averroes is segregated as a learned classical figure, and Averroistic ideas used to enhance the understanding of Christian revelation are rewarded, whereas Averroism as gratuitous, self-indulgent intellectual speculation is condemned alongside other forms of Epicureanism. But here, it is not Arabs or Muslims who are condemned, but Christian deviants from Christian orthodoxy.

In an apparent recanting of earlier philosophical positions found in the *Convivio*, Dante has Beatrice reject in *Paradiso* 4 the potential mistakes in the Greek-Arabic philosophical legacy, which had resulted from Islamic intellectual dialogue with the Aristotelian corpus. In a retrospective glance at *Inferno* 4, Dante here distances the *Commedia* from Greek and Arabic philosophy. In the *Convivio*, Dante seemed to align himself with the philosophical traditions of both the Arabs and the Greeks. Speaking of Beatrice for the last time in *Convivio* (2.7.7),[4] in fact, he enlists all the philosophers (Aristotle, the Stoics, Cicero), the gentiles, and the followers of diverse laws—Jews, Saracens, and Tartars—who all agree to assert how stupid and harmful are the beliefs that the afterlife does not exist and that something eternal does not reside in us (*Conv.* 2.8.8–16). Later in the text, citing Avicenna, Al-Ghazali, Plato, and Pythagoras as his authorities on the nature of the soul, Dante writes that arguments about the nature of the soul might differ among the philosophers, but we might find truth in all of them (*Conv.* 4.21).

Several points follow from this concerning Dante's relationship to Greek philosophy and to its preservation, commentary, and further development by the Arab philosophers. First, he does not separate classical Greek learning from Arab learning: thus he names Avicenna and the Sufi Al-Ghazali (450–505 AH / 1058–1111 CE) alongside the Greeks. Second, he clearly considers them all thinkers who, in a debate, could point to the common truths in their ideas. Third, he presents the classical philosophers' ideas about the soul and the role of the heavenly bodies in their predilections as somehow all capable of being reconciled even though the "classical" view denied individual freedom to the soul. But by the time Dante was writing *Paradiso*, he had clearly come to distinguish Christian views on the question of the soul and its destiny from the more general views he held in the *Convivio*.

Whereas in the *Convivio* Dante had attempted to accommodate the differences about the relative influence of heavenly bodies on the human soul as outlined by ancient Greek and Arabic philosophers, by the time he was writing the *Commedia*, he had clearly rejected this more pluralist position in favor of Christian revelation. Following the Christian synthesis developed by Thomas Aquinas, in which Christ is the means to unite nature and the transcendent, he distinguishes orthodox Christian views on the soul and the freedom of the will from the legacy of the Greeks and the Arabs.

In fact, as a palinode for parts of the *Convivio* and as a look back to *Inferno* 4, *Paradiso* 4 addresses why Plato, Aristotle, Avicenna, and Averroes find themselves in Limbo. Dante in a radical intellectual and theological gesture had placed Averroes and Avicenna among the virtuous pagans, together with Socrates, Plato, and Aristotle. But in *Paradiso* 4, Beatrice's answer to Dante's question about whether the soul returns to the stars, as Plato had expounded in the *Timaeus*, corrects the *Convivio*'s failure to distinguish between the various thinkers on the trajectory of the human soul (*Par.* 4.22–24). In the answer, Beatrice specifically states that Plato's view of the soul returning to its star of origin is wrong, as Dante can see in examples before him in Heaven: "che qui si vede" ("as here is seen"; *Par.* 4.50). Still, she is willing to concede that if Plato had meant that some influence emanates from the stars, then there might after all be some truth in his views (*Par.* 4.55–60). But beyond this small concession, the Platonic view (held by numerous other ancient and Arab philosophers, according to Dante), once led "tutto il mondo quasi" ("almost all the world"; *Par.* 4.62) into error. Dante here makes us look back to Limbo so we understand why the virtuous pagans, who did not believe in freedom of the will, remained there after the Crucifixion and why the ancient Jews, who believed in the coming Messiah, were liberated. In *Purgatorio* 16, in a direct answer to Averroistic ideas about the stars and human freedom, Marco Lombardo answers Dante's question and receives the absolute answer that if the stars controlled our actions, free will would be destroyed (*Purg.* 16.70–71). *Paradiso* 4, in a retrospective look back at *Inferno* 4 thus emerges as a correction or a recanting of the philosophical pluralism in the *Convivio* and as an explanation of the philosophical limitations of Plato, Avicenna, and Averroes, whose arguments lacked the theological revelation that Dante receives through Beatrice. Because of free will, the stars cannot direct human souls. In clearly stating the Christian view of the freedom of the soul and will, Dante simultaneously explains why the ancient philosophers and their Arab followers are domiciled in Limbo (Schildgen, "Philosophers").

Salvation of Pagans and Theology

Some scholars have argued that when Dante raises the issue of the salvation of non-Christians in *Paradiso* 19 (70–78), he may be expressing doubts about the condemnation of the virtuous pagans in Limbo (Foster; Sanguineti 235–54). Of course, Dante does select certain figures from the ancient world as redeemed pagans—Statius (*Purg.* 21 and 22), Cato (*Purg.* 1), Trajan (*Par.* 20.44), and Ripheus (*Par.* 20.68). Therefore, Dante's decision to exile the ancient poets and philosophers shows that he chooses to distinguish pagans he deemed worthy of salvation from those he assigned to Limbo.

From the twelfth century on, strong arguments, reaching back to Pauline and Augustinian statements, held that moral Jews and pagans who had lived before the coming of Christ had equal access to salvation (see Capéran; Sullivan). For, if all humanity had the same roots and the same creator God, they all had to have access to the same possibility of salvation. Peter Abelard, among others, partly due to the rediscovery of Aristotle, argued that the Greeks—Plato, Aristotle, and Socrates—as well as the great Latin writers must have access to heaven under the same rules as the Hebrew patriarchs. Hugh of Saint Victor (*Par.* 12), Albert the Great (*Par.* 10), Thomas Aquinas (*Par.* 10), and Bonaventure (*Par.* 12) argued that for those who had not received the sacrament of baptism, a conversion of heart might be sufficient, for the providence of God was deemed most merciful (Capéran 170–200; Schildgen, *Dante and the Orient* 92–109). Thus, widespread belief held to the possibility of non-Christian salvation, particularly for those who had lived before Christ, or for those who had never encountered Christianity but were nonetheless just.

Dante is more restrictive on the salvation of pagans than the theology of his own time gave him license to be (Capéran 206–12). He invents Limbo as a place to house those just people who were not baptized Christians. Still, in *Paradiso* 19 and 20, with the appearance of Ripheus, a pre-Christian pagan character (*Par.* 20.68) from Virgil's *Aeneid* (2.339, 394, and 426–27), and Trajan, a post-Christian pagan (*Par.* 20.44–45), he raises a question about salvation outside of Christian time. Likewise, the appearance of Cato when the poem turns from the damned to those on the way to salvation in Purgatory undermines any narrow version of Christianity. Dante finds Statius among the penitents (*Purg.* 21–22) and, in an ironic twist since Virgil is not saved, has him claim that Virgil's poetry made him both a poet and a Christian (*Purg.* 22.73). The presence of these figures on the way to salvation or already saved disrupts the claims to an exclusively Judeo-Christian heaven. Moreover, Statius's claim that Virgil's poetry converted him to Christianity gives a stunning justification of the secular liberal arts curriculum for Christian conversion.

When teaching how Dante explores the issue of the status of the secular or "classical" past in the *Commedia*, one must recognize that, although we tend to read the poem one canto and one canticle at a time, to understand its dynamic movement requires continual looking forward and backward even while reading canto-by-canto. Dante's use of the "classical" past in the poem foregrounds the subtle divisions he sets up between those figures confined to Limbo and those he uses as startling exceptions to what he leads us to expect. The poem both uses and reflects on the salutary ends of the liberal arts curriculum and advanced studies in philosophy and theology, all of which stem from the "classical" legacy, whether pagan, Jewish, Islamic, or antique Christian.

NOTES

[1] On Saladin, see Paris; Castro.

[2] Quotations from the *Commedia* in Italian and English translation come from the Singleton edition of *The Divine Comedy*.

[3] On this point, see Mazzotta, *Dante's Vision*.

[4] Citations for *Convivio* are to the edition by Vasoli.

Teaching Dante, Beatrice, and Courtly Love in the *Divine Comedy*

F. Regina Psaki

Seeing generations of students encounter the *Divine Comedy*, resist it, be stunned and then fascinated and then absorbed by it, has been one of the great privileges of my teaching career. Certainly the context of the encounter determines the kind of teaching materials we can use, the assignments we can design, and the learning outcomes we can aim for. Students may encounter the *Comedy* in many course formats from high school to graduate school: a high school advanced placement course of twenty-five students taught in English, a 150-student first-year general education course taught in English, an early-advanced literature survey of twenty-five students taught in Italian, an intimate advanced literature seminar taught in Italian, a noncredit seminar offered in English to interested adult learners, or many others. But at every level teachers have the option of assigning supplemental primary sources that can enrich students' understanding of the poem far more vividly than a mere footnote summary can do. These may be sources that Dante knew and invoked, or they may be representative parallels that clarify or enhance a transaction in the poem. Bringing primary sources to bear on other primary sources is one of the fundamental analytical processes that help students participate in the formation and defense of an interpretation. Bringing those primary sources in from the cold—that is, from their reduced and incidental paraphrase in the endnotes to a canto—is one of the most immediate and energizing ways I have found to activate student engagement with the poem and thus ratchet up student learning.

In the *Comedy* Dante pointedly invokes primary sources that were recognizable to his original audiences and thus able to shed light on the poem. Seven hundred years on, however, biblical, classical, and medieval narratives (and their exegesis) are no longer common knowledge. The current events and recent history of Dante's time are forgotten. The physical and moral worldview that was consensus for Dante's first audience is no longer ours and not widely understood. We are obliged to try to backfill all this knowledge for ourselves and our students using a combination of propaedeutic material, scholarly commentary, and selected primary sources (textual and visual). Because the *Comedy* can in so many ways introduce students to the Middle Ages in general, the challenge of teaching it usually lies in sifting and sequencing the abundance of material available: we end up discarding masses of materials in favor of a manageable workload and a coherent big picture. In my experience, the result is necessarily selective and uneven, a kind of pan-and-zoom in which deep core samples (e.g., *Inf.* 5, 10, 13, 15, etc.) are examined in detail and the cantos between them glossed over, with those summary endnotes doing a lot of the heavy lifting, unthematized in class discussion.

My approach is slightly different. I like my students to walk away not with a coherent big picture of Dante's poem and his period but with an irreducibly complicated one, and with a more direct acquaintance with the primary sources the poem imports as its backdrop. The *Comedy* is notoriously complex and inconsistent, repeatedly presenting its readers with contradictions as *calls to interpretation*. Walt Whitman's formulation in *Leaves of Grass* can characterize elements of Dante's *Comedy* that trouble the poem's foundations and premises: "Do I contradict myself? Very well then, I contradict myself; I am large. I contain multitudes" (87). When we think we have reached an understanding of Dante's position on suicide, on the Roman Empire, and on the fate of pagan souls after death, we encounter the republican suicide Cato as the guardian of Purgatory (*Purg.* 1–2). When we think we understand the status of homosexuality in the moral stratification of *Inferno*, we encounter the homosexual and heterosexual lustful in the same terrace (*Purg.* 26–27). When we think we are clear that repentance, absolution, and (especially) Christ are needed for salvation, we encounter the saved soul of the Trojan Ripheus (*Par.* 20.67–72). I'm not interested in finding—creating—a position from which all Dante's incongruities dissolve away, leaving a clean, clear picture. If we highlight its incompatible verities the poem is infinitely richer and more beautiful, and infinitely closer to Dante's notion that only beyond the perceptual grid of time and space can the plenum of God's universe be grasped in any real sense. To be meaningful and lasting, each reader's understanding of the poem must be reached through individually wrestling with those incompatible verities, not borrowed in wholesale from a learned commentary or an authoritative teacher.

The poem presents many puzzles that will not be resolved simply by the application of additional information, perspective, or argumentation. In particular, one central element of the *Comedy* that I foreground in my teaching has generated sharply contradictory readings in the poem's reception: the nature of Dante's love for Beatrice, both in time (as he has loved and loves her in his life) and in eternity (as he postulates he will love her after his own death). Critics construe this love in subtle and varied ways, but the most popular (and popularly taught) understanding of that love is simplistic: that Dante's early, earthly love for Beatrice has been sublimated and purified, so that she has become a conduit to God rather than an object of love in herself. Or so the clichéd version runs, assisted by the early equation of Beatrice with Theology and Virgil with Human Reason[1] that lives on in manuals, introductory humanities textbooks, and even some specialist writing.

We will never reach a definitive and static right answer on *how* the poet (let alone the historical author) construed his love for Beatrice, or how that love related to the "courtly love" tradition to which Dante was responding in making Beatrice—a woman desired erotically in life—into the medium and mover of the pilgrim's very salvation. The historical author claims to have loved a woman for whom he wrote love poetry and praise poetry, and the *Vita nova* recapitulates that poetry and its place in his biographical, literary, and ethical itinerary.

The poet figure in the *Comedy* identifies this woman with the saved soul who visits the poet Virgil in Limbo—in Hell—to induce him to rescue her "friend" ("amico"; *Inf.* 2.61)[2] already nearly beyond rescue. With *Inferno* 2 begins a master thread that traverses the *Comedy*, the thread of human love and its relation to divine love and to salvation. And by choosing the complex figure of Beatrice to send the equally complex Virgil, "to whom I gave myself for my salvation" ("a cui per mia salute die'mi"; *Purg.* 30.51), Dante set readers the task of deciphering the power and value of erotic love, of *courtly love*, which in the absence of a granular definition we can describe as a love located explicitly outside marriage and exalted in a corpus of lyric song.[3] Because Dante has set his poem outside of earthly life, *sub specie aeternitatis*, he has implicitly set us to puzzling out the power and value of that love *both* in earthly life *and* in the life after death determined by choices made on earth. In play are judgments based on both ontology and teleology: what is inherently right or wrong based on principle, and what is ultimately right or wrong based on outcome.

Although this issue may seem narrowly focused, it affects how students understand not only the *Comedy* but also the Middle Ages as a whole. Reducing Dante's love for Beatrice to a sanitized and etherealized pathway toward a dyadic love between God and Dante risks reducing the entire period's intellectual and philosophical capacity for contradiction, complexity, and indeterminacy. It's this reduction that has given our students catchphrases like "the dark ages" and "the age of faith" to pigeonhole the Middle Ages at the expense of the (apparently superior) nuances of modernity. But the Middle Ages *is* large, it *does* contain multitudes, and nowhere more so than in its greatest poetic monuments, such as the *Divine Comedy*.

I propose an assignment sequence of passages in the poem, most of which are paired with an example of a courtly love song or romance, to mobilize students in actively interpreting Beatrice and the pilgrim's love for her through the lens of both the *Comedy* and its intertexts. There is no implied conclusion for teachers to herd students toward; students may reach, and teachers may endorse, strongly divergent conclusions. The pedagogical goal of this approach is to position students to draw informed conclusions and argue based on their analysis, not to guide them to specific answers to the big questions: Who was Beatrice for Dante—for the pilgrim, the poet, the author? What does the poem suggest about courtly love? About earthly love? And what do students do with the inevitable excess—the evidence that doesn't "fit"? The skills practiced in comparing text and intertext include close reading (focusing in), adducing and applying evidence, devising a thesis, building an argument, illustrating (literally and figuratively) a problem for readers or listeners, and panning back to the ramifications of the analysis just concluded.

It isn't desirable or possible to read the entire *Comedy* solely from the perspective of the role of Beatrice and of the protagonist's, or the poet's, love for her. Thus, the itinerary I suggest here highlights a specific series of passages that would constitute only a subset of the cantos assigned in a course. The notes that would accompany each assigned reading are not exhaustive either; they sketch the issues raised in the *Comedy* that the additional primary sources can illuminate. For that matter, a course that intended to focus on another issue altogether—the proper role(s) of church and state, for example, or the nature and value of pagan antiquity—could deploy the same strategy of pairing specific textual loci with primary sources capable of illuminating them more intensely and more subtly than if the poem were read without them.

Inferno 2.43–142 and Boccaccio's *Esposizioni sopra la* Comedia *di Dante*, literal and allegorical expositions (Boccaccio, *Boccaccio's Expositions* 111–44). In urging the pilgrim to overcome his cowardice and recommit to the journey through Inferno, Virgil details the chain of intercession by which holy ladies, from Mary to Lucy to Beatrice, invoked aid for him. The way Virgil explains Beatrice's role in motivating the rescue places her in a celestial context from the outset. This is a position that students will nuance as the poem moves on, as the pilgrim's emotional investment in her intensifies, and as Virgil's understanding is sometimes shown to need refining. Because these two characters are so often, in introductory materials, set in opposition (reason and theology, for example, or cooperative grace and divine grace), it can be helpful to assign the relevant commentary from Boccaccio's *Esposizioni* (available in English translation as *Boccaccio's Expositions on Dante's* Comedy) or one of the early commentaries. These can show an early gloss that later passages of the poem can actually work against.

Inferno 5.88–107 and Guido Guinizzelli's *canzone* "Al cor gentil rempaira sempre amore" (Marti 57–62; "Love seeks its dwelling always in the gentle heart"; Goldin, *German and Italian Lyrics* 286–91); Dante's sonnet "Amore e 'l cor gentil son una cosa" ("Love and the noble heart are one sole thing"; *Dante's Lyric Poetry* [Barolini] 188–90); Cino da Pistoia's sonnet "Pianta Selvaggia, a me sommo diletto" (Cino da Pistoia 183; "'Wild' tree, my highest pleasure"), which concludes, "A nullo amato amar perdona amore" ("No one loved does Love exempt from loving").[4] The purpose of juxtaposing these courtly lyrics with Francesca's first speech is to open a window onto the courtly lyric register that Dante is having her invoke so pointedly. Francesca implicitly associates the erotic impulses that she and Paolo experienced with the literary production in which the pilgrim had taken part. The reader can see, in the infernal context, evidence that the lovers missed a very important point; the pilgrim's loss of consciousness takes on more varied connotations, including not only his continuing susceptibility to this kind of love and to Francesca's rhetoric, but also his recognition of his potential responsibility in her fault.

Inferno 5.121–38 and prose *Lancelot* (Corley 314–27); Andreas Capellanus, *De arte oneste amandi*, bk. 1, chs. 1–5, on love as suffering (Capellanus

28–33); Alain of Lille, *The Plaint of Nature*, on love as paradox (Alain of Lille 149–53). This small subset of intertexts will contextualize Francesca's understanding of love as the poet has constructed it for her.

Inferno 10.52–72 and Guido Cavalcanti's *canzone* "Donna me prega, perch'eo voglio dire" (Marti 183–191; "A lady asks me please to speak"; Goldin, *German and Italian Lyrics* 322–28). Although the great doctrinal poem may seem a bit of a digression at this point in the *Comedy*, it will keep present both the question of Cavalcanti's "altezza d'ingegno" ("height of intellect," *Inf.* 10.59) and rival definitions of love current in Dante's circles.

Inferno 28 and Bertran de Born, "Be.m platz lo gais temps de pascor" ("I love the joyful time of Easter"; Goldin, *Troubadours* 242–47): the "I love war" song that takes off on a springtime trope of rebirth.

Purgatorio 2.76–133 and Dante's *canzone* "Amor che ne la mente mi ragiona" ("Love, speaking fervently in my mind"; *Dante's Lyric Poetry* [Foster and Boyde] 1: 106–11). The nostalgic encounter between the pilgrim and Casella, and the performance of the former's poem that spellbinds all the souls, begs for a reading of the *canzone* itself, which Cato's indignant accusation of negligence and forgetfulness indicts as something they all need to set aside.

Purgatorio 11.82–120 and Guinizzelli, "I' vogl' del ver la mia donna laudare" (Marti 76–77; "I wish to truly praise my lady"; Wilhelm 141); Cavalcanti, "Chi è questa che ven, ch'ogn'om la mira" (Marti 133–34; "Who is this one that comes, that each man gazes on"; Goldin, *German and Italian Lyrics* 316–17); Dante, "Tanto gentile e tanto onesta pare" ("So noble and so virtuous she seems"; *Dante's Lyric Poetry* [Barolini] 231). Juxtaposing these three sonnets with analogous themes allows students to compare not only their artistry (more clearly visible in Italian) but also their approaches to love and praise poetry. In addition to noting how Dante wrote himself above the "two Guidos" (11.97–99), students will note the added value of Beatrice's apparently universal effect on all around her, not only Dante.

Purgatorio 23.76–133: Dante's "Chi udisse tossir la mal fatata" ("Anyone who heard the coughing of the luckless"; Alfie 34) and Forese Donati's "L'altra notte mi venne una gran tosse" ("The other night I had a great fit of coughing"; Alfie 38–39), the *tenzone* or (in this case) hostile exchange of sonnets that the poet seems now to regret. The focus in these poems on the public life and personae of the poets, including their families, is a useful counterpoint to the personal and private function of Beatrice in the pilgrim's spiritual maturation.

Purgatorio 24.1–69 and Bonagiunta Orbicciani da Lucca, "Voi che avete mutata la mainera" ("You who have changed the manner"; Goldin, *German and Italian Lyrics* 270–71); Guinizzelli, "Om ch'è saggio non corre leggero" ("A wise man does not rush in thoughtlessly"; Goldin, *German and Italian Lyrics* 294–97); and Dante's *canzone* "Donne ch'avete intelletto d'amore" ("Ladies who have intellect of love"; *Dante's Lyric Poetry* [Barolini] 185–87). The *tenzone* between Bonagiunta and Guinizzelli illustrates not only the poetic and theoretical shift Bonagiunta articulates but also rival goals of pursuing love and poetry in the thirteenth century. How the sonnets are recalled implies the historical author's sympathy with Guinizzelli over the stolid Bonagiunta, whereas the *canzone* exemplifies a stage of Dante's poetic production that the poet was ready to integrate into the *Comedy*.

Purgatorio 26 and Guiraut de Bornelh's *alba* "Reis glorios, verais lums e clartatz" ("Glorious King, true Light and Splendor"; Goldin, *Troubadours* 194–97); Arnaut Daniel's sestina "Lo ferm voler q'el cor m'intra" ("The firm desire that enters my heart"; Goldin, *Troubadours* 220–23); Guittone d'Arezzo, "Ora parrà s'eo saverò cantare" ("Now we shall see whether I can still sing"; Jensen, *Tuscan Poetry* 174–81). The *alba* and the sestina of these two Provençal poets consolidate the lyrico-erotic corpus Dante engages in the terrace of lust. The *alba* thematizes, however ironically, divine protection of transgressive lovers, whereas the sestina foregrounds the cryptic, intimate privacy of the coded bedchamber. Guittone, mentioned deprecatingly in *Purgatorio* 24 and 26, can exemplify the putative conversion away from love that the *Comedy* does not promote, though it is often said to.

Purgatorio 30–33 and "Tanto gentile e tanto onesta pare" ("So noble and so virtuous she seems"): the Earthly Paradise. Beatrice's behavior—unexpected after Virgil's coaxing, urging, pushing, and pulling the pilgrim up the mountain with implied promises of a blissful reunion—repositions her, as Dante emphasizes through biblical and Virgilian intertexts, in a role that will take us the whole *Paradiso* to grasp.

Paradiso 8–9 (Heaven of Venus) and Dante's *canzone*, "Voi che 'ntendendo 'l terzo ciel movete" ("O you who move the third heaven by intellection"; *Dante's Lyric Poetry* [Foster and Boyde] 1: 100–03). This heaven rehearses a spectrum of understandings of human love, from the "folle amore" ("frenzied love"; *Par.* 8.2) invoked at its outset and superseded (if unregretted; *Par.* 9.103), to the cosmological function of love. In yet another call to interpretation, Dante complicates the already complex by citing this *canzone*, which explicitly replaces the poet's lady with Lady Philosophy.

Paradiso 10–14 (Heaven of the Sun) and the *Song of Songs*. Pairing the end of *Paradiso* 10 with the *Song of Songs* allows students to explore the medieval allegorical reading of the latter, whereas *Paradiso* 14's hymn to the body allows them to see the treatment of the post-resurrection body returned to its materiality (though transformed in a way we cannot quite grasp).

The *Paradiso* is famously the most abstruse and challenging of the three canticles—exponentially more so on the first reading. So that students can focus on it, from mid-canticle on I assign no additional primary texts, but rather require them to refer to earlier passages and intertexts as the poem moves to its conclusion. Focus topics and loci include the following:

Frequent references to Beatrice's increasing and unbearable beauty and to the pilgrim's inability to grasp it and the poet's inability to fully remember or articulate it (e.g., *Par.* 30.1–37).

Paradiso 26.1–69: the examination on Love, especially passages querying and resolving the "altre corde" ("other bonds," line 49) that drew the pilgrim to the love of God.

Paradiso 28: the vision of God as a dimensionless point that is not marginal to, but encompasses, the universe: a point that is "not circumscribed and circumscribing all" ("non circunscritto, e tutto circunscrive"; *Par.* 14.30).

Paradiso 31.52–93: the pilgrim's stunned realization that Beatrice has left him.

Paradiso 33: the pilgrim's integrative vision of the divine, beginning with the paradoxes or paralogisms of the Virgin Mary: "Vergine madre, figlia del tuo figlio, / Umile ed alta più che creatura" ("Virgin mother, daughter of your son, / more humble and exalted than any creature"; lines 1–2).

As Beatrice has drawn the pilgrim upward, Godward, her role has become not simpler but more complex, and the contradictions that characterize the Trinity and the Virgin Mary encompass her as well. My students have reached varied and contrasting opinions about how we are to construe Beatrice, God's *pasture* ("lures" or "bait"; *Par.* 27.91) for Dante; the object of the exercise is not that they reach the same, or my, conclusion. They learn to apply cultural evidence active in the poem to arrive at their own interpretation, and to use that evidence to clarify and argue that reading. Given that the *Comedy* is coming up on its seven-hundredth year of vigorous debate, definitive solutions are unlikely, to say the least. Instead, an approach that places the responsibility for comprehending this complex poem on its readers in their focused interaction with Dante's intertexts has the capacity to both illuminate the poem and train its students.[5]

This intertextual approach is suitable for high school, college, and graduate courses focusing on Dante in English or Italian. From the earliest extant commentaries, reading the *Comedy* has always been a collective effort, not one conducted in silence, in solitude, and in the library. Instead of putting all students to work on all the pairings, I suggest distributing writing, presentation, or wiki assignments to give each student a particular text-intertext pairing to concentrate on and to illuminate for the class. Assigning students the task of distilling, analyzing, presenting, and teaching these materials to one another activates their own ratiocination, intensifies their engagement, and (not least) consolidates their recollection of the *Comedy*. What students hear or read is soon forgotten; it's what they teach that stays with them.

NOTES

[1] Boccaccio's *Esposizioni sopra la* Comedia *di Dante* already established this clunky symbolism: canto 1, allegorical exposition §150 (Boccaccio, *Boccaccio's Expositions* 104); canto 2, allegorical exposition §§29–47 (141–44).

[2] Quotations and translations of the poem are from Mandelbaum.

[3] The secondary literature on the amorphous semantic field covered by courtly love (or *fin'amor*) can probably no longer be read in a lifetime. A reading summarizing the historiography of the concept can be a helpful supplement: see Schultz; Karras; and Reddy.

[4] I have found no published translation of this sonnet, which puns on the name given to Cino's beloved Selvaggia (wild).

[5] Martin Eisner's *Dante's Library* (sites.duke.edu/danteslibrary) will introduce and eventually include such primary sources.

Dante and the Spectrum of Medieval Vernacular Poetry; or, How Giacomo and Joyce, Brunetto and Eliot, and Bertran and Pound Rhyme

Martin Eisner

Dante is not only a supreme vernacular poet but also one of the first theorists of the vernacular, from the genealogy of vernacular poetry in chapter 25 of the *Vita nuova* to the historical and rhetorical distinctions of the *De vulgari eloquentia*. Throughout the *Commedia*, Dante engages this vernacular tradition in a variety of ways, staging encounters with his own past poetic production and fellow poets while also testing and challenging his own theoretical principles. Because Dante highlights the importance of these relationships in the *Commedia*, most instructors will want to make students aware of this tradition and its impact on Dante's poetry. Had one but world enough and time, students could read Dante's own account of his poetic development in the *Vita nuova* and his other lyrics, but such additions may only be possible for a course dedicated exclusively to Dante.[1] In this essay, I have selected three moments from *Inferno* that can make students aware of the larger traditions, both medieval and modern, in which Dante appears, giving them a taste of Dante's poetry in the original, along with some key modern texts by James Joyce, T. S. Eliot, and Ezra Pound.

Because most students have had limited exposure to poetry even in English, I begin my first class analyzing translations of the first line of *Inferno*: "Nel mezzo del cammin di nostra vita" ("When I had journeyed half of our life's way"; *Inf.* 1.1).[2] A few minutes before the first class begins, I start playing Caroline Bergvall's performance of her poem "Via" (Bergvall, *Via*), in which she reads the first terzina of forty-seven English translations (Bergvall, *Fig* 63–71), and hand out a sheet with the translations she recites to students as they enter. Students thus begin the class surrounded by poetry as both sound and text—a conjunction crucial to their understanding of Dante's work as poetry. When Bergvall's recitation is done, I ask students to comment on the significance of the differences between the various versions. Observations vary year by year, but they understand immediately the way a translation can inflect one's interpretation. I always make a point of adding Peter Whigham's lapidary, "Life's path half past" (Griffiths and Reynolds 400), not only because it leads into our discussion of the medieval arc of life (see *Convivio* 4.12) but also because it highlights issues of diction, sound, and rhythm that I want them to analyze. This exploration of multiple English translations prepares students for their first assignment, in which they compare three different English translations of three to fourteen verses to identify the differences between them and interpret their significance. The goal of this lesson and the accompanying assignment is to make students aware that they are reading Dante in translation and call their attention to the importance of the translators' poetic choices—a critical concern that they can then apply to their readings of different kinds of medieval vernacular poetry.

Giacomo da Lentini and James Joyce: Inferno 5

Given the richness of *Inferno* 5—for its varied history of interpretation, its significant visual reception (see Eisner), and its paradigmatic examination of sin and agency—it may not seem easy to include a discussion of poetic form. A close reading of Dante's rhymes, however, reveals that the poetic tradition is at the forefront of his concerns. To introduce this point, I share a section from chapter 7 of Joyce's *Ulysses* entitled "Rhymes and Reasons." Joyce writes:

RHYMES AND REASONS

Mouth, south. Is the mouth south someway? Or the south a mouth? Must be some. South, pout, out, shout, drouth. Rhymes: two men dressed the same, looking the same, two by two.
. . . . la tua pace
. . . . che parlar ti piace
. . . . mentre chè il vento, come fa, si tace.
He saw them three by three, approaching girls, in green, in rose, in russet, entwining, *per l'aer perso* in mauve, in purple, *quella pacifica oriafiamma*, in gold of oriflamme, *di rimirar fé più ardenti.* But I old men, penitent, leadenfooted, underdarkneath the night: mouth south: tomb womb.   (175)

Joyce pairs Stephen Daedalus's reflections on the significance of rhyme ("is the mouth south someway?") with the beginning of Francesca's speech in *Inferno* 5, where she greets the pilgrim in the highest possible rhetorical register. Because I teach the poem in dual-language versions, students have easy access to the Italian text, so they can look at Francesca's address to the pilgrim:

> O animal grazïoso e benigno
> che visitando vai per l'aere perso
> noi che tignemmo il mondo di sanguigno,
>
> se fosse amico il re de l'universo,
> noi pregheremmo lui de la tua pace,
> poi c'hai pietà del nostro mal perverso.

Di quel che udire e che parlar vi piace,
noi udiremo e parleremo a voi,
mentre che 'l vento, come fa, ci tace.

O living being, gracious and benign,
who through the darkened air have come to visit
our souls that stained the world with blood, if He

who rules the universe were friend to us
then we should pray to Him to give you peace
for you have pitied our atrocious state.

Whatever pleases you to hear and speak
will please us, too, to hear and speak with you,
now while the wind is silent, in this place.

(*Inf.* 5.88–96)

Students immediately recognize that these verses explain some parts of the passage from Joyce, such as "per l'aer perso" ("through the darkened air"). I do have to explain that others such as "quella pacifica oriafiamma" ("that peaceful oriflamme"; *Par.* 31.127) and "di rimirar fé più ardenti" ("made my eyes more ardent to see"; *Par.* 31.142) come from *Paradiso* 31, where Dante is about to look at the Virgin Mary. The presence of Dante's Italian in this masterpiece of modernism shows students the ongoing importance of Dante's work and the pleasures of a multilingual literary universe. The passage from Joyce also underlines the way rhyme can link apparently unrelated concepts ("mouth south: tomb womb") to create resonance between them. With some prompting, students are usually willing to reflect on how the different languages they know also offer connections based on rhyme.

Keeping these ideas in mind, we look at the next lines of the canto, where Francesca evokes Amor at the beginning of each terzina (100–08) to defend herself, and then describes how she and Paolo fell in love (127–38). We analyze how Dante has Francesca call attention to the act of reading, using the idea of the book as Galeotto to exculpate herself, blaming both author and text without taking responsibility for herself as reader: "Galeotto fu 'l libro e chi lo scrisse" ("A Gallehault indeed, that book and he who wrote it, too"; *Inf.* 5.137). Instead of interpreting the scene as the condemnation of a certain kind of courtly literature, we explore how Dante uses Francesca to frame the act of reading as an analogue to ethical decisions. With this understanding of the content of the verses, students can investigate how the poetic form reinforces these ideas. Asking students to pay particular attention to the sounds and rhymes, I read the following verses:

"Noi leggiavamo un giorno per diletto
di Lancialotto come amor lo strinse;
soli eravamo e sanza alcun sospetto.

Per più fïate li occhi ci sospinse
quella lettura, e scolorocci il viso;
ma solo un punto fu quel che ci vinse.

Quando leggemmo il disïato riso
esser basciato da cotanto amante,
questi, che mai da me non fia diviso,

la bocca mi basciò tutto tremante.
Galeotto fu 'l libro e chi lo scrisse:
quel giorno più non vi leggemmo avante."

Mentre che l'uno spirto questo disse,
l'altro piangëa; sì che di pietade
io venni men così com' io morisse.

E caddi come corpo morto cade.

"One day, to pass the time away, we read
of Lancelot—how love had overcome him.
We were alone, and we suspected nothing.

And time and time again that reading led
our eyes to meet, and made our faces pale,
and yet one point alone defeated us.

When we had read how the desired smile
was kissed by one who was so true a lover,
this one, who never shall be parted from me,

while all his body trembled, kissed my mouth.
A Gallehault indeed, that book and he
who wrote it, too; that day we read no more."

And while one spirit said these words to me,
the other wept, so that—because of pity—
I fainted, as if I had met my death.

And then I fell as a dead body falls.
(*Inf.* 5.127–42)

Students usually hear the repetition of the assonant hard *c* of the final line and, working backward, some call attention to the *b* and *t* of "la bocca mi basciò tutto tremante." Others note the sibilant *s* of "strinse," "soli," "sanza," and "sospetto." For a time, at least, students are able to perceive some of the ways Dante the poet crafts the sounds of his poem. Telling students to keep in mind Dante's rhyme words, I then share Giacomo da Lentini's sonnet *Io m' aggio posto in core a Dio servire* ("I have set my heart on serving God") in Italian with an English translation (Jensen, *Poetry* 38–39). Because students will have at least heard of a sonnet, likely in relation to Shakespeare, they may know that it should have fourteen lines, but they usually do not know that the form is an invention of medieval Sicilian poets. The English word "sonnet," which derives from the Italian "sonetto" meaning "little sound," not only encodes this significant literary historical fact but also calls attention to the aural element that I want students to explore. Students have little difficulty identifying the coincidence of the rhymes *riso–viso–diviso* in Giacomo's poem. We then consider other ways these poems might rhyme, not only in terms of form but also in terms of theme. Reading the sonnet in English translation, students observe the similarities between the dramatic situation of the sonnet where the poet wants to go to paradise but does not want to be divided ("diviso") from his lady and the situation of Francesca who, although not separated ("diviso") from her lover, winds up in Hell. Students are now prepared to address the significance of Dante's decision to have the episode of Francesca rhyme with the sonnet of Giacomo da Lentini. Francesca gets just what the speaker of Giacomo's poem wants, but it is achieved in Hell. Following the fine analysis of Teodolinda Barolini ("Dante and the Lyric Past"), I emphasize how Giacomo's sonnet describes the basic courtly dilemma between love of lady and love of God that Dante transforms by combining these loves in the figure of Beatrice.

Brunetto Latini and T. S. Eliot: Inferno 15

While Dante's evocation of the tradition of the courtly lyric represented by Giacomo da Lentini's sonnet occurs implicitly through his deployment of the same rhymes, his engagement with Brunetto Latini could not be more explicit. As the pilgrim tells Brunetto, "m'insegnavate come l'uom s'etterna" ("you taught me how man makes himself eternal"; *Inf.* 15.85). Students immediately grasp the irony of the pilgrim's remark, since Brunetto's teachings have landed him in Hell, not Heaven. I take Brunetto's final lines, where he claims that he lives on in his *Tesoro* 119–20), as an occasion for students to read Brunetto's Italian poem. I note that some commentators argue that Brunetto refers to his French prose *Trésor*, despite Brunetto calling his Italian poem *Tesoro* twice in the text (*Inf.* 15.75 and 113). Brunetto's production in both French and Italian introduces students to the multilingual world of medieval Italy, where the vernacular did not mean a single idiom but instead any language that was not Latin.

Students read Brunetto's poem (his *Tesoro*, our *Tesoretto*) in Julia Bolton Holloway's translation, which not only has the Italian on the facing page but also includes folio numbers for the Strozzi manuscript and footnotes that alert students to accompanying illustrations in the codex. These allusions to the medieval manuscript provide an opportunity to discuss the labor involved in the production of these manuscripts and the challenge of transmitting knowledge in a world before the printing press and public libraries, let alone the search capabilities of the modern Internet. A discussion of these historical questions can help make students more receptive to the medieval world of knowledge represented by Brunetto's poem and his encounters with allegorical figures such as Nature. Although Brunetto's extensive use of personification allegory signals a major difference between his poem and Dante's, these questions about the diffusion of knowledge make students more willing to consider Brunetto's ideas about psychology, cosmology, and ethics, which they can then compare to what they find in Dante's poem.

Although a number of topics could deserve further scrutiny, I ask students to examine Brunetto's treatment of love. In Giacomo da Lentini's sonnet students observe the courtly conflict between the love of the lady and the love of God; in Brunetto they notice the problematic relation between love, reason, and authority. Contrary to post-Romantic ideas of inspiration, Brunetto expresses the medieval anxiety about love's relation to reason. If love means the displacement of reason, how can one be an authority in love? We examine how Brunetto deals with this problem by staging an encounter with Ovid (in contrast to, but also in anticipation of, Dante's Virgil), who frees Brunetto from his desires, thus making him capable of writing the encyclopedic poem that we are reading. Just as Dante collapses Giacomo's distinction between love of lady and love of God by joining them in the figure of Beatrice, Dante asserts that he can be an authority while in love. Dante insists that his love for Beatrice is reasonable at the beginning of the *Vita nuova* where he claims that he never loved Beatrice "sanza lo fedele consiglio de la ragione" ("without the faithful counsel of reason"; 2.9). Whereas Brunetto contrasts love and reason, Dante joins them in his extraordinary love for Beatrice.

Finally, I discuss Brunetto's poetic form and use of rhyming couplets. Hearing a few of these verses read in Italian, students recognize their aphoristic or epigrammatic quality that recalls both the concluding couplet of a Shakespearean sonnet and various nursery rhymes. The brevity of those rhyming couplets written in short verses of seven syllables (*settenario*) provides an occasion to investigate Dante's decision for longer, hendecasyllabic lines that ideally recall Virgil arranged in tercets of terza rima. Brunetto thus provides an important reference point as a poetic model that Dante does not follow in terms of both content (personification allegory, the relation between love and authority) and form.

I continue the analysis of the canto examining Dante's final image of Brunetto running away, which Eliot discusses in his "Tradition and the Individual Talent" as an example of how a poet can have "numberless feelings, phrases, images, which remain there until all the particles which can unite to form a new compound are present together" (49). Eliot's remarks open up a discussion about the valence of this final image and introduce the issue of Eliot's own relationship to Dante. To conclude the class we look at Eliot's recasting of Dante's encounter with Brunetto in part 2 of "Little Gidding" (1942), where Eliot tries to replicate Dante's terza rima in English, as he claims in his 1950 essay "What Dante Means to Me." What Eliot doesn't mention in his essay is that he begins the section with rhyming couplets and continues in terza rima, thus staging in one poem the formal poetic development from Brunetto's couplets to Dante's terzine that we discussed earlier. The section begins:

Ash on an old man's sleeve
Is all the ash the burnt roses leave.
Dust in the air suspended
Marks the place where a story ended.
(Eliot, *Poems* 202; lines 1–4)

He then shifts to tercets to describe his own encounter with "some dead master,"

Whom I had known, forgotten, half recalled
Both one and many; in the brown baked features
The eyes of a familiar compound ghost
Both intimate and unidentifiable.
So I assumed a double part, and cried
And heard another's voice cry: "What! are *you* here?"
(*Poems* 204; lines 40–45)

Just as Dante had created a "new compound" in his representation of Brunetto at the end of the canto, Eliot recalls Dante's question, "Siete voi qui, ser Brunetto?" ("Are you here, ser Brunetto?"; *Inf.* 15.30) to craft his own encounter with "a familiar compound ghost."

Bertran de Born and Ezra Pound: Inferno 28

Brunetto introduces the question of other vernacular languages that Dante explores further in the *De vulgari eloquentia* (1.8), where Dante classifies the Romance languages into the *lingua di sì* (Italian), *lingua d'oc* (Provençal or Occitan), and *lingua d'oïl* (Old French), and identifies three themes, each of which he associates with a Provençal and Italian poet: for love, the poets are Arnaut Daniel and Cino da Pistoia; for "rectitude," Giraut de Borneil and Dante Alighieri; and for war, Bertran de Born and no Italian because, Dante writes, "as for arms, I find that no Italian has yet treated them in poetry" (2.2.8 [Botterill]). Dante's notation of this absence in the *De vulgari* helps students understand the bloody beginning of *Inferno* 28, where Dante describes the dismemberment of the sowers of schism in terms of a series of historical battles. They recognize that in *Inferno* 28 Dante turns himself into the Italian poet of arms to match Bertran.

I used to give students Bertran's celebration of warfare in "Be•m plai lo gais temps de pascor" so students could see how Dante uses rhymes from Bertran's poem in the canto, but I have found that having them read Pound's "Sestina: Altaforte" can be equally productive. Pound's poem is quite difficult: its strident tone; the strange, impersonated voice; odd diction; complex poetic form; and singular structure all challenge students, but each element contributes to the poem's value as an introduction to some distinctive characteristics of the Provençal tradition. Pound's strange prose preface, for example, imitates the prose *vidas* and *razos* that frequently accompany Provençal poems to mediate them to a different cultural world. These texts are especially important because they inform Dante's construction of the *Vita nuova*. The peculiar voice and its call for battle remind students that warmongering is not just something from the medieval past but a fundamental feature of modernity. Equally challenging is Pound's language and his use of words, such as "stour," that require students to use a dictionary and make them aware of the historicity of English and its strangeness. Finally, we discuss the poetic form of the sestina, which Pound imitates (with one slight imperfection), and which gives students the experience of hearing the repetition not of rhymes but of rhyme words, which creates an obsessive atmosphere. Although Pound knew no sestina by Bertran, Pound shows students the kind of formal experimentation that Dante himself discovered in these Provençal poets and that that found its fullest realization in Dante's *rime petrose*.

Because these readings of poetry in multiple genres and vernaculars derive from Dante's own poem, they enrich students' interpretations of Dante's work. Introducing these medieval materials in the company of Joyce, Eliot, and Pound also shows students the continuing vitality of these poetic forms. These three moments from *Inferno* give students a solid foundation for more detailed or extensive explorations of the tradition. As students move further into *Purgatorio*, they see these topics return and develop further. I use these later encounters to add to the repertory of themes and forms that we have discussed so far. The encounter with Forese Donati on the terrace of gluttony, for example, gives students an opportunity to read Dante's use of the register of the insult in his exchange with Forese. Because these sonnets challenge the familiar image of the moralizing Dante, students are amazed by them. In the Earthly Paradise, Dante's recasting of Guido Cavalcanti's "In un boschetto trova' pastorella" ("In a little wood I found a shepherdess"; *Purg.* 588–89 [Durling trans.]) can be the occasion for an analysis of the uncourtly genre of the pastorella, in which desires can, in fact, be physically satisfied. The ambition of all these assignments is to achieve what Seamus Heaney said Osip Mandelstam accomplished in his "Conversation about Dante": "he makes your mouth water to read him" ("Envies" 194).

NOTES

[1] My choices are Mortimer's translation of the *Vita Nuova* and Barolini's *Dante's Lyric Poetry*.

[2] Quotations from the *Divine Comedy* in Italian are from Petrocchi. Unless otherwise noted, English translations are from Mandelbaum.

Transnational Dantes

Nick Havely

The *Commedia* has been rendered into around fifty different national and ethnic languages—from Afrikaans to Welsh and from Arabic to Yiddish—so there is ample scope and material for extending the teaching of transnational Dantes. Much of the focus of such teaching so far has been Anglophone in its orientation,[1] yet considerable resources for a broader study of the subject have accumulated over the past half century, and university courses on Dante reception have recently begun to take advantage of such wider resources.[2] The three courses this essay chiefly draws on are all the products of English departments across the Northern Hemisphere: from the United Kingdom to Switzerland to the United States. The earliest of them was a module, Dante in English, which I taught for second- and third-year bachelor's degree students at the University of York from 1991 to 2011. This was followed in 2013 by David Wallace's more subtly named course, After Dante, which ran for a semester in the English Department at the University of Pennsylvania. And at the University of Basel in the spring of 2015, Julia Straub taught fourteen weeks of classes on Dante in Victorian Literature.

To focus on the content, aims, and outcomes of these three examples is not, however, to belittle the importance of the various comparative literature and great books courses that preceded them, especially in the United States. The present book's predecessor some thirty-five years ago included essays on the place of the *Commedia* in a range of courses on literature in translation.[3] For example, in "A Comparative Approach to Teaching the *Divine Comedy*," Marie Giuriceo described classes that formed part of "Landmarks of European Literature" at Brooklyn College in the early 1980s. That course looks very much as if it might have grown out of (or been related to) the Great Works of Literature class, through which—also at Brooklyn College—Dante came to influence a major African American novelist, the late Gloria Naylor.[4] Naylor's second novel, *Linden Hills*, was published a few years after she graduated from Brooklyn College, and, as she acknowledged, its account of two black poets' winter journey through a middle-class neighborhood develops "along the lines of the *Inferno*."[5] The appropriation of Dante in *Linden Hills* has been the subject of much comment and interpretation,[6] and in its turn Naylor's "modern *Inferno*" has become a popular item for student discussion—as it was in my own Dante in English course at the University of York.

That York course grew out of the teaching and research culture of a department that since its inception in the 1960s had been committed to the study of related literatures and drew on the precedent of a course on Dante in Italian that has continued to run since those early years. In the early 1990s the initial aims of Dante in English were to expand the student readership for the poem by offering an introduction to the *Commedia* in translation and to discuss the various forms and media through which it was appropriated and reinvented in Anglophone cultures. Thus, after several weeks exploring themes in the *Commedia* itself (alongside selected translations and imitations, from Chaucer to Heaney), students would encounter the reception of Dante from his rehabilitation in the late eighteenth century to his presence in contemporary culture. Typically, seminars would then focus on topics such as Romantic and pre-Romantic responses (translation, criticism, illustration, allusion); the Victorian cult of Beatrice and the *Vita nuova*; and reinventions of Dante's work in modern poetry, narrative, and the visual and performing arts.

After twenty years the Dante in English course came to an end when I left York in 2011, but two years later After Dante at the University of Pennsylvania took up the story and expanded its chronological and cultural range. Taking a cue from his groundbreaking essay on the subject in the *Cambridge Companion* (Wallace, "Dante"), David Wallace proposed an experimental approach to the "engagement with Dante by poets and artists coming after him" (Wallace, Course description). After Dante took account, for example, of the earlier appropriations of Dante by Chaucer and Milton, along with his recruitment by Protestant polemicists as a writer against Rome and the ways in which he "gets folded into anti-Catholic discourses" during the eighteenth century (Wallace, Course description). Like the York module, After Dante focused on certain key topics from the early nineteenth century to the present: the first complete English translations by Henry Boyd and Henry Francis Cary and their reception; Samuel Taylor Coleridge's criticism, William Blake's illustrations, and Percy Bysshe Shelley's *dantismi*; the Victorian "turn to the *Vita nuova*"; T. S. Eliot's and Ezra Pound's modernist appropriations, and so on. It also explicitly invited students to address a wider range of cultures: nineteenth-century American appropriators, from Lorenzo da Ponte to H. Cordelia Ray; along with Irish, Caribbean and modern African American Dantes—notably Amiri Baraka's *System of Dante's Hell* and (again) Naylor's *Linden Hills*.

More recent still was Julia Straub's course Dante in Victorian Literature (University of Basel, spring 2015) which drew on Straub's own important study of Dante's Beatrice as "Victorian muse" as well as Alison Milbank's indispensable research on the subject. Its chronological range was narrower than those of the York and the University of Pennsylvania courses, but as well as investigating the engagement with Dante on the part of major Victorian figures, the Basel course also made space for closer study of the relevant Dantean texts (the *Vita nuova* and parts of the *Inferno*); moreover, Straub's syllabus encouraged students to "theorize the Victorian Dante" by explicitly inviting discussion of intertextuality and intermediality.

An enlivening feature of working on the present essay has been the readiness of students to respond to questions and send examples of their work. Like the content, structure, and methods of the courses themselves, the cultural and intellectual backgrounds of such students have been diverse and transnational. Dante in English at York drew students with commitments to disciplines other than literature (especially history, linguistics, and philosophy), and it attracted overseas students (Argentine, German, Italian, Singaporean, and Slovenian) who were well accustomed to moving between languages. Both of the more recent courses have each run for only a single semester, but their intake too has reflected considerable diversity. In the University of Pennsylvania After Dante course, one of the participants had already completed a doctorate in Italy, and the course was to some extent reshaped, for example, to fit the interests of several Germanists, one of whom was engaged in a dissertation on Dante and Goethe. The makeup of the class for the University of Basel course Dante in Victorian Literature reflected Switzerland's multilingual culture in several ways, as an Italian-speaking student from Lugano suggests:

> I found discussions in [the Dante in Victorian Literature] class to be stimulating because we all had different cultural backgrounds, and we got the chance to exchange views with people who had read Dante for the first time and could link some aspects to their previous knowledge, for example, of German literature. This challenged the perspective I had on Dante, which maybe had been more taught than actively discussed during classes at high school.   (Mondia)

Part of the challenge issued to students by all three of these courses was to develop a substantial essay project. Here too a sampling of outcomes reflects a striking diversity and perhaps indicates directions that future courses might take. Thus the essay by the Lugano student at Basel, Michele Mondia, titled "Francesca da Rimini's Reception amongst Romantics," set up a dialogue between nineteenth-century appropriations (by Lord Byron, Leigh Hunt, John Keats, et al.) and modern critical interpretations while also engaging in close analysis of discourse, narrative, and translation or mistranslation. In the same Basel class, another student, Kevin Erni, used Harold Bloom's theories of influence appropriately as a framework for an account of Alfred Tennyson's "Ulysses" as a text "in Battle with Homer and Dante"—a "modern myth" based on a story "as diverse as its protagonists' different names," showing how Tennyson here "deliberately misinterpreted" his two canonical predecessors.

Displaying comparable sophistication of approach, term papers by two students following the After Dante course at the University of Pennsylvania focused on two culturally diverse contemporary writers. In an essay on Haruki Murakami and Dante, Sara Sligar argued that the concern with "physical transition" (and particularly descent) in The Wind-up Bird Chronicle "references the epic form of Dante's Divine Comedy and helps Murakami challenge established norms of novelistic structure," showing also how in this case the text's surrealism "reactivates the epic world-view." This approach might well be applied to some other surreal and katabatic narratives that evoke and revise the

Dantean quest, such as David Lynch's *Blue Velvet* and Mark Danielewski's labyrinthine *House of Leaves.*

In the same University of Pennsylvania class, an Italian student, Andrea Gazzoni, became interested in how responses to Dante's vernacularity have been articulated from perspectives that are (as he put it) "marginal or rooted in local cultures"—for example in Caribbean writing. Taking note of some more general studies of Dante's presence in Derek Walcott's poetry,[7] Gazzoni then focused particularly on the light of *Paradiso* 33 and how in *Omeros* it becomes "a paradigm of poetry's reversible possibilities and limitations" and his ambitious account of the "failure of language" and "going beyond art" built on recent critical accounts of both poems. Comparison here could perhaps be made with "A Dream of Solstice," a poem published ten years later by Walcott's contemporary, Seamus Heaney, writing about Ireland at the turn of the millennium and likewise grappling with the potentialities of the new dawn through what Gazzoni calls the "self-erasing" language of *Paradiso* 33.

Concern with language and its limitations on the part of Dante and later poets—as well as parallels and divergences in quest narrative—had earlier provided fruitful subjects for students of the York Dante in English module. A striking example of a project involving both kinds of approach was an essay by a Slovenian student of (and currently researcher in) linguistics—Moreno Mitrovič—on "Dantean simulacra" in the last four books of Sri Aurobindo Ghose's massive (24,000-line) epic *Savitri*, composed between 1916 and 1951. Drawing on recent comparative studies[8]—and with firsthand knowledge of the Sanskrit contexts of Aurobindo's work—Mitrovič shows how Aurobindo's retelling of a story from the *Mahābāhrata* (Savitri's quest to redeem her husband Satyavan from the world of the dead) develops parallels with the Dantean journey. Citing lines 249–54 of book 10 of *Savitri* (648), he also argues that in the later stages of Savitri's pilgrimage and vision the "limitations of language and mind" can be seen to reflect the paradox in the last lines of *Paradiso* 33.

Encountering this range of skills and accomplishments—along with such diverse and productive backgrounds—has for me been the chief reward of a long career in teaching, and the outcomes of all three programs reviewed here—in terms of student response and research—augur well for the future of courses on transnational Dantes. What directions could such courses take, and at what level(s) might they be taught? They would, of course, need to attend to a range of past and present critical interpretations, translations, and adaptations, as well as developments in the visual and performing arts. Thus, for instance, a seminar about the "rehabilitation" of Dante in European culture around the turn of the eighteenth and nineteenth centuries might begin with theoretical discussion of broader issues such as reception, influence, and intertextuality, then move on to key examples of pre-Romantic and Romantic translation (e.g., Antoine de Rivarol in French, H. F. Cary in English), criticism (the views of August von Schlegel, Ugo Foscolo, Antoine Ozanam, Samuel Taylor Coleridge), illustration (Heinrich Fuseli, John Flaxman, Blake, Jean-Auguste-Dominique Ingres), and performance

(Silvio Pellico's Francesca tragedy and its operatic successors; Gustavo Modena's Dante recitations). A seminar on the *Commedia* in the cinema could start with an early Italian silent movie, the Milano Films *Inferno* (1911) and its national and international impact—and then compare more localized cultural translations, such as Hollywood moralities of the 1920s and 1930s, and many more recent cinematic versions. For an increasing amount of this material, online databases—such as the *Princeton Dante Project*, Columbia's *Digital Dante*, the University of Texas's *Danteworlds* (developed by Raffa), the University of Virginia's *The World of Dante*, and Bowdoin College's *Dante Today: Citings and Sightings of Dante's Works in Contemporary Culture* (edited by Saiber and Coggeshall)—will continue to be crucial.[9]

A very recent example of thinking on the subject is a proposal, by James Robinson at the University of Durham, for a third-year undergraduate module on "Dante's presence within twentieth- and twenty-first century world literature," which describes how such a course could address selected episodes in the *Commedia* and subsequently consider:

> [T]heir appropriation and creative transformation by a range of writers and artists, from Natsume Sōseki and later Japanese engagements to the responses of the Irish modernists, and from early Italian and American film adaptation to the global perspectives of John Kinsella and Derek Walcott. It would use reactions to Dante as a way to explore changing approaches to canonicity and regionalism and to open up questions of cultural and linguistic translation and appropriation.
>
> (Personal communication with Robinson)

Courses following more extended timelines and adopting more advanced approaches could also usefully address factors such as the circulation of manuscripts and printed texts; the role of expatriates in promoting and appropriating Dante's work; Dante's involvement in polemic, propaganda, and censorship from the medieval period through to the present day; and attempts at popularization of the *Commedia* through lectures, festivals, and other media, such as magic lantern slides, movies, and TV.[10] The potency of the Dante "brand" for consumers across various cultures and contexts could be investigated too: from the merchandising at the 1865 *Festa di Dante* in Florence to the present-day use of "the famous Italian name" to market a successful chain of coffee-shops in Taiwan, Indonesia, and the Middle East.[11]

Mention of "advanced approaches" raises the question of setting an appropriate pedagogical level. All three of the existing examples mentioned here have been pitched at the late bachelor's or early master's level, and it is likely that future transnational Dante modules would be similarly challenging.[12] This is not to say that prerequisites would have to be imposed or that all such courses would have to be taught at this advanced level. It would also be possible to construct transnational programs more in line with the great-books tradition, focused substantially on the *Commedia* in translation and accompanied by a much more select sampling of post-Dantean dialogues. But even here some previous experience of exploring a discipline or disciplines in the humanities would still be desirable as a foundation. And at any level, it would have to be recognized that work on such a range of periods, languages, and cultures will be, as one colleague wisely urged, "a collaborative effort; none of us can pretend to know all fields" (Wallace, Course description).

Above all—as the students and subjects featured in this essay demonstrate—diversity of cultural backgrounds and intellectual interests has been crucial to the success of such projects so far and will doubtless continue to be so. "Reading mocks the borders of the nation" (178) was Wai Chee Dimock's assertion in *PMLA* in 2001, in a special topic devoted to global literary studies. Dimock's essay challenged the "almost automatic equation between the literary and the territorial" (175) while arguing that in the case of Dante "the centrifugal force of literature is deeply at odds with the vainglorious talk of the fatherland" (178). During a time in which the volume of such vainglorious talk has been vastly amplified on both sides of the Atlantic and frontiers have been reconstructed or reimagined so as to "take back control" of national sovereignty, it seems appropriate to try to imagine teaching courses in ways that could encourage thinking about Dante beyond borders.[13]

NOTES

[1] For Anglophone reception, other resources (in order of publication) include Toynbee's monumental *Dante in English Literature*; La Piana, *Dante's American Pilgrimage*; S. Ellis, *Dante and English Poetry*; MacDougal, *Dante among the Moderns*; Wallace, "Dante in English"; Hawkins and Jacoff, *The Poets' Dante*; Griffiths and Reynolds, *Dante in English*; Looney, *Freedom Readers*; and Havely, *Dante's British Public*.

[2] A few examples of the broader approach are: Friederich, *Dante's Fame Abroad*; Caesar, *Dante: The Critical Heritage*; Esposito, *L'opera di Dante*; Kuon, *Mio maestro*; the articles on Dante and various national cultures in the *Enciclopedia dantesca* and *The Dante Encyclopedia* (edited by Lansing); and Audeh and Havely, *Dante in the Long Nineteenth Century*.

[3] For approaches to teaching Dante in various comparative and interdisciplinary contexts, see Carole Slade's 1982 *Approaches* volume.

[4] Naylor's untimely death (at the age of 66) was announced by the Associated Press on 3 October 2016.

[5] Naylor and Morrison 582. See also Looney, *Freedom Readers* 158, as well as the essay by Suzanne Roszak in this volume. Naylor also received her MA (in African American studies) at Yale in 1983, the year in which A. Bartlett Giamatti, then president of Yale, published (as editor) an important collection of essays representing Dante's reception in the United States from 1813 to 1981: *Dante in America*.

[6] See the works cited by Looney, *Freedom Readers* 167 and 235 (nn 3, 5, 9).

[7] For example, G. Davis; Balfour; Fumagalli; and Austenfeld.

[8] For example, those by Nandakumar, *Dante and Sri Aurobindo*; and Schildgen, "Dante and the Bengali Renaissance," "Dante in India."

[9] Most of the online databases mentioned are conveniently accessible (along with the *Dartmouth Dante Project*'s commentaries and the Società Dantesca's digitized manuscripts) through the portal of the *Dartmouth Dante Lab* at dantelab.dartmouth.edu/. These resources are discussed in greater depth in the "Materials" section of this volume.

[10] See, for example, some of the essays in Iannucci's *Dante, Cinema, and Television* (3–73, 129–52, 213–23) and in Braida and Calè's *Dante on View* (23–51, 153–92).

[11] On the promotion of Dante at the 1865 festival, see Barlow; O'Connor; and Yousefzadeh. For the Taiwanese Dante Coffee franchise (founded in 1993), see dante.com.tw; I am grateful to Joe Havely of the National University of Singapore Business School for directing my attention to the latter brand.

[12] Other relevant recent courses or parts of courses include those taught by Alison Milbank at Nottingham and by Dennis Looney at Pittsburgh. Milbank includes Dante in an undergraduate religion and literature module which encourages students to engage in "critique of reception through creative projects" (Message). Looney's master's-level graduate class From Hell to Harlem addressed the categories of African American reception that would shape his *Freedom Readers* and aimed to "consider how these imitations, adaptations, rewritings, responses to Dante's *Divine Comedy* call into question the poem's canonical status and at the same time often reaffirm it" (Syllabus).

[13] The same expansive phrase features (as this essay goes to press) in the title of a conference at Verona: Dante oltre i confini (20–21 Oct. 2016). Papers listed on the program focus on Dante's presence in France, Germany, Hungary, Russia, Spain, and the United States, but (perhaps significantly?) not Britain.

Sodomite, Homosexual, Queer: Teaching Dante LGBTQ

Gary Cestaro

The LGBTQ in my title is adverbial. I want to give teachers some ideas about how to approach Dante, sexuality, and gender identity in the classroom—when and how the poem engages these issues, how scholars have talked about them, what is at stake. Drawing examples mostly from *Inferno*, I'll review some of the places where Dante and LGBTQ studies might speak to one another. I'd also like to open up more of the poem to queer reading and urge us away from what Eve Kosofsky Sedgwick called a "minoritizing" view of (homo)sexuality, something of localized interest only to a small few (1–63). That means moving beyond an exclusive focus on Brunetto Latini and the sodomites of the desert plain, whose heavy stone embankments have walled off something of a critical ghetto (if I can use a Venetian word for the Florentine poet) in Dante studies.

We can think of modern gay identity as genealogically descended from several perdurable premodern discourses, most prominently pederasty, gender inversion, and friendship (Halperin, esp. 104–37). Modern gay identity owes something to each but is identical to none. We should invite our students to understand Dante as lodged at a dynamic moment in this historical trajectory. In *Inferno* 15 and 16, Dante condemns sodomites to eternal torment in round three of circle seven, where they wander about cyclically in troops on a lifeless desert under a rain of fire. Today's mostly queer-friendly students may very well be put off by the imperious judgment, particularly if for "sodomites" we read unthinkingly "homosexuals" or "gays and lesbians," as so many even astute critics of the poem continue to do. But with Dante the cartoon picture of a stern moralist masks something richer. As a professor of Dante and LGBTQ studies, I encourage students to discover in Dante a moralist and supreme rationalist, to be sure, but above all a poet. Dante's poetic voice—realist, deeply empirical but at the same time mystical and awed by creation—moves in delicate counterpoint to the impressive strictures of his invention. This tension animates the text and offers opportunity for classroom conversations about history, identity, and the sexual politics that are common currency in our students' daily lives.

This brings us to the three words in the first half of my title. The discipline of LGBTQ studies has concerned itself centrally with theorizing and historicizing the very notion of sexual identity we tend to take for granted. We might even say this is a founding tenet. So the medieval sodomite (not to mention the ancient pederast) is a fundamentally different creature from the modern homosexual. A curious Greek-Latin admixture, the word *homosexual* wasn't cobbled together until 1869 and in some significant sense so, too, the human type, born of the new scientific craze for taxonomy in the latter nineteenth century. Sodomy was a forbidden act, a crime, and anyone harbored the potential for perversion. True, some individuals gained reputations, but that differs from the deep personhood imposed by modern homosexuality. And so in his landmark *History of Sexuality*, Michel Foucault famously quipped: "the sodomite had been a temporary aberration; the homosexual was now a species" (43).

The historical narrative LGBTQ studies describes from ancient pederasty or medieval sodomy to modern homosexuality suggests a movement from mere acts or variant tastes to something called identity, a fundamental component of individual being. Interestingly, the last word in this series, *queer*, tends to move back in the other direction. Sometimes just a catchall for LGB or T, *queer*, as reclaimed by AIDS activists and then harnessed by academics, asserts critical resistance to gender or sexual identity as eternal, fixed, stable. It's fair to say that this usage has trickled down, especially on university campuses. When our students say or identify as *queer*, there's a good chance they're not just using a hipper new word for *gay*. The word comes with a whiff of resistance—an allowance that sex and gender are complicated and on the move. In this way, today's student may very well be more open in her everyday experience to less fixed notions of sexual identity than, say, students of my generation, who came of age in the heyday of strongly claimed identity politics. *Queer* also does useful critical work by training attention on the instability of gender and sexuality binaries of a piece with other discursive structures in ways that seem apt for Dante. In *De vulgari eloquentia* 1.14, for instance, he jokes caustically that the idiolect spoken in Romagna is so distorted in its inflections that it causes its speakers to change sex spontaneously—a notable trans moment in a treatise ostensibly about language.

Dante certainly has the mysteries of the larger physical universe in mind when sketching his portrait of sodomites in *Inferno* 15–16. Nonprocreative sexual intercourse, sodomy was by definition a violation of "nature," and so Dante's sodomites are among the violent in the seventh circle. Sodomy was thought of largely as a male-male act, but more than one early commentator pictures women walking these scorched plains as well, taking a cue from Paul.[1] Of course, Paul wrote centuries before anyone really made much of a connection between same-sex intercourse and the Sodom story in Genesis 19, and long before the word and sin "sodomy" were invented (probably by Peter Damian in the eleventh century[2]). The stunning imagery of these cantos—tides, rivers, earth, moon, and stars—projects condemnation and wonder all at once. Nature is here portrayed not as linear, benevolent, and procreative, but rather destructive in her procreative force, exuberant and excessive, resistant to a straight reading, forever at twists and turns. A divine agent like her sister minister Fortuna, Natura is queer in ways that defy simple classification (Cestaro, "Queering"). Yes, Dante is condemning a sexual infraction, probably the sexual and disciplinary abuses of power he knew from the medieval grammar classroom (not by coincidence all grammarians and men of letters in this section of circle seven). But he also chooses these very cantos to showcase the inscrutability of the natural world.[3]

At the same time, Dante's encounter with his onetime mentor-master Brunetto Latini channels ancient sexual energies while reflecting anxiously on the humanist educational legacy, which fantasized the transmission of wisdom's seed from father (surrogates) to son (surrogates): patriarchy, pedagogy, pederasty. Although Dante could not have known directly Plato's overtly pederastic dialogues, he was surely aware of the intergenerational erotics of Greek men and their intellectual heirs, if only through Ovid and Virgil. And he knew the realities of medieval schools and city life (Cestaro, "Pederastic Insemination" and "Is Ulysses Queer?"). What his relationship with the older Brunetto was can only fall into the realm of speculation, but, to the extent that the text nudges us in this direction, it's not idle speculation. *Inferno* 15 features the promising young poet as object of an intense homoerotic gaze, the apple of his mentor's eye, a thoroughly sexualized "dolce fico" ("sweet fig"; 15.66).[4] This gaze persists in the following canto among the second group of sodomites, Florentine statesmen, here transformed into naked oiled wrestlers eyeing one another for advantage as the poet evokes yet another deeply homoerotic ancient tradition. These cantos provide a case study in polyvalent reading for students. No wonder they gave rise to a modern critical tradition that in some instances tried to deny that they are about sex at all. Though untenable, such resistance nonetheless reflects how in Dante sexuality fuses with broader concerns: language, politics, history, time.

Some readers have detected a change of heart when Dante comes back to sodomy in *Purgatory* 26 on the terrace of lust, now the least serious sin on the doorstep of Eden (see Pequigney). The terrace's symmetry appears to divide the penitent lustful into two large and—can it be?—equally numbered groups, same-sex and opposite-sex desire (*pace* Kinsey and, more recently, the Williams Institute).[5] In Purgatory, gender of object choice seems a minor and relatively benign variant on human sexuality, the flip of a not particularly consequential switch, lightly inscribed by contrary motion and a mostly invisible line. Dante's moral focus here on lack of reasonable measure does more to unite than to divide the two groups. This has prompted some to conclude not implausibly that Dante is leaving space for same-sex attraction that is not "intrinsically disordered."[6] It's certainly worth noting with Teodolinda Barolini that in any case the poet didn't need to reintroduce sodomitic themes in Purgatory for any compelling historical or structural reason.[7] No one would have missed it. At the same time, we don't really need to imagine Dante undergoing a dramatic reversal on sodomy from *Inferno* to *Purgatorio*, since for all their mystery the sexual acts the poet had in mind in Hell had more to do—like the Sodom story itself—with violence, not love.

Dante's encounter with Brunetto is also about fathers and sons, and those in the symbolic role of fathers and sons. Young Dante is sweet son to Brunetto's kindly father. In a parting gesture, Brunetto recommends his *magnum opus*, his life's work and lettered offspring, his *Treasure* (damningly ironic in this context). A charged analogy between biological (straight) and cultural (queer) reproduction informs humanist thought since Plato. Intergenerational male-male cultural intercourse recapitulates symbolically the real eroticism so central to Greek pedagogy, confusing identity and desire. Dante is surely at grips with some remnant of this legacy in his encounter with Brunetto.

Or wherever he is contemplating his own relationship to Virgil, his literary spiritual father (and sometime nurturing mother), which is to say just about everywhere. Virgil is deeply implicated in the schemes of classical pederasty, both personally and in his texts, to an extent Dante could not have ignored. Virgil spent time in Athens and was a devoted student of Greek culture. An authoritative early biography confirms his sexual and romantic preference for young men.[8] His *Eclogues* (most prominently the second) emulate the homoerotics of the Greek pastoral. And throughout the *Aeneid*, Dante's "other Bible,"[9] we discover Virgil's admiration for male-male erotics—from the unnecessary intrusion of Ganymede and Jove in the poem's opening lines to the closing slaughter of Turnus, motivated (according to at least one eminent classicist) by Achilles-like love grief for Pallas (Putnam; see also Pequigney 37–39).

Then there is the *Aeneid*'s great love story. I'm referring to the heroes Nisus and Euryalus, whose drama takes up a good chunk of book 5 and fully half of book 9. A number of Virgil critics have explored the significance of this queer romance for the epic, though Dante readers have hardly noticed.[10] This is odd, since Dante chooses to feature the couple in the *Comedy*'s very opening canto (*Inf.* 1.106–08). There we find the lovers alongside Amazonian gender warrior Camilla, herself an acolyte of the proto-lesbian Diana and—like Nisus and Euryalus—a kind of second-hexad queer foil to Dido. Virgil's fawning portrait blends distinct traces of classical pederasty into the sort of epic heroic friendship better known to history from Homer's Achilles and Patroclus. The ancients debated whether Achilles and Patroclus were sexually involved, but that they might have been is something that has occurred to generations of readers.

Dante himself may be thinking of Homer's warrior lovers when he spots Achilles among the lustful at *Inferno* 5.65–66. More than one early commentator contemplates this same-sex reading, thus linking ancient heroic friendship to medieval sodomy and making it clear, at least, that medieval readers were in on the implicit sexuality of these ancient relationships.[11] But the portrait Virgil gives us of Nisus and Euryalus is vastly more elaborate and romantically intense than anything in Homer. Despite their creator's admiration, Nisus and Euryalus fall short somehow in the race for Roman destiny. They lose themselves in a dark and tangled wood, lose sight of the straight path, and perish. I'm by no means the first reader to point to this wood as at least one possible intertext for the "selva oscura" of *Inferno* 1. It's surely no coincidence that these men's names appear later in the same canto. I would, however, underscore the decidedly queer provenance of the image, the enabling metaphor and substrate of Dante's entire vision.

Dante's text reflects notions of same-sex desire that both reinforce and undermine the gender binary, that are both (again, with Sedgwick) gender separatist and gender transitive.[12] Hypermasculine warrior lovers mix with feminized boys like Euryalus, Narcissus, Hyacinth, and Ganymede.[13] At *Purgatorio* 26.76–81, the poet goes out of his way to include a scandalous reference from Suetonius (via Uguccione) that pictures young Julius Caesar hailed as "queen" in mock triumph after sexual submission to the king of Bithynia—imperial Roman manhood in thrall to more Eastern predilections. In any case, trans bodies populate the *Comedy* as they did ancient texts. Virgil's nuanced depiction of Camilla in *Aeneid* 11 blends Amazonian gender inversion with the all-female separatism of Diana and her nymphs, whose contiguous naked bodies—though technically chaste—summoned an intense erotic gaze.[14] In Virgil, Diana oversees the fate of Camilla, her longtime beloved (see 11.535–38), just as the nighttime escapades of Nisus and Euryalus are bathed in the poignant half-light of her moon (see 9.402–09). At the same time, through Camilla Virgil unmasks gender identity as an accident of upbringing, nurture not nature, while according the warrior maiden enormous respect. Dante echoes this tribute in *Inferno* 1 and places Camilla in the company of Nisus and Euryalus, as if reuniting Virgil's queer family. He again pays Camilla great honor in *Inferno* 4 by placing her in Limbo's noble castle with other ancient heroes, this time joined by her Amazonian ancestor Penthesilea. Dante thus exalts an entire lineage of illustrious male women.

Hermaphroditus looms large in the sexualized Ovidian transformations of *Inferno* 24–25 where bodily appendages morph and boundaries dissolve. Ovid's story affirms the instability of sexed bodies while constructing heterosexual desire itself—a compulsion to erase the male-female divide—as queer. Can it be mere coincidence, then, that Dante chooses the peculiar and deliberately confounding adjective "ermafrodito" to describe "heterosexual" lust at *Purgatorio* 26.82, where, as we have seen, the line between same- and opposite-sex desire apparently so crucial in *Inferno* 15 has begun to give way?[15] Nor does the poet overlook Ovid's other great trans protagonist, the prophet Tiresias (whom Guido da Pisa identifies as "hermaphroditum" at *Inf.* 20.40–45). Tiresias's saga affirms the widespread notion that those who transcend gender limits enjoy extrahuman vision. Dante imports Tiresias into his text in *Inferno* 20 through Statius's *Thebaid* (another richly queer intertext for Dante, along with the *Achilleid*) as father of the prophetess Manto, "vergine cruda" ("harsh virgin"; *Inf.* 20.82), namesake of Virgil's hometown. At once picture of feminine seduction and hostility to men, Manto appears to have inherited a version of her father's queerly gendered sexuality. The soothsayers' pornographic bodies and retroflected heads literalize the backward-glance poetics of the sodomy cantos. *Inferno* 20 also shares the sexualized poetics of the metamorphosis cantos 24–25, with their primal scenes of knotted snakes, crude references to pubic hair, male and female genitalia, gender bending and gender separatism. Of course, in *Inferno* 20 Dante uses sexual confusion to reproach classical enthusiasm for wizardry. But he later grants Manto, too, the dignity of Limbo, naming her explicitly as daughter of a trans father, "la figlia di Tiresia" ("Tiresias's daughter"; *Purg.* 22.113), so putting her in two places at once, the rare instance of a textual inconsistency.

We can be certain anyway that Dante was uncertain—of at least two minds—when it came to Tiresias's queer progeny. Once again we detect an exacting moralist and endlessly curious humanist poet. I hope the preceding has illustrated some of the many places where Dante studies and LGBTQ studies can cross paths. We should help students discover a poet engaged in deeply personal dialogue with ideas and individuals he admired from the past and timeless human, social, and physical realities. Though it may seem paradoxical to some, LGBTQ studies can help us ward off presentism by getting students to think critically about gender and sexual identity in ways that are both more historical and theoretically nuanced. In this way, attention to gender and sexuality in Dante can encourage the sort of dynamic reading we aim to model for students generally while inviting urgent, contemporary conversations in the classroom.

NOTES

I thank Teo Barolini, Chris Moevs, and Justin Steinberg for logistical support and useful feedback during the preparation of this essay.

[1] See the *Dartmouth Dante Project*, Boccaccio's commentary on *Inferno* 15.115–18; and Landino's on *Inferno* 15.100–20. For Paul, see Romans 1.26–27.

[2] For Dante's portrayal of Peter Damian, see *Paradiso* 21.

[3] Northern Italian Aristotelians of the time (like Pietro D'Abano) debated the exact relationship between same-sex desire and "nature"; see Cadden, *Nothing Natural is Shameful.*

[4] Quotations and translations of the *Divine Comedy* are from Durling and Martinez's three-volume edition.

[5] The American sexologist Alfred Kinsey's famous postwar studies estimated the homosexual population at 10% for males, 2–6% for females; the UCLA School of Law Williams Institute's current estimate for the LGBT population of the United States is 4.5% (Kastanis et al.).

[6] For this objectionable formulation, see the 2006 pastoral letter issued by the United States Conference of Catholic Bishops, "Ministry to Persons with a Homosexual Inclination."

[7] See especially Barolini's conclusion in *Dante and Heterodoxy* (edited by Ardizzone and Barolini), esp. 263–65.

[8] Aelius Donatus (possibly derived from Suetonius), *Life of Virgil*: for a recent edition in English, see Copeland and Sluiter 82–103. For Donatus in Dante, see *Paradiso* 12.137–38; interestingly, Priscian, the other great Latin grammarian, is with Brunetto Latini in the circle of the sodomites.

[9] I believe Bruno Nardi was among the first to define the *Aeneid* as a sort of secular scripture for Dante; for resistance to Virgil's homoerotic tendencies, see Nardi, *La giovinezza di Virgilio*.

[10] In addition to Putnam, see the excellent edition and commentary of *Aeneid* 9 by Philip Hardie.

[11] See the Ottimo Commento, 1333; Boccaccio; Benvenuto; the Anonimo Fiorentino; and Landino *ad loc* on the *Dartmouth Dante Project*.

[12] For a broad consideration of gender and the role of women in Dante, see the essay by Kristina Olson in this volume.

[13] Queer young *eromenoi* all. For Narcissus in Dante, see *Inferno* 30.127–29, *Purgatorio* 30.76–78, *Paradiso* 3.16–18; for Hyacinth and the queer classical convention of the beautiful young boy's death (*pulchra mors*), see *Inferno* 2.127–32; for the pilgrim as ravished Ganymede figure from *Purgatorio* 9 through the upper reaches of *Paradiso*, see Holsinger, "Sodomy."

[14] For queer Diana, particularly in the early modern period, see Traub, esp. 229–75; Drouin. At *Purgatorio* 25.130–32 and *Paradiso* 31.31–33, Dante references Ovid's homoerotic tale of the nymph Calisto's desire for Diana (*Metamorphoses* 2.401–507).

[15] On the queerness of all sexual desire, see Aristophanes's famous speech in Plato's *Symposium* at 192c–e. Dante's use of "ermafrodito" here has confused many scholars, even, initially, the brilliant and pioneering John Boswell in *Christianity, Social Tolerance, and Homosexuality*, 375n50; cf. Holsinger, "Sodomy" 261.

Conceptions of Women and Gender in the *Comedy*

Kristina Olson

Conveying the innovative nature of Dante's approach to women and the female gender is one of my priorities in the general education classroom. When students begin to view Dante as an original voice that cannot be labeled either misogynist or feminist tout court, they leave the classroom with the necessary understanding that medieval literature is not dismissive of women's importance. By casting "historical" women, both real and fictive individuals with their own literary pedigrees, as characters in his poem, in addition to engaging with explicit antifeminist rhetoric and discussing literary works and the vernacular as maternal objects, Dante conveys that women and the female gender serve an essential function within his elaborate vision of politics and language itself.

Yet, for an epic love poem written in honor of a woman who appears within it as guide, philosopher-theologian, and Christ-like figure, the critical reception of the *Commedia* has only sporadically examined Dante's innovative approach in this regard. Only over the past three decades has the representation of women and the feminine received sustained attention from scholars. Instructors of Dante in a range of classrooms, from survey and general education courses to stand-alone courses, could benefit from reflecting on this critical history as a way to approach the idea of how women and the female gender are represented in the poem in innovative ways.

To begin, let us remember that the first edition of the MLA *Approaches to Teaching Dante's* Divine Comedy (1982) does not feature an essay treating women.[1] An animated discussion of women and gender had already begun in the scholarship, however, namely with Marianne Shapiro's *Woman Earthly and Divine in the* Comedy *of Dante* (1975) and Joan Ferrante's *Woman as Image in Medieval Literature* (1975), both of which were groundbreaking works in addressing representations of women and matters of misogyny in the poem.[2] Reflecting on the conceptual differences between these two early volumes can prepare an instructor for the polarized preconceptions of women in the Middle Ages that one often encounters in the general education classroom.[3] Shapiro categorizes female figures in the *Comedy* in three telling groups: wives and virgins, lovers, and mothers and maternal figures. Her mode of considering gender as binary is likewise oppositional in ascribing traits to one sex or the other; for Shapiro, Dante views the masculine as the embodiment of that which is holy and good, and the feminine as its opposite. As Ferrante herself notes in her review of Shapiro's book, Shapiro believes the women in the *Comedy* are only marked by sex or motherhood; yet there are numerous characters (such as Beatrice herself) who do not fit this classification (322). According to Shapiro,

Dante adheres to a misogynist strain that she ascribes to patristic and scholastic sources (28), an assumption that is often made by students unfamiliar with Dante and with contemporary scholarship on women and feminism in the medieval period.

It is therefore beneficial to juxtapose Shapiro's volume at the beginning of a course with Ferrante's approach as a way of defusing assumptions about medieval misogyny and Dante's own participation in those traditions. In *Woman as Image*, Ferrante urges us to reflect upon how Dante broke with tradition in ways that also distinguish him from thirteenth-century literary culture (Ferrante, *Woman* 14–15). One such aspect of this departure from tradition is in Dante's insistence that the journey to God can only be made possible by love of a woman, who possesses "both a symbolic and an active function in the salvation of man" (Ferrante, *Woman* 131). Ferrante shows how Dante endows women (such as Beatrice) with this power, yet also how he treats women as realistic human beings, capable of both moral and immoral actions, and not merely as projections of masculine fear or hate.

In my teaching experience, students in the general education classroom come to Dante's poem with hazy generalizations about medieval misogyny similar to those espoused by Shapiro in her book. But those assumptions are tested by the loquacious, learned figure of Beatrice—"*Beatrix loquax*," as Barolini writes,—who possesses an "absolutely unprecedented and masculine authority" (Barolini, *Undivine* Comedy 303n36).[4] Similarly, students often perceive both negative and positive aspects of the feminine in Dante's poem, which Ferrante observes as setting the author apart from his contemporaries. First-time readers of the poem might find it challenging to reconcile these seemingly contradictory representations of women: the eloquent Francesca da Rimini (*Inf.* 5) with the "femmina balba" ("stammering woman"; *Purg.* 19.7)[5]; the damned prostitute of Thaïs (*Inf.* 18) with the saved prostitute, Rahab (*Par.* 9); and so forth. There is also the matter of misogynist language against specified and unspecified groups of women. How are students supposed to judge the creation of exceptional women characters such as Beatrice and Piccarda Donati (*Par.* 3) alongside invectives that indulge in antifeminist language and rail against the immorality of contemporary Florentine women (*Purg.* 6 and *Purg.* 23)?[6] Finally, there is the matter of gender at the linguistic level, above and beyond the mere gendering of nouns: what does it mean that Dante chose to write in what he himself called the "maternal" vernacular (*De vulgari eloquentia*)?

In an attempt to lead students beyond designations of feminism and misogyny, I encourage them to approach the representation of women and the female gender in three different modes: first, to understand his women characters in terms of a historicized poetics that redeems them from the totalizing conclusions in misogynist rhetoric (*à la* Barolini, who in "Dante and Francesca da Rimini" shows how Dante saves Francesca da Rimini from certain oblivion as the protagonist of local political and familial sensations); second, to read the rare moments of misogynist rhetoric as inherent to a historiographical mode (such as in Ferrante, who views the insistence on both female and male morality as a sign of Dante's progressive stance); and, finally, to view language as a gendered construction (the significance of a maternal vernacular that becomes a literary language, as I argue elsewhere [Olson, "Language"]). In the rest of this essay, I share how I integrate these three approaches in the general education classroom, which either reads the *Inferno* alone or the *Commedia* in its entirety. Generally, these students have never read anything by Dante before, nor any works of medieval literature.

First, whenever we encounter a female figure in the poem I insist on the character's historicity: both her record in outside narratives (literature), as well as the realism with which Dante renders her as an individual and not an abstraction. I normally dedicate ten to fifteen minutes of my opening lecture in a given semester on the figure of Beatrice as a character that developed over the course of Dante's lyric production: from the beloved courtly lady in his early lyrics whose subjective voice is not depicted (i.e., in the *Vita nuova*) to the hybrid Platonic and Aristotelian guide that spouts philosophy and theology with astounding conviction and condescension in the *Paradiso* (one might offer her explanation of lunar spots in *Par.* 2 as an example). By insisting on Beatrice as an innovative departure from the archetypical courtly lady, I invite students to view the female characters in the *Comedy* as hybrid figures with a function in this world and in Dante's afterlife. Figures like Pia de' Tolomei (*Purg.* 5) and Piccarda Donati (*Par.* 3), in addition to Francesca da Rimini, are the protagonists in political dramas, a consideration that differs from the totalizing misogynistic narratives that group women into categories based on virtues or vices (see Barolini, "Dante and Francesca"). Broadly speaking, women characters in the *Comedy* are real, historical beings who were significant political figures for Dante as he alludes to a web of inter- and intrafamilial conflicts that dominated civic and peninsular history.

This idea can be presented during the very first class when discussing Beatrice within the context of Dante's biography, but it can also be done when discussing her first textual appearance in *Inferno* 2, or the catalog of virtuous pagans in Limbo (*Inf.* 4). I present the following list of women who come from history or literature and female mythical beings, monsters, and goddesses who appear or are alluded to in the poem (see appendix). Students could also make comparisons to Victoria Kirkham's list of women the pilgrim encounters in his journey (38–41). By drawing students' attention to the nature of these characters (i.e., if they were contemporary Italians or Florentines, or if they came from ancient sources), I show that Dante incorporates historical women from literature, legend, scripture, and contemporary chronicle, just as he does with male characters, and incorporates them alongside classical monsters and abstract personifications of classical literature. Should he have wished to ignore the role of women in history, he would not have included these individuals, especially the contemporary Florentine and Italian women whose biographies are intertwined with Dante's political vision. To this end, it is important to note that "historical" women outnumber the female soothsayers and monsters from antiquity—whose own literary origins, one might argue, Dante drastically revises, as in the case of Manto in *Inferno* 20 and her sources in Virgil and Statius. Thus, they serve Dante as a way to make his mark on literary history rather than as a way to represent the feminine in a negative light.

One might successfully teach this by detecting patterns in the distribution of women (both women and female souls the pilgrim encounters) across the three canticles. Dante bookends the *Commedia* with large concentrations of women at the relative beginning of Hell (Limbo, first circle) and at the end of the voyage, in the Celestial Rose (Empyrean). Yet *Purgatorio* is filled with women, from both ancient and contemporary Italian history. Instructors might ask their students what distinguishes these groups from each other, as well as from other damned women in terms of certain elements: the literary source (e.g., Virgil or scripture versus Statius or Ovid); the regional provenance of the women (e.g., northern, central, or southern Italy versus Florence). Dante populates each canticle with female characters from a variety of ancient sources, yet he includes many women from Florence and Siena. Was this choice motivated by political considerations, since Florence (a Guelph city) and Siena (a Ghibelline stronghold) experienced similar political conflicts within their city walls? These patterns also include the scattered locations of family members throughout the three realms. Francesca da Rimini appears in the first circle but her husband will be in Caïna (ninth circle). Sapia is on the Terrace of Envy, whereas her nephew, Provenzan Salvani, is on the Terrace of Pride. Piccarda Donati is located in Paradise, but her brother Forese is in Purgatorio, where he discusses the future death of their brother Corso. Cunizza da Romano is likewise among the blessed in Paradise, but her brother, Ezzelino, suffers eternity in the circle of the violent (circle 7), and her lover Sordello passes time in the Valley of Rulers (*Purg.* 6–8). In most of these cases the women are in arguably better locations than their relatives for eternity. One can also point out this deliberate strategy in courses that treat the *Inferno* only by gesturing to the complex family networks that extend throughout Dante's vision of the afterlife.

There are occasions in the poem when the feminine is an abstract concept, and a traditional, misogynist tone surfaces in the poem. I have argued elsewhere that these moments, such as when Dante speaks of the dissolute ways of Florentine women in *Purgatorio* 23.101 ("le sfacciate donne fiorentine"; "those immodest ones—Florentine women"), are motivated by a sharp political critique of the wealth and greed of elite families whose conflicts have cast Florence into turmoil (Olson, "Shoes" and "Uncovering"). In order to convey this to students, I contextualize Forese Donati's diatribe in the conflict between the

Donati and Cerchi families (*Inf.* 6 and 16) and gesture toward the shift in social groupings that led to feuds between traditionally aristocratic families and the burgeoning mercantile class, now rising in power. Forese targets women's dress as a way of pointing to the overall decadence in Florence, one expressed by an indulgence in extravagant displays of luxury, as we know from sumptuary statutes at the time. Thus, misogynist rhetoric is a vehicle for political critique. Yet here the historical context is not entirely foreign to today's students: one only need allude to the numerous discussions recently in the media of leading American political figures (men and women) in terms of clothing and displays of wealth. For Dante as well the visual language worn by women refers to conflicts between the families to which these women belonged. The true targets, therefore, extend beyond the women themselves to their families and relatives.

One can see this use of misogynist language for political invective again in the antifeminist descriptions of Italy and Florence that appear in *Purgatorio* 6. Here the poet inveighs against the belligerent state of a leaderless Italy and Florence, exclaiming: "Ahi serva Italia, di dolore ostello, / nave sanza nocchiere in gran tempesta, / non donna di province, ma bordello!" ("Ah, Italy enslaved, abode of misery, / pilotless ship in a fierce tempest tossed, / no mistress over provinces but a harlot!"; *Purg.* 6.76–78). Rome is likened to a widow, alone and crying out for her Caesar (*Purg.* 6.112–14). By the end of this canto, the poet likens Florence to a sick woman tossing and turning in her bed: "vedrai te somigliante a quella inferma / che non può trovar posa in su le piume, / ma con dar volta suo dolore scherma" ("you will see that you are like a woman, ill in bed, / who on the softest down cannot find rest / but twisting, turning, seeks to ease her pain"; *Purg.* 6.149–51). He draws analogies between political decadence with sexual decadence, between a widow and the widowed political state, and between human infirmity and the ailing city. The female body is the body politic for Dante. For if one looks at the actual prostitutes in the poem, one finds that one is damned (Thaïs, *Inf.* 18), whereas another is among the blessed (Rahab, *Par.* 9). To talk generally and disparagingly about unspecified women is almost not to talk about women at all, one might say.

One last approach that highlights the importance of women and the feminine for Dante touches on gender from a linguistic viewpoint. Dante writes that the vernacular is a maternal language ("materna locutio"; *De vulgari eloquentia* 1.6.2 [Botterill]), but that literary language is an evolved form of this maternal language. It is useful to present students with this linguistic history when reading *Purgatorio* 21.97–99, where Dante casts the *Aeneid* as his mother and nurse: "de l'Eneïda dico, la qual mamma / fummi, e fummi nutrice, poetando: / sanz' essa non fermai peso di dramma" ("I mean the *Aeneid*. When I wrote poetry / it was my *mamma* and my nurse. / Without it, I would not have weighed a dram"; my emphasis).[7] If a literary work can claim a maternal origin, then this would speak to Dante's positive view of the feminine. In fact, it is by this blend of the feminine and the masculine, a maternal language crafted by a male author, that literature is born. For this, and for all the reasons given earlier, students should understand the intrinsic importance of women and the female gender in the poetic realization of Dante's afterlife.

NOTES

I would like to thank Teodolinda Barolini and Christopher Kleinhenz for their valuable comments during the preparation of this essay, especially in the compilation of the lists of women in the appendix.

[1] As an interesting point of comparison, the MLA volume dedicated to the teaching of Boccaccio's *Decameron*, published in 2000, features not one but three essays dealing with women, gender, and sexuality (McGregor).

[2] This is not to speak of the numerous treatments of the figure of Beatrice, such as those by Barolini, "Beyond (Courtly) Dualism" and "Notes toward a Gendered History of Italian Literature"; Harrison, *The Body of Beatrice*; Jacoff, "Transgression"; Kirkham, "A Canon of Women in Dante's *Commedia*"; Psaki, "The Sexual Body in Dante's Celestial Paradise"; and C. Williams, *The Figure of Beatrice*. I touch on some of these contributions here but encourage instructors to consult these works in the works-cited list. As a point of interest for the field of Dante Studies, I note that four of the authors referred to in this essay (Shapiro, Ferrante, Barolini, and Olson) earned their doctoral degrees from Columbia University.

[3] See also Ferrante's review of Shapiro's book in *Italica*. Ferrante concludes by writing, "I am worried about the dangers of this approach. It can be valuable and productive to look at the classics of our culture from the perspective of attitudes toward women and to be aware of the basically negative attitudes in our tradition, but such a study must be made without distorting the text and with a balanced consideration of the context" (323).

[4] Also see Barolini, "Dante Alighieri" (190), "Notes"; and Ferrante, *Dante's Beatrice*. Beatrice's eloquence has been targeted by later critics within a misogynist vein. As Barolini writes in response to Harrison, "We note one critic's claim that the 'Beatrice [of the *Vita nuova*] appears far more persuasive, enigmatic, explosive, than the recreated and cantankerous figure' of the *Purgatorio*. To this we must reply that the 'explosive' Beatrice of the *Vita nuova* is silent, while the 'cantankerous' Beatrice of the *Commedia* speaks" ("Notes" 368–69).

[5] For quotations in Italian from the *Divine Comedy*, see Petrocchi's edition; quotations in English come from the Hollander translation.

[6] This conundrum might have caused the earlier impasse on critical work treating women in the *Commedia*, when these differences were neatly reconciled by viewing women as poetic abstractions. As Kirkham writes, "Interpretative tradition on the *Commedia*, in other words, has most to say about a woman when it sees her as something else: Allegorical Reality, a Lyrical or Dramatic Moment, a Problem-in-the-Text. The others, those women who seem just to be a woman, remain by comparison in obscurity, their status reduced to nominal items" (19).

[7] See Cestaro, *Dante and the Grammar of the Nursing Body*, and his contribution in this volume for many intersecting issues addressed in this essay.

APPENDIX: WOMEN, GODDESSES, AND FEMALE MONSTERS IN THE *COMMEDIA*

Names in italics refer to figures who are mentioned in the canto indicated but who are not, however, located in that area of the afterlife. Names not in italics indicate women actually located in the given canto. I do not always list when the Virgin Mary, Eve, or Beatrice are mentioned, as these occurrences are numerous.

Figure or figures	Location in poem	Description of figure or figures
Inferno		
Camilla	*Inf.* 1	figure from Virgil's *Aeneid*
Beatrice (mentioned here but dwells in the Empyrean)	*Inf.* 1 and 2	contemporary Florentine
Virgin Mary; St. Lucy; Rachel (all mentioned here but dwell in the Empyrean)	*Inf.* 2	figures from scripture and hagiography
Camilla; Cornelia; Electra; Julia; Lavinia; Lucrezia; Marcia; Penthesilea; *Rachel* (*Rachel* mentioned here but dwells in the Empyrean)	*Inf.* 4	figures (leaders, wives, warriors) from antiquity and the scriptures
Cleopatra; Dido; Helen; Semiramis	*Inf.* 5	figures (leaders, wives, warriors) from antiquity
Guinevere	*Inf.* 5	legendary character from the medieval period
Francesca da Rimini	*Inf.* 5	contemporary Italian
Fortuna	*Inf.* 7	ahistorical abstraction; figure from classical and medieval traditions
the Furies; *Erichtho*; Medusa	*Inf.* 9	figures from mythology and Lucan's *Pharsalia*
Ariadne; Deianira	*Inf.* 12	figures from mythology
Harpies	*Inf.* 13	mythical monsters
Gualdrada; wife of Iacopo Rusticucci	*Inf.* 16	contemporary Florentines
Arachne	*Inf.* 17	mythical figure
Ghisolabella	*Inf.* 18	contemporary Italian
Hypsipyle; Medea	*Inf.* 18	mythical figures
Thaïs	*Inf.* 18	figure from Terence's play, *The Eunuch*
Manto	*Inf.* 20	character from Virgil and Statius; heavily revised by Dante
"le triste che lasciaron l'ago, / la spuola e 'l fuso" ("the sad women who had left their needle, / shuttle and spindle to become diviners"; lines 121–22)	*Inf.* 20	[uncertain]
Santa Zita	*Inf.* 21	hagiography
Deidamia; Penelope	*Inf.* 26	figures from myth and Trojan legends
Hecuba; Ino; Juno; Myrrha; *Polyxena;* Potiphar's wife; *Semele*	*Inf.* 30	figures from antiquity, scripture, and mythology
Atropos	*Inf.* 33	mythical figure

Figure or figures	Location in poem	Description of figure or figures
Purgatorio		
Calliope	*Purg.* 1	mythical figure (Muse)
The Pierides	*Purg.* 1	mythical figures
Marcia (mentioned here but located in Limbo)	*Purg.* 1	Roman history
Constance of Sicily (mother of Frederick II; mentioned here but located in the Heaven of the Moon); *Constance* (Manfred's daughter and wife of Pedro III of Aragon)	*Purg.* 3	contemporary Italians and Europeans
Pia de' Tolomei; *Giovanna* (wife of Bonconte)	*Purg.* 5	contemporary Italian (Siena)
Marie of Brabant	*Purg.* 6	contemporary Frenchwoman
Beatrice di Provenza (first wife of Charles I of Anjou); *Constance* (daughter of Manfred and wife of Peter III of Aragon); *Margaret of Burgundy* (second wife of Charles I of Anjou)	*Purg.* 7	contemporary Italians and Europeans
Beatrice d'Este (sister of Azzo, daughter of Obizzo II d'Este, widow of Nino Visconti); *Giovanna* (daughter of Nino Visconti and Beatrice d'Este)	*Purg.* 8	contemporary Italians
Saint Lucy (mentioned here but dwells in the Empyrean)	*Purg.* 9	hagiography
concubine of Tithonus	*Purg.* 9	mythical figure
Michal (mentioned in exemplum of David); *la vedovella* ("the widow," mentioned in exemplum of Trajan; line 77)	*Purg.* 10	scripture
Arachne; *Niobe* (mentioned here as exempla)	*Purg.* 12	mythical figures
Eriphyle (mentioned here as exemplum)	*Purg.* 12	Statius's *Thebaid*
Pallas Athena	*Purg.* 12	mythical figure
Queen Tomyris (mentioned here as exemplum)	*Purg.* 12	historical character
Sapia	*Purg.* 13	contemporary Italian (Siena)
Aglauros (mentioned here as exemplum)	*Purg.* 14	mythical figure (Ovid's *Metamorphoses*)
Gaia (daughter of Gherardo da Camino)	*Purg.* 16	contemporary Italian
Procne (mentioned here as exemplum)	*Purg.* 17	mythical figure (Ovid's *Metamorphoses*)
Amata; *Lavinia* (*Amata* mentioned here as exemplum and her daughter *Lavinia* in the context of the exemplum)	*Purg.* 17	characters from Virgil's *Aeneid*
Esther (mentioned in context of exemplum)	*Purg.* 17	scripture
la dolce sirena ("the sweet siren"; line 19)	*Purg.* 19	[uncertain]
Alagia de' Fieschi (niece of Adrian IV and wife of Moroello Malaspina)	*Purg.* 19	contemporary Italian

Figure or figures	Location in poem	Description of figure or figures
Purgatorio (cont.)		
Beatrice d'Anjou ("sua figlia," youngest daughter of Charles II, married to Azzo d'Este); *Latona*; *Sapphira* (*Sapphira* is the exemplum in line 112); *le pulcelle* ("maidens," mentioned here in context of the exemplum, with Saint Nicholas, who gave them dowries; line 32)	*Purg.* 20	scripture (Acts); mythology; contemporary Italian
the Samaritan woman	*Purg.* 21	scripture
Antigone; *Argia*; *Ismene*; *Deidamia*; *Deiphyle*; *Hypsipyle*; *Jocasta*; *Thetis*	*Purg.* 22	characters from Statius and mythical figures
Manto (whom we meet among the soothsayers in *Inf.* 20, though Dante seems to indicate she dwells in Limbo)	*Purg.* 22	figure from Statius
"le romane antiche" ("the ancient Roman women"; line 145)	*Purg.* 22	[uncertain]
Mary of Eleazar	*Purg.* 23	scripture
Nella Donati; *"sfacciate donne fiorentine"* ("brazen women of Florence"); *"le femmine sue"* of the Barbagia	*Purg.* 23	contemporary Florentines and Italians
Gentucca; *Piccarda Donati* (*Piccarda* is mentioned here but located in the Heaven of the Moon)	*Purg.* 24	contemporary Italians
Diana (goddess); *Helice*; *Venus* (all mentioned here as exempla)	*Purg.* 25	mythical figures (Ovid's *Metamorphoses*)
Pasiphae; *Hypsipyle*	*Purg.* 26	mythical figures (Ovid's *Metamorphoses*)
Leah; *Rachel* (mentioned here but located in the Empyrean); *Thisbe*	*Purg.* 27	scripture (Genesis); mythical figures
Matelda	*Purg.* 28–29; 21, 33	contemporary Italian? (Canossa)
Eve (mentioned here, but located in the Empyrean); *Delia*; seven dancing "women"	*Purg.* 29	scripture; mythology
"la puttana" (line 149)	*Purg.* 32	allegorical figure
Beatrice	*Purg.* 30–33 (also throughout *Par.*)	contemporary Florentine

Figure or figures	Location in poem	Description of figure or figures
Paradiso		
Daphne	*Par.* 1	mythical figure (Ovid's *Metamorphoses*)
Pallas Athena	*Par.* 2	mythical figure (Ovid's *Metamorphoses*)
The Muses	*Par.* 2	mythical figures (Ovid's *Metamorphoses*)
Constance of Sicily; Piccarda Donati; *Santa Chiara*	*Par.* 3–4	contemporary Florentines and Italians; hagiography
Eriphyle	*Par.* 4	mythical figure
Iphygenia	*Par.* 5	mythical figure
Cleopatra; Lavinia; Lucrezia; "quattro figlie" ("four daughters" of Raymond Berenger IV; line 133)	*Par.* 6	antiquity; contemporary European history
Dido	*Par.* 8–9	Virgil's *Aeneid*
Creusa	*Par.* 9	Virgil's *Aeneid*
Iole	*Par.* 9	mythical figure
Cunizza da Romano; Clemence	*Par.* 9	contemporary Italians and Europeans
Rahab	*Par.* 9	scripture (Joshua)
Lady Poverty	*Par.* 11	allegorical figure
Giovanna d'Aza (mother of Saint Dominic)	*Par.* 12	hagiography
Juno	*Par.* 12	mythical figure
Ariadne	*Par.* 13	mythical figure
Cianghella	*Par.* 15	contemporary Florentine
Cornelia; mother of Cacciaguida	*Par.* 15	figures from Roman and Italian history
Guinevere; Dame de Malehaut	*Par.* 16	legendary medieval figures
Clymene; Phaedra	*Par.* 17	mythical figures
Semele	*Par.* 21	mythical figure
Latona; Maia	*Par.* 22	mythical figures
Polyhymnia	*Par.* 23	mythical figure
Latona	*Par.* 29	mythical figure
Virgin Mary; Eve; Judith; Rachel; Rebecca; Ruth; Sarah; St. Anne; St. Lucy	*Par.* 32	scripture; hagiography
Cumaean Sybil	*Par.* 33	mythical figure; Virgil's *Aeneid*

Teaching Dante's *Divine Comedy* in a History Course

Joanna Drell

This essay suggests approaches to teaching Dante's *Divine Comedy* in under-graduate medieval-Renaissance history courses. Whether assigned in European or medieval history surveys or for a focused examination of Italy, Dante's unique and often highly personal depiction of historical personages and events both complements the study of medieval-Renaissance history and presents chal-lenges in historical interpretation.

On the one hand, the *Divine Comedy* is invaluable for understanding the pivotal, turbulent thirteenth and early fourteenth centuries in Italy. Dante's spiritual allegory of a Christian Everyman's journey through *Inferno-Purgatorio-Paradiso* not only found its wellspring in Dante's historical moment but also offered trenchant commentary on the day's events. Dante did not conceal his perception of disintegrating social order and endemic political factionalism: Guelfs versus Ghibellines, Black versus White Guelfs, Papal versus Imperial power, family versus family, Florence versus her neighbors, *popolo* versus *mag-nati*. Although students shouldn't learn Italian history exclusively from the *Divine Comedy*, it undeniably reflects a contemporary's understanding and cri-tique of his reality—his views on continuity and change in economic, social, and religious norms and institutions.

On the other hand, study of the *Divine Comedy* can serve as an introduction to historical study. In an introductory course, careful unpacking and dissection of the poem develop tools and sharpen ways of thinking essential to historical study. Evaluation of sources, close reading and critical analysis, disentangling and rec-onciling conflicting contemporary accounts of an event, progressive sharpening of historical understanding through scholarly dialogue, and weighing the benefits and limitations of literary sources are crucial to reading the *Divine Comedy* in-telligently and productively. Moreover, as a provocative primer on the storytell-er's role in the interpretation and transmission of the past, the *Divine Comedy* invites both students and instructors to consider what constitutes historical evi-dence and how best to use it. Such expertise is particularly important for the study of premodern history, where paucity of evidence necessitates judicious use of every available source, whether documentary, narrative, or literary, regardless of potential authorial bias. These foundational skills are both transferable and indispensable to other academic disciplines and to life beyond the institution.

The *Divine Comedy* can be read in different levels of history courses. This is appropriate not only in an intermediate-level course (sophomores and juniors with no prerequisites) but also in smaller seminars for advanced students.[1] The balance of this essay is an overview of my goals in teaching the *Divine Comedy* and the practicalities of its incorporation into my classes over the years. I address the positioning of the *Divine Comedy* in a course, the challenges inherent to the text, the value of foregrounding Florentine history through Dante's biography, the historical prophecies in the text, and the exploration of Dante's historical memory.

My undergraduate course on medieval Italy (c. 1050–1350) offers a case study of using Dante in the classroom, though many of the following suggestions can be adapted for use in surveys of the Renaissance and early modern Europe. For this three-week Dante unit, I assign the entire *Inferno* along with selections from *Purgatorio* and *Paradiso*.[2] In my experience *Inferno* is generally the most accessible and appealing to the students, both on account of the linear narrative and the lively descriptions of the horrors of Hell. When introducing the text I underscore the significance of Dante's work as poetry and his choice to use the Italian vernacular, in itself a reflection of a historic moment in the development of language and early Italian literature. Within the architecture of this medieval Italy course, the study of Dante follows detailed examination of the rise of the communes in northern Italy and the foundation of the Norman kingdom in southern Italy, primary-source-heavy considerations of the intersection of political, economic, social, and religious institutions. With this historical context in place, the class excavates Dante's attitudes toward politics and political discourse, the challenges facing Florence, and issues of *fama* and remembrance.[3]

The *Divine Comedy* poses several immediate challenges in the classroom. Dante places on his stage so many historical players that it is not easy to decide which to highlight before having students explore others on their own. Students (and instructors) can become overwhelmed by the text's litany of names and events, even with the aid of textual notes. Careful targeting of classroom discussions is necessary in order to avoid random skipping back and forth among cantos, characters, and punishments. Distinguishing between Dante the poet and Dante the pilgrim can get tricky as well. Inspired by Giovanni Cecchetti's provocative and perhaps hyperbolic claim that the *Divine Comedy* is "the greatest work of political protest ever written" (42), we concentrate on the political *Divine Comedy*. Most discussion is framed around Dante's notion of a political hell and his relationship with Florence.[4]

Dante's political and personal opinions indeed informed the very geography he created for the Inferno. The gravest sinners, found in the lowest circles of Hell, were sowers of civil and political discord, those who had committed fraud and treason. Here Dante's biography is especially relevant. Exiled from his beloved city in 1302 for his political beliefs—he belonged to the White Guelfs when the Black Guelfs came to power—he injected into the *Divine Comedy* his anguish over what he deemed unfair punishment and the disintegration of his city's values. Historian Gene Brucker observed that writing the *Inferno* "must have been a salutary catharsis for the poet, to gain release from the passions that seethed within [him]" (*Renaissance Florence* 131). It is no coincidence that, in Dante's political vision of the afterlife, many Florentines are consigned to Inferno.[5]

Florence's political fortunes, tending toward decline in Dante's opinion, were a central theme in the encounters Dante the pilgrim has on his otherworldly journey. The class consequently focuses on identifying the problems Florence faced. When asked by a Florentine sodomite, Jacopo Rusticucci, if "cortesia e valor . . . dimora / ne la nostra città sì come suole, / o se del tutto se n'è gita fora" ("courtesy and valor still / abide within our city as they did / when we were there or have they disappeared completely"; *Inf.* 16.66–69), Dante the pilgrim mournfully responds, "La gente nuova e i sùbiti guadagni / orgoglio e dismisura han generata, / Fiorenza, in te, sì che tu già ten piagni" ("Newcomers to the city and quick gains / have brought excess and arrogance to you, / o Florence, and you weep for it already"; *Inf.* 16.73–75).[6] Viewed through the Dantean lens, Florence fell on these hard times from the greed, corruption, and ostentation inherent in a new social order largely created by rustic immigrants. From the late twelfth century onward, artisans and merchants—new money—displaced Florence's traditional landed aristocracy economically and politically. *Inferno* speaks to these tensions when the pilgrim encounters the glutton Ciacco, a Florentine, in the third circle of Hell. Having previously described Florence as a "città, ch'è piena / d'invidia" ("city—one so full / of envy"; *Inf.* 6.49–50), Ciacco declares that "superbia, invidia e avarizia" ("envy, pride and avariciousness"; *Inf.* 6.75) were the "[f]aville" ("sparks"; *Inf.* 6.74) that first divided Guelf from Ghibelline and then White from Black Guelf, the latter resulting in Dante's exile.

The episode with Ciacco is the first of three prophecies for Florence's future that Dante introduces in *Inferno*, a highlighting of Dante's views on Florence's impending fate and his personal destiny. The second prophecy takes place during the pilgrim's encounter with Brunetto Latini, where Dante's mentor warned of the Florentines whom he describes as "quello ingrato popolo maligno" ("that malicious that ungrateful people"; *Inf.* 15.61), "avara, invidiosa e superba" ("presumptuous, avaricious, envious"; *Inf.* 15.68) who would reject Dante in his lifetime. Vanni Fucci of Pistoia, in the third prophecy, foretells a dark fate for Dante's Whites in their struggle with the Blacks:

> apri li orecchi al mio annunzio, e odi.
> Pistoia in pria d'i Neri si dimagra;
> poi Fiorenza rinova gente e modi.

> open your ears to my announcement, hear:
> Pistoia first will strip herself of Blacks,
> then Florence will renew her men and manners

> e con tempesta impetüosa e agra
> . . . fia combattuto;
> . . . .
> . . . ogne Bianco ne sarà feruto.

. . . the clash between them will be fierce, impetuous, a tempest,
and every White be struck by it.

E detto l'ho perché doler ti debbia!

And I have told you this to make you grieve.

(*Inf.* 24.142–44; 47–48, 50; 51)

A useful exercise is for students—either in writing or in discussion—to compare these prophecies piece by piece and identify differences in language, tone, and intent. Why does Dante use the device of a prophecy to convey this material? How do the prophecies work with the conception of time in the text where the figures in Hell can see the future and the past but not the present (see *Inf.* 10.67–69)?

Close study of the political prophecies in *Inferno* invites comparisons with the prophecy for the futures of both Florence and the poet declaimed by Dante's ancestor Cacciaguida in *Paradiso* (cantos 15–17). Reinforcing the miserable futures that await, Dante through Cacciaguida's voice offers a sentimental commentary on a supposed Florentine golden age, when people exercised fiscal, political, and social restraint (*Par.* 15.97–135). Back then Florence was "sobria e pudica" ("sober and chaste"; *Par.* 15.99), its citizens "si stava in pace" ("lived in tranquility"; *Par.* 15.99), and families were not torn asunder by "division" ("factious hatred"; *Par.* 16.154). Sharpening a contrast between the past and what Dante perceived as his present, Cacciaguida recalls when women and men were modest, girls did not marry too young, and wedding celebrations were not the epitome of excess. Cacciaguida's cantos, full of Florentine familial detail and implied critique, are a rich font of material for an upper-level seminar on medieval family, women, and society.[7]

The theme of Florentine discord and party conflict echoes throughout the *Divine Comedy* and is not limited to prophecies. The pilgrim's encounters with Filippo Argenti in the fifth circle (*Inf.* 8.33–48), and with Farinata degli Uberti and Cavalcante dei Cavalcanti in the sixth circle (*Inf.* 10.31–114) are good examples. In the eighth circle of Hell the pilgrim meets, along with other "sowers of scandal and schism," Mosca de' Lamberti, the Ghibelline who, according to legend, started the Guelf-Ghibelline conflict. (*Inf.* 28.106–09). In the ninth circle, at the bottom of Hell, the pilgrim finds (or steps on) traitors to their parties, both Guelf and Ghibelline, frozen in ice. Episodes like these allow students to compare Dante's vision of Florence with that found in other primary and secondary texts, such as the chronicles of Dino Compagni and Giovanni Villani and scholarship by Edward Coleman, George Dameron, and John Najemy.[8] How does Dante's portrait of his time compare with other contemporaneous accounts and with scholarly reconstructions of Florentine life? In an upper-level course—in fact, in any course requiring a larger research paper—each student selects a historical figure from the *Divine Comedy* and compares Dante's presentation of the individual with what is known from the historical record. The students must elaborate on Dante's larger purpose(s) for incorporating the personage in his vision of the afterlife, in essence, to examine Dante's awareness and possible revision of history for his own purposes. For example, what other figures from the Guelf-Ghibelline conflict appear in the *Divine Comedy*? How do Dante's portrayals of the battles of Montaperti, Benevento, and Campaldino compare with other contemporary accounts and with scholarly reconstructions of them?

Dante's bitterness toward Florence and the Florentines stands in sharp contrast to his admiration for classical Rome. Though Florence occupies the central stage of the *Divine Comedy*, Rome—both Republic and Empire—is as prominent as any historical actor in the text. This leads to the second major topic I underscore with my history students when teaching Dante: Dante's use of history and, more generally, the role of historical memory in shaping the past. I remind students that Rome's legacy would have been as visible in the fourteenth century as in the twenty-first, if not more so (consider the Colosseum in Rome). Virgil serves as the pilgrim's guide through *Inferno* and *Purgatorio*. Brutus and Cassius, the betrayers of Julius Caesar, find themselves in the lowest recess of Hell, along with the ultimate Christian traitor, Judas (*Inf.* 34.55–68). Though Dante reached maturity just as Florence's communal pattern of governance reached its zenith, he came to believe that monarchical rule was the only path to stability (Najemy, "Dante" 238). We identify and discuss Dante's incorporation of the classical past to inform his political messages.

Classical Rome offers just one case study of Dante's historical memory. Closely linked with Dante's ideas of the Roman Empire is his attitude towards the other, closer "Roman Empire" of his day, the Holy Roman Empire. Dante's historical memory, moreover, was not limited to classical antiquity or relatively recent Florentine events. The southern Italian kingdom, the Byzantine Empire, the papacy and church, and the Carolingian Empire offered Dante the opportunity to employ laudatory or condemnatory language in the service of expressing his political view. Drawing on these examples of monarchical and quasimonarchical authority, more advanced students explore Dante's not always consistent ideas on the necessity and legitimacy of centralized political power.[9]

Models of good governance or not, Dante's inclusion of wide-ranging political references encourages students to reflect on the nature of historical study: its creation and purpose and how historians deal with issues of source bias and author subjectivity. For the history student and teacher, Dante's masterpiece strikes at the core of what it means to practice history. Rich in historical detail, the text requires the historian to evaluate, analyze, and question that evidence. Just because the author had a personal axe to grind does not mean his work should be dismissed. The pleasure is made all the greater by the challenge that Dante poses. Whether delving into the complexity of medieval politics or exploring aspects of the historical process (or doing both), students will engage with the distant past through a provocative, memorable, and entertaining poem.[10] While developing skills to understand the past, students gain lessons for their future.[11]

NOTES

[1] I have experimented, with limited success, teaching *Inferno* as part of a first-year seminar course focusing on historical epics. Students read *Inferno* along with selections from the *Aeneid, Gilgamesh, Beowulf, Song of Roland*, and Arthurian Romances (the last not being an actual epic). Here the objectives are close reading and critical analysis.

[2] I currently use Mandelbaum's translation of the *Divine Comedy* in my classes. In the past I have also used Musa for *Inferno*. Mandelbaum offers a facing-page Italian-English translation. I have found it valuable to compare different English interpretations of Dante's Italian in class. Both editions require students to become familiar with the scholarly apparatus of different editions and translations, footnotes, and endnotes.

[3] Many secondary and primary teaching texts about Florence are available. Secondary works include Najemy, "Dante" and *History*; and Abulafia. Primary source collections in translation that complement teaching the *Divine Comedy* include Jansen et al.; and Dean, *Towns* (which provides primary sources in translation about the urban civilization of medieval Italy).

[4] In weighing Cecchetti's claim, I ask the students to write an essay about the politics of Dante's vision of Hell. Each student selects three figures Dante the pilgrim encounters on his journey through Inferno—specific characters Dante the poet placed there for political reasons. They must consider the specific reason the figures are in Hell, the sins they committed according to Dante's political vision, and the eternal punishments they suffer and why. At a minimum this requires students to review their understanding (or not) of Dante's organization of Hell.

[5] Najemy quotes Joan Ferrante, who observed that *Inferno* was "full of Florentines, and Florence almost seems to be the model for the corrupt society displaying in the *Inferno*" ("Dante" 239).

[6] All quotations in this essay come from the Mandelbaum edition.

[7] In particular, *Par.* 15.97–136 and *Par.* 16.46–60 allow students to examine Dante's attitudes towards family politics. It is in combination with passages like these that I encourage students to consider the placement of crimes committed against kin in Dante's schema of Hell.

[8] For Compagni and Villani, see P. Clarke; Aquilecchia; and Green. In class I often assign the Bornstein's translation of Dino Compagni's *Chronicle*. For the text of Villani, see Porta's edition of *Nuova cronica*. For Villani in English, I use selections in Jansen et al. To introduce students to current scholarship on Florence, I assign selections from Coleman, "Italian Communes"; Dameron, *Florence and Its Church*; and Najemy, *History*.

[9] I examined some of these issues insofar as they related to the Norman Kingdom of Southern Italy (Drell 62). Excellent discussions of this issue can be found in Ferrante, *Political Vision*; and Davis, *Dante's Italy*.

[10] For further reading, see Beneš's *Urban Legends*, for an examination of the making of myths in the Italian communes; and Wickham's *Early Medieval Italy*, for the classic study of social and economic development of medieval Italy.

[11] I conclude our Dante discussions by asking students to reflect on the legacy of the *Divine Comedy*, not only in the broader university curriculum but also in popular culture, anything from art to cinema to video games to advertisements.

Dante and the Papacy

George Dameron

Teaching Dante, especially the *Commedia*, provides us with a unique opportunity to explore with our students some of the most important issues in medieval church history of the thirteenth and fourteenth centuries. Dante the artist was also Dante the political and ecclesiastical theorist and partisan. He cared deeply about secular and ecclesiastical governance, as he considered them both necessary to sustain the kind of ordered and stable environment that facilitated the pursuit of virtue in this life and salvation in the next. By the early fourteenth century, Dante had, however, concluded that the papacy had lost its way, straying from its original calling. He became one its fiercest critics. The failure of the papacy to fulfill its mission was imperiling souls. Concrete outcomes for advanced undergraduate and graduate students regarding this topic should therefore include both an understanding of the context for the development of the poet's views and a familiarity with the principal passages in the *Commedia* that display them.[1] During the Middle Ages (c. 600–c. 1400), Western European (Latin) Christians looked to the popes in Rome as the leaders of their institutional church and spiritual community. Teachers will want to help guide their students to understand that by the mid-1200s, the height of what many historians call the "papal monarchy," the papacy had become an institution with profound and wide-ranging political, institutional, and material interests. Among those deeply troubled by the apparent conflict between the New Testament message of poverty and the worldly reality of the existing institutional church was Dante himself. For him and for many of his contemporaries, including a faction of the Franciscan Order (the Spirituals), the papacy had come to exemplify the worst vices of which humanity was capable: greed and avarice. It had not only degenerated from its original purely spiritual mission but also become a principal instigator of contemporary chaos, conflict, and moral corruption. Correcting the ills of the world, Dante argued, required the return of the papacy to its original commitment to temporal poverty and the emergence of a strong emperor to rule Italy. Dante's assault on the cupidity of the papacy is, therefore, a practical pathway for the classroom to explore a key conflict present throughout medieval church history: the tension between those within the existing church who represented the status quo on one hand, and the dissenters who wanted change, arguing that the "carnal" church was a corrupt inversion of its original calling, on the other.

To examine Dante's contributions to these contemporary debates, there is obviously no better place to start than the text of the *Commedia* itself. That said, there are, however, a number of excellent secondary sources that can provide students with important background information about the politics of thirteenth- and fourteenth-century Italy (including Florence), the evolution of

Dante's ideas on the proper relation between church (*sacerdotium*) and state (*regnum*), and the history of the papacy.[2] Depending on the pedagogical approach that instructors prefer, they may wish to assign secondary texts such as these before, during, or even after a close reading of portions of the *Commedia* itself. Reading and discussing these texts can contextualize for students some of the most important developments in the political and ecclesiastical history of medieval Italy during Dante's lifetime. They include the growing factionalism with the north Italian communes, the Guelf-Ghibelline conflict, and the intense clash between empire and papacy for hegemony on the peninsula. In late antiquity (c. 200–c. 600) the pope as bishop of Rome was actually only one of several major leading Christian bishops in the late Roman Mediterranean world. With the rise of Islam and growing isolation from the Byzantine Empire in the early Middle Ages (c. 600–c. 1000), the Roman papacy came gradually to assume jurisdictional primacy over the Christian community. It derived its claims to leadership from its direct connection to its founder, the first bishop of Rome, Saint Peter, and through the Donation of Constantine. This eighth-century forgery purported to be a fourth-century imperial grant by the emperor Constantine giving the papacy supreme authority over the Western Roman Empire. By the eleventh century the papacy had become one of the most powerful institutions in Western Europe, rivaled only by the German kings who by the tenth century also claimed the title of emperor as heirs of Charlemagne (died 814). In the second half of the eleventh century, however, the schism with the Eastern churches occurred (in 1054), and a movement within the Christian community emerged to purify or purge the church of major sources of pollution and corruption: simony (the buying and selling of church offices), Nicolaitism (clerical marriage or concubinage), lay investiture, and control by the laity of church property and tithes. This reform movement was largely successful by the early twelfth century and resulted in an expansion of papal power as well as the significant recovery of property by ecclesiastical institutions. From the end of the twelfth through the thirteenth centuries, we can trace the emergence of a papal monarchy, an institution that presided over vast economic resources and oversaw an elaborate legal network of church laws and courts. Innocent III relied on the Donation of Constantine to argue for the legitimacy of his secular and spiritual calling. The most extreme version of this argument came in 1246, just nineteen years before Dante's birth, in a papal bull issued by Innocent IV (1243–54). *Eger cui lenia* argued that Constantine had ruled illegally before becoming a Christian and was actually simply restoring to the papacy what had originally been in its possession from the beginning. Apologists for the emerging contemporary monarchies disagreed.

For almost two and a half centuries, from roughly the middle of the eleventh to the early fourteenth century, the papacy and the German monarchy vied for influence if not outright hegemony in Italy, the most prosperous region of Europe. This story is complicated, but both undergraduate and graduate students will best understand Dante's views of the papacy if they have at least a general sense of the historical context that follows. Here, another set of recent secondary sources can assist the instructor and help guide students through the most important stages of this complicated history.[3] North Italian city-states (communes) managed by 1183 (the Peace of Constance) to fend off the emperor Frederick I Barbarossa of Germany. For the next 150 years, however, the kings of Germany, who also claimed the title of emperor, continued to press their claims to sovereignty over Italy, even in the face of determined papal opposition. In the early decades of the thirteenth century, by the 1240s, those factions within the Italian city-states who recognized that their local interests were best served by aligning themselves with the papacy were known as Guelfs. Most were members of a rising urban cohort of prosperous and nonnoble men known as the *Popolo*. Those who aligned with the cause of the emperor, who primarily (but not totally) came from the aristocracy, were known as Ghibellines. Only after the death of Emperor Frederick II in 1250 did the Ghibelline cause weaken significantly. Nevertheless, later German emperors never relinquished their efforts to press their claims in Italy. Determined to maintain its own independence and security in central Italy and avoid any interference by the German emperors from the north or south, the papacy sponsored an invasion of Italy in the middle of the thirteenth century by an army led by a younger brother (Charles of Anjou) of its close ally, the king of France (Louis IX). Bankrolling this effort were Guelf bankers, primarily from Florence. By 1266 Charles of Anjou had helped establish Guelf regimes in most of the city-states in central and northern Italy and had seized control of the Kingdom of Sicily in the south. Dante was born the year that Charles invaded Italy (1265), and the future poet was two years old when Charles marched his army into Florence, formerly a Ghibelline but now a Guelf city (1267).

Dante's lifetime coincided with unprecedented economic growth and crippling factional disputes. By the time opponents had exiled Dante (1302), the population of Florence had doubled from what it had been at his birth. In addition, the city had surpassed Lucca and Pisa as the dominant city of Tuscany. Yet, paradoxically, Florence remained deeply divided and factionalized throughout the poet's life. Inevitably Dante himself became personally caught up in these partisan conflicts.[4] He was born into a Guelf family of modest background from the lower aristocracy. Ghibellines had exiled his grandfather twice from Florence in 1248 and 1260. Dante also came from a familial tradition deeply engaged in the governance of the city. He continued that tradition, beginning with his matriculation into the Physicians and Apothecaries Guild in 1295. In both 1295 and 1296 he served as a member of two major city councils. His service coincided with a sharp anti-aristocratic (and pro-*Popolo*) political turn in 1293 and 1295, exemplified in the promulgation by the government of the anti-aristocratic Ordinances of Justice in 1293 and 1295. This was legislation directed against those members of the elite called "magnates." They had a reputation for violence directed against the *Popolo*, and their claim to elite status derived from their close association with knighthood.

Between 1295 and 1300 growing division within the ranks of the Guelf elite intensified, culminating in a full split in 1300 into two Guelf factions: the Blacks and the Whites. Reasons for the split remain obscure, although it is possible that rivalries between the major banking families might have helped precipitate it. The Cerchi supported the Whites, whereas the Blacks included the Spini family, prominent bankers and creditors of Pope Boniface VIII (reigned 1294– 1303). In 1300 Dante began serving a normal term of two months as one of six priors in the Florentine government. The priorate was the principal magistracy of the city. In May or June of 1300, either just before or during Dante's term, the priorate banished the leaders of both factions in an effort to quell the disorder and appear politically balanced. Shortly thereafter, Dante found sympathy with the Whites, as he supported the decision as prior to allow the White faction, led by Vieri de' Cerchi, to return to Florence. Meanwhile, the Spini and Corso Donati approached Pope Boniface VIII for support. The pope asked Charles of Valois, brother of King Philip IV of France, to lead an army into Florence on behalf of the Blacks. In a clear indication that Dante was troubled by the role the pope was playing in the internal affairs of his city, he urged one of the legislative councils in June of 1301 to vote against advancing further military aid to Pope Boniface VIII. He failed in this effort, and sometime in the summer of that year Charles of Valois led an army that included five hundred knights into Tuscany. Dispatched by the then White-controlled government, Dante led a diplomatic mission to Rome to convince Pope Boniface VIII to avoid any further involvement in Florentine internal politics. Meanwhile, a new priorate in the closing months of 1301 chose to consult the seventy-two guilds about whether to welcome Charles into the city as a "peacemaker" or not, and the decision on behalf of all the guilds but one (the bakers) was positive. Charles therefore entered the city with his army in November of 1301 and restored the Blacks and Corso Donati to power. White partisans and property came under attack, and the Black regime exiled over five hundred Whites, including Dante. Charged with financial extortion and corruption, Dante faced a fine, two years of exile, and exclusion from holding further public offices. His failure to pay the fine led eventually to the confiscation of his property and his condemnation in March of 1302 to be burned at the stake. By June he was in San Godenzo (east of the city) at a meeting of Whites as they were planning assaults on the Blacks. In the fall he traveled with White partisans across the Apennines to Forlì, a Ghibelline stronghold. He spent the rest of his life in exile.

This was the context for the development of Dante's views on the papacy that appear in both his prose and poetic works from at least 1310. These include *Epistles* V, VI, and VII, associated with the invasion of Italy by the emperor Henry VII (reigned 1308–13); the *Monarchia* (1308, or 1312, or 1317–18), *Inferno* (1314), *Purgatorio* (1315), and *Paradiso* (1320–21). Throughout the two

decades of his exile, Dante came to use the language and values of the *Popolo*
to criticize the violent and divisive behavior of the Florentine aristocracy, but
he was also critical of the *Popolo* for their displaced loyalty to family and faction
rather than to city and empire. For the exiled poet, both the papacy and the
emperor drew their authority and legitimacy from God, and both were necessary for the moral development, happiness, and salvation of humanity. Based on
his understanding of Christ's New Testament commands regarding poverty,
however, Dante argued that the papacy should have no worldly powers or prop-
erties and should focus exclusively on its spiritual mission to save souls. Regarding the emperor, Dante argued forcefully for the return and restoration of a
universal empire that could unite the human race, bring an end to the destructive factionalism within the Italian city-states, and provide a safe and secure
environment in which men and women could pursue virtue and personal salvation. It was a position largely consistent with the views of the White Guelfs. In
Epistle V Dante expressed faith in the empire and in particular the emperor,
Henry VII, as the best remedy to end the corrupting divisions afflicting Italy.
Although Henry VII failed in his attempt to take Florence in 1312, Dante placed
him in Paradise and predicted the damnation of the pro-Black pope Clement V
(*Par.* 30.133–38, and *Inf.* 19.82–84). In 1314, following the death of the emperor
Henry VII (died 1313) and Pope Clement V (died 1314), Dante wrote to the cardinals as they were considering the election of a new pope (*Epistle* XI). This was
five years after the papacy had moved to Avignon. He argued for the election of
a new Italian pope and accused the cardinals of being led by their own greed
and avarice. The necessity of a return by the church to evangelical poverty had
become a major theme in Dante's thinking. His own concerns were consistent
with the views of dissident Franciscans or Spirituals like Pietro Olivi (died 1298)
and Ubertino da Casale (died by 1341). Both were critical of the papacy for
weakening the commitment of their order to evangelical poverty.

Dante's argument for a return to universal empire as a cure for the factionalism in Italy is evident not only in his letters but also in the *Monarchia*, written
at the same time as he was composing the *Commedia*. For advanced students
interested in his views on the papacy, teachers may wish to supplement the
Commedia with a reading of this text, especially the third of its three parts (this
details Dante's views on empire and papacy and argues against any temporal
power of the church). His essential argument is that the pursuit of salvation and
moral virtue in this life requires nothing less than the kind of social peace and
stability provided only by universal empire and the rule of a single monarch.
This is the principal theme developed in book 1. In book 2, Dante argues that
Rome emerged in history before the Christian church to promote the common
good, consistent both with nature and with the will of God. Furthermore, he
observes, Christ could atone for the sins of humanity only by being executed by
a (Roman) judge with universal jurisdiction. In book 3, he attacks the legal validity and legitimacy of the Donation of Constantine itself and argues that Saint
Peter's Christ-given power to "bind and to loose" did not include temporal

power. No emperor could relinquish his God-given responsibility to govern the empire, he argued, and no pope could accept it because he was forbidden to have any temporal authority and worldly property by Christ. In other words, Constantine had made a strategic mistake, and nothing less than a repauperization of the papacy and the church were necessary. Ecclesiastical property was therefore illegitimate.[5] The *Monarchia*, therefore, stakes out Dante's position regarding an issue that had roiled medieval church history for centuries: the vexed conflict between the ideal spiritual mission of the papacy and its real-world temporal claims. Instructors who wish to follow this theme will find its fullest development in the *Commedia*.

In the three canticles of the *Commedia*, written in the second decade of the fourteenth century, Dante's criticisms and attacks on the avarice and greed of the contemporary papacy became more insistent and fierce. To explore these perspectives, students might want first to read and discuss *Inferno* 19 and 27, and then move on to *Purgatorio* 19, 32, and 33, and finally, *Paradiso* 17.[6] In *Inferno* 19 Dante demonstrates his sympathy with the legacy of the eleventh-century church reform tradition by portraying Pope Nicholas III (reigned 1277–80) among the simoniacs, those who buy and sell church offices and resources for personal gain. Here, in the Malebolge (circle 8), in Dante's most fervent attack on the papacy, all those who use their intellects to satisfy their desires and temporal passions are punished. Three thirteenth-century popes come under criticism for their greed, with their bodies inverted head down inside a tube-like structure that resembles a baptismal font. Nicholas III suffers upside down as the heels of his feet burn. Soon, Nicholas III says, he will drop out of the receptacle into the recesses of the earth to make room for his corrupt and temporally minded papal successors: Popes Boniface VIII (reigned 1294–1303) and Clement V (reigned 1305–14). Dante's indictment of Nicholas III is harsh:

> Deh, or mi dì: quanto tesoro volle
> Nostro Segnore in prima da san Pietro
> ch'ei ponesse le chiavi in sua balìa?
> Certo non chiese se non "Viemmi retro."

> Pray now tell me how much treasure did our lord require
> of Saint Peter before he put the keys into his keeping?
> Surely he asked nothing save: "Follow me."
> (*Inf.* 19.90–93)[7]

Dante had in mind the "great whore" mentioned in Revelation 17: 1–7 when he condemned Nicholas III for his great avarice, for his "calcando i buoni e sollevando i pravi" ("trampling down the good and exalting the bad"; *Inf.* 19.105). An evil moment indeed was the day Constantine made his donation: it marked the origin of the corrupting accumulation of temporal power and material wealth by the papacy (*Inf.* 19.115–17). In canto 27 (circle 8, bolgia 8), the

Ghibelline leader, Guido da Montefeltro, condemned for evil counsel, curses Pope Boniface VIII as the "Lo principe d'i novi Farisei" ("Prince of the New Pharisees"; *Inf.* 27.85). The pope had taken Guido's evil advice and tricked his rivals, the Colonna.

Dante's criticism became even more pronounced and symbolically complex in *Purgatorio* and *Paradiso*. Teachers may read out loud in class some of the passages mentioned here, to help students both appreciate fully Dante's artistic skill at complex symbolism and follow, carefully and slowly, the rich and complicated images with which these two canticles end. In canto 19 of *Purgatorio*, the cornice of the avaricious, Dante comes upon another of his contemporary pontiffs, Pope Hadrian V (reigned 1276). Speaking to Dante as he lies flat on his stomach in the dust, bound hand and foot, the pope says:

> Quel ch'avarizia fa, qui si dichiara
> in purgazion de l'anime converse;
> e nulla pena il monte ha più amara.
> Sì come l'occhio nostro non s'aderse
> in alto, fisso a le cose terrene,
> così giustizia qui a terra il merse.

> What avarice does is displayed here in the purging of
> down-turned souls, and the mountain has no more bitter
> penalty. Even as our eyes, fixed upon earthly things, were not
> lifted on high, so justice here has sunk them down to earth.
> (*Purg.* 19.115–20)

In *Purgatorio* 32 and 33, Dante elevates his assault on the corruption of the church and contemporary papacy to an even more complex, allegorical level. The cantos describe a sacred procession at the top of the mountain of Purgatory, involving a chariot (the Church Triumphant) led by a griffin (the animal-human hybrid, perhaps symbolic of the human and divine Christ), accompanied by the three theological and four cardinal virtues. In canto 32 the griffin ties the chariot to a tree (most likely the tree of the knowledge of good and evil in the Garden of Eden). The participants in the procession then leave. An eagle (perhaps representing the empire) attacks the tree and chariot, joined by a fox. The eagle returns, the earth opens up under the chariot, and a dragon, symbolizing since antiquity the disorder-causing forces of cupidity and greed, emerges to tear apart the bottom of the chariot. Then, the chariot itself is transformed into a many-headed monster on which sits a whore, identified as the papal court by some of the earliest commentators of the poem. The whore is in turn beaten by a giant, a mythical figure perhaps representing the arrogance of the French monarchy. He pulls the chariot into the forest, reminiscent of the move of the papacy to Avignon. In *Paradiso* 27, Saint Peter himself condemns his successors for having "fatt' . . . del cimitero mio cloaca / del sangue e de la puzza" ("made my burial-ground a sewer of blood and of stench"; *Par.* 27.25–26). According to the saint, the papacy continues to engage in factional strife and has permitted wars against other Christians to be fought under the papal banner. These popes are "[i]n vesta di pastor lupi rapaci" ("[r]apacious wolves, in shepherd's garb"; *Par.* 27.55), motivated by the kind of greed (*cupidigia*) that Beatrice nevertheless confidently prophesies will soon disappear: "e vero frutto verrà dopo 'l fiore" ("and good fruit shall follow on the flower"; *Par.* 27.148). After echoing many of the typical fourteenth-century criticisms directed at ecclesiastical authorities and institutions for their corruption and greed, Dante acknowledges optimistically in the voice of Beatrice at the end of *Paradiso* that history is after all in the hands of God, and a corrupt and worldly minded papacy will soon pass from the earth.

NOTES

[1] For what follows, appropriate for reading assignments and for general background, see Rosenwein 241–82 (ch. 7). For information on the institutional church and religion at the time, undergraduate students will benefit from Briggs 177–228 (pt. 3). For the Florentine church, see Dameron, "Church." For Dante's criticism of the papacy, advanced undergraduates and graduate students should consult Burr, "Heresy"; Pertile, "Life" and "Works." Advanced students may also benefit from more detailed analyses of Dante's apocalyptic themes: Dameron, "Angels"; Havely, *Dante and the Franciscans*; C. Davis, "Poverty"; and McGinn 170–72.

[2] For proper background on Dante's pro-imperial politics, the Italian factionalized political and intellectual context, and the history of the temporal authority of the papacy, the following are particularly excellent resources for students: Caferro; Canning 137–53; Colish 335–40; Ferrante, *Political Vision*; and Bolton (with extensive bibliography, 260–61). For the church reform movement, see M. Miller. For a recent history of the papacy for all levels of undergraduates, see Whalen 111–32, 152–73 (chs. 5, 7).

[3] For background on the medieval Italian commune at the time of Dante, appropriate primarily for advanced undergraduates and graduate students, see Coleman, "Cities"; Takayama; and Dean, "Rise." For the history of medieval Florence, they should consult Caferro; Day; Najemy, *History* 5–155, esp. 60–95 (chs. 1–5); and Dameron, "Florence."

[4] For the information on Dante's life and works that follows in the rest of this essay, see Pertile, "Life" 461–72 and "Works," esp. 488–90, 505; Havely, *Dante and the Franciscans* 2–4; Najemy, "Dante and Florence" and *History* 88–95; and C. Davis, "Poverty" 48. For Dante's views on the spiritual Franciscans, see Burr, *Spiritual Franciscans* 332 and 392.

[5] For the *Monarchia* in particular, see Colish 338–39; Pertile, "Works" 488–89; and Canning 150–53.

[6] An excellent, online (with notes and illustrations), and bilingual collection of the *Divine Comedy* for use in class or individual study is *The World of Dante*.

[7] The original quotations and English translations come from *The Divine Comedy*, translated with commentary by Singleton. For what follows in this section, see Dameron, "Angels"; Pertile, "Works" 501–05; Havely, *Dante and the Franciscans* 2–7, 104–21, 149–84; Pertile, "Introduction to *Inferno*" 76; Jacoff, "Introduction to *Paradiso*" 122; Hawkins, "Dante and the Bible" 136–37; and C. Davis, "Poverty."

The Quest for Ethical Self-Reflection

Sherry Roush

In writing the *Divine Comedy* and figuring himself as a character in the work, Dante deliberately foregrounds two distinct but interrelated notions. The first is a creative ethical imperative. Dante the poet not only acknowledges a profound intellectual and cultural inheritance but also asserts his willingness to adapt or rewrite tradition in order to compose an otherworldly realm that compels his readers to consider in an immediately accessible (and vernacular) way the consequences of human decisions. The second is a vulnerable, curious openness to a life quest. Here, Dante the pilgrim dramatizes a process of individual learning, erring, and growth, which has through the ages prompted his readers to read themselves into the ethical hierarchical scheme of his masterpiece, particularly his *Inferno*. My approach to teaching Dante in Translation embraces Dante's two overarching concerns by emphasizing active student participation to deepen ethical awareness and the production of two interpretive creative projects that prompt students to think critically, ponder virtuous decision-making, and relate Dante's text to contemporary American society.

Dante in Translation is an upper-division, semester-long seminar taught in English typically to twenty to thirty undergraduates—predominantly Italian majors and minors and students from other disciplines aiming to satisfy a Penn State University ethics requirement. Because most of my students encounter Dante's work for the first time here, I focus their attention on the close reading of the *Vita nuova* and the *Comedy* while relinquishing any expectations they will read secondary sources on Dante or be exposed to the many influences of Dante's works on subsequent writers or in other disciplines.[1] I organize the fifteen-week syllabus as follows. In the first week I provide an orientation of Dante's biographical, historical, literary, political, religious, and cultural worlds.[2] For the second week of classes, students have read the *Vita nuova* with the aim of acquainting themselves with Dante's interests, his views of love and God, and his self-representation.[3] We spend the remaining thirteen weeks exploring the three canticles of Dante's *Comedy*, naturally engaging some characters and topics in greater depth and inevitably passing over others in relative silence.[4]

To teach Dante's work is to be compelled to make difficult choices, since no course will exhaust the subject. Students retain what matters to them, and there are no guarantees that a medieval poem of 14,233 lines with enough morals and allegory to intimidate even the most avid readers of the classics will hold the attention of a diverse pool of young adults in this fast-paced, non-Eurocentric world. Each year as I prepare the course syllabus, I am initially tempted to remove the *Vita nuova* so the class can spend one more week on the *Comedy*. Each time, however, I reject this option because the *Vita nuova*—as brief and ever bewildering as it is—helps today's students relate to Dante as another young adult with big dreams and a strong sense of obligation. He represents all the wonder, pain, and confusion of first love; he struggles in the throes of grief; and he experiences peer pressure in an array of social situations (wedding and funeral gatherings, encounters with groups of men and women on the streets of the city, etc.). Moreover, he expresses frustration in not being able to articulate his authentic self or perhaps even to find a way to live according to it. I encourage students to focus on the narrative, more than the poetry and divisions, to discern the choices that Dante makes at this point in his life. I dedicate particular attention to Dante's conversation with an unnamed gentlewoman in chapter 18 because this scene also highlights how Dante the author represents the vulnerability of Dante the character. Dante the character claims an intrinsic motivation for composing poetry in praise of Beatrice, but he is shamed by the gentlewoman who points out the discrepancy between his theory and practice. Dante claims he puts his bliss in something that cannot fail him (praise of Beatrice without any expectations), but the gentlewoman helps him understand that his unarticulated expectations are in fact the source of his unhappiness. This episode provides an excellent prompt for students to discuss the motivations for their own choices and how they anticipate their own bliss from the expectations they have. As different as Dante's cultural context is, I invite students to imagine his personality in their own terms (e.g., What would Dante include on his social media page?). In short, what is the foundation of Dante's and students' respective attempts at what today is termed "self-branding"?

As we move to the *Comedy,* students are aided in their understanding of Dante through his interactions with the guiding figure of Virgil, and I shamelessly tell them that I see my role in guiding them through the *Comedy* much as Virgil does Dante. Virgil has some experience of this other world, but he does not have all the answers. At one point he must return to Limbo and leave his charge to continue along an upward trajectory without him. Dante's journey is one of education itself—from dark, solitary lostness to the light of harmoniously shared knowing—and it offers a model for interactions with my class.

Emphasis in the discussion of Dante's Hell falls squarely on understanding the ethical hierarchy, especially as it is explained by Virgil in *Inferno* 11. Students learn that, unlike convicted criminals in the American correctional system, sinners in Dante's Hell find their place and punishment according to the intentionality of their actions. For example, assault is an act attributed to various shades, though their collocational destinies depend on whether the act was committed out of incontinent greed or wrath, violence, or one of the many forms of simple or complex fraud, including the betrayal of one's political party represented by Bocca degli Abati in *Inferno* 32. The pusillanimous souls of *Inferno* 3 receive an unusual amount of attention in a course dedicated to an ethical approach to Dante's poem because the exquisitely tragic refusal of the pusillanimous to make a choice and commit themselves to a personal destiny throws into stark relief the great importance of free will throughout the *Comedy*. I focus student attention on the ways the damned use language in an attempt to excuse their sins. Finally, together with an understanding of Dante's notion of *contrapasso* as an extension of each soul's motivational pursuit in life (at some times represented quite literally, at others more symbolically or abstractly, requiring students' interpretive efforts), these focal points provide the preliminary foundations for the students' first project, which I call the Dante Today project.

The purpose of the Dante Today project is for students to apply their knowledge of Dante's ethical hierarchy to a contemporary and controversial political, moral, philosophical, or criminal issue not already addressed in Dante's *Inferno*. During the first eight to ten minutes of each class period for most of the remainder of the semester (beginning in the seventh week, when the class has finished the final cantos of the *Inferno*), one pair of students presents a Dante Today project, recommending a place in Dante's *Inferno* (or a new circle or bolgia within it) for a person (historical or fictional—from a work of literature, television, or cinema) who exemplifies a present-day vice or crime. Some examples of Dante Today topics include drug dealing, illegal music-downloading, bullying, racial profiling, college-apparel sweatshop manufacturing, texting while driving, and catfishing. Students are invited to see themselves almost as legal prosecutors of their sinner; in their presentations to the jury of their peers, they argue for the guilt of their figure, based on the sinner's own words, which the students have researched in history books, newspapers, other literary works, movie or television scripts, celebrity magazines, or Web sites. Spirited in-class debates ensue, and I guide discussion by asking students to compare each sinner's words or actions to specific passages and characters in Dante's text. I also ask the presenters to suggest an appropriate *contrapasso* for their sinner by interpreting their figure's actions and motivations in allegorical or symbolic ways. Thus, as a class, we practice applying these interpretive skills to a modern figure and vice in each lesson. Student presenters follow up their oral arguments in class with individually written reports of approximately five pages to receive personalized assessments. No two pairs are permitted to address the same present-day vice.

Meanwhile, the class continues its study of *Purgatory*, endeavoring to understand, for instance, how infernal punishments differ from purgatorial penances, the basis for the structure of the mountain in *Purgatory* 17, and the role of individual intent as represented in the contrasting rhetoric of the souls of the saved and of the damned. Asking students to compare the lives and postmortem destinies of Guido da Montefeltro (*Inf.* 27) and his son Buonconte (*Purg.* 5) offers another potentially illuminating discussion topic on the illusory status of worldly honor (that is, our virtue does not derive from how other people view us). Ethical issues also remain at the forefront of discussions in Dante's *Paradise*: How does Dante both maintain and subvert the notion of a moral hierarchy in the final canticle? How can blessed souls who abide in one truth not agree with one another (*Paradise* 4)? Why does an all-loving and all-powerful God not just redeem all human beings? What is the place of an individual's free will?

Throughout the semester, I remind students of how Dante represents himself both as poet and as pilgrim. He was a highly experimental poet, inventing his own rhyme scheme and the space of Purgatory, as well as many brilliant neologisms. Moreover, Dante has the courage to figure his character as flawed, vulnerable, and emotional, and, in the final canto of *Paradise*, he acknowledges that he has failed (the wholeness of his vision remains ineffable). Dante also deliberately chooses to forgo Latin in favor of the Florentine Italian vernacular, indicating how much he wanted to reach an audience well beyond elite academic circles. All these considerations are at the heart of the second project, which students produce in lieu of a research paper: the individual imaginative, interpretive final project.

Students' final projects have both creative and analytical components; the latter explains the work's creative inspiration by referring to specific passages from Dante's text(s) and demonstrates an advanced understanding of Dante's allegorical or symbolic mode of signification. Projects consisting of visual art pieces are thus accompanied by an interpretation of the kind displayed next to each piece in museums and art galleries. For creative writing projects, students typically include a foreword, postscript, and/or series of footnotes to explain their compositional choices, and for journalistic projects, the analysis might appear on an editorial page. Other creative projects include some form of interpretive equivalent, which need not be written. For example, an audio project's analysis might take the form of recorded liner notes, or a video might include a director's commentary track.

Students benefit from producing highly self-directed creative and interpretive projects inspired by Dante through a vast array of formats—sometimes freeingly creative for students in highly analytical major fields of study, at other times as applications of students' preferred disciplinary epistemologies. In addition to the visual, aural, and creative or journalistic writing approaches mentioned above, examples of student project formats include tongue-in-cheek tourist brochures promoting Dante's infernal realms, amusement park ride concepts, reality television show pilots, new video or board games, modern psychological assessments of Dante or his characters, interpretations of Dante's poetry in dance or figure skating, public relations proposals figuring God as a client, satirical skits in the style of *Saturday Night Live* based on scenes from the *Comedy*, and blogs and social media sites maintained by selected *Comedy* characters.

Since the scope of the creative contribution and the length of the analytical component vary depending on the type of project selected by each student, I require students to submit a one-page description of their plans approximately three weeks before the submission deadline for the final project. This step assists students in identifying their objective and medium and dissipates any blocks they might be experiencing at the prospect of producing a creative work.

The description also gives me the opportunity in my assessment to deepen their engagement with Dante's text by suggesting potential research questions they might address in the analytical component of their final project submissions.

In recent years I have set aside the last day of term for students to share with the rest of the class their work in progress on their individual final projects (due during the following week of exams). Given the typical enrollment size of my class, I do not have enough time in one class period for each student to individually present to the entire class. Instead, I divide the class in half, asking the first group to present their projects to the second group cocktail party style, that is informally to individuals and small groups circulating about the room at their own speed and asking questions and making suggestions according to their interests. When the class period is nearly half over, the two groups switch, and the presenters become the audience in circulation. During the last few minutes, I ask students to write a brief assessment of the most impressive projects and the reasons the format, subject, or methodology had a positive impact on them. Experience has shown that the activities of this final day of class help students perceive qualitative differences in the interpretation of creative projects. As a consequence, some struggling students endeavor to improve their final projects before consigning them to me the following week, and fewer students report frustrations about perceived arbitrariness in the grading of such personal projects, when I can opt to include excerpts from the peer assessments of their work.

In retrospect, students report they are proud of their Dante projects, which compel them to read Dante's text very closely and practice their interpretive skills at the highest levels in order to reimagine aspects of the *Comedy* in a contemporary and personal way. In doing so, they also come to a profound appreciation for Dante's procedure of figuring himself in his work. For my part, after nearly two decades of the privilege of offering this and other Dante courses to students ranging from faculty auditors and graduate and honors students to undergraduates of every background, I am continually reminded to meet my interlocutors where they are: in the *medias res* of life. Often it is the student in crisis or the one whose intellectual spirit has not yet taken spark who receives the greatest benefit from this course and its approach. I can fathom no greater lesson to have learned from my best teachers—my Virgils—and no more important legacy to leave to my next group of students than a deeper awareness, inspired by Dante, of one's responsibilities, boundaries, and potential as an individual in this world.

NOTES

[1] I provide detailed bibliographies as well as a series of Web links for students to explore on their own Dante's legacy in the arts and sciences, as well as in popular culture.

[2] Scott's *Understanding Dante* is an excellent reference for new teachers.

[3] I adopt Musa's 1973 translation of the *Vita Nuova*.

[4] For the *Comedy*, I recommend the Oxford University Press edition translated by Robert M. Durling, which provides an appropriate balance of scholarly detail and accessible notes for undergraduates. Most weeks students will study approximately eight cantos with periodic reviews of the material covered.

Teaching the Theological Dimension of Dante's *Comedy*

Paul J. Contino

I am a practicing Catholic who has taught Dante for over twenty-five years in two church-related schools: in Christ College, the Honors College of Valparaiso University (Lutheran), and in the Great Books Colloquium in Pepperdine University (Church of Christ). My students come to Dante having read Saint Augustine, who, in *Confessions*, exhorts his readers to imitate the incarnational pattern of Christ: "Come down so that you may ascend, and make your ascent to God" (4.12 [19]). In the prologue, Dante thinks he can ascend the mountain alone; instead, he must humbly accept guidance, and descend into Hell to see sin for what it is. Only then can he ascend the terraces of Purgatory and the spheres of Paradise. In this essay, I discuss each canticle in light of a persistent theological puzzle: the relation between divine grace and human freedom.[1] Created in the image and likeness of God, persons have free will, as affirmed by both Marco Lombardo (*Purg.* 16.65–90) and Beatrice (*Par.* 5.19–30). God's love respects human freedom; and yet all forms of Christianity—Catholic, Orthodox, Protestant—affirm that we are saved—granted the gift of eternal communal beatitude—through God's divine and loving grace, and, historically, through Christ's kenotic, salvific suffering, death, and resurrection (see Beatrice's rendering of classic atonement theory in *Par.* 7).[2] How does human freedom respond to this gift of grace? Does the poet's account of the pilgrim's arduous journey suggest that human effort matters more than grace, or somehow earns grace through meritorious work? My mostly Protestant students sometimes need to be reminded of the Pelagian heresy, which claimed that grace is earned by our own hard work, and which was soundly rejected by Saint Augustine and the church magisterium. And yet if we are free and not predetermined, how do a person's actions affect his or her eternal destiny?[3] Reading the whole *Comedy* over the course of six weeks, students discern the perennial paradox given poetic form by Dante: redemption is realized by humble acceptance of the gift of grace, often mediated by other people, and by free cooperation with the Giver through love of God and neighbor.

Love is at that heart of Dante's vision, the divine love that moves not only the sun but also Dante's heart, as he writes his *Comedy* as an act of love for his fellow pilgrims. But the *Inferno* poses a challenge to any complacent claim of God's love. How can Dante imagine the maker of this place of eternal pain to be "PRIMAL LOVE" ("e 'l primo amore"; *Inf.* 3.6)?[4] Rarely does a church-goer hear a sermon on hell these days; theologians like Hans Urs von Balthasar ask whether we dare hope for the salvation of all, given those scriptural passages that insist that "God's will for salvation applies for men, especially since Christ gave himself as a ransom for all (1 Tim. 2.1–6)" (*Dare* 21).[5] Here C. S. Lewis, whom many students know, can be helpful. In *The Great Divorce*, denizens of the grey town are offered a bus ride out of hell. But once they see heaven, most reject it as too real, its flowers and grass "solider" than things in hell (21). Dante, too, emphasizes freedom in his "drama of the soul's choice" (Sayers, Introduction 11).[6] Willfully, the souls perversely choose Hell and are "pronti . . . a trapassar lo rio" over the Acheron ("eager for the river crossing"; *Inf.* 3.124). In the spirit of terza rima, I focus on three characters who reveal their infernal preference by their lack of love: Francesca, Farinata, and Ulysses.

Francesca's words can seduce students much as they do Dante the pilgrim. Reading more closely, however, students notice that Francesca never takes responsibility for "subjecting [her] reason to the rule of lust" ("la ragion sommettono al talento"; *Inf.* 5.39), but blames love: "Amor, ch'a nullo amato amar perdona, / mi prese del costui piacer sì forte, / che, come vedi, ancor non m'abbandona" ("Love, that releases no beloved from loving, / took hold of me so strongly through his beauty / that, as you see, it has not left me yet"; *Inf.* 5.103–05). Later, she blames a literary depiction of two lovers' illicit kiss: "Galeotto fu 'l libro e chi lo scrisse: / quel giorno più non vi leggemmo avante" ("A Gallehault indeed, that book and he / who wrote it, too; that day we read no more"; *Inf.* 5.137–38). Francesca's alibi can provoke an apt question: Do authors bear responsibility for the negative effect their words may have on their readers? Might the pilgrim's swoon suggest a love poet's guilt? Every step of the way, Dante will come to understand love more fully and clearly.

Standing erect among the heated heretics, Farinata seems magnanimous but lacks love. Like Francesca, who never utters the name of her windblown lover, Farinata never notices his sepulchral neighbor, Cavalcante dei Cavalcanti. Even when Cavalcante cries out in grief, believing his son Guido to be dead, Farinata simply "tak[es] up his words where he'd left off" ("e sé continüando al primo detto"; *Inf.* 10.76) and interrogates the pilgrim about his Ghibelline countrymen. As they do with other similarly intense encounters, students present a dramatic reading of the episode, each taking a part. They then write for five minutes, analyzing what they may have heard for the first time upon rereading. Finally, they share their insights in discussion, often discerning Farinata's almost mechanized solipsism, his isolated refusal to recognize his neighbor, much less love him.

So too does Ulysses willfully refuse to love. A student reads aloud Ulysses's speech to his crew: "non vogliate negar l'esperïenza, / di retro al sol, del mondo sanza gente" ("You must not deny / experience of that which lies beyond"; *Inf.* 26.115–16) and "fatti non foste a viver come bruti, / ma per seguir virtute e canoscenza" ("you were not made to live your lives as brutes, / but to be followers of worth and knowledge"; *Inf.* 26.119–20). I ask, "Isn't that why you came to college? If so, why is curious, intrepid Ulysses in Hell?" Students read closely and begin to see that Ulysses's counsel is fraudulent in its destructive *curiositas* and *libido dominandi*: he desires knowledge to grab solitary, God-like power.[7] Ulysses's quest for divine omniscience and omnipotence travesties the divine attributes.

He manipulates his crew through his rhetoric and severs himself from any human attachment:

> né dolcezza di figlio, né la pieta
> del vecchio padre, né 'l debito amore
> lo qual dovea Penelopè far lieta
>   vincer potero dentro a me l'ardore
> ch'i' ebbi a divenir del mondo esperto

> neither my fondness for my son nor pity
> for my old father, nor the love I owed
> Penelope, which would have gladdened her,
>   was able to defeat in me the longing
> I had to gain experience of the world.
> (*Inf.* 26.94–98)

Students note the contrast between Ulysses's journey of autonomous assertion, and Dante's grace-guided pilgrimage toward conversion.

After we have climbed with Dante and Virgil over the Trinitarian travesty that is three-faced, frozen Satan, we are relieved to reach the sunny shores of Purgatory, with its "miglior acque" ("kindly waters"; *Purg.* 1.1) and serene sky. I ask students to create and write a "Postcard from Purgatory" to a loved one. These take various, typically comical forms (e.g., "It's beautiful here, Mom, and people are very friendly, but I'd like to move on, so if you could spare a prayer or two"). But by the time we reach the three steps of Purgatory proper—white for penitence, purple for confession, and (especially) bloodred for satisfaction by penitential works—my mostly Protestant students reprise Luther's question: What is the purpose of this place? Hasn't the work been accomplished on Calvary hill, by which we are "cleansed of sin" ("dove l'umano spirito si purga"; *Purg.* 1.5) by the red blood of the Lamb? The Protestant C. S. Lewis again proves helpful as he defended the doctrine, insisting, "Our souls *demand* purgatory, don't they?" (C. S. Lewis, *Letters* 108–09). I ask students to reread passages that suggest Dante's similar insight, and they gradually see how the poet envisions God's grace as deeply respectful of human freedom: grace grants the soul's desire to rehabilitate through penitential suffering and communal prayer, until the soul itself feels free and ready for heaven. Thus, when the souls sing the "Our Father," they emphasize the free "sacrifice" of their will in union with Christ, whose sacrifice is definitive: "Come del suo voler li angeli tuoi / fan sacrificio a te, cantando *osanna* / così facciano li uomini de' suoi" ("Just as Your angels, as they sing Hosanna, / offer their wills to You as sacrifice, / so may men offer up their wills to You"; *Purg.* 11.10–12). Dante's friend Forese Donati explains that his hunger and thirst is freely joined to and participates in the pain of Christ on the cross:

> io dico pena, e dovria dir sollazzo,
>   ché quella voglia a li alberi ci mena

che menò Cristo lieto a dire *Elì*,
quando ne liberò con la sua vena.

(Purg. 23.72–75)

I speak of pain but I should speak of solace,
for we are guided to those trees by that
  same longing that had guided Christ when He
had come to free us through the blood He shed
and, in His joyousness, called out: "Eli."

(Purg. 23.71–75)

The graced freedom entailed in penitential offering is especially highlighted in the story of Statius who appears after the earthquake. Like Jesus on the road to Emmaus, he joins Dante and Virgil, and explains the recent events:

Tremaci quando alcuna anima monda
sentesi, sì che surga o che si mova
per salir sù; e tal grido seconda.
  De la mondizia sol voler fa prova,
che, tutto libero a mutar convento,
l'alma sorprende, e di voler le giova.
  Prima vuol ben, ma non lascia il talento
che divina giustizia, contra voglia,
come fu al peccar, pone al tormento.
  E io, che son giaciuto a questa doglia
cinquecent' anni e più, pur mo sentii
libera volontà di miglior soglia.

. . . for [the earth] only trembles here
when some soul feels it's cleansed, so that it rises
or stirs to climb on high. . . .
  The will alone is proof of purity
and, fully free, surprises soul into
a change of dwelling place—effectively.
  Soul had the will to climb before, but that
will was opposed by longing to do penance
(as once to sin), instilled by divine justice.
  And I. . . .
. . . just now have
felt my free will for a better threshold.

(Purg. 21.58–69)

Divine justice respects human freedom, and allows each person to fulfill his or her wish—Purgatory as a strenuous spa experience, if you will. In each of the seven terraces, the assigned vice is partly purged by the presence or invocation of the countering virtue, the prime exemplum of each being drawn from the life of Mary, the Mother of God. Here, showing students paintings from Dante's own time can be edifying, especially those of Dante's friend Giotto, who is mentioned in the first terrace of pride (*Purg.* 11.95). I show the students the Arena Chapel frescoes that depict Mary's counteracting virtues: humility (Annunciation), generosity (Cana), mildness (Jesus in the Temple), zeal (Visitation), poverty (Nativity), temperance (Cana), and chastity (Annunciation).[8] As many of my students come from Protestant traditions in which the figure of Mary is deemphasized or ignored, it's salutary for them to be reminded of her scriptural provenance; Giotto's images help prepare students for Mary's prominence in the final canto of *Paradiso*.

Mary's face is the one most like her Son's (*Par.* 32.85–86), and she mediates grace from the beginning. Moved by Divine Love, she appeals to Lucia, who speaks to Beatrice, who inspires Virgil to help Dante. But as they near the Earthly Paradise, Virgil—whom most students come to love—must make way for Beatrice. The students expect a dewy lovers' reunion, but at the end of the scriptural, sacramental procession they are jolted by the entrance of Admiral Beatrice: why is she so harsh? We enact the confrontation-confession scene in class—Balthasar calls it "the dynamic goal of the whole journey" (*Glory* 61)—and the students perceive the pilgrim's need to tearfully confess and cleanse himself before ascending to God. Whatever their doctrinal beliefs, students can come to see Dante's Purgatory as an allegory of this life—the human inclination toward misdirected love (see *Purg.* 17.85–130) and deeper desire to reform through the graced habits of virtue, repentance, and prayer—in both its individual and communal forms.

Communal beatitude illuminates all of Paradise—its smiling, dancing, singing silence.[9] Practicing patience and attention, students can develop a taste for the "pan de li angeli" ("bread of angels"; *Par.* 2.11) and Heaven's varied degrees of luminosity. But why degrees? The students meet Piccarda Donati and, like the pilgrim, want to know: "Ma dimmi: voi che siete qui felici, / disiderate voi più alto loco / per più vedere e per più farvi amici?" ("Though you're happy here, do you / desire a higher place in order to / see more and to be still more close to Him?"; *Par.* 3.64–66). Or, as they are more apt to protest, Why, after so many levels and terraces, does Dante have hierarchy in Heaven? Part of the answer, of course, is provided by Beatrice: all souls are united with God in the Empyrean; their appearance in the Ptolemaic spheres is simply a "command performance" (Freccero, *Dante* 226) for the pilgrim's edification. In fact, the "punto" ("point") that is God marks the true center of the universe (*Par.* 28.41–42).[10] But a further answer lies in Dante's love for the reality of diversity. Persons vary in talents and gifts (*Par.* 32.65), and how receptive they are to grace (*Par.* 29.64–66). Some, because of human limitation, have been less receptive than others. Piccarda broke her vow under duress; Folco fell in love too easily (*Par.* 9.94–99). Even in Heaven, each personality remains particular, and community is both "structured and diversified."[11] But everyone "si ride, / . . . / del valor ch'ordinò e provide" ("smiles" for "the Power that fashioned and foresaw"; *Par.* 9.103, 105).

There are other related theological questions I raise in class but cannot fully address in this brief essay. For example, how does Dante the Christian respond to the reality of religious pluralism?[12] The Eagle of Justice knows Dante's question about the man born along the Indus River:

> e tutti suoi voleri e atti buoni
> sono, quanto ragione umana vede,
> sanza peccato in vita o in sermoni.
>   Muore non battezzato e sanza fede:
> ov' è questa giustizia che 'l condanna?
> ov' è la colpa sua, se ei non crede?
>
> *(Par.* 19.73–78)

> in all he seeks and all he does is good:
> there is no sin within his life or speech.
>   And that man dies unbaptized, without faith.
> Where is this justice then that would condemn him?
> Where is his sin if he does not believe?
>
> *(Par.* 19.74–78)

With this very challenge many reject Christianity, unsatisfied with the "scandal of particularity"[13] affirmed in the Eagle's response: "A questo regno / non salì mai chi non credette 'n Cristo, / né pria né poi ch'el si chiavasse al legno" ("No one without belief in Christ / has ever risen to this kingdom—either / before or after He was crucified"; *Par.* 19.103–05). But Dante the theologian's answer doesn't end with that declaration; in the next canto first-time readers are puzzled and, perhaps, delighted to discover the pagans Trajan and Riphaeus shining on the Eagle's eyebrow. (Dare we hope that Virgil will have a place there, too?) At the end of the canto, "the pair of blessed lights together, / like eyes that wink in concord, move their flames / in ways that were at one with what he said" ("le due luci benedette, / pur come batter d'occhi si concorda, / con le parole mover le fiammette"; *Par.* 20.146–48). Mandelbaum renders "wink" for "batter d'occhi," and this seems an apt poetic image for the divine response to the human cry for justice, as if to say, "It's OK, I've got this. All will be well." In Dante God's love encompasses all, although it wasn't until Vatican II that the Catholic Church gave the Eagle's "wink" a more fully doctrinal form.[14] And what of the Christian response to violence and war? Dante's ancestor, Cacciaguida the Crusader, is among those warriors who form a red cross in canto 14. But in canto 11, Saint Thomas Aquinas describes the cross-marked Saint Francis of Assisi's visit to the sultan, which has emerged for many as an image of interreligious peace. For most of the last fifteen years I have taught this canto while United States' troops have fought in Muslim countries. Early in 2003, Pope John Paul II pleaded with President George W. Bush to refrain from war with Iraq and, in what seemed a shift away from traditional just war theory, declared that "war is always a defeat for humanity." The contrasting images of Cacciaguida and Francis provide an occasion to discuss the developing and conflicted understanding of war in the Christian tradition.

And what of sexuality? Students are acquainted with Dante's story: how he fell and remained in love with Beatrice, even as they both married other people (he married Gemma Donati). At the end of the *Vita nuova*, he promises to write a poem worthy of her and depicts their reunion in the *Comedy*. But does the pilgrim experience Beatrice's beautiful presence as an idol, in whom his love rests, or as an icon, who reorients his love to its divine source? The pilgrim comes to see that she smiles most radiantly when Dante shifts his attention from her to Christ (*Par.* 10.61–63). The incarnation, within the interrelation of the Trinity, is Dante's final focus and the moment when pilgrim becomes poet. And what of Dante's understanding of homosexuality, which remains a vexed issue for many Christians? In *Inferno*, he walks above his beloved teacher Brunetto Latini among the sodomites; later Dante joins both heterosexuals and homosexuals in the flames, as they purge the same sin with a chaste embrace and kiss.[15] In an age when *eros* can be debased and held cheaply, students may be surprised by the role it plays in holiness. After all, Virgil entices the pilgrim to enter the flaming terrace with erotic Ovidian references, reminding him of beautiful Beatrice waiting on the other side. Indeed, Beatrice's beauty only grows as the poem proceeds. In Dante's imagination *eros* is not merely sublimated but sanctified; united with *agape*, it yields *caritas*.[16]

Engaging theological questions through close attention to Dante's miraculous poem has been a singular gift throughout my vocation as a teacher. I might add that this gift has been enriched by the experience of teaching Dante's *Comedy* twice in Florence. Visiting the city's churches is especially moving: the octagonal Baptistery of San Giovanni, where Dante received his vocation as a Christian; the Duomo, in which Domenico di Michelino portrays Dante presenting the *Commedia* to his native city; the church of Santa Margherita where he first saw Beatrice; Santa Maria Maggiore, where his teacher Brunetto lies entombed; Santa Croce, where he read Bonaventure with the Franciscans; Santa Maria Novella, where he studied Thomas Aquinas with the Dominicans.

I have taught the poem in two Christian universities, but these theological questions can and ought to be engaged in any university if students are to achieve a full understanding of Dante's poetic purpose. Moreover, even in our postsecular age, college students continue to care about the enduring existential questions of life's purpose, and the possible fulfillment of that life in eternity.[17] Students desire to engage these questions in the classroom, and Dante's poem offers a profound occasion for doing so, and it may even offer the "vital nodrimento" ("living nourishment") promised by Cacciaguida (*Par.* 17.132). Many will be moved by Dante's vision of the Love that moves the sun and other stars, and that moves the poet himself to compose his *Comedy* as an act of love for his fellow pilgrims, his attentive readers.

NOTES

[1] In "The Theology of Dante," Ryan claims "that the central quest of Dante's understanding in the poem, and indeed in his *oeuvre* as a whole, was to grasp how the divine is present in the human" (136). In "The Theology of the *Comedy*," A. N. Williams emphasizes the ways "Dante tries to hold together human freedom with divine redemption and grace" (213). Also highly recommended are Montemaggi; Montemaggi and Treherne; and Mazzotta, "Liberty."

[2] *Paradiso* 7 itself can inspire theological discussion, as some theologians have challenged Anselm's explanation of the atonement. For a lucid discussion of soteriology, and other theological themes discussed in this essay, see Bauerschmidt and Buckley.

[3] Dante grapples with the question of predestination. See, for example, *Par.* 20.130–39.

[4] Here and throughout, I use Mandelbaum for quotations and translations.

[5] See especially Balthasar, *Dare We Hope*, but also the more popular evangelical Bell, *Love Wins.*

[6] Sayers's helpful introductions to both *Hell* and *Purgatory* remain available in Penguin editions. See also O'Connell Baur who points to "the *Commedia*'s overriding claim that souls enjoy the afterlife that they themselves have chosen" (224–25).

[7] See P. Griffiths for a helpful analysis of the differences between *curiositas* and *studiositas.*

[8] Showing students images inspired by the *Comedy* itself, from early illuminators to contemporary painters, is always an edifying delight for visually alert students. See Kleinhenz, "On Dante." See also some of the excellent Dante Web sites, including Guy Raffa's site, *Danteworlds.*

[9] See Hawkins, "All Smiles"; and Russell 151–85.

[10] For an extensive analysis of "the point," see Moevs.

[11] Here I draw a bit from my introduction to Raffel's translation of the *Divine Comedy*. The description of Catholic community as "structured and diversified" is from Greeley (141).

[12] See Barolini, "Dante's Sympathy" and "Medieval Multiculturalism."

[13] *Scandal of particularity* is an oft-used theological phrase, but its origin has only recently been identified: it appears to have entered English only in 1930, as a translation of *das Ärgernis der Einmaligkeit*, a term coined by the twentieth-century biblical theologian Gerhard Kittel to describe the "scandal" to rationalism of the uniqueness of Jesus Christ (Doherty 15n7).

[14] Dulles's summary is helpful: "In several important texts, Vatican II took up the question of the salvation of non-Christians. . . . God's universal salvific will, it taught, means that he gives non-Christians, including even atheists, sufficient help to be saved. Whoever sincerely seeks God and, with his grace, follows the dictates of conscience is on the path to salvation." See also Fredericks.

[15] See the essay by Gary Cestaro in this collection.

[16] See Hawkins, "Dante's Beatrice." In his 2005 encyclical "Deus Caritas Est," Pope Benedict XVI writes, "*Eros* and *agape*—ascending love and descending love—can never be completely separated. The more the two, in their different aspects, find a proper unity in the one reality of love, the more the true nature of love in general is realized" (7).

[17] See, for example, Astin et al.; and Jacobsen and Hustedt Jacobsen.

Dante, Poet of Loss

Peter S. Hawkins

For contemporary readers, much of the *Commedia*'s appeal lies in the fact that, like so many of us, Dante pilgrim knows himself to be profoundly confused and disoriented: "Nel mezzo del cammin di nostra vita / mi ritrovai per una selva oscura, / che la diritta via era smarrita" ("Midway in the journey of our life, / I came to myself in a dark wood, / for the straight way was lost"; *Inf.* 1.1–3).[1] For people of a certain age, the poet is describing a midlife crisis: once there had been a clear path, a way through the dark places, but suddenly it is gone. The death-do-us-part relationship dies, perfect health suddenly fails, the secure job is either no longer secure, or no longer bearable. Yet even students far from the expected midpoint of a lifespan—Dante's "mezzo del cammin"—can easily find in his story a version of their own condition: the "dark wood" practices no age discrimination. A quick Internet perusal of popular culture reveals how often the term has become shorthand for speaking about disorientation, addiction, frustration, fear, clinical depression, and personal crises of all kinds.

But more than merely a confirmation of what ails us, the poem has also inspired contemporary readers to leave the dark wood behind. In *Darkness Visible*, for instance, William Styron recounts his struggles with suicidal depression by appropriating Dante's "selva oscura" to describe his own desperate condition. He concludes the book with the closing lines of the *Inferno*, suggesting the poem's role in his recovery: "E quindi uscimmo a riveder le stelle" ("And so we came forth, and once again beheld the stars"; *Inf.* 34.139).

Two quite recent books go further in bearing extensive witness to the therapeutic value of the *Commedia* as charting a path from despair to hope: Rod Dreher's *How Dante Can Save Your Life* and Joseph Luzzi's *In a Dark Wood: What Dante Taught Me about Grief, Healing, and the Mysteries of Love.*[2] Like the author of the *Commedia*—who writes a story about himself from the perspective of someone who has not only survived to tell the tale but also been transformed in the process—Dreher and Luzzi share their accounts of rescue and deliverance from profound personal losses, which in both cases is the unexpected death of a beloved (Dreher a sister, Luzzi a wife). Dreher, a journalist, finds religious inspiration in the poem; Luzzi, a professor of Italian, takes a more humanist turn. In both cases, Dante became their Virgil, their Beatrice. Thanks to the poem, each can say, in the words of John Newton's "Amazing Grace": "I once was lost, but now am found, / was blind, but now I see."

A Dante course might well begin by sampling one of these books to pose the issue of the students' own "dark wood" or by asking them to identify the nature of the "beasts" that prevent them, like Dante pilgrim in *Inferno* 1, from moving upward toward the light. Dante always links the individual to the collective, as he does in the poem's opening lines by situating his personal narrative "midway in the journey of *our* life" (my emphasis). For him, the personal is inevitably political. How, then, might students identify not only the forces that hold them back personally, but that also keep our society in the dark? In *Inferno* 6, one of the gluttons, Ciacco, names "superbia, invidia e avarizia" ("pride, envy, and greed"; 74) as the sources of Florence's corruption. What would the students say are the forces that currently compromise our wellbeing and hold us captive?

Beyond taking this inventory of our dark wood, a study of the *Commedia* might open with the poet's loss of home, livelihood, and cultural identity—the devastation that precipitated the poem's composition and that in many ways determined what it would become. In the summer of 1300, Dante became one of the six priors of Florence, a coveted civic position that marked his prominence in the commune's political sphere. After his formal arrival on the literary scene five years earlier with the appearance of his *Vita nuova*, he was apparently at the height of his powers at age thirty-five. Not long after he served his July–August term as prior, however, a shift in Florentine political power led to the vilification of those who had recently held office. In January of 1302, Dante and three others were accused of trafficking in public offices, as well as bribery, acts of vengeance against opponents, and other unsubstantiated crimes. His property was confiscated; he was exiled for two years and barred from ever again holding public office. Two months later, another decree condemned him to be burned at the stake should he ever return to the commune. Others who shared this sentence eventually made their way back to Florence, accepting the humiliating terms extended to them and, as best they could, picking up the wreckage of their lives. For complex reasons, stemming no doubt from a mixture of integrity and pride, Dante was not among them. For the rest of his life and until his death in 1321—moving from place to place throughout north-central Italy—he suffered the indignity and alienation of exile.

Dante expressed what the loss of his home felt like in the *Convivio*, written just a few years into this exile: "Truly I have been a ship without sail or rudder, brought to different ports, inlets, and shores by the dry wind that painful poverty blows" (*Conv.* 1.3.5). In the *Commedia* this pain of displacement becomes even more specific. Because the poem is set in April 1300, a couple of years before his exile, what Dante would come to know all too well is foreshadowed gradually. Toward the end of the *Paradiso*, the disaster merely hinted at over the poem's course is finally clarified:

> Tu lascerai ogne cosa diletta
> più caramente; e questo è quello strale
> che l'arco de lo essilio pria saetta.
> Tu proverai sì come sa di sale
> lo pane altrui, e come è duro calle
> lo scendere e 'l salir per l'altrui scale.

You shall leave behind all you most dearly love
And that shall be the arrow
First loosed from exile's bow.
You shall come to learn how salt is the taste
of another man's bread and how hard is the way,
going down and then up another man's stairs.

(*Par.* 17.55–60)

Dante loses, in other words, the privileged, well-connected world he had known until the midpoint of his life. After it, Florence was no longer "his": its distinctive local accent and familiar unsalted cuisine, his comfortable family residence (compared to the indignity of living as a perpetual guest, beholden to climbing up and down "another's stairs"), his identity as an esteemed citizen rather than as a political refugee. All the easy pleasures of being at home and in place were lost.

Therefore, one way for students to enter into the heart of the poem (and perhaps to make more palatable the daunting intricacy of Florentine politics) would be to imagine the particular social displacements that would devastate them were they in a similar situation. What would it be like to be exiled or made a refugee, as millions of people in Africa and the Middle East currently are? What would it feel like for them to be uprooted? What would they miss most? Who would they even be once all the familiar guarantors of identity were taken away?

Students should be encouraged to make personal reflections and to be curious about the particularities of Dante's life, insofar as we can know them from the remove of centuries.[3] This is because all of his writing—the *Vita nuova*, certainly, but also the *De vulgari eloquentia*, the *Convivio*, and even *Monarchia*—is to one extent or another autobiographical. The reader is never far away from Dante's life story. This is especially true of the *Commedia*, written in the first person, where Dante Alighieri, the author of every word, stands behind both the narrator of the tale (Dante poet) and the character who makes his way within it (Dante pilgrim). We move forward with the pilgrim, look backward with the poet; we learn from the experience of the one, benefit from the hindsight of the other.

Loss as a theme runs through Dante's literary project from its very beginning, the *Vita nuova*, when he must deal with the death of Beatrice, who not only opened him to the reality of someone other than himself but also gave him his first hunger and thirst for God. In the *Convivio*, at the point of exile (1.17), he turns from the theological reality of Beatrice, "a lady in glory" to another affection—the allegorical Lady Philosophy. Whereas it was Beatrice and all she represents in the *Vita nuova* to whom he turned in his youth, upon mature reflection, and after the disaster of his banishment from Florence, there is someone else who commands his allegiance: "the daughter of God, queen of all things, most noble and beautiful Philosophy" (*Conv.* 2.12.9). He finds in her the same consolation she offered to Boethius, when he, like Dante, was the victim of political malfeasance and false accusation (Mills Chiarenza, "Boethius").

But if the philosophic mind rescued Dante from despair in the early days of his exile, it was the rediscovery of Beatrice, and a return to theology, that animates the *Commedia*. As we know from Virgil's flashback in *Inferno* 2, it was she—prompted by the Virgin Mary and Saint Lucy—who begins the rescue that becomes Dante's path from the dark wood to the paradisiacal white rose of its conclusion. It is she, in effect, who helps transform the profound loss of his exile into a spiritual exodus. The Old Testament Exodus is, in fact, a biblical paradigm that undergirds the entire poem, as Dante himself makes plain in the *Letter to Can Grande della Scala*. The journey of the pilgrim is from Inferno's Egypt to the promised land of Paradise.[4]

But if Dante, given his life circumstances, is in many ways a poet of loss, his *Commedia* as a whole charts the experience of being found: retrieving the "diritta via" ("straight way"; *Inf.* 1.3), progressing from perpetual stasis in Hell to follow the "onward and upward" trajectory of the rest of the poem. The *Inferno* is the starting point of this trajectory—an exploration of what it means to be lost absolutely. As Hell's gate declares so dramatically, "LASCIATE OGNE SPERANZA, VOI CH'ENTRATE" ("Abandon all hope, you who enter here"; *Inf.* 3.9). The damned are collectively "la perduta gente" ("the lost people"; *Inf.* 3.3), who are wretched primarily because they "hanno perduto il ben de l'intelletto" ("have lost the good of the intellect"; *Inf.* 3.18). In a technical theological sense, this means that they have forfeited the beatific vision of God for which the intellect was formed: to know God "face to face" (1 Cor. 13.12 [Douay-Rheims]) is the ultimate goal of all rational creation in Dante's universe. More broadly, however, losing the good of the intellect means forfeiting the opportunity to know anything new, to become anyone different, or to move forward. The damned are all stuck within themselves and their past histories. This is what the pilgrim incrementally discovers as he descends "lo cammino alto e silvestro" ("the deep and savage way"; *Inf.* 1.142). Soul after soul is given the chance to speak to him but in doing so only relives the past, unable to exist outside its strictures. Hell is an endless replay.

Purgatory reverses this downward direction in every possible way, even as it shows the ability of the penitents to move beyond where they were in mortal life. The souls regain the true selves they lost to sin by moving from vices to virtues, from imperfect sight to ever-clearer vision. On the terrace of pride, for instance, they suffer under the heavy burden of their past egos, which are represented by the stone under which each is bowed down. Their punishment is to carry this increasingly oppressive and false persona until they can willingly let go of it. When they are able to do so, they stand tall—that is, humbly—free at last from what they mistakenly thought to be their true selves. The imprisonment of the vice is transformed into the freedom of the virtue. The self-important worm becomes the angelic butterfly it was always meant to be.

The penitents also learn to be in community. Whereas the damned are radically alone, no matter how dense the crowd, the penitents discover one another. *Inferno*'s relentless "I"—the song of myself that is sung from bolgia to bolgia—

is gradually replaced by the sense of a corporate "we." Infernal soloists become part of a purgatorial chorus chanting psalms, singing hymns, and reciting the prayers of the church.

Typically, the damned hold fast to all the makers and allegiances of where they came from, as if being from Florence or Siena, or belonging to the Ghibellines or to a particular brand of Guelph, summed up their identity. In Purgatory, however, the pilgrim discovers a new sense of identification. When he asks on the terrace of envy if anyone there is Italian, presumably so that he can pray for them, he is told that whereas all of them used to be from here or there, now "ciascuna è cittadina / d'una vera città" ("each one here is a citizen of a true city"; *Purg.* 13.94–95). The loss of one identity, both civic and personal, leads to the discovery of another.

Loss and rediscovery are also a way to understand what awaits the pilgrim at the Edenic summit of Mount Purgatory. For it is there in *Purgatorio* 30, in the long-anticipated presence of Beatrice, that Dante turns to share the excitement of the experience with Virgil only to discover that his beloved guide is no longer there. We have been alerted to this exchange from the opening canto of the poem, when Virgil foretold this very moment: "anima fia a ciò più di me degna: / con lei ti lascerò nel mio partire" ("you'll find a soul more fit to lead than I: / I'll leave you in her care when I depart"; *Inf.* 1.122–23). No fair warning, however, mitigates the loss of Virgil—not the resurrected presence of Beatrice nor a return to the beauties of Eden and "né quantunque perdeo l'antica matre" ("all that our ancient mother [Eve] lost"; *Purg.* 30.52).

Here, too, students may be invited to enter into this moment by reflecting on their personal histories. Is there someone like Virgil in their lives who taught them to know themselves, or to move beyond obstacles with steady encouragement and the occasional tough love? Is there a Beatrice, not necessarily a romantic interest but someone who helped them move beyond the "dark wood," who taught them to love?

In the final heavenly leg of the journey, Dante learns not only of what he will come to lose on earth but what he will gain as recompense: a commission to write the poem we are reading. That command comes first from Beatrice at the end of *Purgatorio* (32.103–05 and 33.52–54). Beatrice charges him, once he returns to mortal life, to write down what he has seen during the journey, and to do so for those who are alive—for his future readers—whose life is most likely "un correre a la morte" ("a race to death"; *Purg.* 33.54). In *Paradiso* 17, his great-great grandfather, the Florentine Cacciaguida, emboldens him to make his entire vision plain (127–29) regardless of the consequences to doing so. He is not to be a "al vero . . . timido amico" ("timid friend of truth"; 118). Similarly, no less a figure than Saint Peter charges him to open his mouth and hide nothing of what has been revealed to him (*Par.* 27.64–66).

The city Dante loved and to which he devoted himself may have forever closed its doors to his return; nonetheless, he will venture back another way. The *Commedia* will serve as his means of entry, as he suggests in the poignant address to the reader in *Paradiso* 25.1–12. And yet, from the final perspective of the *Paradiso*, all that he lost on earth has been compensated for by a new and ultimate sense of belonging elsewhere, in "quella Roma onde Cristo è romano" ("that Rome where Christ is a Roman"; *Purg.* 32.102). Or, as the pilgrim himself reflects with amazement, standing in the midst of the City of God: "ïo, che al divino da l'umano, / a l'etterno dal tempo era venuto, / e di Fiorenza in popol giusto e sano" ("I, who had come to things divine from man's estate, / to eternity from time, / from Florence to a people just and sane"; *Par.* 31.37–39).

Students who do not share Dante's faith in an afterlife may not find his religious consolation for earthly loss compelling. What they should all be able to recognize, however, is how writing the poem enabled him to use his negative experience to shape a "vita nuova"—a new life. What he gave up as a prior he gained as an author. Out of his devastation came the work of which we are the beneficiaries.

NOTES

[1] All citations of Dante are to the editions found on the *Princeton Dante Project*: Hollander and Hollander's translation of the *Commedia*, Lansing's translation of the *Convivio*.

[2] See also Elizabeth Coggeshall's essay in this volume for a slightly different take on these two books.

[3] An excellent source for biographical information and insight is Santagata's *Dante: The Story of His Life*.

[4] The Exodus "sails" into the *Commedia* in *Purgatorio* 2 in the form of the opening line of Psalm 113, "In exitu Israel de Aegypto" (Vulgate), or "When Israel went out of Egypt" (*Biblia sacra*). This is only the most overt reference to this Old Testament event with its New Testament interpretations. Dante also uses the psalm to instruct his readers how to interpret his poem the *Letter to Can Grande della Scala*, paragraphs 20–25. For Dante's relation to the Bible, see Hawkins, *Dante's Testaments* 36–53.

Teaching Dante and the Visual Arts

Aida Audeh

There are numerous reasons to teach Dante with the visual arts. Artists working in visual media have been inspired by Dante's text for centuries, from the earliest illuminated manuscripts of the fourteenth century to postmodern animated film. Students are drawn to imagery, particularly in this increasingly visual world, and the wide variety of imagery inspired by Dante can in turn inspire students to understand the text more deeply through examination of these various artistic interpretations, especially when they turn on key moments in the narrative.

Organizing a Course on Dante and the Visual Arts

When teaching Dante and the visual arts, the first consideration is to decide which aspect will guide the organization of the course: the art itself or Dante's poem. If the artworks themselves are the guide, then the instructor familiar with art historical development can organize the course chronologically, discussing Dante's influence on art beginning with the Middle Ages and early Renaissance and working through the centuries and their movements to the present day. This approach might work best in a course taught by two instructors, one an art historian and one a specialist in Dante or comparative literature, as it is rare to find one instructor with expertise in both fields.

Because most instructors interested in teaching Dante and the visual arts will be proficient in textual analysis rather than art history, however, the remainder of this essay provides guidance for courses driven by Dante's text, where the instructor intends to incorporate visual imagery as a complement to robust literary analysis. The model is tailored to a semester-long course, though it certainly would work well in a yearlong class. A course of this kind can be adapted for any level of college student of any specialization and is even appropriate for graduate students.

When I teach the course, more experienced students with backgrounds in art history write research papers investigating three artists' interpretations of a single canto and are expected to incorporate critical literature on Dante's poem as well as art historical secondary literature. All students in my class, whatever their background, must complete a study workbook as they read each canto and take essay exams in class on specific cantos and associated imagery. I am not so much interested in testing students' memory in this class as I am in inspiring enthusiasm in them for Dante's poem as one of the most significant achievements in Western culture and introducing them to art historical analysis and interpretation through focus on this text.

Thus, assignments, exams, and so on can vary depending on the individual instructor's goal(s) for the course. I look for students to relate the imagery to the complexity of Dante's poem in their own words in a plausible and accurate manner—given the multiplicity of meanings possible with Dante—not to regurgitate class discussion or assigned readings. I want to know students have absorbed Dante's way of thinking as expressed in the poem and can work intelligently with it in relation to imagery of different periods inspired by it, incorporating in their analysis aspects of traditional art historical method.

Art Historical Method

A mistake I've seen too often in non–art historians' use of art in approaching Dante is to equate formal choices or characteristics in visual art with the artists' personal expression or psychological state. This would be false—as false as to approach the poem itself solely as an expression of Dante's personal psychology devoid of larger context. Thus, a course on Dante and the visual arts should attempt to help students understand the poem within its larger context through text and imagery while weaving in the art historical developments that parallel the literary, theological, philosophical, and political developments that frame and inform our approach to it.

As an art historian, I recommend using the compare-contrast method of stylistic categorization and analysis for elucidating important similarities and differences in imagery. Pioneered by Heinrich Wölfflin in the late nineteenth and early twentieth centuries, this approach is a foundational method for art historical analysis. For the purposes of understanding Dante's poem, and the works of art inspired by it, presenting carefully selected pairs or groupings of images is most effective.

Further, it is essential to introduce students to Erwin Panofsky's concept of "iconography-iconology" (Adams 43–64; art historians tend to use the term "iconography" to refer to both Panofsky's iconographic and iconological analyses) in visual art early in the semester so it is understood that art should be considered a shared visual language, a visual dialogue, with certain approaches to form and content, which embody meaning in Western arts passed down through centuries, from the classicism of antiquity on through the twentieth century and beyond. Students' understanding of how iconography works to communicate meaning in visual art is parallel to their understanding of Dante's use of literal and allegorical meaning in language. The word signifies multiple meanings simultaneously, as does the image. And the word/image has resonances with other words/images outside itself, which layer that meaning across various contexts, creating a dialogue through time and taking part in a larger tradition of literature/art.[1]

With these analytical approaches one can begin to take students through the poem with meaningful discussion of artistic interpretation over time. Just as Dante's poem is layered with meanings drawn from myriad literary sources, art inspired by it is layered with meanings drawn not only from the poem itself but also from visual sources external to it, some of which may have been in Dante's mind as he crafted his highly evocative descriptions of characters, dialogue, locations, actions, and events.

Applying Art Historical Method: Inferno Canto 1

To begin with a highly charged example: Dante's description of his presence in the dark wood opens the first canto of the *Inferno*: "Nel mezzo del cammin di nostra vita / mi ritrovai per una selva oscura, / che la diritta via era smarrita" ("Midway in the journey of our life I found myself in a dark wood, for the straight way was lost").[2] Dante addresses the question of authorship immediately upon beginning his poem: "mi ritrovai" ("I found myself"). He takes the unique position of narrator and protagonist of the narrative at once, as he tells his story as memory. Dantists are familiar with the "Pilgrim/Poet" as a literary device and introduce this to students as crucial to understanding the poem. How is this dual role represented in visual art?

I have found that the most astute understanding of this dual role is found in the fifteenth-century Venetian manuscript found in the Biblioteca Nazionale Marciana, Venice, Cod. It. IX, 276 (=6902) (reproduced in Samek-Ludovici and Ravenna 21). On this single page Dante is presented in both roles. In the upper left corner, most immediate in time, Dante is shown as the poet writing the *Divine Comedy* in the position—and with the typical writing desk—of scribe or, more appropriately here, saint/prophet.

An apt visual comparison to demonstrate the iconographic tradition that the Venetian illustrator references is provided by the *Aachen Gospels* of the ninth century, featuring typical early medieval evangelist portrait prototypes of the divinely inspired saint noting his transformative experiences for posterity.

This iconographic tradition itself derived from the secular-classical precedent for depictions of author-philosophers, such as found in the fifth-century Roman Virgil (see Vergilius Romanus). From here, the instructor can go into further detail, with reference to *Inferno* 2, regarding Paul and Aeneas as precedents for Dante's journey to the afterlife and back, thus his placing of himself in the footsteps of both a saint and an epic hero (though he questions his suitability to undertake the journey). Drawing the context out further, both Dante and the Venetian illustrator rely on classical pagan and medieval Christian precedents and prototypes, consistent with larger Renaissance developments from the fourteenth and fifteenth centuries.

Similarities and differences between the two images can be brought out during discussion. Important to mention is the historical and personal specificity given to the Dante image versus the generalized image of the evangelists in this case: Dante is presented in a blue cloak and red cap, is seated in a wooden writing niche and desk, and sees before him the starry skies he references in his poem. The evangelists, on the other hand, are presented in a natural setting to indicate the larger world, and their divinity is represented by the figuration of a halo encircling the head of each. Thus, Dante's secular identity is preserved while the *allusion* to a divine calling or mission is made through the iconographic reference to evangelist portraits without naming his explicitly as such through the presence of a halo or the wearing of prophet-like garb. In this sense, Dante poet is nearly prophet, but not quite. The placement of the image of Dante as poet in the upper left corner of the page signals its primary placement in the narrative—we are to recognize Dante in his role as the author before we read his words that begin just below.

But Dante is also the pilgrim who undertakes the difficult journey. The Venetian artist represents this on the same page in two places (both below and a bit larger in format than the initial poet image), presenting the dramatic incidences of the text that are at the foreground of our attention as we read. On the lower left of the page there is a quite large image of Dante attempting to climb the hill toward the light and facing the three beasts that drive him back, the she-wolf given prominence as the uppermost of the three and to which Dante points specifically.

A bit higher on the page, to the right, the Venetian artist represents Dante beginning his journey toward knowledge of sin with Virgil's guidance—his pilgrimage. In this image, the artist references compositions associated with pilgrimages common in the Middle Ages and early Renaissance, such as the German pilgrimage woodcut of the fifteenth century (gettyimages.com/photos/566451825). Using the compare-contrast method, the instructor can draw out from students the essential similarities in these two images, which communicate the idea of pilgrimage: moving, in pairs, one seeming to guide toward something (there is a goal to which they move—they are not aimlessly wandering). They walk in space that is believable as an earthly plain, as something of actual and direct physical experience, analogous to the spiritual work and transformation that occurs through physical suffering. The act of pilgrimage communicates a sense of experiencing the attainment of salvation—pilgrimage—as a time-based process, very typical of the Western approach to spirituality as something measurable, organized, and hierarchical. The Venetian artist's reference to the iconography of pilgrimage emphasizes Dante's role in the journey as pilgrim—as human in his weakness and seeking to achieve salvation.

Differences in the images can be elicited through discussion as well. The roughness of the pilgrimage image is a reflection of its medium as a woodcut—a cheap and easily reproducible form in the Middle Ages, which communicates the commonness or universality of the pilgrimage experience at that time. Woodcuts and guides to pilgrimage were produced in the Middle Ages and were available at little cost. In contrast, the illustrated manuscripts of the *Divine Comedy* available in the late Middle Ages and early Renaissance were luxury objects—rare and available only at great expense. The exquisite nature of the hand-painted imagery of the Venetian artist speaks to the socioeconomic privilege of the owner of the manuscript and the devotion given to the text of Dante as nearly equal to that which one would give to Holy Scripture at the time. Most people living on the Italian peninsula were illiterate and were familiar with Dante's poem through public readings of the work, whereas those of wealth could perhaps afford to purchase or commission their own illustrated manuscript copy. Thus, it can be elucidated through discussion of the two images that Dante's poem was both elite and popular, as it has been since its writing, with a broad audience enjoying it through various visual, written, and aural forms.

Moreover, the specificity of Dante's clothing, the exact repetition of that of Dante as poet in the upper left corner of the page, emphasizes his individuality—he is not just any pilgrim—and also highlights his dual role as pilgrim-poet. In addition, we note Virgil's double presence in the pilgrimage image: Virgil walks near Dante but is also pictured turning to observe Dante's failure to climb the hill as he is driven back by the three beasts in the image below, thus providing a link between the two illustrations. The doubling of Virgil in the pilgrimage image is referred to as *continuous narrative* and is a technique common to visual art of the medieval and early Renaissance periods. We do not see that in the pilgrimage woodcut.

To jump to a late-nineteenth-century comparison, very different in approach, I would bring in Auguste Rodin's representation of Dante on his *Gates of Hell*. The *Gates* were commissioned as a sculpted illustration of the *Divine Comedy* in the form of bronze doors by the French state in 1880 for a planned but never realized museum of the decorative arts. The representation of Dante on the *Gates* is known independently as the *Thinker* but was created originally to sit atop the lintel of the *Gates*, observing the actions of hundreds of nude human forms above, below, and behind him. Rodin does not present the figure of Dante more than once in the work—he does not resort to the medieval technique of continuous narrative—but he also does not observe any traditional sort of single-point perspective space within his sculpted relief. In this he partakes of medieval traditions typical of Last Judgment imagery such as that of the tympanum at Saint Lazare Cathedral at Autun. In Rodin's interpretation Dante-Thinker in fact takes the position traditionally given to Christ sitting in judgment in medieval and Renaissance imagery. In this sense Rodin enlarges Dante's poet-prophet allusion to one that is more Christ-like yet ties his Dante to the others on the *Gates* through their common nudity.

Rodin also rejects the use of historically specific costume in presenting his Dante, so that his Dante becomes the modern everyman: "Midway in the journey of *our* life" (*Inf.* 1.1; my emphasis). Dante's quest is a universal one, as Rodin presents it, in contrast to the traditional presentation of Dante with his red cap, aquiline nose, and so on. In this way, working in the late nineteenth century, with many years of artistic innovation from which to draw, Rodin communicates Dante's dual role of pilgrim-poet through his placement, alluding to Christ as omnipotent creator of the narrative and judge of the actions he witnesses but addresses through his vulnerable, naked form; humanity; weakness; and position as seeking pilgrim, like the hundreds of others on the *Gates* who in their nudity engage in gestures ranging from pure torment to bliss. Rodin's use of nudity is at once a reference to classicism and a rejection of its idealized perfectionism as he uses it as a vehicle of expression, the way Dante used classical allusion as a means to express his profoundly Christian worldview. The freedom with which Rodin approaches his interpretation, drawing from centuries of artistic tradition yet breaking it at will, reflects the state of French art in the Postimpressionist era, where the stranglehold of the strict classicism of the French Academy had been challenged and largely overcome in painting and sculpture.

To broaden the view to a larger context, Rodin's late-nineteenth-century interpretation reflects the interest in Dante that has continued to the present day, where the medieval poet has taken on significance for the modern world. By the late nineteenth century, Dante had come to mean many things, from representing political radicalism in service of the Risorgimento in Italy to religious conservatism for the Catholic right in France. In Rodin's work Dante represents the hapless modern person, nearly paralyzed by angst while seeking God in a godless industrial society on the brink of the First World War. Rodin also sought, and achieved, a name for himself, through taking on this monumental poetic work in a creation of an equally monumental sculpture, working with that staple of classical art and tradition—the nude—but reconfiguring it to question the belief in the possibility of an ideal world in contemporary France.

In *Inferno* 1 alone I could go on with examples of how artists represent the "dark wood" and the "straight way," how visual precedent relied on concepts of landscape going back to visions of classical Arcadia, biblical Eden, the meanings communicated in Western visual and literary traditions through allusion to wild, untamed nature versus controlled, enclosed gardens, and so on. A discussion of a single work of art in relation to Dante's poem can easily fill a class hour, so it is important to pace discussion to be sure that what the instructor deems most significant in text and image is touched on during class discussion or lecture.

Selecting Works of Art

The definitive work on Dante imagery of the Middle Ages and early Renaissance is, of course, the two-volume *Illuminated Manuscripts of the Divine Comedy* by Peter Brieger, Millard Meiss, and Charles S. Singleton, for it provides a good basis to begin an exploration of the iconographic traditions associated with each canto. There is more in these two volumes than can ever be covered in a single semester, or even in a yearlong course on Dante and the visual arts, so I suggest that each instructor consider first which elements of the text are most important to discuss at length in a classroom setting and investigate with Brieger et. al. the basic iconographic tradition associated with that particular passage or concept in Dante. Identify what to focus on—perhaps one significant aspect from each canto or from groups of two or three cantos where a certain pattern in Dante's journey is emerging: I suggest one major concern or event from *Inferno* 1–3 and two or three noteworthy encounters or moments of understanding from the cantos of Incontinence (5–8), Violence (12–17), Fraud (18–30), and Treachery (32–34).

Moving forward to art of the eighteenth through the twenty-first centuries, one can select from any number of printed and digital resources for comparative imagery for a particular canto. There are, of course, the well-known illustrated editions by John Flaxman, William Blake (see Klonsky), and Gustave Doré, but for those seeking more challenging comparisons there are individual works of art by significant artists such as Henry Fuseli, Eugène Delacroix, Ary Scheffer, Dante Gabriel Rossetti, Jean Baptiste Carpeaux, and Rodin, to name but a few. The most significant interest in Dante in modern art (c. 1800–1950) was shown in nineteenth-century France, which produced over two hundred works of painting, sculpture, and minor arts exhibited at its annual state-sponsored exhibition (the "Salon") between 1800 and 1921. England is a close second, with significant interest borne by the Pre-Raphaelite Brotherhood and artists inspired by them. Germany also had its share of interested artists earlier in the nineteenth century in the works of the Nazarenes. French and English interest is most thoroughly documented, although not all images are readily available in digital format for easy incorporation into a *PowerPoint* class lesson (see the list of sources at the end of this essay). For those interested in the twentieth century, there are several films that could be analyzed in relation to art—as the influence of Doré is very clear in them—most particularly the Milano Films *Inferno* of 1911 and Sandow Birk's postmodern animated interpretation of 2007.

Depending on what an instructor feels comfortable discussing in relation to Dante's poem and on that person's own interests in and knowledge of certain periods of art, the selection of works of art (or even film) will be highly individual. As I am a specialist in European painting and sculpture of the eighteenth and nineteenth centuries, I place my focus there in relation to medieval and Renaissance imagery as a basis for the iconographic traditions. Others may be more comfortable with modernist interpretations of the twentieth century such as Rico LeBrun, Salvador Dalí, and others, to use in comparison with earlier imagery culled from Brieger et al.

Some Considerations

Note that the imagery of the selected works is not subservient to Dante's text, but parallel to it, and participates in visual culture's larger development, as artists find inspiration in the poem and seek to interpret it in various contexts, from illustration alongside text to stand-alone works of art such as paintings or sculptures.

For example, the earliest illuminated manuscripts of the *Comedy* with substantial imagery beyond historiated letters beginning each canticle are believed to originate along with the commentary traditions on the poem and sometimes responded directly to specific commentary. In other instances it is thought that imagery directly contradicts commentary associated with a particular manuscript, or even contradicts Dante's text itself. The instructor should make careful choices with regard to relation of text and commentary.

Keep in mind that often the artists working on illustrations in the Middle Ages and early Renaissance were for the most part not known by name, were part of a larger workshop, and may have worked on more than one manuscript. Duties were divided and probably undertaken in this order: calligraphy, gilding, painting (illustrating). In many cases it is not known for certain exactly how or even whether these artists working on illustrations were advised or given guidance in their approach to the creation of imagery. Thus, in all but a few cases, making definite claims about an artist's intention with respect to illuminated manuscripts is not advisable.

And although eighteenth- and nineteenth-century creators of illustrated editions were usually considered commercial and therefore not serious artists at the time, some were in a class apart by virtue of their work in other media, such as Blake, who was also a poet in his own right. It is also important to point out that for a commercial illustrator like Flaxman, the subject was one of many he illustrated on commission, whereas for Doré, the subject was his choice (self-funded) and, unusually for his time, was taken up as a calculated risk on which he meant to stake his claim as a serious artist alongside his individual large format paintings based on Dante's *Comedy*.

When we consider painters and sculptors of the eighteenth, nineteenth, and twentieth centuries who took up Dante and his writing as subject matter for their work, an entirely different situation is at play. Delacroix, for example, selected a subject from Dante's *Inferno* not to participate in the workshop illustration tradition and render the entire poem but as a means to make his mark as an up-and-coming painter circa 1822. At that time, Dante as author was recognized in France as of the same caliber as Shakespeare and as an equally valid but progressive alternative to classical authors of antiquity favored as a basis for subject matter. Thus, like Delacroix, an artist seeking to create a name for himself in the late eighteenth or early nineteenth century would use a scene from the *Comedy* as a way to showcase his technical ability, whether in painting or sculpture; provide legitimacy for his efforts through his choice of subject; and stake his claim to originality through some variation in approach to it (though not departing too far from what would have been acceptable at the time). By the mid– to late nineteenth century, however, taking a subject from Dante would be considered more mainstream than progressive, and an artist would be doing so for different reasons than did Delacroix earlier in the century. By the early twentieth century, a literary subject such as Dante's *Comedy* could be seen as downright old-fashioned in the context of movements such as fauvism, cubism, and dadaism, for example. An artist's choice to take the *Comedy* up at that point would be a definite strike against some of these movements moving toward abstraction and conceptualism in art, a sort of nod to a bygone era of art based on a canonical textual source.

In discussing Dante and the visual arts in a classroom setting, it is crucial to point out that artists took up the subject for varied reasons, patrons, and audiences, and in widely differing circumstances. Thus, the approach should not simply be one of whether or not the image in question is an accurate rendition of Dante's text. Rather, unique aspects of an image should be used to draw out this larger context within which the artist was working.

Finally, in teaching Dante and the visual arts the instructor need not inundate students with hundreds of images, nor feel the need to cover everything, for that is not possible. Rather, instructors should select those images that best generate the most productive discussion given the focus for the course or for the particular canto or group of cantos for that day.[3]

NOTES

[1] For those wishing to teach Dante and the visual arts but who are unfamiliar with the basic art historical method, I suggest reading a quick summary of two primary analytic approaches: *stylistic analysis* and *iconographic analysis*. Readings on these approaches could be assigned to students in the class as well, to establish a foundation for analyzing works of art shown in class. I suggest Adams's *The Methodologies of Art* for its highly readable summary of these important analytic approaches. When I teach Dante and the Visual Arts to a class composed primarily of non–art history majors, I devote an entire session to discussion of these methods. For those unfamiliar with iconography or imagery generally, I suggest consulting online resources, such as the digitized version of Bartsch (www.artstor.org/collection/illustrated-bartsch/) or other comprehensive sources. For handy but limited references that can be obtained individually I suggest

Hall's *Dictionary of Subjects and Symbols in Art* and Ferguson's *Signs and Symbols in Christian Art*. For those seeking a general guide to art historical development for their own information as they develop the course, I recommend the well-known series *Gardner's Art through the Ages*, available in multiple editions and in various configurations. Each period is given a chapter with good historical background to set the context, and the major monuments are pictured and thoroughly explained. The bibliography is helpful if the instructor seeks more specific information on any particular period, movement, work, or artist.

[2] All quotations and translations from the *Divine Comedy* come from Singleton's edition.

[3] Though certainly not an exhaustive list, I find the following sources on visual arts in relation to Dante useful in preparing my course on the subject: Adams; Audeh, "Dante in the Nineteenth Century," "Dante's Ugolino," "Dufau's *La Mort d'Ugolin*," "Gustave Doré's Illustrations," "Images," and the essays on Rodin's *Gates of Hell* and on Van Gogh's interest in Dante; Barricelli; Bindman et al.; Braida and Calè; Brieger et al.; Clark; Doré; Ferguson; Flaxman; Fugelso; Hall; Havely, *Dante in the Nineteenth Century* and *Dante's Modern Afterlife*; Holbrook; Iannucci, *Dante, Cinema, and Television* and *Dante: Contemporary Perspectives*; Klonsky; Le Normand-Romain; Mather; Nassar; Samek-Ludovici and Ravenna; Schulze Altcappenberg; Taylor and Finley; Volkmann. The following Web sites have substantial imagery: *Divine Comedy Image Archive*; *Dante Today* (Saiber and Coggeshall); *Danteworlds* (Raffa); the *Princeton Dante Project*; *The World of Dante*.

Reading Dante's *Comedy* with Giotto

Heather Webb

It is a commonplace among those who teach undergraduates to claim that our students today are more visually than textually inclined. They have an easier time, we say, talking about images than texts. For this reason, at the University of Cambridge, we begin our first-year course in Italian Literature and Culture with Giotto's Arena Chapel. Students quickly learn to analyze what they see in each scene, pointing out color, gesture, and the ways Giotto directs the eye around the scene. From there, we teach them to make connections between separate bands of narrative, looking above, below, and across from the scene they might be analyzing. How does Judas's embrace of Christ, along with all the other notably outstretched arms in that scene, create a strong contrast with the outstretched arms in the scene directly above, the presentation of Christ at the temple? How do all the bristling spears in the lower panel direct the eye upward, to the tender scene of a mother and child reaching toward one another? And what might this link do to reinforce the central messages of the chapel? The students thus acquire the skills to look closely at the particular, but also to put their close attention to the particular into a broader context.

As Christopher Kleinhenz notes in his essay "On Dante and the Visual Arts," it seems entirely possible that Dante borrowed structural techniques for his poem from the visual arts. Kleinhenz focuses on the mosaics of the Baptistery in Florence that Dante would have looked on in childhood. The habit of reading typological or allegorical relations between scenes that are placed one above the other at the same time as one reads storylines horizontally would have been further reinforced by Dante's viewing of major fresco programs such as that of the Arena Chapel in Padua (Kleinhenz, "On Dante" 282–83). The pervasive use of vertical parallels between scriptural (and indeed classical and mythological) events and persons through different visual media—from mosaics and frescoes to the architecture and sculptures of churches and cathedrals—highlights, therefore, a familiar medieval exegetical practice.

At Cambridge, we have recently engaged in an experiment to test fully, for the first time, the degree to which the entire *Comedy* might be profitably read in this way, by looking for vertical parallels.[1] If we keep multilevel visual programs such as the Baptistery mosaics or the Arena Chapel in mind, it is easy to imagine the three canticles of the *Comedy* inscribed one above the other in bands so that—literally—we could read either horizontally (reading each canto in numerical order) or vertically (reading cantos of the same number in sets of three upward from *Inferno* to *Paradiso* or downward from *Paradiso* to *Inferno*).

As Brenda Deen Schildgen puts it in her introduction to a recent issue of the journal *Pedagogy* on teaching Dante, "This systematic approach to interpreting the poem provides a wholly new way, not just to read the poem, but to teach it across the three canticles. Teaching the *Comedy* vertically offers a way to address issues that cross the poem and to select cantos that deal with Dante's principal concerns" (Introduction 452). Schildgen suggests that for a core curriculum or great-books course, rather than teaching *Inferno*, so often perceived as the most accessible canticle, and leaving the other canticles untouched, one might follow a thematic structure instead. The edition of *Pedagogy* offers essays that facilitate teaching the poem vertically, for the purposes of a context in which Dante is taught as part of a general curriculum with a number of canonical authors. Schildgen notes that "teaching the poem by extricating a single canticle unfortunately gives a distorted view of what Dante strove to achieve in his monumental work" (Introduction 453). The essays in that volume look at teaching Brunetto Latini through Cacciaguida (Monica Keane) and teaching justice and vision in the *Comedy* through the cantos numbered 19 (Jessica Wilson), to give just two examples.

I had the luxury of teaching a final-year undergraduate course at Cambridge that focused entirely on Dante and therefore did not face any of the pressures of fitting Dante into a great-books course. Nonetheless, in conversation with the students, we decided that a vertical approach would be most useful. The students felt that if we proceeded horizontally, starting with *Inferno* and moving from there to *Purgatorio* and then to *Paradiso*, we ran the usual risk of running out of time when we got to *Paradiso*, in precisely the canticle where students need the most help. They thought they had a reasonable grasp on *Inferno* but felt most at sea and in need of guidance for *Paradiso*. The vertical approach provided clear points of access to the *Paradiso*. Thus, from the very first class, we discussed the *Paradiso* alongside the other canticles.

For our discussion of all three cantos 10 and all three cantos 11, we held a joint seminar with students in art history who were studying Giotto that term with Donal Cooper. Cooper and I cotaught a class in which we explored the shared conditions between viewership and readership in a vertical reading with Giotto. Cooper has been working on the relation between preaching and pictures, on the one hand, and the visual links between tiers of the program at Assisi on the other (see Cooper and Robson; Cooper). There was, therefore, a natural affinity of research interests in this research-led seminar. We began by thinking about how we might explore analogies between the structure of the *Comedy* and fresco and mosaic cycles of the period, above all the possibility of reading through visual and verbal texts in different ways. For instance, Cooper's book on Assisi, coauthored with Janet Robson, discusses the ways the *Stigmatization* depicting Saint Francis reveals links between the fresco cycles of the basilica at Assisi. In the *Stigmatization*, Francis kneels and looks up and to the right at the Christ-Seraph but "if the diagonal of his gaze is continued beyond the limits of the pictorial frame, it leads up to the first scene on the middle tier of the next bay, the *Crucifixion*" (131). Francis can thus be witnessed experiencing a double vision that extends beyond his own narrative band and into the

Passion cycle. As Cooper and Robson put it: "By means of such visual links between the tiers, the overall nave program continually becomes more than the
sum of its individual parts" (131). Likewise, the *Comedy* is a text that continu-
ously points from one moment in the narrative to another moment in the narrative, often in another canticle. When we read the poem beyond the limits of the
frame of the canto or of the canticle, we see how it constructs itself as much
more than the sum of its individual parts. The poem's insistent self-referentiality
can be intimidating to students, as this self-referentiality is often discussed in
the criticism by means of long lists and a dense network of references. But what
happens if we take this as a new way of seeing? What if we find a new way to
look at and in the poem?

In *Purgatorio* 10, in fact, Virgil tells Dante, who is gazing in awe at the bas-
reliefs on the Terrace of Pride: "non tener pur ad un loco la mente" ("don't keep
your mind fixed only on one part"; *Purg.* 10.46).[2] For Michel Alpatoff, this admonition shows "how Giotto's contemporaries were accustomed to regard reliefs or frescoes" (154). But there may also be reasons to suspect that Virgil's
instructions here could be meant more broadly for the reader of the poem.
Gervase Rosser argues, "The *Divine Comedy* used the medium of poetry to
educate its Trecento reader in how to see" (482). Thus, although much of the
critical tradition has worried the problem of the primacy of text over image or
vice versa as asserted in the text, it has proved much more profitable in the
classroom to think of the *Comedy* as working in much the same way as visual
art (see Barolini, "Re-presenting What God Presented"). Our engagement with
visual art can teach us to see the *Comedy* as a program made up of many parts
that point to one another in various ways. We can then train our eyes to move
between those parts in the most fruitful ways, opening up new hermeneutical
possibilities. So if we read the *Comedy* in the same way that we read one or
more fresco cycles in a single architectural space, we must think of ourselves as
viewers as well as readers.

Our collective research has shown that there are particularly strong links
between cantos of the same number, and that these cantos tend to send our
gaze from one to the other in particularly compelling ways. And of course the
cantos numbered 10 and 11 make for a perfect case study, as they explicitly
theorize the visual and even create a visual pattern. In what remains of this essay, I present some reflections on the three cantos 10 that lend themselves well
to discussion in a seminar setting with students who have read *Inferno* 10, *Purgatorio* 10, and *Paradiso* 10 in preparation for the class.

One can begin with Farinata:

"Vedi là Farinata che s'è dritto:
da la cintola in sù tutto 'l vedrai."
    Io avea già il mio viso nel suo fitto;
ed el s'ergea col petto e con la fronte
com'avesse l'inferno a gran dispitto.

"And see there, upright, risen, Farinata.
From cincture upwards you will see him whole."
 My gaze was trained already into his,
while he, brow raised, was thrusting out his chest,
as though he held all Hell in high disdain.
(*Inf.* 10.32–36)

Here it is helpful to show an *Imago pietatis*, such as that of Filippo Lippi, even though it is later, to give a sense of the genre. The description of Farinata rising from the tomb would, for many late medieval readers, conjure up known images of Christ rising from the tomb, visible from the waist up.[3] Farinata appears to us as a perversion of a known and familiar sacred image. The word "arte" itself is foregrounded here, in Dante's response to Farinata: "'S'ei fur cacciati, ei tornar d'ogne parte,' / rispuos'io lui, 'l'una e l'altra fiata; / ma i vostri non appreser ben quell'arte' ("'Scattered,' I answered, 'so they may have been, / but all came back from all sides, then and now. / And your men truly never learned that art.'"; *Inf.* 10.49–51). The "arte" here is the art of party politics, and, as K. P. Clarke notes in his essay "Humility and the (P)Arts of Art," features what will be a repetition of three rhyming words of a terzina, *parte-parte-arte*, which appear in *Inferno* 10.47, 49, 51; *Purgatorio* 10.8, 10, 12; and *Paradiso* 10.8, 10, 12. As Clarke highlights, this parallelism must be deliberately constructed, given that two of the instances in question occur in the same line numbers (206). They are, visibly, in the same place across canticles.

   The move from *Inferno* 10 to *Purgatorio* 10 transports us from the political arts and perverse images of resurrection to a glimpse of God's art, beginning with the bas-relief of the Virgin: "e avea in atto impressa esta favella / 'Ecce ancilla Dei', propriamente / come figura in cera si suggella" ("[a]nd from her stance and bearing there shone out / (exactly as an imprint sealed in wax) / '*Ecce ancilla Dei*,' word for word"; *Purg.* 10.43–45). How does the image create speech, rendered for us in text, and how does the text create the image? Here we might ask students to visualize the Virgin's stance and bearing. This calls for some historical reconstruction. I show the students Giovanni Pisano's 1298–1301 pulpit (Church of Sant'Andrea, Pistoia) and the detail of the Annunciation there for an example of bas-reliefs from the period. The Virgin recoils, her arms inward across her body, one hand tipped back. But this is only a contextual data point. Bodily postures and gestures are eloquent in *Purgatorio*, and they must be read carefully with as much density of medieval visual vocabulary as possible.[4] Giotto's Annunciation scene in the Arena Chapel shows the Virgin with her arms crossed in a show of humility. It is notable that Giotto also depicts the Virgin in this pose in the Presentation of the Virgin in the temple scene. This pose becomes something of an emblem for the Virgin's humility, a self-crossing that also foretells her Son's Crucifixion and resurrection. It is the same pose featured in the Coronation of the Virgin mosaics in the Duomo of Florence, dating from around 1300. With the students, we look through these images and discuss their connotations. How does the posture speak? How does Dante's text depend on our catalogue of visual images? Does Dante need Giotto or others here to communicate an image of God's art? How can we see the Virgin's stance here? How can we read her humility against Farinata's emblematic pride? How does Dante harness images and words together in his own "visibile parlare" ("visible speech"; *Purg.* 10.95)?

From discussion of these questions, we move on to instructions for both looking and reading, in which viewership and readership are productively conflated: "Non attender la forma del martìre: / pensa la succession; pensa ch'al peggio / oltre la gran sentenza non può ire" ("Don't dwell upon the form their sufferings take. / Think of what follows, and that, come the worst, / it can't go on beyond the Judgement Day"; *Purg.* 10.109–11). Just as earlier we noted how Virgil instructs Dante to move his eyes from one place to another and "non tener pur ad un loco la mente," here we receive similar instructions on how to read. We are to move beyond the particular, beyond the individual moment in time, beyond the individual instance, as Farinata resoundingly fails to do, and to contemplate a broader picture. The reader is asked to see this form within an expanded temporal scale, to see this scene within the context of the events that take place before and after. When reading and viewing, the detail must always be held in balance with the wider perspective.

This becomes even clearer when we move from here to *Paradiso* 10. Here, the *parte-parte-arte* rhyme recurs to again contemplate God's art, but this time on a cosmic scale:

> Leva dunque, lettore, a l'alte rote
> meco la vista, dritto a quella parte
> dove l'un moto e l'altro si percuote;
>   e lì comincia a vagheggiar ne l'arte
> di quel maestro che dentro a sé l'ama,
> tanto che mai da lei l'occhio non parte.

> Lift up your eyes, then, reader, and, along with
> me, look to those wheels directed to that part
> where motions—yearly and diurnal—clash.
>   And there, entranced, begin to view the skill
> the Master demonstrates. Within Himself,
> He loves it so, His looking never leaves.

> (*Par.* 10.7–12)

Here, if we gaze upon this divine art created by mutual love within the Trinity, simply to see this art is to participate in its perfection. We are contemplating another cross here, the cross where the equatorial circle and the ecliptic meet. In light of the *Imago pietatis* and the Virgin's pose of humility, this celestial cross reveals the role of love in creation, providing us with the greatest possible picture. Across the canticles, we redirect our gaze from the divisive, factional warfare of Montaperti to the humility of the Virgin's acceptance at the Annunciation to the love within the Trinity and the cosmic scale of creation.

I hope this essay has suggested some ways it may be helpful for students to learn to read Dante with Giotto. Rather than pushing questions of influence or citation that have been of interest to Dante scholars, the approach I outline focuses on empowering students to think of the poem as a structure within which they can choose lines to move through as they seek out connections. It also encourages them to think through the visual, whether investigating medieval images that could have informed the poem or its readers, or thinking of the poem as a visual text that takes visual art as its model as much as it does other texts. The *Paradiso*, I have found, is less forbidding for students when they can compare images, moments, or rhymes from within it with parallel or contrasting instances in *Purgatorio* and *Paradiso*. Instead of suggesting they must only move through the poem horizontally and comprehensively, this approach allows them to pick out strands of signification and compare the perspectives of each of the canticles. Above all, a vertical, visual approach, offers a new way to look.

NOTES

[1] Thirty-four speakers from the United Kingdom, the United States, and Italy came to present readings of each of the conumerary cantos and subsequently reworked their lectures as essays for three volumes of *Vertical Readings in Dante's* Comedy. In the same years as the lectures took place (2012–16), I tested vertical readings for pedagogical purposes in the classroom.

[2] I use the Petrocchi edition of the *Comedy* and Kirkpatrick's translations.

[3] On this image, see Cassell, "Dante's Farinata"; and Durling, "Canto X" (esp. 147–48).

[4] I discuss gestures in *Dante's Persons* and the postures of *Purgatorio* and some possible devotional contexts for those postures in "Postures of Penitence in Dante's *Purgatorio*."

Rewritings and Relevance:
Teaching Gloria Naylor's *Linden Hills* alongside Dante's *Inferno*

Suzanne Manizza Roszak

One pedagogical problem that arises in the world literature survey course is the need to cultivate student investment in premodern texts that may feel far removed from the contemporary moment in which students themselves are immersed. In my world literature course, an introductory-level lecture course at a large state-supported university, students are expected to immerse themselves in texts that range from the fourth century BCE to the early seventeenth century CE. Many of them will have at least a little bit of experience with ancient Greek texts like Sophocles's *Oedipus the King*, which seems to be commonly assigned in area secondary schools. Beyond that, however, my students tend to have little previous experience navigating either the Western or the non-Western texts that make up the curricular options for this general education course. Shakespeare's *The Tempest* is as unfamiliar as *The Ramayana*—and as tempting to tackle through SparkNotes rather than through close reading, as my students themselves have admitted to me. Some of this potential for alienation from the texts comes from their more foreign uses of language, and I try to mitigate that problem by choosing the most accessible translation of each. Yet there is no denying that on the surface, these dramas and narratives can also seem to take place in very strange worlds, centered on beliefs and values and conflicts and struggles that appear rather different from those of my student readers. I see it as my job to counterbalance this understandable impression, which only partly captures the rich realities of each text.

One way I address this teaching issue is by pairing Western and non-Western texts with their contemporary rewritings by American and global postcolonial authors, as I have found that this solution helps give students a sense of the continuing literary and cultural relevance of the earlier works. At the start of the course, for instance, we read *Oedipus the King* alongside portions of Ola Rotimi's *The Gods Are Not to Blame* and Euripides's *Medea* together with scenes from Cherríe Moraga's *The Hungry Woman*. Once students are able to identify the thematic links between Sophocles's vision and Rotimi's postcolonial commentary on the British presence in Nigeria, it becomes more difficult to claim that Sophocles's contemporary relevance is limited to his role in the development of psychoanalytic theories that raise eyebrows today. Moraga's reenvisioning allows students to draw connections between intersectional issues of gender, ethnicity, and nationality in Euripides (Medea herself is racialized as foreign in the play) and colliding currents of prejudice based on ethnicity, citizenship, linguistic identity, gender, sexual orientation, and other factors that can make Chicanx children and adults vulnerable to marginalization in the

United States. That the two plays can be understood through similar cultural-theoretical lenses despite their stark differences tends to prove surprising and intriguing for students.

This essay addresses one particularly fruitful pairing of texts from later in the course: Gloria Naylor's 1985 novel *Linden Hills* and Dante's *Inferno*. By making room for students to examine the echoes of Dante's text in a relatively recent work of American fiction, this approach to teaching Dante helps students become better able to identify the echoes of a premodern text in the present day. As a result, students become more engaged and invested in the material, which they perceive as more relevant to their own context. At the same time, in considering how Naylor reimagines Dante's circles of Hell as the streets of an affluent black bourgeois suburb, students also learn important lessons about literary adaptation, appropriation, and rewriting. They learn to analyze how an important African American novel adapts and reshapes a premodern European text, subversively challenging the primacy of the European literary tradition. In the process, they gain insight into the role of literature as a tool for social protest.

Contemporary readers might rightly challenge Catherine C. Ward's assertion that *Linden Hills* uses the architecture provided by Dante's original to "give . . . a universalizing mythic dimension to what otherwise *might be considered a narrow subject*, the price American blacks are paying for their economic and social 'success'" (67; emphasis mine). It would be absurd today to characterize questions of economic and social assimilation in black America as "narrow" or as insufficiently pressing on their own—especially in an era when police brutality is rampant and white supremacists are gaining access to the highest positions in the federal government, reintroducing urgent questions about the need for black Americans to divert their socioeconomic resources away from businesses and communities that directly or indirectly uphold racial inequality and white aggression. For a more satisfying overview of Naylor's text, we might turn to Bernard W. Bell, who describes the novel as "a Dantesque allegorical journey and critique of the crass materialism and spiritual alienation of the black Talented Tenth" (278). Whereas writers like Ward have suggested that a good deal of what is intriguing about *Linden Hills* comes from its connection to Dante's *Inferno*, I would suggest the opposite: that Dante's work becomes newly interesting and relevant for my students when read alongside Naylor's fiction.

My students do not read excerpts from *Linden Hills* until they have already read *Inferno*, although in another course with a less predetermined focus on the premodern texts, it would be possible not only to assign the entirety of Naylor's novel but also to have students read the two texts side by side. On the day when the first chapter of Naylor's novel is assigned, students arrive ready for a discussion of the correspondences between the two texts; since Dante falls near the end of the course, they have already had a few experiences with this type of comparative analysis and discussion. Still, instead of throwing them into the deep end of the pool, I begin with a bit of contextual grounding, providing some fundamental information about Naylor's work and her place in literary history, the type of information that my students have specifically mentioned that they enjoy learning in class. I like to make sure they're aware of the Black Arts–era precedent set by Amiri Baraka's own appropriation of Dante in *The System of Dante's Hell* as well as Naylor's own literary trajectory and the place of *Linden Hills* in the relative shadow of Naylor's National Book Award-winning *The Women of Brewster Place*. Mel Watkins's *New York Times* review of *Linden Hills*, I tell them, damned the novel with a kind of faint praise, calling it "ambitious . . . [a]lthough flawed" ("Circular Driveways"). Somehow, knowing that a book they are reading has been lauded as well as torn down a bit by critics seems to put my students at greater ease in discussing the text, as though this discontinuity in the critical responses to the book reinforces the acceptability of multiple readings of the novel and thus, in this way, makes class discussion a less risky proposition.

This background established, my students are ready to launch into a simple discussion of parallels and discontinuities between the two texts—what similarities to Dante does Naylor preserve? What more superficial changes does she make to the setting and time period, and how do they set the stage for larger adjustments to the central concerns of the book? We will have already discussed the political resonance of Dante's text in its original context; how might *Linden Hills* have functioned similarly or differently in a historico-political moment in which racial equality and justice for black Americans remained very much in doubt in the United States, and how might these aspects of the novel continue to resonate with contemporary readers in a national context in which not nearly enough has changed since 1985? Often, I have students work in pairs or small groups to discuss the more basic of these questions; as they share out during large-group discussion, we start to mull over the more intricate and complex topics.

One of the important effects of this approach is that it provides students with a very concrete illustration of the lasting impact of Dante's work. Naylor's example helps demonstrate to students that Dante's *Inferno* continues to have a wide readership into the present day; it is not just a book that grumbling students are obligated to read at the behest of crotchety English professors but a book that some of America's most exciting creative writers have themselves dived into as readers. In this way, Naylor becomes a sort of retroactive role model for my students as they finish their reading of Dante and begin to think about quizzes and papers centered on this material. Being exposed to Naylor's work with the book also helps show students that *Inferno* is worth reading not just for its own sake but because this reading process makes it possible to better understand the creative output that responds to it. Their reading of *Inferno* becomes more meaningful because it provides this valuable insight into Naylor's oeuvre and her distinctive contributions to contemporary American literature.

It would be a serious mistake to cast Naylor as a simple beneficiary of Dante's influence, and it is critical that students come to understand this as the discussion progresses. Some scholarly approaches to rewritings of canonical texts by American or global postcolonial writers of color threaten to reproduce a highly problematic worldview in which the earlier Western text is viewed as the valuable original and the rewriting as a derivative or imitative copy. A more helpful theoretical approach to understanding these rewritings is one that acknowledges the power of subversive appropriations in which the canonical Western text is turned on its head, used as a tool for critiquing the very culture from which it sprang and for collapsing the supposed distinctions between the dominant and nondominant cultures. This is a concept that my students are already familiar with by this point in the quarter, but for instructors who are just beginning to introduce this idea to students, excerpts from Homi Bhabha's *The Location of Culture* may be helpful. As Bhabha writes, "the exercise of colonial authority . . . requires the production of differentiations" between the colony and the colonizer "through which discriminatory practices can map out subject populations that are tarred with the visible and transparent mark of power" (158). The same, we might argue, is true of the United States as a settler colonialist nation that has long overvalued white Western cultural artifacts while aggressively attempting to distinguish them from those of indigenous, black, and other nonwhite communities. A rewriting like Naylor's disrupts this conveniently exaggerated vision of difference. At the same time, in reimagining a canonical text, *Linden Hills* redirects attention away from the canon itself and demands to become the center of the conversation, effecting a change that is still urgently needed in the education system of the United States, where not too long ago, for instance, the first-year literature course required as part of Columbia University's core curriculum included not a single American writer of color.

Although these ideas are rich fodder for large-group discussion, it can also be helpful to carve out opportunities for students to work introspectively with the material, thinking and freewriting in moments of solitude that appeal to students who might be a bit more intrapersonal in their strategies for processing and generating ideas. With this in mind, I like to ask students to think about the social justice issues that are closest to them personally, the ones they are most invested in bringing to light and ultimately eradicating. Once students have had a moment to reflect on their own values, I ask them to think about how they themselves might rewrite Dante's *Inferno* to make the rewritten text into a tool in these struggles. Given these instructions, students might reenvision Dante's work as a one-act play exposing the layers of ableist ideas and rhetoric in contemporary American society, or as a short story in which Dante's sinners morph into unrepentant mansplainers explaining women scientists' and historians' academic specialties for eternity. Depending on the course, there may even be some possibility of giving students a creative writing assignment that lets them enact one of their ideas more directly. When I do give this type of assignment, I ask students to compose a reflective companion essay in which they analyze their own rhetorical strategies in their creative piece; the results are often exciting.

Depending on the approach to literature that my students were exposed to in high school, some of them may never have really thought of literature—whether premodern or otherwise—as relevant to social protest. Other students may be used to the idea that contemporary texts have this type of social resonance and relevance, but they may feel alienated from premodern texts precisely because they find it difficult to visualize them as having this sort of engaging importance. Does it really make sense for us to invest our time in these earlier texts when there are such pressing current issues for us to consider, and when we have much more recent texts to help us address these issues? For students who are not used to thinking of literature as a vehicle for pursuing social justice, learning about Naylor's novel in itself has the potential to open up new avenues of thought. Meanwhile, for students who simply need a little encouragement to see that premodern texts, too, can be relevant to our current conversations surrounding social resistance and change, pairing Dante with Naylor creates a new perspective on the earlier text.

Large general education literature courses like the ones I teach can be challenging for instructors and students alike. At my university, these courses bring seventy students together in an auditorium-style setting with a single instructor and no teaching assistants, creating the danger of unengaged students feeling so anonymous in class that they risk falling asleep in the back of the room during tiring weeks. Especially in these contexts, I think, it is important to do the simple things: learn students' names and faces, occasionally crack a joke or two so that our humanity as instructors can still be visible to students who are sitting twenty rows back. These contexts, where anonymous disengagement feels like a risk, are ones where it is especially helpful to use somewhat unconventional methods like the one I've outlined here to make premodern texts come alive. Although *Linden Hills* technically falls outside the purview of my pre-1700 literature course, I've found that a little deviation from the standard curriculum is more than worth it. From the front of the room, I can see the engagement on my seventy students' faces as they turn to one another to talk in pairs about the correspondences and the discontinuities between Dante's and Naylor's texts. I can also see every single hand that flies up when I ask my students, after they've finished freewriting, to share the social issues that they are personally committed to and can imagine raising awareness of through their own rewritings of *Inferno*. Although I ask my students to speak in front of sixty-nine of their peers in these moments, even some of my shyer students will find their nervousness about public speaking overcome by their excitement about their own ideas. Naylor's novel, when paired with Dante's text, has done more than make the relevance of premodern literature more palpable to my students. It has also brought lessons to the forefront about the nature of literary rewritings, the importance of challenging the Western canon and subverting myths of cultural supremacy, and the essential role of literature in processes of social protest that remain as critical today as they were when Naylor published *Linden Hills*.

Teaching Dante through Music

Francesco Ciabattoni

Studying Dante and music may help students develop their knowledge of European history, art, philosophy, and literature, but, more important, it will provide them with a multidisciplinary perspective. Ideally, a course on Dante and music would be situated at the upper level in a program of Italian, European, or medieval studies or in a music curriculum. Students would probably need previous instruction in a relevant branch of the humanities in order to best succeed in a course focused on Dante and music. It could function as a lower-level course as well, but this would require more class preparation from the teacher. A course on Dante and music would be excellent to satisfy a general education requirement, especially if the teacher is willing to explore Dante's musical reception during the nineteenth and twentieth centuries. Teaching Dante and music will provide reinforcement and solid interdisciplinary skills on content pertaining to literature, history, art, philosophy, and, of course, music. It will inspire students to see a literary work in its broader cultural context and would be an ideal course to cross list as part of a strong multidisciplinary education. A course on Dante's *Commedia* with a musical focus could be approached in two ways: music in Dante's *Commedia* or the *Commedia* in music (i.e., musical settings of Dante's work). Such a course could easily be offered over a year, but a sensible selection of the material can fit into one semester.

Music in Dante's Commedia

In his poetry and prose, Dante refers to both the theory and the practice of music. The *Commedia* features many musical episodes, especially sacred songs in liturgical use. One teaching issue that a musical approach can address is an exploration of the *Commedia* from a structural standpoint: the *Inferno* sets the stage for the programmatic reversal effected by purgatorial and paradisiacal music. In my experience, contrasting musical episodes from *Inferno* to those in *Purgatorio* and *Paradiso* can generate fruitful discussions of the symmetrical aspects of Dante's poem. The music of the *Inferno* is, of course, cacophonous and harsh, but not without logic: it is the logic of ironic reversal and parodic recasting.

This approach, based in historiography and musicology, would be the most useful to illuminate Dante's text, especially the parts that refer to liturgical or secular songs. It is extremely beneficial for students to reconstruct and understand the contexts of Dante's musical quotations. One good Web resource is "Music" from *The World of Dante* (www.worldofdante.org/music.html), which lists the texts and translations along with audio clips of Gregorian chants of all the sacred songs in the *Commedia*. Sensible guidance is advised, however, since different versions of lyrics and music existed throughout Europe, and what we listen to today may not be what precisely filled Dante's ears. Another good Web resource is my "Musical Instruments in Dante's *Commedia*: A Visual and Acoustic Journey," on Columbia University's *Digital Dante* site.

One of the most extraordinary musical topoi in the *Commedia* is Dante's evocation of the Pythagorean-Platonic music of the spheres in *Paradiso* 1, when "the heavens you made eternal, / wheeling in desire, caught my attention / with the harmony you temper and attune" ("Quando la rota che tu sempiterni / desiderato, a sé mi fece atteso / con l'armonia che temperi e discerni"; 76–78)[1] and "the newness of the sound and the bright light" ("la novità del suono e 'l grande lume"; 82) surrounds the pilgrim as he ascends with Beatrice to the first Heaven. The *Commedia* is punctuated by oblique references to the music of the spheres, a theory rejected by Aristotle and Christian Scholastic theologians, and which Dante could therefore hardly endorse officially. But its echo rings distinctly in the singing of the angels in the terrestrial paradise: "they sang who always are in tune / with notes set down in the eternal spheres" ("anzi 'l cantar di quei che notan sempre / dietro a le note de li etterni giri"; *Purg.* 30.92–93); in Justinian's account of the harmony among the blessed: "differing voices make sweet music. / Just so our differing ranks in this our life / create sweet harmony among these wheels" ("diverse voci fanno dolci note; / così diversi scanni in nostra vita / rendon dolce armonia tra queste rote"; *Par.* 6.124–26); and again the music of the spheres is metonymically adumbrated in the angelic choirs:

> L'altro ternaro, che così germoglia
> in questa primavera sempiterna
> che notturno Arïete non dispoglia,
>   perpetüalemente 'Osanna' sberna
> con tre melode, che suonano in tree
> ordini di letizia onde s'interna.

> The second triad thus blossoming
> in this eternity of spring
> which no nocturnal Ram cuts short
> 'ever sings hosannas, the threefold strain
> resounding in the threefold ranks
> of bliss by which they are intrined.
>   (*Par.* 28.115–20)

The music of the spheres exerts a special fascination on students, and some have asked me if it is possible to listen to such music. The surprising answer is that it is indeed possible today. One way to hear the music of heavenly bodies has been made available by artist Jeff Talman and scientists Daniel Huber and Ralph Wenzl, who recorded radiation and seismic data from stars and then converted them into music (NPR Staff). A possible class activity could consist of readings on the Pythagorean myth and its fortune in the Middle Ages, including the Dantean passages about the music of the spheres; then students would listen to Talman's rendering and offer their comments. The aim would be to present the students with the Pythagorean music of the spheres and its place in the Aristotelian universe of Dante's *Commedia*.

A more formal study of music and its symbolic implications for the poet might consider how Dante employs polyphony as a metaphor of the ideal reconciliation of the world's differences and multiplicity with divine unity and harmony. The dance of the theologians in *Paradiso* 10–14 is one of the most musically inspiring and poetically rich sections of the entire poem, on which critical pages by John Freccero ("Dance") and Ciabattoni ("Musical Ways") will be helpful. Dante has his favorite theologians dance and sing in a marvelous double garland that imitates the sounds and movements of a medieval clock, reconciling poetically theological issues between the Franciscans and Dominicans.

Sacred Chants in the Commedia

The liturgical context of medieval life cannot be separated from its musical aspects. Time was measured by monks singing to the book of hours, and the proprium of the Mass included different prayers and songs for each day. In terms of pedagogical approaches, how does Dante's text speak to these cultural aspects of medieval life? And how did the daily liturgy shape the writing of the *Commedia*? I have found that these questions work especially well in a Catholic university such as Georgetown, where students are required to take two theology courses. Even at secular universities, however, students would likely be interested in considering the importance of measuring time and performing ritual actions in everyday life. In addition to the Mass, the medieval liturgy had another set of daily prayers: the liturgy of the hours, largely based on the psalms that monks intoned musically. Starting with lauds at dawn, every set is spaced about three hours apart: prime, tierce, sext, nones, vespers, compline, and the night office, also called vigils or matins, the latter taking place near midnight and closing the cycle while opening the set for the new day. The teacher could invite comparison between the psalms sung by penitents in *Purgatorio* and Thomas Aquinas's commendation of penitential practice, in which he states, "through praying we get closer to God" (*Summa Theologica*, 2a2ae, q. 83, c. 12). In fact, several passages in *Purgatorio* contain elements of liturgical drama and ceremonial directions as would take place in Italian cities during feast days.[2]

Once again, online sources may help students acquire some familiarity with Gregorian chant, a unisonal musical style whose symbolic meaning for Dante achieves a choral dimension in the expiation of sins. Among the many recordings of Gregorian chants on *YouTube*, one of Dantean interest is the *Agnus Dei*, recorded by the Alfred Deller Consort from the *Graduale Romanum* published in 1961 with transcriptions by the monks of Solesmes. This performance reflects the musical setting in the *Graduale Romanum* (101), intended for the Mass for the Dead. A Gradual collects songs for the *ordinarium missae*, the portion of the sung liturgy that is repeated, unvaried, every week, but with different musical settings. The prayers of the *ordinarium missae* include *Kyrie eleison, Gloria in excelsis Deo, Sanctus,* and *Agnus Dei.* Several different settings of each prayer are included in the *Graduale Romanum* for different times and occasions of the liturgical year. For example, the *Agnus Dei* appears with fifteen different melodies, and so we wonder which one would have been sung by the penitent wrathful in *Purgatorio* 16. In the fictional chronology of the poem, the pilgrim crosses the terrace of the wrathful on Easter Monday 1300, so the tune that we should imagine in *Purgatorio* 16 may be the one found either on page 7 or on pages 10–11, since these two are prescribed for Easter week. Dante specifies that for *Agnus Dei* the souls "una parola in tutte era e un modo, / sì che parea tra esse ogne concordia" ("with one voice and intonation sang the words / so that they seemed to share complete accord"; *Purg.* 16.20–21). Thus, we can form a rather precise idea of this unisonal and peaceful-sounding performance. The *Te deum laudamus* is sung twice in the *Commedia*: at the entrance of the penitential section of Purgatory (*Purg.* 9.140) and after Saint Peter examines Dante on faith, sung by the angels "ne la melode che là sù si canta") ("with such melody as is only sung above"; *Par.* 24.114). The *Graduale Romanum* has three monophonic settings of *Te Deum, tonus solemnis, tonus simplex,* and *juxta morem Romanum* (141–50), and the angels' song in *Paradiso* would definitely adhere to the solemn tone of the *Graduale.* Gregorian tunes are not difficult to learn, so if students wished to learn them, the teacher could encourage a choral performance.

Secular Music in the Commedia

When I propose a historical reading of music in the *Commedia*, I warn my students that not all music is sacred in Dante's poem. A case of great musical interest is when Casella sings one of Dante's *canzoni*—"Amor che ne la mente mi ragiona" ("Love that converses with me in my mind")—in *Purgatorio* 2.112, a famous autocitation that has sparked critical debate among scholars and students alike. When discussing whether Dante's own song is a celebration or a recantation of his former poetics, I encourage students to keep in mind the fact that "Amor che ne la mente" is presented in a musical guise, not merely as a "spoken word" performance. Casella's song is often examined in relation to the siren's song of *Purgatorio* 19, another even more aberrant musical temptation. I then invite discussion of the different effects of presenting a text as music or simply as a verbal utterance, and of the differences between such a presentation on the written page or live from a stage.

In the *Commedia*, several troubadours are included: Guido Guinizzelli declares Arnaut Daniel's superiority to Giraut de Bornelh (*Purg.* 26.115–23), who had received praise in *De vulgari eloquentia* (2.2.9); in *Inferno* 28 Bertran de Born, who loved the poetry of war, arms, and bloodshed, stands as a memento of his bellic verse, holding his own severed head; Sordello of Goito acts as guide in the Valley of the Princes (*Purg.* 6–8); and Folquet of Marseilles is among the blessed in the heaven of Venus (*Par.* 9). One exercise that students find stimulating is reading some of the most significant verses by Bertran or Arnaut—for example, "Be'm plai lo gais temps de pascor" ("The gay time of spring pleases me well") and Arnaut's "En cest sonnet coind'e leri" ("In this song gracious and gay") or "Quan chai la fuelha" ("When the leaf sings")—and then comparing these authors' style and content with Dante's treatment of them. Bertran's "Be'm plai," with its exaltation of violent combat, serves particularly well to exemplify the *contrapasso* for the sowers of discord in *Inferno* 28. It is no wonder that Dante, a poet and a soldier, would condemn Bertran, the man who instigated a rift between Henry II of England and his son and who wrote such a gory description of the battlefield, as the following lines from "Be'm plai" demonstrate: "eating or drinking or sleeping hasn't such savor for me as the moment I hear both sides shouting 'Get 'em!' and I hear riderless horses crashing through the shadows, and I hear men shouting 'Help! Help!' . . . and I see the dead with splintered lances decked with pennons, through their sides" (Bertran de Born 342). This approach works very well also with Sordello, who in his lament (*planh*) on the death of Blacatz named Europe's monarchs one by one in order to shame them by exalting the virtues of his dead patron, and who identifies for Dante the princes in the valley (*Purg.* 7–8).[3]

Another musical consideration can be made on what is allegedly the *Commedia*'s most famous episode. The second circle of Hell (*Inf.* 5) resounds with the bird-like sounds of those who committed sins of lust: "E come i gru van cantando lor lai" ("Just as cranes sing their mournful songs"; *Inf.* 5.46). As Giovanni Boccaccio wrote in his commentary on this line, however, the word "lai" might contain a veiled reference to an entire literary and musical genre of chivalric love songs in vogue among the French trouvères and troubadours in the twelfth and thirteenth centuries. One of Marie de France's *Lais*, *Chevrefoil*, tells the story of Tristan, whom Dante includes among the windswept souls a mere twenty-one lines after he uses "lai" to describe their laments. Marie's lai could also provide the opportunity to reflect on Dante's allusion to the danger of erotic literature for lovers like Francesca and Paolo, who fail to disassociate real life from fiction.

Musical Symbolism

The medieval mind placed great importance on allegory as a way of reading the world and the Scriptures: historical facts, objects, images, and words could all be interpreted as signs pointing to moral or metaphysical meanings. Music represented no exception to this vision of the world. Indeed, early Christian writers developed a complex system of musical symbolism, attributing values and meanings to musical instruments on the basis of their shapes, sounds, and origins. One practical exercise is to identify the Dantean passages referencing musical instruments and then assign students the task of finding, either on the Internet or in a print source, an image of each, quoting the source. Subsequently, the instructor can give students relevant bibliography to unearth the symbolic values attributed to those instruments in the Middle Ages.[4] This would generate a discussion about how and to what symbolic end Dante employs the representation of musical instruments in the *Commedia*.

The Commedia *Set to Music*

Over the centuries many composers have either set Dante's text to music or were inspired by it to write pieces in a variety of musical genres and styles that vary from the madrigal to the cantata to the symphony. This happened not only because the *Commedia* is a visionary poem with great individual stories to recast but also because of its intrinsic musical nature: "The vast majority of the earliest receptors of Dante's masterpiece would have experienced it as an oral-aural work, and its recitation would have been a public, indeed social act" (Armour, "The *Comedy*" 19). In *The Dante Encyclopedia* Lansing provides a very inclusive appendix of musical settings of Dante's *Commedia* across the centuries ("Musical Settings" and "Recorded"), which can orient interested students; Maria Ann Roglieri's *Dante and Music* provides an in-depth analysis of nineteenth- and twentieth-century musical settings of Dante's *Commedia*.[5] Given that some of these musical compositions—such as Pyotr Ilyich Tchaikovsky's symphonic poem *Francesca da Rimini* or Giacomo Puccini's opera *Gianni Schicchi*—became milestones of Western music history, this approach could also function as a *fil rouge* through the history of Western music.

Composers, however, developed an early interest in Dante's lyrics. If we are to believe Dante himself, a notable case in point is the setting of "Amor che nella mente mi ragiona" (*Purg.* 2.112) by the Florentine musician and Dante's personal friend Casella. According to Giovanni Mario Crescimbeni,[6] the now lost *codice boccoliniano* contained a rubric stating that a musician coeval with Dante by the name of Scochetto set to music the ballad "Deh, Violetta, che in ombra d'amore" ("Ah, Violetta, you who . . . in Love's shadow")[7] and Dante himself asked a musician named Lippo to "dress" one of his ballads with music in "Se Lippo amico se' tu che mi leggi" ("If you who read me are friend Lippo"). Then, for more than two centuries we have no indications that Dante's verses received musical treatment; later, during an era poetically dominated by the Petrarchan model, some composers nonetheless chose to set Dante's verses to music. One original madrigal is by Luca Marenzio, who in his *Ninth Book of Madrigals* from 1599 turned to Dante's *Rime petrose* rather than the *Commedia*, setting to five-voice polyphony one of Dante's harshest treatments of love,

"Così nel mio parlar voglio esser aspro" ("I want to be as harsh in my speech"). Marenzio was inspired by the theory of interval affects, spearheaded by Nicola Vicentino (*L'antica musica ridotta alla moderna prattica*, 1555) and Gioseffo Zarlino (*Istitutioni harmonice*, 1558). This theory, which drew only from the greatest poets, consisted in imitating the poetic affects by the careful choice of melodic and harmonic intervals and rhythmic figurations, taking Cinquecento polyphony to extents never before heard and leading to the development of a specifically musical rhetoric.

A long list of Renaissance composers chose to set portions *Inferno* 5 to polyphonic madrigals. The superlative example among this group is Luzzasco Luzzaschi's 1576 "Quivi sospiri pianti e alti guai" ("Now sighs, loud wailing, lamentation"), which masterfully applies the theory of interval affects. The madrigals by Marenzio and Luzzaschi can be studied quite profitably in parallel, with the aid of Anthony Newcomb's "Luzzaschi's Setting of Dante: 'Quivi sospiri, pianti, ed alti guai'" and Paolo Fabbri's introduction to *Il nono libro de madrigali a cinque voci (1599)*. In fact, one could track the shift from polyphonic madrigals to the rise of monody simply by following the musical settings of Dante's poetry: the canto of Count Ugolino (*Inf.* 33) seems to be closely connected with the birth of the cantata, since Vincenzo Galilei set it for a single-voice melody in 1581 or 1582 (Abramov-van Rijk 450). Galilei's music is now lost, but his role in the Florentine Camerata de' Bardi, which essentially invented Baroque opera, is well known. Just as successful as *Inferno* 5, the episode of Count Ugolino was set to music in the Romantic era by Nicola Antonio Zingarelli in 1805; Francesco Morlacchi in 1806, and again in 1832; and Gaetano Donizetti in 1828, who in 1837 also wrote a song about Pia de' Tolomei (*Purg.* 5). A stylistic comparison of these songs would show the students the incredible potential of the *Commedia* as a source of musical inspiration and how composers of different ages favored different episodes and differently rendered the lyrical expression.

Some nonmusical, performative adaptations—for example, Silvio Pellico's play or Gustavo Modena's *Dantate*—could be used to illustrate the historical context of Risorgimento Italy. In 1839 the Venetian actor Modena (a friend of Pellico's), considering Dante "a heretic disguised as a Catholic" and using his poetry to satirize the modern Hell of the Savoy regime (Pieri 70), exploited the anticlerical potential of certain cantos (*Inf.* 19, *Purg.* 30). The years before the sixth centennial of Dante's birth (1865) were particularly prolific for Dante-inspired music, also thanks to the nationalistic impulse of newly unified Italy. In 1863 Giovanni Pacini composed a *Dante Symphony* in four parts ("Inferno," "Purgatorio," "Paradiso," and "Il ritorno trionfale di Dante sulla terra"), and this work was then followed by Teodulo Mabellini's *Lo spirito di Dante* in 1865 and Enrique Granados's symphonic poem *Dante* of 1866.

Franz Liszt's 1856 *Dante Symphony* (*Eine Symphonie zu Dante's* Divina Commedia, S. 109) stands out among the symphonic repertory inspired by Dante for the originality of its musical inspiration and its technical solutions. In this short work, vocal parts incorporate famous lines from the poem,[8] marking key passages, but otherwise no extended vocal parts exist in the symphony until the *Magnificat*, which Liszt included instead of a section dedicated to the *Paradiso*, since Richard Wagner had suggested that no music could express Dante's Paradise. The first movement of Liszt's *Dante Symphony*, "Inferno," represents five passages from Dante's first canticle: cantos 3, 5, 21–22, 24, followed by 3 again. Based on the sonata form (with alternating themes A-B-A), the damned souls' torments are expressed by low-key instruments such as bass clarinet, contrabassoon, bass drum, and gong, and by the piercing sounds of cymbals, harps, harmonium, and organ (Roglieri, *Dante and Music*, 27). Restless motion is rendered through fast-descending scales, dissonances, and irregular rhythmical patterns. Furthermore, as Roglieri observes, "the movement as a whole has no stable key, which produces an effect of purposeless motion" (*Dante and Music*, 27, 29). In the second movement, "Purgatorio," no specific episodes are mentioned, but the general sense of spiritual purification is expressed through ascending melodic phrases, culminating in the final *Magnificat* for female and boys' voices, the third and last movement. One possible exercise on Liszt's *Dante Symphony* is a guided exercise of reading and listening to the score. The musically versed instructor will be able to guide the students through the score as they listen to the symphony (available on *YouTube*), stopping at salient passages to focus on the musical scales and figures of different instruments and encouraging the students to describe both graphically and aurally how the music expresses the passages from the poem. Furthermore, a comparison can be made with Tchaikovsky's 1876 *Francesca da Rimini* and with Riccardo Zandonai's *Francesca da Rimini* from 1914.[9] The twentieth century also gave birth to Giacomo Puccini's 1918 opera *Gianni Schicchi*, Mario Castelnuovo-Tedesco's songs on *La vita nuova* and *Purgatorio* 8 (*La sera*), Luigi Dallapiccola's opera *Ulisse*, and a great number of other musical settings, symphonies, and ballets in Europe and North America, a complete list of which can be found in the *Dante Encyclopedia* ("Musical Settings" and "Recorded").

In addition to classical musicians, Dante has elicited the interest of popular music artists as well. During the 1970s some Italian songwriters targeted Dante as an icon in a cultural and generational battle: such artists as Roberto Vecchioni ("Alighieri," *Ipertensione*, 1975) and Antonello Venditti ("Compagno di scuola," *Lilly*, 1975) associate the Tuscan poet with Italy's old school system in need of modernization, while Fabrizio De André ("Al ballo mascherato della celebrità," *Storia di un impiegato*, 1973) makes him a voyeur who spies on Paolo and Francesca, not having the courage to live his own love story to the full. More recently, however, Angelo Branduardi ("Paradiso Canto XI," *L'infinitamente Piccolo*, 2000), Gianna Nannini (*Pia come la canto io*, 2007), Caparezza ("Argenti vive," *Museica*, 2014) and Vinicio Capossela ("Nostos," *Marinai, profeti e balene*, 2011) have set to music or rewritten famous episodes from the *Commedia* without polemical intent and with a sincere interest for the poem. Outside Italy, several pop and rock artists have written songs or entire albums inspired by Dante's *Commedia*, in particular by the first canticle, the most recent being Dante's *Inferno* by the Greek death metal band Spetiflesh. But such artists as Loreena McKennit ("Dante's Prayer," *Book of Secrets*, 1997), Sepultura (*Dante XXI*, 2006), Eminem ("Rap God," *The Marshall Mathers LP 2*, 2013), and many others have taken more than one page from Dante's works.[10]

Teaching Dante and music is directly related to the multimedia approach of the medieval mind. Whereas in today's overspecialized world we may struggle with the idea that a literary work might draw from different disciplines and cross the boundaries of one genre or artistic medium, learned medieval readers did not perceive music, astronomy, or the visual arts as foreign disciplines. Indeed, the curriculum was based on a combination of the seven liberal arts: the *trivium* (grammar, logic, and rhetoric), more focused on what we call the humanities, and the *quadrivium* (astronomy, arithmetic, geometry, and music), with a more scientific emphasis. Music, as a quadrivial art (and "art" in the Middle Ages indicated any technical branch of knowledge, including the sciences), was therefore one of the subjects in which medieval pupils received instruction, and the texts used were theoretical: Augustine's *De musica* and Boethius's *De institutione musica* (*Fundamentals of Music*). Students today need to read and understand the *Commedia* as the product of this dynamic medieval interdisciplinary culture, and a consideration of music in Dante's poem will help them achieve this goal.[11]

NOTES

[1] Texts and translations of *The Divine Comedy* are from the *Princeton Dante Project*, which reproduces Giorgio Petrocchi's critical edition and the translation by Robert Hollander and Jean Hollander.

[2] La Favia's essay is very useful to help students realize how in Dante's *Purgatory* earthly ceremonies and otherworldly penitence are united by the same liturgy, while Ciabattoni's volume (*Dante's Journey to Polyphony*) provides interpretation and musicological context.

[3] As a way of acquainting students with a musical aesthetic quite different from today's, the teacher can find Arnaut Daniel's songs "En cest sonet" and "Lo ferm voler" on *Gérard Zuchetto chante les Troubadours des XIIe et XIIIe siècles*, as well as on YouTube. Arnaut Daniel's melodies, including these, are contained in the thirteenth-century Italian manuscript known as Canzoniere G (fol. 73r), which is partly viewable online at www.filmod.unina.it/cdg/G.htm.

[4] See, for example, van Schaik.

[5] Roglieri (*Dante and Music*) also provides an extensive appendix of "Tables representing the compiled data on musical settings of the *Commedia*," 279–304.

[6] Crescimbeni quotes these words from the rubric: "Parole di Dante, e Suono di Scochetto." The Boccolini manuscript is now lost, but Crescimbeni's annotation is available in vol. 5, p. 220 (viewable online at books.google.it/books?id=0BK1XH3ZyX0C&pg=PA 215&dq=Mario+Crescimbeni+codice+boccoliniano&hl=en&sa=X&ved=0ahUKEwijj On92rvaAhVMr6QKHQp-CMIQ6AEIKTAA#v=onepage&q&f=false).

[7] Texts and translations of these three poems are from Foster and Boyde's *Dante's Lyric Poetry* (40–41, 18–19, 170–71).

[8] See the following examples, which can be found in the complete score of Liszt's *Dante Symphony*, available online (p. 55: *Inf.* 3.9; p. 41: *Inf.* 5.103–05).

[9] Most opera librettos are available online at opera.stanford.edu/iu/librettim.html. Roglieri's *Dante and Music* (especially pp. 26 ff. and 91 ff.) will be of great help to frame the critical discussion.

[10] A helpful list of popular musicians who wrote about or quoted from Dante's works can be found on the Web site *Dante Today*.

[11] I recommend the following studies for their pertinence to the topic of this essay: Aubrey; Audeh and Havely; Barnes; Barolini, "Dante and the Troubadours" and *Dante's Poets*; Bergin; Bertoni; Birge-Vitz; Bowles; Burgess; Christensen; Ciabattoni, Review of the conference Dante and Music; Fassler and Jeffrey; Fosca; Freccero, "Casella's Song"; Gerbert; Gracyk and Kania; Hawkins, *Dante's Testaments*; Holsinger, *Music*; Jeffrey; Kleinhenz, "Biblical Citation"; Mahrt; Martinez, "'Amoroso Canto'"; Mathiesen; McCracken; Moore (esp. 2: 152–208, 246–68); Picone, "Giraut de Bornelh," "*Paradiso*," and "Trovatori"; Povoledo; Roglieri, "'Dolce Sinfonia,'" "Music," and "Twentieth-Century Musical Interpretations"; Santangelo; Sesini; Smith; Strohm and Blackburn; Swing; Van Deusen; and Walker. Also recommended are the following Web sites: *Petrucci Music Library* (imslp.org); *Partifi*, a publicly accessible library of musical scores (partifi.org); *Dante Today* (Saiber and Coggeshall); *The World of Dante*; *Church Music Association of America* (musicasacra.com).

Dante's Afterlife in Popular Culture

Elizabeth Coggeshall

On first encountering the *Divine Comedy*, many American undergraduates find the poem unapproachable, a monolith of a past age that bears little resemblance to our fast-paced, eclectic, digital one. Students often read literature in search of characters they find relatable, and messages that are relevant to their personal lives. These reasons drive the largest numbers of literature majors toward specializations in modern or even postmodern literatures. This was especially true of the students in a course I taught at the University of California, Santa Cruz, whose classroom experiences will be the focus of the present study. At the time, the UCSC Literature program required all majors to take at least one course in premodern literature, and the majority of my students indicated their interest in the Dante course was primarily to satisfy this requirement. Like many who first encounter Dante in a required course, most of my students came to the course expecting to find premodern literature at best intriguing but alienating; worse, irrelevant but historically necessary; and, at worst, dogmatic, preachy, or outright boring.

Armed with the knowledge that many students register for introductory courses on Dante with some mixture of these adjectives coloring their expectations, I set my course objectives to address these precise concerns. In large part, I focus my attention on the psychological and philosophical dimensions of the text, presenting the *Divine Comedy* as a work of ethics, which aims to instruct its readers in the best ways to live. The poem, however, does not give such instruction through direct, straightforward messages; rather, it invites readers to work through its fourteenth-century Italian references to draw out a meaning applicable to their own situations. With careful analogies, such lessons can resonate with the contemporary lives and questions of students. To achieve this resonance, I weave in a variety of cross-disciplinary references to Dante that span a long historical and cross-cultural arc, culled from high and low culture alike. In addition to canonical authors such as T. S. Eliot or Primo Levi, I rely heavily on examples from *Dante Today: Citings and Sightings of Dante's Works in Contemporary Culture*, a curated, crowd-sourced Web archive, created by Arielle Saiber in 2006, which I have coedited with Saiber since 2012. Of popular examples, the Web site provides a wide variety from which to choose: *New Yorker* cartoons; t-shirts; blog posts; restaurant names; candies; and the infamous Electronic Arts video game "Dante's Inferno," with its crusader pilgrim and damsel-in-distress Beatrice.

Much like the typological approach that Rachel Jacoff outlines in the 1982 *Approaches* volume, reading contemporary popular examples alongside the original text uncovers the poem's "psychological and phenomenological validity," in which "[t]he poem's literary futurity might be thought of as its anagoge"

(Jacoff, *"Divine Comedy"* 83). The primary goal of such juxtapositions is to develop a critical comparative reading practice: to see how a single text can invite multiple interpretations and to analyze how texts negotiate with one another to create meaning. This practice not only helps refine students' literary study but also promotes their literacy as savvy cultural consumers, bombarded as they are by a constant stream of content, presented in diverse media, and made available to them often without any trusted system of curation or cataloguing.

The pop culture examples I bring to the classroom vary in medium, kind, and quality, as well as in the depth of their appropriation of and their attitudes toward the original, which may range from pious reverence to superficial mimicry.[1] From the beginning of the term, I prime students for the kind of critical comparative work they will do in their end-of-term research projects, in which they discuss an example of "pop Dante" and the light the example sheds on a specific aspect of the *Comedy*. To prepare them to analyze the poem's transmedia resonance, I present a daily *PowerPoint* that relies on visual media to supplement the textual material under discussion. As do many instructors of Dante, I make frequent use of Gustave Doré's illustrations, as well as of Dante-inspired works by canonical artists, such as William Blake, Sandro Botticelli, Salvador Dalí, Dante Gabriel Rossetti, and others. But I also incorporate images from graphic novel adaptations of the *Comedy*, such as those of Sandow Birk, Seymour Chwast, or Hunt Emerson, to name a few. Birk's *Inferno* models his Hell on earth on contemporary Los Angeles. Chwast adapts the entire *Comedy*, following a noir-detective-style pilgrim through encounters in each of the three realms. Of the three adaptations, Emerson's *Inferno* reads the most like a classic comic strip, with illustrations accompanying discussions of what his stout, gruff Virgil repeatedly calls the "metaphysics" of Hell. These images are good for a shock or for a laugh—a welcome break in the middle of a lecture—but they are more than merely frivolous and often warrant more extended discussion.

Of these graphic adaptations, Sandow Birk's has garnered the most critical attention from Dante scholars.[2] Birk's multiphase *Divine Comedy* project took shape over the course of five years of work, including a series of paintings and lithographs modeled on Doré's illustrations of each of the three canticles.[3] In the illustrations, Birk reimagines the landscapes of Dante's—or, more accurately, Doré's—Hell as what Rebecca Solnit aptly calls the "leftover spaces" of an infernal Los Angeles: parking lots, fast-food restaurants, freeway underpasses, corner stores (32). The images were then assembled to accompany an adaptation of the text into a contemporary American idiom, written by Birk and Marcus Sanders. The project's final phase is the 2007 toy-theater film *Dante's Inferno*, produced by Birk and Paul Zaloom and directed by Sean Meredith.

In my classes I typically devote a lesson to screening a portion of Birk's film, around the midpoint of the *Inferno*, after students have prepared the first few cantos of the Malebolge. The early encounters in the Malebolge can be particularly bewildering for students, and they may respond much like Birk's pilgrim, who, shortly after entering the eighth circle, exclaims in disbelief, "You go to hell for *flattery*?" In order to underscore the severity of these sins, I ask the students to articulate the reasons the poem presents a sin like flattery or seduction as more grievous than something like manslaughter. I steer the conversation toward those aspects of the sin that are distinctly human: the reliance on language and on intellectual faculties, the social and political repercussions of such sins, and so on. Once students have an idea of what might make such sins so menacing to the human community, we turn to Birk's film.

I begin the screening with Birk's figure of Geryon, a Fox News helicopter that arises from the depths of the circle of fraud. We watch the following eight minutes of the film, concluding with the encounter with the flatterers, whom Birk reimagines as lobbyists serving on Capitol Hill in Washington, DC. After watching the clip, I ask students to discuss the comparison Birk sets up: is this an apt comparison for the kind of flattery Dante has in mind? How does the comparison shed light on the political or social impact of flattery? How does it change students' view of flattery as a vice? I encourage students to think about other ways Birk updates the *Inferno* for a contemporary American audience, especially with regard to American politics. I claim that Birk's political agenda is similar to Dante's own: to use local cases and historically specific interpretations of sins to bring about cutting political commentary. Birk's work, I argue, challenges its viewers to look more closely at the "leftover spaces" of their own urban landscapes—and especially at the people trapped within those "leftover spaces"—as the infernal by-product of a collective cultural apathy, a vast indifference figured by Birk's pilgrim: a dimwitted, hungover, unobservant everyman. Birk seems to shift the blame from the sinners themselves to the system in which they are trapped and to the public's complicity in replicating the patterns that enable such a system to persist. I encourage students to consider Birk's commentary on the culpability of cultural institutions as they continue to read *Inferno* and *Purgatorio*.

At the close of this discussion, I show the students an image from the 23 September 1998 edition of the satirical newspaper *The Onion*. The headline reads: "Tenth Circle Added to Rapidly Expanding Hell," and the image shows a traditional map of Dante's Hell with an additional ring inserted just above Cocytus. The new circle is called "Corpadverticus," wherein are punished the "Total Bastards": lobbyists, marketers, and awards-show hosts. The *Onion* headline leads into the introduction of the students' first writing assignment for the course: to imagine and describe a new tenth circle of Hell. This creative assignment appears on many syllabi, and it is adaptable for students at different levels of instruction, from middle school to college. My version of the assignment asks students to focus on the *contrapasso*, keeping in mind the landscape; the weather; the group(s) of individuals found in the circle; the types of language and gestures these characters exhibit; and the psychology expressed in that physical, behavioral, and intellectual language. The sin should be reflected on each of these counts, manifesting the will of the sinner through his or her body and the environment in which that body is found. I offer students the chance to write in the genre of their choice: dialogues, essays, news reports, additional cantos in verse or prose. I have, on occasion, even received cantos composed entirely in terza rima, such as the UCSC undergraduate Luis Rodriguez's 101-verse canto recounting the fate of souls marked by the sin Rodriguez identifies as "pessimismo."

On the day students hand in their creative assignments, I schedule a full lesson on the role of the *Divine Comedy* in contemporary—and especially popular—American culture. I begin the lesson with a slide displaying an Internet meme. I project an image of the young man from the Dell computer ad campaign of the early 2000s, finger pointed gleefully at the camera, over which is written the phrase, "Dude, you're going to Hell!" With this aggressive image on the screen, I ask students to describe their visions of the "tenth circle," explaining in detail the *contrapasso* devised for the assignment and its relation to the sin at hand. I then ask students to discuss the role they had to embody as authors of that *contrapasso*. Perhaps prompted by the jubilant expression on the young man's face, my UCSC students ventured into this discussion even before my next slide elicited it; some students spoke about devising their punishments with a similar delight, while others expressed discomfort at playing the judge in their invented circle.

The vacillation between desire and discomfort that students feel at playing the judge leads us to one of the most distinct uses of Dante's work in contemporary popular culture: the judgmental power of the "circles of hell" as a persistent meme, especially in Internet culture. I show the students a number of examples of the "circles" meme: we have already seen Sandow Birk's lobbyists and *The Onion*'s Corpadverticus, and I add examples such as Nat Towsen's "Nine NEW Levels of Hell" (e.g., "Level 4: Internet Commentators"), Jorge Cham's *Dante's Inferno: Academic Edition* by PhD Comics, or Dan Moreau's "The Nine Circles of Adjunct Hell." I spend several slides looking at "Twenty-Three Circles of Hell That Should Exist for the Modern Age," by the *BuzzFeed* staff writer Adam Ellis, which claims that we need to expand Dante's outdated nine circles because they were conceived "like a million years ago." Ellis adds fourteen circles, which include "People Who Walk Too Slow on the Street" (eleventh circle), "Able-Bodied People Who Take the Elevator a Single Floor" (sixteenth circle), and "People Who Bring 11 Items to the 10 Item Express Lane" (nineteenth circle).

Why, I ask my students, do Dante's circles make the right vehicle for airing grievances about the modern world? In the American imagination, the title, map, schema, and format of the poem, as well as the name of its author, all conspire to provide a point of reference for passing judgment on behaviors that annoy or irritate us. Particularly within Internet culture, with its anonymous trolls and cyberbullies, Dante and his poem represent a cipher that commentators use to code their passive-aggressive critiques of modern life. The austerity and monumentality of the poem lend the bloggers' moralizing the severe critical legitimacy of the original and, at the same time, provide the cachet that accompanies flippant appropriations of canonical forms.

It is not only the punitive aspect of Dante's poem that electrifies the contemporary imagination; the redemptive elements of the poem's themes, strategies, and structure also take a primary place among many popular reworkings of the poem. These reworkings tend to fall into two, sometimes overlapping, categories: memoir and self-help. Of the many examples of redemptive readings of the *Comedy*, I briefly mention two of the most recent: Joseph Luzzi's memoir *In a Dark Wood: What Dante Taught Me about Grief, Healing, and the Mysteries of Love*, and Rod Dreher's *How Dante Can Save Your Life: The Life-Changing Wisdom of History's Greatest Poem*, both published in 2015.[4] Luzzi's memoir uses the lens of Dante's life and works to explore his own grief and healing process after the sudden, tragic death of his wife in 2007. The memoir presents a strikingly personal and intimate portrait, even in its readings of the *Divine Comedy*, which it relates to episodes in the poet's biography. The memoir reads the author's mourning process by analogy with Dante's own.

Dreher is similarly motivated by a personal experience of profound depression and grief, but, in contrast to Luzzi, he presents the *Comedy* as an outwardly focused narrative that means to dispense practical, actionable wisdom to its readers. Despite Luzzi's definitive proclamation that "*The Divine Comedy* was not a self-help manual" (130), many writers have treated it as one, most emphatically Dreher, who, in an essay for the *Wall Street Journal* goes so far as to claim that the *Comedy* is "the most astonishing self-help book ever written" ("Ultimate Self-Help Book"). Whereas Luzzi focuses on the redemptive beauty of the *Comedy*, Dreher emphasizes the salvific power of the poem's moral wisdom to draw the reader from despair. A brief discussion of these two conflicting examples allows us to revisit two questions I raise at the beginning of the term. First, I introduce the poem by emphasizing that it is a first-person epic, the narrative of an individual's passage through a physical space that gives form to his inward examination of conscience. In other words, the poem presents itself as a memoir of a distinctly personal experience. Second, at the same time, I discuss the poem as a version of a psychological diagnostic manual, identifying pathologies of the will that may be found across cultures and times. I ask the students to pay attention to the question of whether the poem seeks exclusively to diagnose, or if there is any therapeutic aspect to its presentations. We could think of this therapy as akin to the self-help manuals in our present-day bookstores. At this midpoint in the term, I ask the students to consider where they might catalogue a contemporary *Divine Comedy* in a bookstore: in the "Memoir" section, or in "Self-Help"? Answering this question—and defending the answer persuasively—requires students to articulate what each one sees as the major thrust of the poem. Is the *Divine Comedy* written for its author's redemption, or for ours?

At the end of the lesson on "Dante Today," I distribute the prompt for the final research project: a relatively short, critical comparative essay on an example of "pop Dante." The research essay assignment challenges students to put into practice the comparative methods they have been developing all term. They have free choice of topic, and I encourage them to seek out subjects that appeal to their specific tastes or interests. I suggest they peruse the eight categories on the *Dante Today* Web site—"Consumer Goods," "Dining and Leisure," "Music," "Odds and Ends," "Performing Arts," "Places," "Visual Art and Architecture," and "Written Word"—or to search for tags or keywords that intrigue them, such as "poetry," "apps," "puppets," or "hip-hop."

Once students select a topic, they should also identify a single aspect of the *Comedy* that this example elucidates. It is not enough for a paper to claim that the example takes much of its influence from Dante's poem; the thesis should articulate how the dialogue between the medieval poem and its popular analogue gives insight into Dante's claims about love, justice, politics, poetry, freedom, gender, or any other problem with which the poem grapples. The best theses are even more precise: the popular example may contrast with the deeply psychological *contrapasso* system, or it may exploit its poetic form to ends similar to Dante's terza rima. The point of the exercise is not merely to see Dante's resonance in popular culture but also to use that resonance to understand something about his poem more clearly.

The fifty-nine students in my class at UC Santa Cruz wrote about a wide variety of subjects, each confronting the original poem from positions of reverence, irony, or superficiality. I highlight here a few of the projects that engaged most clearly with pop examples. Samantha Hamilton writes about the type of redemptive reading I discussed above, which she identifies as "bibliotherapy." Using the self-help guide *Dante's Path: A Practical Approach to Achieving Inner Wisdom* as a point of comparison, Hamilton addresses the practice of developing empathy through reading as a therapeutic means of healing from psychological trauma. She relates this to both the pilgrim's and the reader's struggles for redemption through identification with the sinners, the penitents, and the saved. Micaela Accardi-Krown chose to write about Italian prog rock band Metamorfosi's 1973 album *Inferno*. Her analysis focuses on how the instrumentation of the album maps both the motion and the emotion of the pilgrim as he progresses through Inferno. Victoria Jones analyzes the opening episode of the third season of NBC's *Hannibal*, in which the cannibalistic protagonist's administration of so-called justice to his victims complicates the view of the poet's position as author of punishments in the *Comedy*. Both Hannibal and Dante, she claims, emphasize aesthetics over ethics in their distribution of justice, but they differ on which system gives rise to the other; she argues that for Dante aesthetic principles arise from ethical ones, whereas the inverse is true for Hannibal. One of the most popular research subjects was Zander Cannon's 2013 graphic novel *Heck*, which follows characters Heck and Elliot on their adventures running a courier service transmitting messages to the recently deceased in Hell. Aside from the appealing artwork and narrative, students enjoyed working through the differences between Dante's protagonists and Cannon's. Analie Bet-Yadegar, for example, uses the graphic novel to explore the role of memory (or lack thereof) in the construction of the hero figure at the center of each narrative. Each of these projects identifies and analyzes patterns that emerge from the original all the more clearly when contrasted with a contemporary counterpart.

Such comparative readings, I admit, may easily run into the danger of anachronism. It is for this reason that I work throughout the term to set up our analogies between past and present very carefully. In class and in office hours, I emphasize the tensions that emerge between the contemporary examples we consider and the original poem, whatever the ostensible similarities may be. Regardless of the danger, I find the exercise of comparative readings such as these to be particularly effective at rendering the poem both more and less familiar to students. Incorporating particular case studies of Dante's continued presence in popular culture helps to render more intelligible to undergraduates the ethical and psychological dimensions of the poem, allowing them to understand Dante's locally and historically specific cultural critique by analogy with the conditions of twenty-first-century American life. Such a practice welcomes newcomers into Dante's medieval cosmos, which they can begin to see as coherent and coextensive with their own.

NOTES

[1] On the distinction between "respect" and "reverence," see Parker and Parker (139–40).

[2] To name just a few, see De Rooy, "A Cardboard Dante"; Hawkins, "Moderno Uso"; Olson, "Dante's Urban American Vernacular"; and Parker and Parker (esp. 155–64).

[3] See *Dante's* Inferno; *Dante's* Paradiso, and *Dante's* Purgatorio, adapted by Sandow Birk and Marcus Sanders.

[4] See also Peter Hawkins's essay in this volume for a slightly different take on these two books.

From Poem to PlayStation 3:
Teaching Dante with Video Games

Brandon K. Essary

This essay describes teaching Dante's *Inferno* alongside the 2010 Electronic Arts video game *Dante's* Inferno. The essay describes my approach from the first offering of the course entitled Dante's *Inferno*: from Poetry to Video Games at Elon University in spring 2017. The course is an interdisciplinary Core Capstone Seminar for third- and fourth-year undergraduate students. The capstone serves as a culminating experience that engages the modes of inquiry, knowledge, and communication skills acquired throughout students' academic formation at Elon. The seminar is also writing intensive, utilizing a variety of writing approaches to promote critical thinking. Finally, it counts toward Elon's interdisciplinary Italian studies minor.

The seminar has students from a variety of disciplines, most of whom have little or no prior experience with Dante, *The Divine Comedy*, or the video game *Dante's* Inferno. Thus, the primary course objectives are to read critically and analyze the entirety of Dante's *Inferno*, understanding its place within the *Divine Comedy* and in the historical context of medieval Italy; analyze critically video game recordings of *Dante's* Inferno as a digital narrative based on the poem; and compare and contrast a classic literary work and a popular video game. These goals will help students to understand how to read, interpret, and write about a masterpiece of world literature and a video game based on it; evaluate the interaction of literature and popular culture; and reflect on the growing importance, complexity, and pedagogical potential of video games in contemporary society.

The course is taught on Mondays, Wednesdays, and Fridays for seventy minutes each day with a total of thirty-nine class sessions. It is capped at twenty-three students. The course has the following grade categories: participation, discussion groups, research papers, game journal, core capstone project for the Elon core curriculum, and a final oral exam. The Monday and Wednesday sessions are dedicated to discussion of Robert Hollander and Jean Hollander's translation of *Inferno*. The cantos of the poem are divided evenly across these sessions, and students must read the assigned cantos prior to class. Friday classes are game labs, for which students watch *YouTube* videos—recorded and produced by me—of the video game *Dante's* Inferno, and read academic articles on, for example, game design, gender studies, digital humanities, play theory, and so on (see Essary). The game recordings typically correspond to the assigned cantos of that same week, and are less than an hour in viewing length for each week.

Why use a video game as an approach to teaching Dante? is a good and expected question, especially given popular misconceptions about the video game medium. First, as much as seventy percent of college students play video games at least "once in a while," with some sixty-five percent reporting being regular or occasional game players, according to a Pew Internet Research survey (Jones). Beyond the college context, another such survey reports that some forty-nine percent of American adults play video games, with an almost identical share of men (fifty percent) and women (forty-eight percent) reporting ever playing video games (Duggan). So, the medium is ubiquitous in the college experience and life as an adult, and video games are a medium that our students on the whole are interested in and whose language (visual and written) they speak and understand as "digital natives."[1] The element of quantity, the number of people playing games and engaging with these stimulating, interactive, multimedia worlds, however, is not the only or best reason. The quality element regarding the kind of engagement that takes place when playing video games is far more important. Students who use video games to learn about academic subject matter are likely to report high levels of agreement regarding willingness to take our courses on Dante; learning a lot from our courses; learning well through a variety of mediums, pedagogical approaches, and leadership opportunities; and learning more through studying a literary text alongside a video game than alongside traditional scholarly sources. Finally, students are likely to report high levels of transferable knowledge applicable after the class regarding the way they think, in general, about literature and about video games. As evinced by student data from my courses that teach Dante with video games, students find that the video game medium gives new life to literature, a medium many of them perceive to be dying or in decline.[2]

A fundamental tenet of the course, and of teaching and learning at Elon University, is active student engagement, which video games not only encourage but also require of players. Thus, my approach resonates with the "students as partners" model elaborated in Alison Cook-Sather, Catherine Bovill, and Peter Felten's 2014 study, *Engaging Students as Partners in Learning and Teaching.* They "define student-faculty partnership as a collaborative, reciprocal process through which all participants have the opportunity to contribute equally, although not necessarily in the same ways, to curricular or pedagogical conceptualization, decision making, implementation, investigation, or analysis" (6–7). So, in class we often begin with the aforementioned discussion groups of approximately four groups of five students. Each group has a leader who prepares questions on key elements, passages, and footnotes from the day's reading, and cites secondary sources. The leader prepares answers to the questions and is ready to lead the group's discussion based on them. Each group member writes a brief reflection on the day's reading to prepare for the discussion. During class, the professor visits each group at least once. During each visit, the professor responds to students' questions, draws attention to quality observations, and mines the discussions for talking points that align student interests with the class-wide discussion that takes place during the second half of class. At the end of class, the professor collects each group leader's preparations and grades them closely according to a detailed rubric. Group members' reflections are spot-checked for participation.

The capstone seminar serves as a culminating experience that engages skills acquired throughout students' academic formation. These daily discussion and leadership opportunities, together with the detailed feedback provided to student leaders by the professor, allow students to practice regularly modes of inquiry (into primary and secondary sources), sharing of knowledge with peers and the professor, and honing of clear communication skills with on-the-spot feedback from peers and the professor. I use this "students as partners" approach to varying degrees in all my classes, whether Italian language, cinema, or literature. It is rewarding to see students practice these skills daily and to give them numerous opportunities to learn and improve. It is also rewarding to see students become invested, passionate coleaders of the course.[3]

The capstone seminar is also writing intensive, utilizing a variety of writing approaches to promote critical thinking. In the discussion group assignments, students experience a variety of evaluations, both high stakes (closely graded writings of the leaders) and low stakes (members' spot-checked, participatory writings). Both can lead to critical thinking in small-group and class-wide discussions. Writing and critical thinking is also promoted in the game journal and the more traditional research papers. The game journal is a low-stakes assignment due once per week in preparation for the Friday game labs. Students must write a brief reflection on the game segment, in which they describe what is happening and what part of Dante's poem it corresponds to (with a screen shot from the recording and the quotation from *Inferno* it illustrates); briefly analyze the transformation of the poem to a game (Is it true to the text? Is it an effective visual representation? Would you do it differently? why or why not?); and, finally, students articulate a connection between the game segment and the day's reading on video game studies or from a related discipline. These readings and reflections require students to think critically about both the process of transforming a literary work into a video game and the original poetic text.[4] Since the capstone seminar is interdisciplinary in nature, the game lab readings offer various keys for interpreting the game. These readings connect to the students' disciplines, other courses, and broader education.

Some examples of the game lab readings will give an idea of this interdisciplinary potential. Harry Brown's *Video Games and Education* treats some of the "literary" elements found in good video games: poetics, aesthetics, and rhetoric. With *The Ecology of Games*, edited by Katie Salen, students confront race portrayal with S. Craig Watkins and Anna Everett's "The Power of Play: The Portrayal and Performance of Race in Video Games" and other studies. We discuss gender and the representation of women—in our case, Beatrice—with readings from Yasmin Kafai's *Beyond Barbie and Mortal Kombat* and Alison Harvey's *Gender, Age, and Digital Games in the Domestic Context*. We study the sounds of Hell while reflecting on Helen Mitchell's "Fear and the Musical Avant-Garde in Games." We observe Gustave Doré's *Inferno* illustrations and their influence on the game's art. We discuss play theory, Johan Huizinga's *Homo Ludens*, and Roger Caillois's *Man, Play and Games*. Finally, we discuss the pedagogical potential of video games—for Dante studies and beyond—with James Gee's seminal study *What Video Games Have to Teach Us about Learning and Literacy* and Kurt Squire's *Video Games and Learning*. This selection should give a sense of how rich and diverse video game studies and the disciplines they intersect with are, and, from what follows, why this approach is important.

First, on a personal note, I have been playing video games since I was about four years old, starting with *Super Mario Bros.* on the original Nintendo Entertainment System (NES), and I like games. When I was a kid, and now as an adult, video games inspired me to read, write, and interact with people, sources, and disciplines I might not have otherwise. They are a fun, engaging, interactive and social medium that gets people talking and thinking. As Gee states, "Games for learning work pretty much the same way as books for learning. Kids learn with books or games (or television or computers or movies or pencils) when they are engaged in well-designed and good interactions with adults and more advanced peers, interactions that lead to problem solving, meta-critical reflection, and connections to the world and other texts and tools" (*Good Video Games* 3). Thus, games can be powerful motivators, not just to play more games, but to engage with peers, texts, disciplines, and activities connected to them. For these reasons, I want students to experience the fun, engagement, and poetic content built into *Dante's Inferno*.[5] These elements, in turn, can be used to motivate them to reflect critically on the poem vis-à-vis its transformation into a complex digital narrative that shares with it countless similarities: from verbatim references to the *Comedy* to visualization of grotesque hellscapes (e.g., circle 3's environs, drenched in what the poet calls a "piova . . . greve"; "heavy rain"; *Inf.* 6.7–8) that evoke in the video game churning bowels with monstrous intestinal worms and gluttonous giants, stomachs bursting at the seams, impeding Dante the Crusader's path). One might worry that the video game's captivating setting might replace the poem's imagery. More often than not, however, my students remark that the game sparks their imagination, giving them the power to see Dante's imagery of Hell.

Second, I agree with Gee and others who argue for a broad interpretation of literacy in today's multimedia world. To be literate nowadays, one should be able to read and interpret traditional written texts alongside images, Web sites, film, television, radio, and, as the medium becomes more widespread and complex, video games.[6] Video game technology has evolved tremendously since my childhood. On the one hand, they are a lot more realistic and sophisticated from a graphics standpoint. On the other hand, video games now tell stories that engage increasingly diverse player demographics to think about and experience vicariously serious, often academic topics.[7] My course seeks to train students to recognize and think critically about these topics and the way video games portray them. As we will see in the case of the game *Dante's* Inferno, not just entertainment is at stake. Education is at stake, too, as players are led through complicated and, at times, thought-provoking landscapes based on a medieval Italian literary work. Many critics ignore (or do not see, for not having actually played the game) *Dante's* Inferno's countless connections to the poem. They disregard the rich interplay—intertextuality, even—between the poem and the game. In doing so, a ripe opportunity to teach a new generation about Dante is lost. This teaching should be done using both accuracies and inaccuracies as valuable, engaging, and entertaining learning moments.

Let us take the cantos, video game segment, and topics of week one in the class to reify these moments. During week one, students read *Inferno* 1 and 2 in preparation for Monday and *Inferno* 3 and 4 for Wednesday. I explain the discussion group assignment in class on Monday. On Wednesday, we do a practice run of the discussion groups to prepare them to begin in earnest during week two. For Friday's game lab, students watch the video recordings of the game that correspond to *Inferno* 1 through 4 and Circles 0 and 1, and read Harry Brown's chapter "Video Games and Storytelling" from his *Video Games and Education* (3–20). On day one, we discuss in class the prologue of the poem and the reason for and structure of Dante's journey. On day two, we will discuss the architecture of the *Inferno* and how Virgil and Beatrice fit into the journey. These discussions lay the groundwork for comparison and contrast of this part of the poem as interpreted in the first part of the video game.

Students watch the game recording for Friday, and they write their first game journal entry. They inevitably notice that the video game's protagonist is Dante the Crusader and that a different story is unfolding. The year is 1191. Dante the Warrior has just returned home to Florence from the Crusade to be with his wife, Beatrice. Dante the Warrior's home is ransacked and his beloved slain. Beatrice's spirit rises out of her body, and intimates to Dante she made a deal to save his life. A dark spirit appears behind that of Beatrice, and dashes away into Hell with her soul. Needless to say, the Crusader races after them. He must battle to the center of Hell to defeat Satan and save her. That synopsis leaves little hope for meaningful dialogue with the poet's original story. And, unfortunately, many critics of the game stop here. They point out the obvious: this is not the narrative, or time period, of Beatrice of *Inferno*. The entire game is judged and dismissed based on a few moments at its beginning.

In the first game lab, the students—and I, too—investigate the obvious and use such inaccuracies to engage the poem, to reinforce what actually happens, and compare the two.[8] But we go beyond the obvious and confront also the countless ways the video game utilizes the poem to inspire the game's dialogue, construct its settings, design its maps, and give order to and populate the various circles of Hell. The game's writers adapt and modernize Henry Wadsworth Longfellow's translation to create Dante the Crusader and Virgil's dialogues. Their first exchange takes place at the Gate of Hell and is based on Dante the Pilgrim and Virgil's exchanges in *Inferno* 1 and 2. The Warrior begs of Virgil's shade: "Have pity on me, whatever you are!" (*Inf.* 1.65–66). Virgil agrees and explains how Beatrice sent him to help Dante: "A lady called. I prayed for her to command me" (*Inf.* 2.53–54). The dialogue continues to be inspired by Dante's poem throughout the game. Virgil quotes it to guide Dante the Crusader and the player through Hell and explain what is happening, the settings, the punishments (*contrapasso*), the souls being punished, and so on. One also encounters condemned souls and demons in the game, usually in the order in which they appear in the poem. Amid the neutrals, Dante the Warrior finds Pontius Pilate. This and other shades lure the player to them by talking about their misdeeds, and the player must choose to punish them to stay in Hell as Dante the poet intended or, defy the poet's judgment, absolve them, and send them to Paradise. This scene unfolds after Dante the Warrior asks Virgil about the neutrals, and Virgil clarifies: "Mercy and justice disdain them. Let us not speak of them. Move on!" (*Inf.* 3.50–51). Charon is in the background, foreshadowing the next leg of the journey, transfigured into a giant ferry that takes souls across Acheron. His head, complete with "occhi di bragia" ("eyes like embers"; *Inf.* 3.109) is the animated, nautical figurehead of the ship. He admonishes the shades: "Woe to you, wicked souls. Do not hope to ever see Paradise!" (*Inf.* 3.84–85); and the Crusader: "You there, stand aside from those that are dead" (*Inf.* 3.88–89).

In-class discussions of the poem make up the majority of class sessions and are dedicated to the essential goal of students' understanding Dante's masterpiece. These days also prepare them to identify the countless and meaningful ways game designers utilized that same poem to make it relevant to a new generation of readers through a new, interactive medium. Students' citation of primary and secondary sources in the discussion and game lab activities lead to and culminate with their three research papers on the poem and game. The process of reading and thinking critically about the poem, the game, and their interaction will prepare students for a creative core capstone project for the Elon core curriculum. In it, groups pick a work of literature or course from their academic discipline to transform into a blockbuster video game title, applying the lessons learned from *Inferno, Dante's* Inferno, and the interdisciplinary game readings. They must make a sales pitch to the rest of the class to garner imaginary funding for their proposal. The class votes for the most compelling proposal, and we discuss what elements make it persuasive (from the point of view of story, visuals, and market viability). The course ends with individual oral exams in which students elaborate to the professor what they have learned, how they learned it, and how they foresee that knowledge impacting their future learning and life beyond college.[9] I ask them about Dante's *Inferno* (poem); *Dante's* Inferno (video game); and the interaction between literature and popular culture. They consistently share with me the key findings of their literary research in the course, the unique and manifold ways in which a popular digital medium provoked thought about and interaction with that research, and how analyzing that interaction will help them understand and interpret similar literary transformations in the future.[10]

NOTES

[1] Marc Prensky refers to today's students as "digital natives" because, in contrast with previous generations, they are often highly proficient "native speakers of technology, fluent in the digital language of computers, video games, and the Internet" (9).

[2] As of May 2018, I have taught the course twice, once in spring 2017 and once in winter term 2018, and have demonstrable evidence of the positive outcomes of teaching Dante and the *Inferno* with the video game *Dante's* Inferno. Students from both courses agreed or strongly agreed regarding these statements (with agreement rate in parentheses): "I learned a lot from the course" (ninety-five percent); I learned actively through a variety of mediums, teaching approaches, and in-class leadership opportunities (ninety-five percent); "I learned more about Dante and his poetry [with] a video game than [with] the text by itself or alongside traditional, written scholarly sources" (eighty-five percent); "The course will affect the way I think in the future about literature, about games" (ninety-seven percent). Students perceive by the end of the course that video games have a unique potential to give new life to literature as a medium. As one student eloquently put it: "I have always loved video games and literature and being able to find ways that these things could do learning and socialization have done wonders for what I think they could do for the future of humanity. It also leads me to believe that literature, which is my favorite medium, won't completely die out due to its ability to live on through video games."

[3] In *Good Video Games and Good Learning* Gee refers to these environments as "passionate affinity spaces," in which "[w]hat matters are interest, passion, practice, mastery, talk, shared experiences, feedback, mentoring, production and not just consumption. Leadership is porous; on some days a person leads or mentors and on other days he or she follows or gets mentored" (68).

[4] Students in the course often state directly that the game "forces them" to read the poem more closely and think more critically about it. As one student put it: "I did learn more about Dante by studying the video game as well because it forced me to study the poem more. I was able to recognize aspects of the poem that were not in the game, aspects of the poem that were in the game, what they changed and how it affected the learning of the poem. This comparison between game and poem also helped for the final group project because I knew how to design a game better and learn from the mistakes the creators of *Dante's* Inferno the video game made."

[5] Students with an Xbox 360 or PlayStation 3 can play the game for a direct experience. Also, in 2018, the Xbox 360 version of the game was also made playable on the newer Xbox One console, both as a disc and as downloadable content. I made the recordings so everyone is welcome to the course and can experience the game at least indirectly.

[6] Gee defines this literacy: "Learning to use any technology—whether this be video games, digital video, digital fabrication, social media, blogs, web quests, or anything else—is a 'literacy' in the sense that, just as with books, we need to learn to 'read' (consume meanings) and 'write' (produce meanings)" (*Good Video Games* 65).

[7] As of October 2016, Entertainment Software Association statistics show the demographic diversity of game players, which goes well beyond the stereotypical teenage boy, as sixty-three percent of households in the United States have at least one person who plays three hours or more a week; the average game player is thirty-five years old; fifty-nine percent are male, forty-one percent are female; women age eighteen or older rep-

resent a greater portion (thirty-one percent) than boys age eighteen or younger (seventeen percent).

[8] H. Brown's statement for studying history holds true for literature in this case: "Studying history interactively is not simply more fun—it invites students to consider a new range of issues, such as identity, perspective, agency, and causality" (119).

[9] Students will "describe, examine, and articulate learning" as described in Ash and Clayton (34).

[10] Other writings on the topic include the following: Barolini, "Ivy League Professor"; Bregni, *"Assassin's Creed"*; A. Brown, *Sexuality*; Damrosch; Steinkuhler et al.; and Weaver. Also worth consulting is Saiber and Coggeshall's Web site *Dante Today*.

INSTRUCTIONAL CONTEXTS
AND PEDAGOGICAL STRATEGIES

On Selecting the "Best" Translation of Dante

Madison U. Sowell

> All great poets . . . must be read in their native tongue. . . .
> To understand Dante, then, it is absolutely necessary to
> understand the Italian language.
> —Henry Wadsworth Longfellow

Over the course of a four-decade career teaching the *Divine Comedy* to undergraduates and graduate students, as well as to occasional high school students, fellow faculty members, and adult learners, the most common question posed to me by non-Italian-speaking teachers and students has been either, "Which translation of Dante is the best?" or "Which translation do you recommend?" My standard reply, which revolves around two words ("it depends"), inevitably has disappointed those expecting a rapid one-word response, such as (to cite but a baker's dozen in alphabetical order) "Binyon," "Ciardi," "Durling," "Hollander," "Kirkpatrick," "Longfellow," "Mandelbaum," "Musa," "Phillips," "Pinsky," "Sayers," "Sinclair," or "Singleton."[1] For me, as for the more sentient questioners, the answer depends on the objective(s) and preparation of the teacher or reader. It depends on the primary goal(s) of the course and at what level the course will be offered. It depends on whether we are talking about high school, undergraduate, or graduate students. It depends on whether poetic form or narrative content will receive primary attention during the course, whether extensive or limited commentary is desired, whether illustrations are welcomed or not, and whether community standards (values and guidelines) are an issue. It depends on whether students will be reading Dante's *New Life* as background to the *Comedy* or starting *ex abrupto* with the *Inferno*.[2]

Furthermore, the answer depends on whether teachers will be dealing with only one canticle or all three major divisions of the poem. (For example, the translations by Phillips and Pinsky, cited above, include only the *Inferno*.) It depends on whether canticles will be studied in toto or in excerpts. (Anthologies of medieval literature tend to include only selected cantos.) It depends on whether the course focuses exclusively on Dante or more broadly on great books or epic tradition. It even depends on the level of fluency the students may have with Latin, conversational Italian, or a Romance language other than Italian. In some cases a bilingual edition (e.g., Durling, Hollander, Kirkpatrick, Mandelbaum, Musa, Pinsky, Sinclair, or Singleton), with Italian on the facing page, may prove valuable in deciphering cognates in Dante's medieval vernacular or fostering interest in mastering fourteenth-century Italian. The answer to a query about the best translation can even depend on something as ostensibly mundane as whether cost is an insignificant or a determining factor in the selection process. Some readers may prefer to consider only translations available in Kindle editions. Of the thirteen translations cited above, the cost to purchase new or unused paper copies just of the *Inferno* ranges from under ten dollars to several times that amount.

When the questioner evinces sincere interest and time allows, I usually begin a more extended response to the question with a brief overview of the purist notion captured in the Tuscan adage "Traduttore traditore" ("every translator, a traitor"). This concept resounds in the bold proposition made by Longfellow, who ironically completed the first American translation of the entire *Comedy*, that to understand Dante one must know the Italian language. I acknowledge that the most reputable translators strive to balance the goal of faithful reproduction with the necessity of artful creativity; as Jiří Levý writes, "The translator's goal is to preserve, capture and convey the original work, and not to create a new work having no precedent in the source. Therefore, the goal of translation is reproduction. In practice, the procedure involves substituting one set of verbal material for another—this entails autonomous creativity involving all the artistic means of the target language. Translation is therefore an original creative process taking place in a given linguistic environment" (57). Levý goes on to postulate, "A translation as a work of art is artistic reproduction, translation as a process is original creation and translation as an art form is a borderline case at the interface between reproductive art and original creative art" (58). I underscore in particular the difficulties a translator of Dante faces in rendering hendecasyllabic terza rima into a non-Romance language. Nonspecialist or non-Italian-speaking teachers of Dante usually are unaware of how many syllables are prescribed in each terzina or tercet of the poem's original 14,233 verses. Therefore, I outline that, according to Italian rules of versification, every three-line stanza is limited to thirty-three syllables. On the microcosmic level of syllabification Dante mirrors each macrocosmic canticle of thirty-three cantos, a number that emphasizes the Trinity but more specifically refers to the years of Christ's mortal life. The *Commedia* is intended as a testament of the life of Christ, not only thematically and allegorically but also structurally and numerologically.

A translator invariably finds it easier to convey the structural import on the grand scale of cantos and canticles than on the scale of eleven-syllable lines. This situation results in part because each verse in Italian has fixed or tonic accents either on the fourth, seventh or eighth, and tenth syllables, or on the sixth and tenth syllables. The celebrated opening line, for example, accents the sixth and tenth syllables, "Nel mezzo del cam*min* di nostra *vita*" ("In the middle of the journey of our life"; my emphasis),[3] thus drawing attention to the poem's dominant metaphor that life ("vita") is a journey ("cammin"). Then there is the matter of whether or how to reproduce the intertwining rhyme scheme (ABA BCB CDC DED, etc.) that Dante invented specifically for the *Divine Comedy*. While Italian words typically end in vowels, English words do not—a fact that makes Dante's penchant for rhymes almost impossible to reproduce.[4] Nevertheless Gilbert Cunningham, in a two-volume study, identified over thirty English translations between 1782 and 1962 that were in some form of terza rima. If we exclude from consideration John Ciardi's defective terza rima (rhyming only the first and third verses in each tercet), the only ones readily available today are by Laurence Binyon and Dorothy L. Sayers.

How does a translator of Dante deal with such complex linguistic, stylistic, and aesthetic issues? Fortunately, answers do exist and are found in translation theory, which has evolved significantly over the past half century, as has the academic (inter)discipline of translation studies. The latter has enjoyed since 2008 a homonymous journal, *Translation Studies*, and most modern translators have come to agree that the most viable translation should privilege as accurately as possible the original author's message. Whether the translation copies or imitates the grammar or syntax of the original remains up for debate and invariably relates to or hinges on the question of the purpose of the translation or its intended audience.

For teachers selecting a translation either for personal pleasure or for a course requirement, it is helpful to keep in mind well-known translating techniques such as *adaptation* (freely translating the original text into terms culturally relevant or familiar to readers of the translation), *borrowing* (repeating the original word and usually placing it in italics), *compensation* (which may take the form of using colloquial or archaic forms, formal or informal registers to capture the tone, if not the word-for-word meaning, of the original), and the use of *periphrasis* (paraphrasing or replacing one word in the source text with a group of words that explain the meaning).

While most translators rely on all these techniques, some tend to emphasize one approach over another. *Compensation*, to cite an obvious example, occurs as soon as the translator has to deal with Dante's use of the personal pronouns: "tu" ("thou") versus "voi" ("you [plural]"). For "tu" and its derivative forms, does one employ the archaic "thou," "thee," and "thine"? Binyon takes this approach, as when he has Dante the pilgrim address Virgil in the line, "Thou art my Master and my Author thou" ("Tu se' lo mio maestro e 'l mio autore"; *Inf.* 1.85) and has Beatrice inform Dante that "Thou'rt not on earth, as thou supposest thee" ("Tu non se' in terra, sì come tu credi"; *Par.* 1.91). The poet and translator Robert Fitzgerald, my professor of the epic tradition at Harvard, strongly recommended the Binyon translation, quoting Ezra Pound's opinion that it was "the most interesting English version of Dante that I have seen or expect to see."[5] Most high school students and college freshmen, however, would likely snicker at the use of "thou." It will be up to the teacher or professor who selects Binyon to explain why in that translation Dante the wayfarer uses "you" and "your" when he responds to Beatrice's questioning, whereas she uses "thou" and "thine" when addressing Dante. It's a complicated issue, because for most twenty-first-century readers of English the use of "thou" and "thine" is formal, not familiar or intimate, speech; in the original Italian, however, "tu" is the familiar form and "voi" constitutes formal speech.

John D. Sinclair's literal prose translation forms the basis for Charles S. Singleton's and also for the translation by Robert Hollander and Jean Hollander. While a word-for-word prose version can be extremely useful for deciphering Dante's vocabulary, it must be noted that Sinclair also employed a more consistently refined vocabulary (cf. his use of "ordure" and "filthy" to translate Dante's "merda" and "merdose" in *Inf.* 18.116 and 131) that fails to capture some of the grittiness of the *Inferno*. By contrast, Tom Phillips buttressed his cutting-edge and occasionally risqué illustrations of the *Inferno* with a translation that freely adapts Dante's Italian into a modern idiom. The devil who berates the seducer Venedico Caccianemico exclaims in Phillips' version, "Move on, you pimp! / We've no girls here to screw your profit from" ("Via / ruffian! qui non son femmine da conio"; *Inf.* 18.65–66). The use of the word "pimp" rather than "pander" (the usual translation of the Italian word "ruffian," at least from Longfellow to Singleton) and especially the employment of the verb "to screw" are decidedly contemporary adaptations intended to convey to modern readers without any equivocation the devil's crude message. Whereas Phillips' translation and ingenious and complex illustrations might serve an undergraduate senior seminar in the humanities or a graduate course in comparative literature very well, a high school teacher or an instructor of a first-year experience course may prefer to adopt a much less costly version with milder language and fewer or no eyebrow-raising illustrations, such as the one depicting Satan as an erect and ejaculating phallus.[6]

Nearly every translator of Dante into English has to engage in *borrowing*, especially when Dante invents words, such as the opening gibberish of *Inferno* 7, when Plutus cries out on seeing Dante and Virgil approach: "Pape Satàn, pape Satàn aleppe!" What do those words mean? No one can be sure, but such cruxes or scholarly problems—not to mention Dante's myriad classical allusions and scholastic theology—lead to the creation of scholarly notes that attempt to explain Dante's intended meaning. The next question that naturally arises is, at what point are such notes too brief or too long?

For length of commentary, Singleton and Hollander vie with each other for the greatest amount of notes. For example, the Hollander translation of and notes for the *Paradiso* total 916 pages; Singleton's translation and commentary of the third canticle number 1000 pages. So the answer to the question of when are the notes too brief or too long is again "it depends": it depends on the level of interest and preparation of the reader and, more to the point, whether the question is posed to the teacher or the student. Certainly for the mature undergraduate and any graduate student engaged in serious research on the *Comedy*, the commentaries of both Singleton and Hollander are required reading.[7]

Periphrasis is needed almost every time Dante creates a neologism, and he increasingly relies on such newly invented words as he composes the *Paradiso*. In the first canto of the third canticle, Dante creates the verb *trasumanar*, which Binyon translates or paraphrases in a seven-word line: "The passing beyond bounds of human sense." The original context for the infinitive *trasumanar*, which means "to transcend the human," is the poet's statement that one cannot describe by means of words the ineffable experience of going to heaven while one is still alive: "Trasumanar significar *per verba* / non si poria; però l'essemplo basti / a cui esperïenza grazia serba" (*Par.* 1.70–72). That is why Dante invents a neologism; no words existed prior to or after his experience that captured what it means to see the divine, whether in the body or out of the body (to paraphrase Saint Paul in 2 Corinthians 12.2).

The following list illustrates how nine translators of modern editions, listed chronologically according to the date of publication of their version of the *Paradiso*, have attempted to capture Dante's terzina quoted above (*Par.* 1.70–72) on the ineffability or inexpressibility of the pilgrim's experience of seeing God (for a more complete list of modern translations, see the appendix below):

> Longfellow (1867, blank verse): "To represent transhumanize in words / Impossible were; the example, then, suffice / Him for whom Grace the experience reserves."
>
> Sinclair (1939, prose): "The passing beyond humanity cannot be set forth in words; let the example suffice, therefore, for him to whom grace reserves the experience."
>
> Binyon (1943, terza rima): "The passing beyond bounds of human sense / Words cannot tell; let then the example sate / Him for whom grace reserves the experience."
>
> Ciardi (1965, "dummy" *terza rima*): "How speak trans-human change to human sense? / Let the example speak until God's grace / grants the pure spirit the experience."
>
> Singleton (1975, prose): "The passing beyond humanity may not be set forth in words: therefore let the example suffice any for whom grace reserves that experience."

Mandelbaum (1982, "a verse translation"): "Passing beyond the human cannot be / worded: let Glaucus serve as simile— / until grace grant you the experience."

Musa (1984, blank verse): "'Transhumanize'—it cannot be explained / *per verba*, so let this example serve / until God's grace grants the experience."

Hollander (2007, free verse): "To soar beyond the human cannot be described / in words. Let the example be enough to one / for whom grace holds this experience."

Durling (2011, prose set in lines): "To signify transhumanizing *per verba* is / impossible; therefore let the comparison / suffice for those to whom grace reserves the experience."

An honest response to the question of the best translation invariably samples and evaluates the various types of translation available for the *Comedy*; furthermore, it explores the pedagogical implications that instructors or readers make when they select a particular translation. Which of the above is the best translation? Again, the answer in large part will depend on the goal of the teacher or reader. The candid discussion of translations, their pros and cons, should prove a practical guide to teachers and students of Dante at all levels— from high school to college to adult-learning centers.

Which translations have I selected for my classes and what were the bases for my choices? When guest lecturing to high school students in advanced placement English courses who only read the *Inferno*, I have relied on Ciardi's fun and easy-to-read translation, which popularized Dante on American college campuses in the 1960s, much as did Longfellow's version a century earlier.[8] I met Ciardi when I was an undergraduate and listened to his lively discourse about what he hoped to accomplish in translating Dante. He very much wanted to share the *Comedy* with, and appeal to the masses of, general education students.[9] To accomplish this goal he employed what he humorously labeled "dummy *terza rima*," rhyming only the first and third lines of each tercet. This decision allowed him a freedom that neither Binyon nor Sayers enjoyed. Like Robert Pinsky, he was a poet in his own right and felt freer to engage in adaptation and periphrasis than did such literal translators as Sinclair and Singleton. I can invariably keep the attention of high school and first-year college students when I read to them from Ciardi's translation of *Inferno* 21 and 22, the tale of the wayfarer's encounter with the horde of demons who guard the barraters. For example, Ciardi creatively translates the name of the devils in *Inf.* 21.118–23, bestowing on Malacoda's squadron the epithets of Snatcher, Grizzly, Hellken, Deaddog, Curlybeard, Grafter, Dragontooth, Pigtusk, Catclaw, Cramper, and Crazyred.

When I taught a cross-listed course for Italian majors and non-Italian-speaking honors students who read the entire *Divine Comedy*, I had to use a bilingual text. That limited my options, but I soon developed a strategy that allowed students the opportunity to see and judge for themselves how translators engaged Dante's text, both in their translation and in their commentary. I used Allen Mandelbaum's inexpensive translation of the *Inferno*, which has the Italian facing the English, includes Barry Moser's delightful illustrations, and keeps notes to a readable minimum at the end of the book. For the *Purgatorio*, I selected Singleton's more costly two-volume paperback edition. The first volume contains the Italian and English translation; the second volume consists solely of commentary. Singleton's literal prose translation is based heavily on Sinclair's earlier translation, but his commentary is truly magisterial. The only notes in English that approach it appear in the commentaries of Robert M. Durling and Ronald L. Martinez or in Robert Hollander's. I chose Singleton because I wanted my students to understand the difference a renowned scholar-translator can make when approaching Dante. In all cases I recommend the use of the online *Dartmouth Dante Project* commentaries to supplement whatever printed scholarly apparatus students have at hand.

For the *Paradiso*, arguably the most esoteric or challenging of Dante's three canticles, I chose Sinclair's edition in no small part because of the insightful introductions he penned to each of the thirty-three cantos. His actual notes are among the briefest on record, but his two- to four-page explanations of what Dante is attempting poetically, philosophically, and theologically are trenchant and prove invaluable to the undergraduate Italian major or honors student struggling to understand the basic tenets of Scholasticism, monasticism, and the Ptolemaic or geocentric conception of the universe.

Currently, even though I have limited time for teaching because of administrative assignments, I manage to teach every other year an upper-division general education course cross-listed in the English department that is devoted to Dante's world. In part to keep the cost of the books to a minimum, I have adopted the paperback Mandelbaum version for all three canticles of the poem. Although my students rarely have fluency in Italian, they seem to enjoy, as did my earlier honors students, when I draw attention to what Dante is accomplishing in the original Italian. Students who have reading ability in French or Spanish often can follow the meaning of many of the Italian words. Furthermore, the notes, although not nearly as extensive as those of Singleton, Durling and Martinez, and Robert Hollander, are more than adequate for their needs.

For anyone approaching Dante's epic for the first time, I am hesitant to recommend (but wish to cite for experienced readers) two translations. The first is by the Australian polymath Clive James, who eschewed traditional tercets and reproduced the entire *Divine Comedy* in rhymed quatrains. His edition lacks any explanatory notes. The dearth of commentary makes the comprehension of Dante's myriad cast of characters quite challenging, if not impossible, for first-time readers of the poem. The second translation is an adaptation by the American visual artist Sandow Birk, who transmogrified Dante's poem into contemporary slang and relocated the action in urban American cities and ghettos. Although

Birk's accompanying lithographic images aid the comprehension of the re-imagined narrative scenes, what remains of the original *Comedy* constitutes a question mark for newcomers to the poem.

For the reader who is a product of—or consumed by—post-9/11 culture, a final work does deserve consideration. The brilliant postmodern poet Mary Jo Bang has created not so much an idiomatic translation as a highly entertaining "reenvisioning" of the *Inferno*. Anachronistic references to Pink Floyd, *South Park*, Donald Rumsfeld, and *Star Trek* substitute for, or appear alongside, Dante's medieval and classical allusions, to which the vast majority of college undergraduates presumably do not relate. American slang and contemporary references regularly replace attempts at textual fidelity (e.g., the she-wolf in *Inf.* 1.49 has a "bitch-kitty face"; four cantos later Minos's opening words to Dante pilgrim are "Hey, you, who've come to the Hotel Woe" (5.16); the banks of the sodomites were designed by "some Frank Lloyd Wright" (15.10–12); the squadron of demons in *Inferno* 21 take on names such as "Badass" and "Scumbutt," "Killer Clown" and "Ilse the Witch," "Qaddafi" and "Dragan Nikolić" (21.118–23). Dante's archaic literary references are often updated to pay tribute to modernist giants, such as Robert Lowell and Sylvia Plath, as well as to earlier authors who wrote in English but postdated Dante (e.g., William Shakespeare and John Milton).

Unlike James, Bang includes notes to clarify her own literary and historical allusions and those made by Dante that still remain in her revisionist, richly intertextual work. Hendrik Drescher provides wildly clever illustrations that support Bang's nonrhyming, largely nonmetrical (yet unquestionably lyrical) narrative. As might be expected, the response to Bang's creative "translation" has ranged widely, from high-minded horror from purists to rapturous praise from lovers of colloquialism and postmodernism. Whether this unconventional approach to translation will appeal to a particular reader once again depends on background and expectations.

In conclusion, the English-speaking world truly is experiencing the so-called golden age of Dante translations. The variety of translations available to teachers and students presents an opportunity to ask oneself the question: What do I hope to gain from the translation and commentary I choose? Or, what do I want my students to take away from reading Dante's *Comedy* in translation? If a poet-translator such as Fitzgerald is teaching a class on epic poems, he may very well choose the Binyon translation in terza rima so prized by Pound for its poetic nuances. The graduate student of Geoffrey Chaucer, on the other hand, may be more interested in understanding the literal meaning and context of the lines Chaucer borrowed from Dante and consequently may prize a prose translation. Between such options abound several intriguing possibilities. The answer to the perennial question of "the best" invariably relates more to the goal(s) of the individual teacher-reader than to the opinion of a single pontificating professor of Italian.[10]

NOTES

¹ For critical bibliographies of Dante translations in English up to the septicentennial of Dante's birth (1965), see De Sua (*Dante into English*) and Cunningham (Divine Comedy *in English*). For more recent translations see "Selected Bibliography of American and English Dante Translations" in De Rooy (Divine Comedies *for the New Millennium* 135–39).

² Quotations in Italian from the *Divine Comedy* come from Singleton's edition.

³ This essay does not focus on English translations of Dante's *Vita nova*, which remains the best introduction to the *Divine Comedy*. Nonetheless, the question of which version to use of the *New Life* in a non-Italian classroom setting constitutes another oft asked question of dantisti. Readily available options are far fewer in number than for the *Comedy*, but in the last half century they include at least an impressive quintet. For example, the Frisardi translation contains lengthy and highly informative notes and the most up-to-date bibliography; the Slavitt edition is highly readable because of its contemporary idiom and minimalist notes; the Cervigni and Vasta version has the Italian text facing the English, as well as a concordance and glossary; the translation by Reynolds includes an important note on the *Vita nova*'s symmetrical structure; and Musa's 1973 version, which has undoubtedly sold the most copies since it first appeared in 1962, contains his seminal and oft cited study, "An Essay on the *Vita Nuova*" (87–120).

⁴ In a "Translator's Note" John Ciardi discusses his version of Dante's rhyme as "dummy *terza rima*," as he maintains the three-line unit but chooses to rhyme only the first and third lines of each stanza (Ciardi, *Purgatorio*, xxiv–xxix).

⁵ Fitzgerald quotes at length Pound's April 1934 review of Binyon's *Inferno* in *The Criterion* (148).

⁶ In researching the topic of Satan, whom Dante derides as an *uccello* (Italian slang for *phallus*), I found considerable evidence prior to, and contemporary with, Dante's era that supports Phillips' phallic illustration (Sowell, "'Quanto'").

⁷ For a review of the pros and cons of the Hollander translation itself, see Sowell, "'Substantial, Verbatim, (Un)Attributed, Misleading'?"

⁸ Even after a half century, Ciardi remains the translator of choice for many seeking a verse translation. See, for example, the recent assessment by the poet Barbarese, who prefers Ciardi over either Mandelbaum or Hollander.

⁹ Students guffawed when Ciardi claimed in a lecture at Brigham Young University in the early 1970s that he had wanted to translate the alliterative phrase "Più non posso" (*Purgatory* 10.139), describing the thoughts of the prideful who are weighed down by heavy stones, as "Pal, I'm pissed!" He opted instead for a blander but more genteel exclamation: "I can bear no more!"

¹⁰ To give Dante the last word concerning whether poetry can be successfully translated from one language to another, I cite *Convivio* 1.7.14: "[N]ulla cosa per legame musaico armonizzata si può de la sua loquela in altra transmutare sanza rompere tutta sua dolcezza e armonia," which is to argue that "nothing harmonized according to the rules of poetry can be translated from its native tongue into another without destroying all its sweetness and harmony" (Lansing trans.).

APPENDIX: TRANSLATIONS OF
THE *DIVINE COMEDY,*
ARRANGED BY TRANSLATOR

See this volume's works-cited list for full bibliographical information.

Mary Jo Bang, *Inferno* (2012)

Laurence Binyon, *The Portable Dante* (1947)

Sandow Birk and Marcus Sanders, *Dante's* Inferno (2004); *Dante's* Purgatorio (2005); *Dante's* Paradiso (2005)

John Ciardi, *The* Inferno: *A Verse Rendering for the Modern Reader* (1954); *The* Purgatorio: *A Verse Rendering for the Modern Reader* (1961); *The* Paradiso: *A Verse Rendering for the Modern Reader* (1970)

Robert M. Durling, *The Divine Comedy: Inferno* (1996); *Purgatorio* (2003); *Paradiso* (2011)

Robert Hollander and Jean Hollander, *Inferno* (2000); *Purgatorio* (2003); *Paradiso* (2007)

Clive James, *The Divine Comedy* (2012)

Robin Kirkpatrick, *The Divine Comedy: Inferno* (2006); *Purgatorio* (2007); *Paradiso* (2007)

Henry Wadsworth Longfellow, The Divine Comedy *of Dante Alighieri* (1867)

Allen Mandelbaum, *The* Divine Comedy *of Dante Alighieri:* Inferno (1982); *The* Divine Comedy *of Dante Alighieri:* Purgatorio (1984); *The* Divine Comedy *of Dante Alighieri:* Paradiso (1984)

Mark Musa, *The Portable Dante* (1995)

Tom Phillips, *Dante's* Inferno: *The First Part of* The Divine Comedy *of Dante Alighieri* (1985)

Robert Pinsky, *The* Inferno *of Dante: A New Verse Translation* (1994)

Dorothy L. Sayers, *The* Comedy *of Dante Alighieri the Florentine: I:* Hell (1949); *The* Comedy *of Dante Alighieri the Florentine: II:* Purgatory (1955)

Dorothy L. Sayers and Barbara Reynolds, *The* Comedy *of Dante Alighieri the Florentine: III:* Paradise (1962)

John D. Sinclair, *The* Divine Comedy *of Dante Alighieri* (1978)

Charles S. Singleton, *The Divine Comedy* (1970–75)

Damned Rhetoric: Teaching Dante's *Inferno* in Translation to Undergraduates

Suzanne Hagedorn

Studying Dante's *Commedia* in its original Italian best enables students to appreciate its sonority and linguistic fireworks. Still, many students of Italian would never have been inspired to learn the poet's language without first feeling captivated by the breadth and depth of Dante's otherworldly vision—even as imperfectly transmitted in a Modern English translation. Dante's status and enduring influence outside Italian studies has ensured that undergraduates at English-speaking universities are far more likely to encounter the *Commedia* (or portions of it) outside Italian programs than within them, for it is frequently taught in translation in great-books or general education courses.

Instructors teaching upper- and lower-division general education or comparative literature courses can share their appreciation of Dante's monumental poem with their students by incorporating translations of the most renowned canticle of the *Commedia*, the *Inferno*, into a wide variety of classes. Encountering Dante in such environments can attract students to study Italian and to enroll in study-abroad programs and upper-division Italian literature offerings. Moreover, at community colleges and smaller colleges and universities without Italian specialists, studying Dante in translation may be the only exposure some students ever have to this important medieval Italian writer.

Fortunately, instructors teaching the *Inferno* in translation have many different editions and translations from which to choose, including those by Charles S. Singleton, Allen Mandelbaum, Robert Pinsky, Mark Musa, and Robert Hollander and Jean Hollander. Arguably, Singleton's prose rendition gives his readers a more faithful version of the literal sense of Dante's lines than these more recent poetic translations offer. In my experience, however, students have found poetic translations that preserve (at least visually) the feel of Dante's terzinas more accessible and compelling. In particular, the Hollanders' translation, available as an affordable paperback, presents Dante's Italian text parallel to a faithful poetic translation that reads well in its own right, along with extensive explanatory notes, summaries, and diagrams that help first-time readers navigate both the verbal and visual complexities of Dante's poem.

For many instructors, an upper-division great-books survey may be the course in which they most frequently assign Dante's *Inferno* in translation. My most long-running course incorporating the *Inferno* is Epic and Romance, a comparative literature course aimed at junior and senior English majors that introduces students to important classical and medieval examples of these genres in translation. We spend the first half of the semester studying the classical tradition, reading Homer's *Iliad* and *Odyssey* in Modern English translation before considering Virgil's translation and transformation of these Greek poems into the foundational epic of ancient Rome, the *Aeneid*. To make the transition between epic and romance texts, I devote one class meeting to selected epistles from Ovid's *Heroides* (those of Penelope, Briseis, Helen, Paris, and Dido) in which we discuss Ovid's reenvisioning of the epic storylines of Homer and Virgil through the lens of women's experiences and the foregrounding of individual love affairs. With this Ovidian perspective in mind, we turn to medieval romances, in which gender issues and amorous relationships figure even more prominently. We first read and discuss a selection of Chrétien de Troyes's Arthurian romances, specifically *Erec, Yvain, Lancelot,* and *Perceval*; we consider the cultural differences between pagan antiquity and the Christian medieval culture depicted in these texts and reflect on the similarities and differences between the knightly hero's challenges and those faced by epic heroes of classical literature. We then turn to Wolfram von Eschenbach's Grail poem *Parzival*, comparing and contrasting the more epic (and tragic) trajectory of Parzival's father, Gahmuret, in its opening books with that of its eponymous hero. As the poem continues, we consider the parallels and differences between Parzival's spiritual quest and the more secular, courtly adventures of the poem's secondary hero, Gawan.

As our final literary text, we read Dante's *Inferno*, which combines many elements of the individual journey of the romance hero with the dense mythological background of classical epic. Studying Dante's *Inferno* in conjunction with these earlier texts allows us to appreciate the innovation of his autobiographical spiritual quest narrative and to see the way he redeploys figures from the epic tradition in surprising ways. (First-time readers of the *Inferno* tend to be very surprised to encounter Ulysses so deep in Hell, enabling us to have an interesting discussion about the difference between the values of Dante's Christian vision and those of classical epic heroes.) Moreover, students enjoy examining the way Dante engages in a poetic dialogue with the *Aeneid* and analyzing his ambiguous portrait of Virgil, as both an inspirational guide who helps Dante emerge from the "selva oscura" ("dark wood"; *Inf.* 1.2) of despair in which he finds himself at the beginning of the poem and a tragic symbol of the shortcomings of pagan culture. Finally, as an entertaining way to connect the epic and romance motifs we have encountered in our readings to contemporary popular culture, students watch George Lucas's original *Star Wars* trilogy to see how it recycles and recasts various plot elements, character types, and situations we encountered in earlier literature.

Instructors can also find ways to incorporate Dante's *Inferno* in translation into thematically organized general education courses aimed at nonliterature majors. In the past few years, I have taught a course called Monsters, Giants, Fairies and Other Worlds, which uses the fascination with monsters and the monstrous so prevalent in today's popular culture as a lens through which to view older literature. The texts in this course can be understood as precursors to the modern science fiction and fantasy that are the preferred pleasure reading of many students who opt to enroll. In this course, we study the Old English epic *Beowulf* and the Middle English romance *Sir Gawain and the Green Knight*, which focus on encounters with monstrous, supernatural Others in translation. We then turn to the Middle English romance *Sir Orfeo* and Marie de France's *Lanval*, which portray supernatural fairy figures and their landscapes. We continue exploring medieval visions of the supernatural by spending several weeks on Dante's *Inferno*, comparing and contrasting its monsters and hellscape to the imagined worlds we have seen in earlier medieval literature. Last, students read A. S. Byatt's *Ragnorok: The End of the Gods*, a vivid retelling of the Norse creation and destruction stories as seen through the eyes of an autobiographical modern narrator, the Thin Girl, who has been evacuated from London during the Nazi bombings of World War II. This contemporary text allows us to contrast pagan Germanic mythology with classical mythology and Christian culture, and to consider how writers find meaning and inspiration as they encounter the great works of the distant past, as Dante did with Virgil's *Aeneid* and Byatt does with the Norse myths.

Finally, instructors can easily include the *Inferno* in lower-level interdisciplinary survey courses that introduce students to medieval and Renaissance studies. In my version of such an introductory course, students encounter a wide variety of texts from the *Norton Anthology of Western Literature* to give them a sense of the ideas and values central to these historical periods and to consider the continuity and change between them. Our readings include selections from Virgil's *Aeneid* and the Bible, Augustine's *Confessions*, *The Song of Roland*, Chrétien de Troyes's *Perceval*, troubadour lyrics, lais by Marie de France, Dante's *Inferno*, Giovanni Boccaccio's *Decameron*, Petrarch's lyrics and letters, Niccolò Machiavelli's *The Prince*, Baldassare Castiglione's *Book of the Courtier*, Marguerite de Navarre's *Heptameron*, François Rabelais's *Gargantua and Pantagruel*, and Miguel de Cervantes's *Don Quixote*. The breadth and the pace of this survey course preclude us from delving into the *Inferno* as deeply as we do in the other two courses, especially since we read the poem in the excerpts included in the *Norton Anthology* rather than in its entirety. Nevertheless, students do have the option of writing their final course paper on a particular canto of the *Inferno*, which enables them to explore Dante's imagery and themes in more detail on their own.

In these types of courses, instructors should be prepared to give students extensive background information to ease their understanding of Dante's challenging and sometime strange text. I generally begin our exploration of the poem by devoting one class meeting to lecturing on Dante's life, times, and writings other than the *Commedia*. In discussing Dante's radical choice to make his own journey the subject of his poem, I encourage my students to appreciate the difference between the perspectives of Dante the author versus Dante the character so central to modern interpretations of the poem. Like Dante the character, students who are first-time readers of the *Commedia* often find the hellscape confusing. In teaching the *Inferno*, instructors should expect to stop frequently to ask and answer questions to help their students understand and appreciate this rewarding but challenging poem. Most important, for courses that will not study either the *Purgatorio* or *Paradiso*, instructors may find it helpful to remind students that Dante's poem is not all darkness and condemnation. Students reading on their own often tend to focus the most on the poem's plot and the physical and ethical organization of Dante's Hell. In order to encourage them to read more carefully and question the motivations of the speakers Dante encounters as he makes his descent through the circles of Hell, instructors may wish to introduce classroom activities that encourage students to focus carefully on smaller chunks of text. I have found it helpful to use a series of in-class close-reading exercises that require students to look back at important personages in the poem and reflect on Dante the pilgrim's reactions to them.

For the first of these "damned rhetoric" exercises, I divide students into three groups, assigning them particular characters whom Dante encounters in the upper part of Hell: Francesca da Rimini (*Inferno* 5), Cavalcante dei Cavalcanti (*Inferno* 10) or Farinata degli Uberti (*Inferno* 10). I project a *PowerPoint* slide in front of the class with the following questions: How does character X seem to view himself or herself? How does this character speak to Dante? What does this character feel was most valuable or important in life? How does this character appear to think about God? How does Dante the pilgrim feel about or react to this character? I have students look back at their texts and give them ten to fifteen minutes of class time to answer these questions on an index card or a piece of notebook paper (which they will turn in for credit as informal writing). If time permits, the groups gather together to compare their answers before the class as a whole discusses each of these figures.

Students find the questions in this exercise easier to answer when looking at Francesca's speeches than Cavalcante's and Farinata's. They quickly notice Francesca's sense of herself as a victim of circumstances beyond her control and her tendency to project her adulterous impulses on "Love" and forces outside herself. They notice that she seems to blame God for not being a friend to her and Paolo and point out that, ultimately, she faults a medieval romance and its author for her situation in Hell. As we examine her rhetoric and Dante the character's sympathetic swoon in response to it, we look carefully at Francesca's emotional vocabulary. Students in my classes have generally tended to be much tougher in judging Francesca's sins and excesses than Dante the protagonist (who weeps and faints), and thus, this particular episode establishes an important sense of critical distance between them as readers and Dante as a character.

Not surprisingly, students assigned the more cryptic Farinata and Cavalcante speeches in the circle of the heretics generally have more trouble untangling them, since understanding their nuances requires some knowledge of the Florentine political situation (and consequently, careful reading of the footnotes that provide this historical background). Nevertheless, they observe that Farinata seems only interested in Dante's political party and Florentine politics, while Cavalcante lives vicariously through his absent son. In discussing Cavalcante's speech and Dante's delay in answering him, I call my students' attention to Dante's personal relationship to Guido Cavalcanti and the political role Dante played in exiling his youthful friend to the marshlands that eventually led to Guido's death from malaria; we reflect on what Cavalcante's (and Dante's) confusion might reveal about his conflicted feelings about this fateful political decision. Most important, in dissecting these two characters' speeches, we note that neither seems particularly interested in God or spiritual matters; even in the afterlife, these worldly characters only display interest in the present, although God's judgment has denied them this knowledge. Although we are many cantos away from Bertran de Born and Dante's use of the term *contrapasso*, I introduce the concept so that students can use it as they reflect on the spiritual and physical punishments Dante devises for the other occupants of his hellscape.

In subsequent class meetings, I repeat this "damned rhetoric" writing exercise with other major figures, so students can better understand that Dante the poet's decision to place an individual in Hell stems not so much from the actions that a soul has committed but in its spiritual disposition toward God and willingness to admit wrongdoing and take responsibility for sinful behavior. For the second exercise, we discuss Pier delle Vigne, Brunetto Latini, and Vanni Fucci. Here, we look at Dante's sympathetic portraits of Pier and Brunetto, and their own focus on rhetoric. Students notice that, like Francesca, Pier shifts the blame for his own choices: he commits suicide because of the envious voices of others. Students also note his resolute declaration that "not once did I break faith / with my true lord" (*Inf.* 13.74–75; Hollander trans.). Like Farinata and Cavalcante, Pier has fixed his mind only on earthly things; he shows more concern with his reputation, memory, and his fidelity to the emperor rather than with his relationship to God, who should be the Lord with whom he strives to keep faith.

As we examine Dante the character's interactions with Brunetto Latini, students usually point out Dante's surprise at finding this admired scholar in Hell, and the way that he ironically casts him as a father figure in the poem despite the sin of sodomy for which Brunetto is apparently punished. (Here, I note that although Dante, as a medieval Christian, considered same-sex sexual activity sinful, he also decided to put those who committed similar actions but who repented for them among the saved souls in the highest terrace of Purgatory.) As we work through the text, students notice the way in which Brunetto and Dante debate earthly political matters, much as he had with Farinata; they also call attention to Dante's observation that Brunetto "taught me how man makes himself immortal," indicating that Brunetto has made an idol out of human achievement rather than submitting himself to God (*Inf.* 15.85; Hollander trans.). Finally, they note that Brunetto's main concern is the survival of the literary reputation of the *Tesoro*; he has forgotten Jesus's command in Matthew 6:19 to store up treasures not on earth but in heaven.

As we discuss Vanni Fucci, students point out that Dante's portrait of this unrepentant thief lacks the respect and sympathy that we see in Dante's actions with Pier or Brunetto; his speech, in keeping with the physical metamorphosis described in the canto, is replete with animal imagery. Where earlier interlocutors have been polite and even pleading, Vanni goes out of his way to give Dante a negative prophecy. Previous speakers have simply ignored God to talk about their own concerns; in contrast, Dante's encounter with Vanni concludes with the thief offering a much more direct (and physical) manifestation of his continuing contempt for the divine order.

In our final class meeting, students repeat the "damned rhetoric" exercise with three of the most prominent sinners in lower Hell: Ulysses, Guido da Montefeltro, and Ugolino. In general, students tend to be very surprised at Dante's placement of Ulysses in Hell and at Dante's description of Ulysses's watery doom. As we examine his speech, students usually point out Ulysses's pride in his own achievements and his lack of respect for social and familial bonds. In looking at Guido da Montefeltro, we analyze elements of his speech that show his pride in his previous crafty behavior, and willingness to shift the blame for his actions from himself to Boniface, the pope who absolved him (in advance) for his sins. Finally, as we examine Ugolino's rhetoric, students tend to note his self-pity and plea for sympathy from Dante while he exhibits no such empathy for his own children, to whose cries he has hardened his heart.

As we consider these varied characters and their speeches we can delineate some essential characteristics of the "damned rhetoric" that Dante places into the mouths of these characters: they tend to shift any blame from their current situation from themselves to others; moreover, even when they are condemned to spend eternity in close proximity to others, they consider and speak only about themselves. We also observe how certain elements in these speeches gesture at larger Christian meanings that Dante intends his reader to grasp, but that these sinners have misunderstood or ignored, a fateful decision that has led to their present position in Hell.

Although I usually teach only the *Inferno* in translation in my courses, I have also used this approach to teach the *Purgatorio* in translation to upper-division English majors, using a parallel series of exercises on "redeemed rhetoric." For these exercises, I focus on the speeches of Casella, Manfred, Belaqua, Buonconte da Montefeltro, Sordello, Nino Visconti, Currado Malaspina, Oderisi da Gubbio, Sapia, Guido del Duca, Marco Lombardo, Pope Adrian V, and Hugh Capet, a list that could easily be expanded or contracted. Instructors who teach the entire *Commedia* in their courses could take a similar approach and create exercises for various figures in the *Paradiso* in order to illustrate the gap between heavenly and earthly perspectives.

Dante's *Comedy* as First-Year Seminar: From Early Engagement to Self-Reliance

Simone Marchesi

Io voglio che voi non istiate lì con la bocca aperta e
occhi levati a raccoglier le parole dell'oracolo, con niun
altro incomodo che d'imprimerle nella vostra mente.
Voi dovete avvezzarvi a pensare col vostro capo, a trovare
il vero, a sentire la gioia di averlo trovato voi stessi.

(You should not, I insist, simply wait with your mouth
open and your eyes raised to receive the pronouncements
of the oracle, making no other effort but to impress them
in your memory. You should learn to think with your own
head, discover the truth, and feel the joy of having
discovered it yourself.)
  —Francesco De Sanctis, "Ai Miei Giovani" (my trans.)

In the wake of Robert Hollander's seminal teachings, Dante's *Comedy* is taught in several venues at Princeton (Hollander, "Teaching Dante"). Offerings range from dedicated undergraduate seminars conducted in Italian for advanced students in the Department of French and Italian to introductory seminars in English focusing on the *Inferno*. The *Comedy* also enjoys a steady presence in the Humanities Sequence (a great-book, yearlong, cotaught lecture-precept course), which devotes two weeks of its lecture and precept time to the poem, as well as in graduate seminars, where it is taught in a comparative perspective alongside other classical, medieval, and early modern texts. This essay presents a set of active-learning practices that I have adopted at Princeton in the last five years, in teaching Dante's *Comedy* to undergraduate students. The strategies and techniques surveyed here aim at fostering early student engagement with and critical reading of the text, as well as sustained discussion in the seminars. They are based on the interplay between course-long assigned responsibilities to individual students (three strategies) and in-class exercises (three techniques), which take the form of ad hoc activities assigned to small, constantly reconfiguring groups of learners in the course.

In line with recent trends in active pedagogy, the strategies and techniques presented here are designed to help instructors remove themselves as much as possible from the center of attention and become facilitators for independent, independently motivated, and collaborative learning in the course (Bonwell and Eison; Faust and Paulson). By promoting students' personal and critical engagement with Dante's text, these teaching practices have proved instrumental in creating a collaborative and productive atmosphere in the daily life of the courses. Most important, and perhaps more measurably, they have reduced the need for direct instruction during meetings, so that instructor contributions center on channeling the natural flow of the dialogue or directing the students' interactions in class. These practices have also been successful at producing the same degree of information retention during mid- and end-of-semester tests, as well as the same high quality in final summative and critical papers and projects, as more frontal approaches to teaching Dante's *Comedy*. Although focusing on one specific teaching situation, the small-scale and intensive-reading setting that characterizes first-year seminars at Princeton, this essay surveys approaches that may be adopted in and adapted to other discussion-oriented instructional settings.

Promoting Personal and Collective Learning: Yearlong Engagement Strategies

Three reciprocally balancing strategies have proved instrumental in promoting students' active approach to reading the *Comedy*. The first strategy is the progressive memorization and recitation of the first lines of the poem in the original, an exercise conducted at the ideal pace of one new tercet every week. This strategy serves two purposes. For students who take the course in Italian but have spent the rest of the day in an English-speaking setting, reciting Dante becomes an opportunity to reset their communication mode to the target language, isolating their classwork from the pervasive dominance of their first language. This ritual moment of collective recitation from memory does not require much time, but it is extremely effective in preventing relapses into the more familiar linguistic patterns—that is, it helps banish English from the classroom for the duration of the seminar. It has also proved effective in eventually drawing into the conversation students who may be reluctant to make active contributions to class discussions at first. For students who take the class in English, it acts as an additional constant reminder (together with the facing-page edition that is used) that the text they are studying in translation exists first in a different language, a language from which all interpretations should begin and against which they should be measured. In this case, pronunciation accuracy is of course not the goal, though the use of the recordings provided by the *Princeton Dante Project* (in the voice of Lino Pertile) has helped non-Italianists improve the way they sound both when reciting in Italian and, just as important, when pronouncing the many place and personal names usually left unchanged in the translated text of the poem.

This first collective and admittedly mechanical task assigned to all students as a group is accompanied by a second strategy that is designed to promote early personal engagement with more than just the linguistic surface of the poem: the call to becoming the class resident expert on a specific topic related to the *Comedy*. During short in-class self-introductions conducted at the start of each semester, students are given an opportunity to manifest the motivations and goals they set for themselves when they decided to study the *Comedy*. In that setting, it is usually easy to identify what aspects of the poem's encyclopedia will most appeal to each of them. On that basis, each student is asked to commit to studying one particular topic in more depth and thus become the go-to person for relevant questions on that topic that may arise during class discussions.

In practice, the resident expert on a topic knows that, while preparing for class, he or she has to pay special attention to the zones of the text in which their topic is particularly relevant and that they will be called on during discussion to comment and clarify these passages for the class. No matter what level of involvement with their specific topic each student chooses to adopt (ranging from simply being aware that there is something relevant in a specific passage, to being ready to share the results of targeted research on the issues present in the text), all members of the class benefit from having peer-experts in the room. In the past, topics such as Dante's politics, his idea of Rome, his engagement with classical philosophies and literatures, the natural sciences, religious doctrines, the romance vernaculars, his portrayal of gender issues, as well as his deployment of rhetorical and poetic categories have been identified and assigned to students based on their interests and preferences. This list, of course, illustrates only some of the possibilities, and each class produces different sets of resident experts.

The main goal of this technique is to allow students to develop a special relation with the text early on, to angle their reading of it from the start, and to encourage their active participation in the seminars from a position of relative authority. It also serves to dispel the notion that each reader of the poem should know everything and that the point of studying the *Comedy* is to acquire the knowledge on which it is based—a common as well as deleterious misconception. The poem may certainly be conceived of and read as a summative work, one that invites readers to educate themselves, but not at the expense of a genuine personal connection. Dispelling the anxiety that may come from an encyclopedic approach to the text by redistributing expertise responsibilities among a community of learners also facilitates the production of more focused and better-researched final essays and projects. Students actually respond well to the notion that even professional readers of the poem specialize in specific areas of Dante's culture and that omniology is not necessarily a virtue when working on the *Comedy*. As a consequence, their final independent work usually reflects their awareness that Dante studies have a depth of field.

The final strategy adopted in our courses, which I adapted from a similar exercise developed by Susanna Barsella at Fordham University, is labeled the Poet's Corner. Throughout the semester students know that they have the possibility to open a five- to ten-minute Poet's Corner, a time in which (individually or in small groups) they present to the class a specific cultural object from present-day pop culture, connected to the material covered for that meeting. Not unlike the resident expert, the Poet's Corner is a tool aimed at encouraging early individual engagement with the interpretive study of the poem and maintaining it throughout the course. It also balances the mandatory quality of both memorization- and expertise-based strategies with a more spontaneous framework. In addition to bringing awareness of the pervasive quality of Dante's presence in contemporary culture, this exercise helps individual students to showcase their ability to use the poem as a currently relevant phenomenon, rather than learn about it as a simply historical (or, worse, merely archaeological) artifact. For this exercise, beyond the serendipitous finds that every class may produce, Arielle Saiber and Elizabeth Coggeshall's archive of Dante Sightings/Citings remains an invaluable resource, to which students seem eager to go back for inspiration and are always excited to add their own finds.

Depending on the type of class, the Poet's Corner may also take another form. Since it provides students with a framework for individual initiative and active participation in the formation of the lesson plan, the student-initiated activity may be structured so individuals in the class can draw their peers' attention to sections or issues in the text that may have fallen by the wayside during discussions. Resident experts have sometimes felt the whole class could benefit from going back to a passage, an image, a word in the text to which insufficient attention had been paid, and they have taken advantage of the Poet's Corner space to do so. In this instantiation, the activity may take on the function of the often merely perfunctory and always teacher-centered prompt "Any more questions?" at the end of each meeting.

Developing Self-Reliance: Gradual Questioning Techniques

In the second area, that of daily classwork exercises designed to promote discussion of the cantos students have prepared in advance of the class meeting, three class activities based on peer-to-peer interaction have been successfully adopted. The first technique is essentially an ice-breaking exercise and consists in eliciting from each student a so-called one-word lecture on each canto covered that week (usually three). All students in the seminar are asked to identify in advance of each meeting a keyword in the canto (or in the commentary tradition) that, for them, embodies the central idea of the text at hand. They are then asked to brainstorm about the proposed keywords, either collectively or in small groups, discussing which words have received more support statistically, which are ultimately more convincing, and why they think this is the case.

Many different patterns for debriefing may be adopted during the class work. A possible one is the following. The teacher asks the first student to present a one-word lecture for the canto; a second student is then immediately drawn into the conversation by being asked to hypothesize why the classmate has chosen that keyword; a third student may then be asked to assess the force of the explanation given and then to provide a new word. At this point, with two keywords on the table, the first student may be given the option to change the original word and to explain the reasons for this choice; alternatively, the class may be asked to take a vote in favor of each option and to organize a one-minute explanation of their choice. The exercise may then be repeated by soliciting new input from other members of the class or by asking students to evaluate the teacher's own one-word lecture, until the learning goal of the meeting has been achieved.

The exercise, which is most fruitfully used in the first third of the semester, when students have limited or no familiarity with the text they are discussing, serves two purposes. First, by asking for a low-stress kind of reaction to the readings, the instructor affords all students, independent of their preparation for the class, to contribute to the class discussion as equals. Even students who have just (and only) read the canto are, as a rule, capable of and comfortable with venturing out a one-word interpretation of the material they have studied, read, or at the very least skimmed through. Second, by requiring no predetermined direction in the interpretation, the exercise is designed to level as much as possible the playing field for students who come for the first time to a serious interpretive engagement with literary texts. Although some students who decide to take a close reading course on a medieval Italian literary text may have developed in high school reading habits that prepare them for literary analysis, others may not have had the same opportunities. In order for the teaching to be as inclusive as possible and for all reactions to, and points of view on, the text to be equally positioned from the start, this exercise initially makes only a minimal demand on each student.

Although never completely abandoned, the one-word lecture exercise may be gradually paired with a second technique that requires more detailed preparation. Moving from soliciting a simple reaction to the reading to inviting a more active interpretive role, I ask students to engage in a cross fire exercise. Individual students are asked to come to the weekly meeting with a difficult question for their peers; that is, with a question derived from the week's readings for which they have an answer that they believe may have escaped their fellow learners. Organized as an individual challenge to the class, this gauntlet exercise affords students an opportunity to have their various roles as resident experts validated in their reading of the text. When they identify a challenging question for their peers, they each actively note for discussion elements that may elude other readers, who may approach the text with different interests and competencies. In addition, the exercise also serves to deepen students' individual engagement with the text by inviting a reading that dynamically connects the literal understanding of the poetry and narrative to the identification of interpretive questions underlying the text. Finally, by monitoring the questions asked, the instructor can gauge what constitutes a difficulty for the class—that is, what notions, structures, concepts, and features in the text prove challenging for students, and adapt teaching methods to address them.

Various debriefing techniques may be adopted to facilitate cross fire interaction during class. Students may be asked to write out their questions in advance, and the teacher organizes them in chronological order according to the area of the text from which they issue, using each (or some) to prod discussion while moving through the readings assigned for the day. Alternatively, the exercise may start with the teacher inviting a random student to ask a question or by soliciting volunteers; the person who formulates the question may also be asked to evaluate the responses. Finally, the class may be divided into three role-rotating teams: team A is put in charge of asking the first question to team B, and team C is asked to evaluate on a numerical scale how satisfactory the answer was; then team B poses a new question to team C, with team A doing the evaluation, and so on, until all members in the teams have asked, answered, and evaluated a set number of questions and answers. The team that scores highest wins the tournament. The same pattern may be applied to scaled-down groups of three students, in which every participant rotates through the roles of questioner, answerer, and evaluator. Each debriefing option has advantages and drawbacks, especially when it comes to budgeting class time, with the first option guaranteeing the highest coverage at the highest time cost (with each student ideally being exposed to a number of questions equal to the number of students in the class), and the last one ensuring the fastest pace at the cost of comprehensiveness of the exercise (each student is exposed to only three questions—one asked, one answered, and one evaluated).

The third technique, based on the lifeline model (and hence has been nick-named "The Rope"), consists in asking students to come to the meeting having identified a question for which they genuinely do not have an answer (or a passage that utterly confuses or perplexes them) and present it to the class for collective solving. The debriefing options for this last exercise are similar to those suggested for the preceding one. The exercise may be led by the instructor or performed by involving the whole class in the dialogue or by dividing it into small, self-regulating groups. The core objective of this technique is not only the reestablishment of a collaborative atmosphere in the course after the more challenging exercises have been performed but also the invitation to take the text of the *Comedy* as an opportunity to move beyond the pervasive convention of considering literary analysis a solitary exercise. Replacing the habit of matching *una testa a un testo* ("one text with one isolated interpreter") with a collaborative exercise, it dispels the students' anxiety of performance in the class. Furthermore, by allowing exploration into areas of the poem that are subjectively more difficult, the exercise also helps the class to expand coverage of the poem beyond the areas falling within the instructor's predilections and expertise.

Different groups respond differently to these strategies and techniques, and instructors should choose when to have their class engage in either some or all of these exercises. In general, they all generate activities sufficiently flexible to accommodate various types of lesson plans. In this writer's experience, the most effective way of using the techniques has been to introduce them progressively through the semester, staggering them in blocks of four weeks each. All teaching practices reviewed here have been developed for the model and within the scope of an undergraduate seminar, but they may be exported, with small adjustments, to discussion sessions in larger lecture courses or, with more radical alterations, in graduate seminars.

Answering the Text's Call

The strategies and techniques developed in the Princeton Dante seminars strive to balance personal and collaborative approaches to the study of the *Comedy*. In the life of the seminars, the individual motivations and goals that have prompted each student to accost Dante's text are valued as much as the no less necessary efforts to construct a common platform for discussion in the classroom—ideally, but not necessarily, a shared understanding of the text. Mediating between what Dante's text means for each reader and the meaning the poem is designed to convey, the class activities are ultimately conceived as a response to a hermeneutic call at the core of Dante's text.

In addition to responding to new pedagogical principles, these teaching tools invite students to perform one of the tasks to which the poem calls them: to become active readers of the text. In order to convey the notion that the reading relation they are asked to establish with the *Comedy* has philological reasons, it is often useful to remind students that the first identified sinner in the poem is introduced through a formulation that requires an active effort of interpretation and triggers hermeneutic consequences. When reflecting on the possible identifications that may be provided for the one "che fece per viltade il gran rifiuto" ("who, through cowardice, made the great refusal"; *Inf.* 3.60 [Petrocchi; Hollander trans.]), students may be invited to realize that the text puts them in the position to provide a name for that character, asking that they choose among options, a choice that results in a self-positioning. The abstract notion that different readers, with different cultural, political, and ideological agendas, will read the text differently turns into a direct and unavoidable experience when students choose between, say, Celestine V or Pontius Pilate as the characters indicated in the circumlocution. The circumstance that they are asked to make a choice precisely in the context of a direct attack on neutrality (as the unwillingness to make self-positioning choices), which Dante is performing by introducing the category of the "ignavi" ("cowards"; "neutrals") into his afterlife, is a strong reminder that the *Comedy* is designed to produce an active hermeneutic engagement on each reader's part.

Writing like Dante: Understanding the *Inferno* through Creative Writing

Nicolino Applauso

Dante's *Comedy* endures as not only one of the most important masterworks of world literature but also one of the most representative examples of human creativity. Even though scholars and teachers often acknowledge the immense inventiveness of Dante's masterpiece, its creative value has not been the main object of studies in university courses. I propose a new approach to teaching Dante's *Inferno* through creative writing. Based on my personal experience in implementing creative writing assignments in various interdisciplinary courses for undergraduate majors and minors, I explore the potentials of creative writing in the teaching of Dante's *Inferno*. Creative writing constitutes an effective way to gain a deeper understanding and appreciation of literature, as well as a means to gain proficiency in Italian. Alongside its great potential, however, creative writing also poses some challenges to both instructors and students.

I put my approach into practice in three upper-level undergraduate courses. Each of them took place in a different type of institution (a large research university, a small private liberal arts college, and a medium-size private liberal arts university) and was tailored toward different cohorts of undergraduate students. One class was taught in Italian for Italian majors and minors, whereas the other two courses were taught in English for a much wider student audience. By implementing creative writing, I sought to assist students in understanding theoretical concepts in connection with literature and poetry (such as metaphors, rhymes, figures of speech, etc.) and the presence of a well-defined narrative structure within selected cantos of the *Inferno*. My main objective was to empower students to put theory into practice by creating original content through creative writing either in English or Italian and thus develop a deeper appreciation of Dante's masterwork. Students focused on technical aspects of writing, such as experimenting with grammar, vocabulary, and content at an advanced level, and experimented with a variety of stylistic techniques in order to effectively and coherently articulate original ideas through a narrative. My approach also touched on pedagogical objectives such as developing a cultural and historical understanding of poetry as a literary genre and its relevance in medieval culture and society. The main challenge in introducing poetry from the medieval period to a modern audience is overcoming preconceived notions about poetry and the Middle Ages that are established in popular culture, such as that poetry is a simple, inspirational, remote, impractical, and instinctual art and that the Middle Ages is a backward, undeveloped, savage, and inflexible yet lawless period in human history.

In order to meet these objectives, I first experimented with the inclusion of a creative writing assignment in a survey of medieval and Renaissance Italian

literature taught in Italian at the University of Oregon. The class examined selected texts from early Italian literature (c. 1180) to the late 1500s, encompass-
ing different literary genres (poetry, short stories, epic poems, political and
philosophical treatises, and theater). Students had the original text and modern Italian (or occasionally English translations) on facing pages. We spent two
weeks on a selection of representative cantos from the *Inferno*, *Purgatorio*, and
Paradiso, and focused on the moral and narrative dimension of the *Comedy* and
its poetic and rhetorical style (use of hendecasyllable, rhymes, metaphors, analogy, etc.). Regina Psaki first inspired me to implement a creative writing assignment on Dante's *Inferno* when she included it as a topic choice for the first
composition, assigned during midterm. The question was divided in two parts.
In the first part, students were asked to challenge the moral system of Dante's
Inferno by comparing it with one they invented:

> What do you think about the arrangements of the sins according to
> Dante? Are there any sins that you think are more or less severe than
> others? Are there sins that are considered more serious from a modern
> perspective but are not present in Dante's classification of sins? Could you
> find some sins/transgressions in Dante's *Inferno* that you would exclude
> completely?

The second part asked them to include an illustration about their own Hell set
in today's world, exposed though a diagram representing their hierarchy of sins
following Dante's model (i.e., less serious sins at the top of the chart and more
severe sins at the bottom), and a sample of a canto written by them. They had to
include in their canto real people from their contemporary world and try to
mimic Dante's rhyme structure. Even though only a third of the students chose
this topic and developed their own inferno, bringing into the narrative politicians and historical figures from the United States and other countries (e.g.,
United States' President George W. Bush, Iranian President Ahmadinejad or
Venezuela's late president Hugo Chávez) as well as fictional ones (e.g., Mickey
Mouse or the Simpsons), those who participated particularly enjoyed this assignment. Creative writing was implemented throughout the course with other
medieval and Renaissance authors, such as Giovanni Boccaccio and Petrarch,
as they were asked to write a novella in the style of Boccaccio and a comic parody of one of Petrarch's sonnets from the *Canzoniere* (namely an anti-Petrarchan
sonnet). Since assignments were all written in Italian, creative writing was
implemented more as a stimulus to spur them in developing their chosen topics.
Thus, in grading these assignments, I focused on elements pertaining to grammatical accuracy in Italian, the use of the lexicon, organization, and content
rather than the creative aspects of the writing.

Encouraged by this positive experience, I decided to develop the creative
writing assignment as an independent project in conjunction with the final research paper. I launched this initiative during two capstone seminars on Dante's

Inferno taught in English for both Italian and English majors and minors, first at Colorado College and then at Bucknell University. Both seminars focused on the moral organization of Dante's *Comedy* by examining the moral construction and ideology at the foundation of the *Inferno* and linking medieval to contemporary morality. Students examined modern rewritings, artworks, and film adaptations of the *Inferno* and analyzed themes such as the question of evil and satire in the *Comedy*, Dante's moral structure of Hell, and the ethics of the *contrapasso*. My main objective was to have them see the important impact that Dante had on other medieval and modern authors while appreciating the dynamics behind Dante's writing, such as his strategies, word choice, use of reliable and unreliable narrators, as well as the notion of verisimilitude. Special attention was given to the narrative structure of the cantos, examining the order of events in the narration; their arrangement and setting into three parts (the so-called three-act structure of introduction, development, and conclusion); and their relation to the conflict, climax, and resolution.

Prior to reading canto 5, students were provided with a one-page outline to highlight the strategies and structure that authors use to create an effective and persuasive fictional narrative. This guide outlines four main parts to narrative structure. First, the beginning briefly—and with vivid language and descriptions—introduces the setting, the protagonist, and the main characters (including an antagonist). Second, the plot and its elaboration follow; narratives include a *fabula* (the chronological order with sequences related by cause and effect) and an *intreccio* (the plot as arranged by the author, which may diverge from chronological order or introduce digressions through flashbacks, descriptions, invective, etc.). Elaborating the *intreccio* involves the protagonist or other characters confronting a conflict or problem, followed by a climax where the narration reaches its highest peak and the protagonist reaches the highest point of difficulty in the story. Plot revolves around the wants or desires of a character who must pursue that objective, despite resistance or antagonism, to arrive at a denouement. Third, the resolution of the *intreccio* involves a solution or point of closure that sets the stage for the end of the story and the disentanglement of all the events in the story (which involve the protagonist and all the characters in the story). Fourth, the conclusion recaptures the beginning of the story and solidifies the ending or resolution, which could be comic (positive) or tragic (dramatic).

One example of a successful activity to apply narratology to Dante's *Inferno* was to compare three different cantos and examine the application of these narrative components and their effects on readers. After dividing the class evenly into three groups, I asked each group to focus on a single canto and answer given questions about the sequence of the story; its three-act structure; the specific conflict, climax, and resolution presented; the type of conclusion; and finally the use of language portraying both the action and the characters of the given canto. The three groups focused respectively on cantos 13, 19, and 21. At the end of the activity, students were able to identify the various sequences and narrative components of the story and also note different conclusions (either a tragic or comic ending) unique for each canto. They also saw that characters use noticeably different language in their direct speeches (e.g., Pier della Vigna's intricate self-punitive language greatly differs from the arrogantly scornful speech of Pope Nicholas III). Finally, they focused on different narrative devices used in the interaction between the pilgrim and the sinners. This last observation allowed students to realize how Dante sought to accomplish a realistic narration in order to persuade readers of its own authenticity. For example, students commented that in canto 13 the conversation between the pilgrim or Virgil and Pier della Vigna expressed a credible interaction between a man and a tree because of the numerous pauses caused by the ambiguity of the characters' interaction. Della Vigna does not have eyes or a human face, thus listeners are never sure when he finishes speaking (*Inf.* 13.79, 91–92, 109–10). During other class discussions, students noticed how Dante vividly implements realistic descriptions or everyday objects associated with real-life situations. Two favorites were the upward flight of Geryon, which is powerfully compared to the diver emerging from the ocean depths (*Inf.* 16.130–36), or the cord wrapped around the pilgrim's cloak, which is given to Virgil in canto 16 to attract Geryon's attention (*Inf.* 16.106–14).[1] Overall, students started to perceive Dante as a model author of fictional writing and his masterpiece as a masterfully crafted novel. My choice of the Robert M. Durling and Ronald L. Martinez edition of the *Inferno* as the required text for the class greatly contributed to this understanding of Dante. Its effective English prose translation brought Dante's masterpiece closer to a modern reader. Students who could read Italian were also able to compare the English prose to the Italian poetry, as we often referred to the meter and rhyme of the original text.

After all these guided activities and discussions, students completed their first major written assignment, which consisted of writing their own canto (either in prose or in poetry) and articulating their own personal moral structure in an illustrative chart. Here, like Dante, they had to place graver sins and lighter transgressions respectively at the bottom and top of hell. Furthermore, they had to frame their canto within a modern setting and use characters that were both real and fictional. Particular emphasis was also given to the setting of the canto and specific ethical issues pertaining to the question of evil that we discussed in class (e.g., war, holocaust, organized crime, political corruption, homicide, mass murder, etc.). Before the assignment, students had the chance to familiarize themselves with other creative projects when we juxtaposed the *Inferno* to other medieval texts, modern rewritings, artworks, and film adaptations. I organized the creative writing assignment slightly differently at Colorado College and Bucknell University because I had to adapt to the type of students enrolled in each seminar and the specific needs of each institution.

Because at Colorado College the class was cross-listed with the Italian and Comparative Literature departments, it had a wide variety of students. The great majority wrote the assignment in English, whereas the few Italian majors wrote it in Italian. I provided students with a rubric that illustrated the criteria for grading the creative essay, which was evaluated on five aspects: communication, content, grammar, vocabulary, and organization and style. For communication, students were expected to display lucid, effective, and concise writing with effective use of dialogue. Content required rich, dynamic, realistic, and cohesive writing, well-connected to the provided chart of hell and with excellent character development. Under grammar, students had to display fluency with no serious grammatical or mechanical errors. The expectations for vocabulary included an extensive exploration of available vocabulary, using a rich and varied lexicon appropriate to character and narrative. Organization and style required well-organized writing, a strong introduction, a detailed body, and a general conclusion or resolution. The conflict and its resolution were expected to be clearly presented in the story, alongside a fluid flow of ideas and dialogue and a logical sequence and clear connections among paragraphs.

The essays varied in content. Some students based their hell on class topics such as war and political corruption. One student framed his Inferno in the contemporary battlefield of Iraq and chose as a guide Oliver North (the political commentator and military historian). His canto was a well-crafted invective against what he called "mass murdering politicians," and ingeniously merged the connection between violence and fraud, which Dante separates in his moral hierarchy. Another student created an effective journey inside American consumerism (which featured CEOs from big-box retailers and major fast-food restaurant chains) with the interesting choice of Morgan Freeman as guide. Another student treated the issue of religion and created an all-inclusive hell with sinners of all faiths and of no faith. An interesting outcome of this assignment was that a good number of students set their canto in the college environment. This allowed the class to confront delicate issues pertaining to the students' own lives, which often are not addressed in a literature class. For example, one student's moral hierarchy started from lesser evils (such as rude people and vandalism) and ended with honor code breakers, campus thieves, bad professors, and corrupt administrators. Another student framed his Inferno within a college party:

> The pilgrim was traveling through various rooms of the house to find a girl he was interested in. As the party goes on and the guests become more intoxicated, the dialogue and events become more dream-like. The paper begins to focus more on people who prey on the vulnerable, like drug dealers and committers of sexual assault.
>
> (Owen Bean, Colorado College)

In all cases, students had to think about strategies to maintain credibility and consistency in their narration and personal moral hierarchy. Dante's *Inferno* became a vehicle to express students' intimate concerns about their lives and everyday environment.

At Bucknell University the course was offered as an interdisciplinary capstone and comprised students who double-majored in Italian and other disciplines. It was a writing-intensive course focused on the notion of writing as a process, which included specific steps implemented through outlines, multiple drafts, and peer reviews. After they wrote the first draft of their Inferno, we did a peer-review session in which they share their creative work with a classmate. I provided them with guidelines for peer review used first in class and then as a weekend assignment. The guidelines helped students create a coherent narrative with credible characters who would reveal themselves and their personal qualities through their way of speaking. For the peer review, students worked with partners and read drafts of each another's essays. The students focused on giving feedback in four areas: grammar and style, where students commented on clarity, flow, continuity, and coherence, in addition to grammar, punctuation, and spelling; organization, which required discussing the narrative structure, including the conflict, resolution, and conclusion, and the use of dialogue and indirect speech; language and vocabulary, where students examined the complexity and variety of the lexicon used in the story; and content, which asked them to evaluate the quality of the content (rich, dynamic, and informative?) and how well it illuminated the chart of hell provided. After both papers were read, students gave each other constructive feedback on how to improve the paper in key areas.

Students tried to make their characters unique and recognizable by a target reader. This was at times challenging for them when they alternated the narrative of the canto with the dialogues. In earlier drafts, the majority of students wrote excessive character descriptions that ultimately rendered their cantos too cumbersome. In the majority of their second drafts, they were able to limit successfully the input of explicit information by implementing more direct speeches among the characters, thus letting each character speak to the reader in a more effective way. Their cantos followed the example set by Dante, and implemented suspense, surprise, and climactic scenes. Their second assignment was an analytical essay, which was also based on the same premises. I thus tried to create a link between the creative writing assignment and an analytical research paper assignment. Students noticed this link and provided feedback: "The analytic/research paper assignment was definitely linked to the creative-writing assignment, because the research I did sparked many ideas and inspired parts of my creative-writing piece" (Kristina Kalkanis). Structurally, the two essays were similar because in both cases students had to justify their thesis and ideas by providing evidence in order to render their writing convincing. Students' final research papers combined both the creative and analytical aspects of Dante's *Inferno* that emerged from their assignments. They had to compare two cantos in conjunction with a scholarly essay and/or a modern creative project of their choice (e.g., an adaptation or illustration) done by others. At the end of the course they had a *Skype* interview and participated in an interactive online forum with American illustrator and graphic artist Sandow Birk.

By first employing Dante as a model, imitating his narrative language and techniques through creative writing, then focusing on a comparative analytical approach to the topic of Dante and modernity, and finally engaging in a live conversation with a modern artist who adapted the *Inferno*, students developed a deep appreciation of Dante and his importance in contemporary popular culture.[2] Creative writing was thus implemented as a tool to broaden students' admiration and understanding of Dante's *Inferno* and medieval culture in general. Students provided feedback about the creative writing assignment and the course overall:

Mapping out our own version of Hell, in the form of a short story, challenged me to approach and communicate my ideas about morality in a way I hadn't before—analytical essays are great, but they only get so far.
(Robert Heald, Colorado College)

I did enjoy the creative-writing assignment of writing my own Inferno. It was very insightful and a bit challenging for me to imagine my own personal Inferno—who would be there, the setting, etc. It was a unique opportunity for me as a college student. Once I chose an overall plot, it wasn't difficult and I even had fun writing the remainder of the paper.
(Kristina Kalkanis, Bucknell University)

I certainly think this is an effective way of understanding the Inferno, because our creative-writing assignment should mimic Dante's prose or perhaps, play around with it stylistically. We had to go through the same process of developing a system of the Inferno in which we choose our own morals and degrees of evil. This is the exact same process Dante went through and we were putting ourselves in his shoes [. . .] I researched other authors who had written their own creative versions of the Inferno like Giorgio Pressburger in *Nel Regno Oscuro*. I wanted to see his categorization of evil/suicide and how it compared to mine and Dante's.
(Sara Bunker, Bucknell University)

As a teacher, I found these courses rewarding because of the positive response from students, but the experience was not without challenges, mainly coming up with cohesive and clear criteria for evaluating creative writing assignments in a literature class. In some cases, students ventured into very creative projects that sometime diverged too much from Dante's *Inferno*. This challenged the instructor to develop more viable assessment tools in order to balance effectively the level of freedom expected in a creative project with a more rigid set of objectives. Furthermore, the students' enthusiasm for Dante's *Inferno* was sometimes at odds with the objective of contextualizing it within contemporary medieval poetry and the historical frame of the late Middle Ages. In some research papers, Dante's *Inferno* emerged as an exceptional work that is not bound by time.

This suggested to some students that Dante's *Inferno* could be read as a timeless masterpiece.

Overall, I realized that approaching Dante through creative writing brought me back to when I was reading the *Inferno* for the very first time. Back then I sensed through the vivid narrative and dialogue that Dante's masterpiece had a life of its own. Yet its ingeniously effective narrative continued to haunt me. Thus, as many have done before me, I tried to imitate it and understand it. Now, as a teacher, I feel that I am a partner in crime with my students in trying to make them write like Dante. If you are thinking about trying this approach with your students, I recommend the following words of advice from Richard Downing, who has been teaching creative writing for nearly forty years:

> Despite the number of "mistakes" or the degree to which the student may have strayed from whatever I might have expected, I ask myself: How close have I become to these characters? Is there a writing style emerging that seems fresh, different? And the biggest question: To what degree am I excited about this piece? Occasionally, I'll give a superior grade, and I can't really quantify why. The paper just seems to be alive in some way. There was a time when that would have bothered me, but I've become comfortable grading as much from intuition as from objective analysis. *Don't overthink it.* Provide an environment in which students feel safe, feel that they can take risks, make critical comments.
>
> (E-mail message to author, 28 Sept. 2016)

NOTES

I dedicate this essay to Raymond Fleming and F. Regina Psaki, whose teaching has had an impact on very many people and has sown in me the passion for teaching Dante. I would also like to thank Richard Downing, who taught me the power of creative writing in the college environment and beyond.

[1] Raffa's online *Danteworlds* is a very helpful source to highlight the realism of Dante's narrative implemented in the *Inferno*.

[2] A good source to further explore the presence of Dante's *Inferno* in popular culture is Saiber and Coggeshall's Web site *Dante Today*. This site includes a rich repository of references that document the pervasiveness of Dante and his works in contemporary culture, as well as useful teaching resources.

Scaffolding Scholarly Research for a Senior-Level Course on Dante in Translation

Katherine V. Haynes

The Dante course at Aquinas College has been one of two senior-level, semester-length courses required of the English major, and an upper-division elective. In addition to demonstrating knowledge of the primary texts, students are expected to demonstrate potential for graduate work in literature. Class discussion and written assignments scaffold scholarly endeavor using themes from Dante's writings and those of early commentators on the *Comedy*. These works provide insight into the process of literary interpretation and criticism, especially regarding medieval theories important to Dante that can be opaque to modern students. Although this essay narrowly focuses on pedagogy, the course itself is an entrance into Dante studies in translation within a curriculum that seeks to instill appreciation for the intrinsic value of literature for the flourishing of the individual, society, and culture.

Scaffolds in this course provide temporary pedagogical support while students are acquiring and assimilating new information and research skills into their long-term memory to solve more complex problems in literary and textual criticism than they would have accomplished without the support (Wood et al. 90). Beginning with class discussion, the class advances to small-group analysis with oral feedback, followed by formal writing assignments consisting of a reflection paper, three close reading assignments (one for each of the three parts of the *Comedy*), a short-essay midterm examination, an annotated bibliography, a research paper, and a short-essay final examination. The assignments are designed to increase in difficulty as the student acquires the tools to produce an original research paper at the level of an entering master of arts student.

Essentially, scaffolding is practical; it speeds up the learning process for students because it lowers anxiety of the unknown, resolves frustration and confusion associated with the unfamiliar, and builds confidence and self-esteem through understanding and subject mastery. I have found the best way to scaffold is to build a course on a platform of three principles. These principles are not unfamiliar to seasoned teachers, but when brought intentionally to the foreground of syllabus design and lesson plans, prove to be very powerful tools for long-term learning. The first principle is to select secondary educational materials such as textbooks and online resources that serve to move the student from the familiar to the challenging. The second is to plan lessons that incorporate brief, in-class activities to promote confidence in students by eliciting informal peer interaction and student-instructor interaction. These provide on-site intervention when a hurdle appears to confuse or otherwise halt progress, and students' excitement builds up through engagement in a common cause. The third

is to design into the course frequent, increasingly complex formal writing assignments that provide measureable instructor feedback and reinforce earlier
knowledge and skills while creating new understanding. To these I always add a
fourth: guided topic choices. In the various assignment prompts, I require students to demonstrate their own expertise in a field of topics along the way and
to bring their growing expertise to the classroom conversation in both individual and collaborative assignments. Putting personal preferences to work early in
a way that is manageable for undergraduates enhances their confidence as
scholars and leads to intellectual wonder, the very foundation of scholarship.
This essay discusses how I have used these principles in the Dante course, but
I adapt them for all my courses, because they work and because they help make
courses fun.

The electronic course portal offers assignment prompts and evaluation instruments, as well as pertinent external links. Students read, in the required
translation, two primary texts: *Vita Nuova* and *Commedia*. Although many excellent translations are available for both works, I prefer to use Mark Musa's
translation of the *Vita Nuova* (2008) and Robert Hollander and Jean Hollander's translations of the *Inferno*, the *Purgatorio*, and the *Paradiso*. In brief, these
satisfy classroom needs for clarity, affordability, and portability, and especially
for the Hollander edition, offer good teaching tools in the facing-page translation and copious endnotes designed to further student research. For the three
canticles of the *Divine Comedy*, they analyze samples from other twentieth-
century translations. Dante's other works are discussed in class as time allows,
but students are not evaluated on them per se. During the first two weeks, the
class reads the *Vita Nuova*. The remainder of the course is devoted to reading
the *Divine Comedy*. Reading the brief, earlier work at the beginning allows
students to become acquainted with Dante's milieu and his efforts to excel as a
poet and builds confidence that they can assimilate essential medieval concepts that are probably new for many of them. For example, guided classroom
discussion of blog writing can quickly launch a mental connection to Dante's
understanding of authorship and his use of marginal glosses in the context of
the late thirteenth and early fourteenth centuries. This is an opportunity for
students to develop self-confidence in interpretation based on their experience
and will become a platform from which discussion of medieval educational
theory and practice will be introduced. As a generation attuned to social media, students are heartened by Dante's insistence on the value of the vernacular, popular themes and by the do-it-yourself commentary found in the *Vita
Nuova*. If Dante comes across as rather contemporary at this stage of the semester, I see it as a boon. Once we begin the descent into *Inferno*, the process
of complicating, or defamiliarizing, will seem a part of the anticipated encounter. Scaffolding incorporates confidence-building exercises with the emphasis
on the known, or at least the seemingly familiar, in order to create a platform
for new material to be assimilated, not despaired of and abandoned. This concept is extended to text selection, because the ongoing reading assignment is

the core exercise for literature students. Regarding primary texts, the brevity, themes, and experimental quality of the *Vita Nuova*, as well as its relative low risk in terms of the final grade for the course, provide opportunity for platform building so that once the class begins *Inferno* the third week into the semester, they have already settled into the poet's milieu and writing, and the danger of alienating them at the high-risk threshold of the major work and the course grading is reduced. Students frequently remark that they initially did not understand why we were spending so much time on this work when they wanted to begin *Inferno* immediately, but doing so provides necessary information for students with little background in medieval literature. For those who have been introduced to the *Commedia* elsewhere, such as a high school advanced placement class or a home school unit, the delay is also useful, because it sets course expectations at a higher level before the class begins the longer work and their expectations are reset to learn afresh. For this course, the *Vita Nuova* introduces important concepts needed for the *Comedy*, such as authorial command, medieval commentary traditions, medieval dream visions and the imagination, the meditative ascent tradition, prosimetric structure, and contemporary poetic forms.

In the second class meeting, we discuss the development of the vernacular lyric and the expectations of *fin' amors* along with the semiautobiographical and dream qualities of the *Vita Nuova* relative to troubadour poetry and Dante's immediate circle of fellow poets. This lesson introduces the production and circulation of manuscripts in the era and conventions of dream vision literature. In the third class meeting, students are introduced to the medieval meditative ascent tradition, such as in Boethius's *Consolation of Philosophy*, alongside the apologetics of the poet's vocation as differing from his predecessors' and contemporaries' works (McMahon). The fourth class meeting provides visual examples of the medieval gloss and commentary tradition: biblical, theological, and literary. I briefly outline how Dante's treatises *Convivio* and *De vulgari eloquentia* express his developing theories on language and literature and introduce the works of important encyclopedists, such as Brunetto Latini, a character who appears in the *Comedy*. I explain that the commentary tradition on *Commedia* goes back to the fourteenth century and that Dante's sons, Jacopo and Pietro, as well as other fourteenth-century writers, are part of that tradition.[1] Recognizing that the interpretive effort goes back to the first generation of readers gives students key terms and provides an opportunity for them to acknowledge the strangeness of the text, preparing them to be more at ease assimilating Dante's highly developed, imaginative universe. I focus on a few very basic questions addressed in the fourteenth-century commentaries that the students themselves have raised in class, such as Dante's use of allegory, first-person narration, conventions of register and diction, allusion to classical literature, and claims to encompass the whole of reality. As for those topics that have not yet surfaced but will be needed, I save them until students begin to wrestle with them, or when I see they are struggling.

At this point, small groups discuss the kinds of arguments being made in the prose sections of the *Vita Nuova*, using a draft of the first assignment, a short reflection paper. By having produced a draft and by keeping the discussion informal within small peer groups, students contribute actively and gain confidence. After a few minutes, I ask for group-level discussion reports whereby each small group appoints an ad hoc spokesperson to provide tentative oral feedback of the group's growing understanding of the assignment prompts, launching their theories as so many "trial balloons" to the whole class before any individual student submits a response for formal written evaluation. This small-stakes early writing assignment prevents students from becoming over-anxious but reaps benefits that will be evident in the more substantial research assignment later in the term. For the remainder of this class, we discuss how Dante experiments with authority and consider changes in the understanding of authority over the centuries. By the end of the second week, as they begin to read the *Comedy*, the class is aware of several concepts basic to the argument of the poem. Building on their understanding of self-authorizing blogs and authorial glosses, I introduce several important concepts for Dante and his commentators. Furthermore, the background from the early commentaries sets up a discussion of the rise of the university, its curriculum, the production and dissemination of medieval textbooks, and cognition theories. These concepts provide building blocks for future lessons that can introduce any number of subjects important to their chosen research topic and that will be introduced to address the significance of Dante's claim for producing a sacred poem in the *Comedy*, the theme for the course.

By the third week, students begin reading a translation of the *Divine Comedy*, beginning with *Inferno*, which provides both the Italian and English versions on facing pages. Students are instructed to prepare the first of three close reading assignments: an evaluation of an interpretive problem of their choice from a specific section of a canto in the *Inferno* (the assignment is repeated for *Purgatorio* and *Paradiso*). No two students can share a single canto and subject, which encourages them to find their own niche for the research paper. Students are required to choose a canto, summarize it, explain how it relates to adjacent cantos, and identify a short passage within it for comparison and analysis with one other recent scholarly translation. I have found that granting these assignments minimal credit lowers anxiety, particularly since the measured skills are new for many. Furthermore, because these assignments evaluate the ability to analyze and critique recent scholarship, including editorial processes, they provide an opportunity for intervention well ahead of the annotated bibliography and research paper.

If the student so desires, the canto selection may be applied later to the same canto number in *Purgatorio* and *Paradiso*, as the narrative famously revisits similar problems at the same stage of each canticle. Students are asked to recommend where one should go next to research the issue on which they have focused and to predict the likely outcome. The assignment also measures recognition of basic translation decisions and literary interpretive issues within the canto. The written product of the close reading assignment is a guided essay of about three pages with a one-page handout to distribute to the instructor and each classmate. Students can thus report on a sophisticated problem in a particular canto, which helps them identify a viable research issue of interest to them, and they learn by suggesting to others how to pursue a problem by practicing sound methodology at little risk. Students learn to compare and evaluate recent translations and interpretations while practicing other tasks, which they believe to be more oriented toward the goals of locating, evaluating, and applying critical methodology to produce their own original literary research project.

Class discussion is high during and immediately after the three close reading assignments, as students begin to acknowledge their ability to conduct research and recommend reliable sources and methodologies to peers. Dante's works provide an excellent opportunity for students to begin to address the mediation embedded in translation and textual editing. By providing instructor and peer feedback three times, for the three parts of the poem, using three additional translations, students begin to recognize why they should want to know what lies behind questions regarding translation theory and interpretations that direct further research. Usually, the first close reading (*Inferno*) produces a relatively stronger summary and identification of an interpretive issue but has little regard for the latter portion of the assignment. By the third close reading (*Paradiso*), however, students demonstrate more sophistication toward various levels of interpretation, including competing editions and translations.

While reading *Inferno* and *Purgatorio*, students also read Marc Cogan's *The Design in the Wax*; once into *Paradiso*, they take up Christian Moevs's *The Metaphysics of Dante's* Comedy. Cogan's text is designed with undergraduates in mind, but Moevs's monograph is admittedly difficult and requires mediation. Together, they provide essential concepts, arguing from Thomistic-Aristotelian or Augustinian-Neoplatonic theories respectively, thereby providing two very different scholarly interpretations of the poem. Attending a liberal arts college in the Dominican tradition, most of the students at Aquinas will have been introduced to Western philosophy and Catholic theological concepts, and these two texts complement the course description, which is to focus on Dante's claim that the *Comedy* is a sacred poem. Not all students understand how to lay out a strong organizational methodology for original research, and these two texts provide excellent models. When a group of students found Cogan's text repetitive, for example, I questioned their rationale and realized that their observation provided a segue to explore the text as a model for building a careful, scholarly, interpretive argument and the difference between repetition that reinforces as it builds connections and repetition that offers no such enrichment.

During the section of the course devoted to *Purgatorio*, I take up early commentaries as educational texts to engage in questions regarding various expressions of Catholic spirituality, considering differences among the major religious houses of the Benedictine, Cistercian, Franciscan, Dominican, and Carmelite orders. This is a good opportunity to pause, as does Dante in this canticle, to consider the role of the arts and imagination in productions of the *Comedy* over time. The lesson begins by inviting students to discuss their own tastes in representations found in Web sites, books, and video games, with the announcement that they will have an option to contribute an original multimedia component on the final examination. After a few minutes of discussion, we look at some representations from early commentaries and major works of art over the centuries, concluding with a discussion of the concept of ekphrasis in literature and Dante's use of it in *Purgatorio*.

Themes focused on in *Paradiso* are highly abstract. Early commentaries provide insight into the effort of engaging in speculative theology on the nature of the Trinity, cosmology, and angelology. When students begin *Paradiso*, they are concluding Cogan and take up Moevs's text. I do not expect students to assimilate this more difficult text to the same degree that they have Cogan. I spend a full class outlining the introduction, carefully defining philosophical and theological terms so students can respond at least on an average level to the final exam question on Moevs. About a third of the students find this sufficient for their needs. Another third will go further to incorporate concepts in Moevs's work in their research paper and final close reading.

The research paper and the associated annotated bibliography are more substantial assignments. Students write an original essay on an interpretive problem with a specific theme focusing on one to three cantos within the entire poem, addressing how the theme is significant for understanding Dante's claim to be writing a sacred poem. They are instructed to join some part of the ongoing conversation of Dante scholarship within the past twenty years and not simply to repackage known material. This assignment is eye-opening for students who are more comfortable writing a term paper that restates a standard interpretation, so it is important to build into the syllabus prerequisite deadlines, such as a topic sign-up form and an annotated bibliography tutorial outside of class time, as well as to prepare the writing center and reference librarian for their visits.

The two examinations comprise short-essay questions. The midterm evaluates students' understanding of the *Vita Nuova*, the *Inferno*, and the chapters in Cogan's *Design* that discuss *Inferno*. Students demonstrate understanding and application of basic concepts in an open book exam that requires short-essay responses to establish a baseline. A more synthetic understanding of Dante's works and the importance of the early commentaries are developed in the second half of the course. In addition to measuring knowledge of *Purgatorio*, *Paradiso*, and related sections of Cogan's and Moevs's texts, the final examination includes an option for students who want to prepare a multimedia presentation for a portion of this requirement. Usually, students find the final exam less taxing than the midterm because it follows the same structure.

I use the final hours of class for students to share their research paper findings and multimedia presentations with their colleagues. By designing a course around several assignments of increasing complexity with repetition built in for reinforcement, and by fostering questions, discussion, and feedback before summative grades are awarded, students come away with a deeper appreciation of Dante's artistic achievements and their rich literary heritage, but they also sense that they have been on their own journey of discovery. Class discussion and activities provide more than a guided tour of the narrative. So much high-quality information about the *Comedy*'s characters, plot, and structure is easily available online and from library resources. Instead, this course maximizes the strengths available in a traditional small-class setting by fostering an actual community of engaged students and facilitating insights about the earliest generation of readers. Introducing fourteenth-century commentaries into class discussion provides an opportunity to discuss the history of authority and methodologies of scholarship and peer review up to modern editions of the poem. Scaffolding scholarly reading and research methodology, beginning with Dante's own writing and the responses of other fourteenth-century commentators, along with the secondary course texts, improves critical thinking and articulation of complex thought for all students, not just majors, and is measurable. Moreover, these techniques are adaptable to other text-based courses, including large auditorium-sized classes, by designing for peer groups.

Students find the combination of small-group discussion with directed question and answer, scholarly research, and formal writing to be useful for their development. Furthermore, when students understand that their interpretive problems have a venerable history, they can appropriate their predecessors' methodological scaffolds into their own scholarship. Students thus understand they are engaging in the timeless pursuit of literary criticism as part of the larger tradition, gaining insight into sound practices that lead to deeper appreciation and enjoyment. The highly adaptable scaffold techniques presented here prepare students to advance to master of arts programs, but those who do not plan to go on to graduate study or who are taking the course as an elective are pleased to produce meaningful scholarship on a subject that has long held a major place in the larger culture for its reputation as so-called serious literature.

Dante never dumbs down his message for his readers, who from the fourteenth century to today love him for it. The more complex, intricate, and obscure the *Divine Comedy* appears initially, the more tantalizing it becomes, because readers trust its scaffolding to help them produce new, defensible insights, to build another rung in the ladder of understanding, to see analogues to their life, and to make meaning on an epic scale.

NOTE

[1] For this tradition, see Nasti and Rossignoli.

"Cliques in Hell":
Teaching Dante to Nontraditional Students

Susan Gorman

My student Grace looks up from her copy of *The Inferno*, a frustrated expression on her face, and asks, "How you gonna' be havin' cliques in hell?" Grace and I and a dozen other people are discussing several cantos of the *Inferno* in my Great Works of Western Literature class for the Clemente Course in the Humanities. The Clemente program lets low-income students earn a year of humanities credits, tuition-free, from an affiliated college or university, in our case Bard College. Students come to the course with a variety of educational experience: some have tried four-year colleges, others have recently earned their GEDs. In eleven weeks we go from Homer to Junot Díaz, leaving us only one two-hour class on the *Inferno*.

Few, if any, students from this lower-level introductory survey will go on to major in literature. My broad hope is that they will understand some basic literary concepts, engage with textual analysis, and become familiar with some important texts. My major goal is to allow them to demonstrate to themselves how smart and capable they are. I want them to gain a confidence in their own ideas and their own voices that they can bring to other texts, classes, life situations. Because I'm trying to build confidence and general academic skills rather than specifically literary ones, I allow avenues of interpretation I might not in an upper-level class, where I shy away from the biographical approach. I am not too concerned that, because my brief contextual introductions often provide my students' only background information, their interpretations tend to be tied to those few small facts: this week, everything will be about exile and unrequited love. Though I do problematize this to some extent, almost always, whatever their comment, my answer begins with "yes"—even if I go on to add "but can we make it more complicated than that?" or "that was certainly the case with Odysseus [or whatever else they said might be true], but is it true here?" or "it seems that way [go over the evidence for their point] but does anyone have another reading?" They gently mock me for this ("She gets so excited about this stuff!"), but it gets them talking.

My more specific pedagogical aim throughout the semester is to show not only that concepts repeat throughout literary history (ideas like narration and juxtaposition that we covered in our discussion of the *Odyssey* remain important this week and in weeks 3 through 11) but also that texts themselves become ideas that recur. Though this is only the second week of class, already they see last week's protagonist, Odysseus, this week as Ulysses in Dante's canto 26. And Dante's text will reappear weeks ahead in works by William Wordsworth, Harriet Beecher Stowe, T. S. Eliot, and Díaz. I want them to see literature, the humanities, and human knowledge as long, continuing conversations they are able to join.

After I give a brief introductory lecture on Dante and his context, we spend about fifteen minutes coming to terms with the language in John Ciardi's translation. My students are usually intimidated by its unfamiliar syntax and vocabulary, often beginning our discussions claiming they understand nothing of the text. Nevertheless, after I ask a few questions, they realize that they do indeed get the plot. Once they begin to find their voices, inevitably at least one student expresses frustration at what Dante gets wrong. Though many of them have never heard of Dante, most are very familiar with the Bible. Though they doubt their abilities to analyze the former, they're at home with the latter and immediately spot where he diverges from scripture.

This is when Grace asked her question. Grace was being purposely provocative and silly, but she was also voicing honest frustration. A few years later I saw her reading a prayer she wrote at a community rally. She was fearless there. But in class she was indirect, using humor to deflect the tension, the risk of coming right out and voicing her frustration at Dante's unfamiliar language and ideas (a useful reminder that, however laid back, the Great Works of Western Literature classroom can be an intimidating place—even to someone who can captivate a crowd of hundreds and knows her Bible). My using her question literally (yes, why *are* there cliques in hell?) when she meant it ironically (why are we reading this difficult book?) honored her voice and led to a substantive discussion. Avoiding religious argument as much as possible, we historicized, considering the *Inferno* as a text informed by the Bible, but also by thirteenth- and early-fourteenth-century Italy and Dante's own life. They saw that Dante's strict segregation of sinners, their rigid stratification, could signal desperation to find clarity, meaning, and justice in the ways of God that points to a chaos in the earthly realm, a chaos they—like scholars before them—related in part to Dante's exiled state.

My Muslim students have a different set of objections that, admittedly, I have only begun to address. I always point out that Saladin is in the circle of the virtuous pagans despite being born after Jesus and ask them to consider this contradiction. Does it open up a crack in Dante's seemingly unyielding schema?

In recent years, as an attempt to deal more effectively with intertextual and interreligious concerns, I have added five poems by the fourteenth-century Kashmiri Sufi mystic and Hindu saint Lal Ded to our Dante assignment. One poem reads:

You won't find the Truth
by crossing your legs and holding your breath.
Daydreams won't take you through the gateway of release.
You can stir as much salt as you like in water,
it won't become the sea.   (46)

Like Dante, Lalla—as she refers to herself in her poems—was a kind of exile, having left her home and marriage in order to experience the ways of God in the world. Whereas the Dante of the *Inferno*, pursued relentlessly in life by the wolf of incontinence, experiences the world as a nearly unrelenting risk of damnation, Lalla in the above poem and others, experiences the world as an education. My students and I compare that to Dante's Ulysses, who says,

> not fondness for my son, nor reverence
> for my aged father, nor Penelope's claim
>   to the joys of love, could drive out of my mind
> the lust to experience the far-flung world
> and the failings and felicities of mankind.
>   (*Inf.* 26.89–93)[1]

My students usually see the word "lust" right away and note that it is a deadly sin. Ulysses's explorations lead to his death and help damn his soul rather than enlighten it. As my student Tolga said, unlike Dante, "she [Lalla] doesn't limit herself." So, about an hour into class, my students have used concepts they learned in our first class, relied on their outside expertise to produce textual analysis, and worked together to analyze new poems and explain them in relation to Dante. By now, I tell them, they can do anything.

Next we move on to metaphor, where we spend a good deal of time. Because they know and use this concept every day, they feel comfortable, this second week of class, in teasing out meaning aloud. We start with the description of the monster Plutus as a "carnival of bloat" (*Inf.* 7.7). It's a rich image, full of associations they can play with. I ask them to talk about carnivals: What are they like? When do they happen? Then I tell them about fourteenth-century Italy's carnival, the disguises that, in concealing identity, enabled the mixing of classes, genders, nationalities. They start by reading "carnival" as light fun, but come to see its darker subversive possibilities. And what is "bloat"? The image of an overstretched balloon, easily popped, usually comes up. We connect the two and they see the wonderful way the last word undercuts the first—that Virgil, instead of vaguely trash-talking, is specifically saying, you look scary but you're a fraud. I write their ideas on the board, and they see how many concepts are contained in that three-word phrase. Their knowledge, their words, their participation just created hugely complex meaning.

We continue to explore metaphor as we turn to the poem's beginning. The animals seem outlandish, bizarre to them. Often that in itself is enough to make them fear analyzing them. We talk about how and why a wolf of incontinence might menace someone. We talk about our own worldly pleasures, and this is often when they start to emotionally connect with the poem. Previously we've discussed Odysseus's trip to the underworld in book 11 of the *Odyssey* as a metaphor, like having to hit bottom—or go to hell and back—before one can recover from addiction, homelessness, despair. They see that Dante's text might be an elaboration on that point. The more we connect this seemingly foreign text to their lives, the more confident they are in advancing their interpreta-

tions. They start to see Dante, not as an obscure guy they can barely understand, but as someone like them, just telling a story.

Their connecting to the work teaches me. The most powerful instance of this
happened in one of my early years teaching in the Clemente program. We were
discussing Virgil's description of existence as a virtuous pagan: "without hope
we live on in desire" (*Inf.* 4.42). I always get them to free associate with this ach-
ingly beautiful line the way they do with "carnival of bloat." Eventually, they see
that Dante's exile from home, as well as his impossible love for Beatrice, might
have informed this line. One year a student who had been in prison compared
it to the way someone with a life sentence must feel. That contemporary, concrete image of Virgil's plight stuck with me and is part of what makes teaching
this class so revelatory. That night I understood something new about Dante,
about prison, about my students.

I get them to see they are experts in the emotional material Dante mines, so
when we get to the final canto they are quite vocal on the question of why the
center of the Inferno is icy cold. Again, I ask them to draw on their own experiences. How does it feel to be cold versus hot? What's the coldest you've been?
the hottest? We talk about how we, Bostonians all, have experienced waiting for
a bus in mid-January. How did your feet feel? your shoulders? What were you
thinking? None of us, fortunately, have had full-body experiences of boil-
ing. This leads us to discuss the way Dante—and any writer—relies on the
reader's own ideas to create art. One of the loveliest readings I've heard was
from Sandra, who said that being around a coldhearted person makes you feel
undermined, isolated, possibly erased; it makes sense that the damned are tor-
mented, negated by the literal cold heart of hell.

Every year I make sure to call their attention to these lines in canto 18:

> I saw among the felons of that pit
> One wraith who might or might not have been tonsured—
> One could not tell, he was so smeared with shit.
> (*Inf.* 18.115–17)

Some students resist thinking about this last line because the image is so dis-
gusting or the word too offensive. As one of my students two years ago said,
though, if Dante's in a horrible place, it's going to affect his language. I remind
them why Dante wrote in the vernacular, of his project to open literary culture to
wider audiences, which is exactly the Clemente program's mission. We talk
about the radical possibilities of democratized knowledge—all contained here,
in the use of the word "shit." I move quickly past these specific lines this week
but read them again during our final class when we discuss Junot Díaz's story
"Drown." Some students come to that class taken aback by Díaz's language,
wondering why we read his work. I reread the Dante lines above, which helps
them remember what the vernacular looks like, reminds them of its social and
political possibilities, and then ask them to reconsider the language. This often

frees students who felt too shy to defend the use of expletives. They see Díaz's use of untranslated Spanish and English profanity as a way of inventing a unique language for the story's narrator. Many of my students identify with him. One year our class graduation speaker said Díaz made him realize his own life is worthy of literary treatment. Dante, from over seven hundred years in the past, helps these students understand what the political stakes are in a story like "Drown."

They haven't gone nine weeks without hearing from Dante; he helped us read Wordsworth. In Ciardi's translation, Virgil, looking at the hoarders and wasters, tells Dante that in life "[h]oarding and squandering wasted all their light" (*Inf.* 7.58). Similarly, in "The World Is Too Much with Us," Wordsworth warns his readers, "Getting and spending, we lay waste our powers" (line 2). Hoarding and squandering, getting and spending; wasted light, wasted power. Ciardi's translation gives Wordsworth's sonnet a Dantean echo, turning a wistful pastoral dream into a despairing, apocalyptic warning. We may be "standing on this pleasant lea" (line 11) but it's in the fourth circle of Hell.

When we read the first few chapters of Stowe's *Uncle Tom's Cabin*, occasionally a student will have read further and we'll talk separately before or after class about how Tom's journey into the depths of the South can be read as a descent into the Inferno. Dante is also with us, of course, when we discuss T. S. Eliot's "The Hollow Men." I added the Muslim poet Lal Ded in part as a response to the election of Donald Trump.[2] Last year, also in response to Trump, I added in week 10, along with the "December 19th" section of Gloria Naylor's *Linden Hills*, Mitsuye Yamada's poem "Desert Run."[3] *Linden Hills* beautifully plays with *The Inferno.* Naylor's affluent African American suburb is constructed in a series of concentric rings housing sinners who have betrayed community and self rather than king or God.

Such repetitions, I tell my students, the way each century's artists respond to and reuse the works of the past, help form the rich and complicated fabric of our cultural inheritance. So in this semester of echoing texts, I want my students to play with Yamada, who by playing with Eliot becomes a new Dante. Her five-part poem begins in terrain familiar to readers of Eliot's five-part "The Hollow Men":

> I return to the desert
> where criminals
> were abandoned to wander
> away to their deaths
> where scorpions
> spiders
> lizards
> and rats
> live in outcast harmony. (1)

Like Eliot's men, in the desert, Yamada was blind to beauty, surrounded by the vocabulary of death, shivering in the cold presence of stars. Unlike them, however, Yamada has escaped, is there—Dante-like—only for a visit and has come out writing:

> I write these words at night
> for I am still a night creature
> but I will not keep a discreet distance.
>
> If you must fit me to your needs
> I will die
> And so will you.   (5)

If her world ends, with a bang or a whimper, Yamada will take her jailer with her.

Yamada was interned with other Japanese Americans during World War II. As Traise Yamamoto says in her study of Japanese American women's writing, despite the useful fiction that the author is dead, sometimes biographical information on an author is crucial: "Thus, the recovery of history is inextricably tied to the recovery of the voice that recovers history" (Yamamoto 203). In other words, if a reader does not understand that Yamada had been interned as a child, a poem like "Desert Run" would make no sense and the ending would lack the power such knowledge brings. Yamamoto's reading supports the pedagogy of our class. The few introductory facts I can give will offer my students more than just a naive first step in reading this poem. Those facts, along with their knowledge of Dante, Eliot, and other literature, will allow them to produce important readings of Yamada's poem.

They might, for instance, note that both Yamada and Dante were unjustly exiled from their homes, that both are surrounded by serpents in their poems, that Yamada does not seem at all dependent on her companion the way Dante is on Virgil, that she in fact becomes a serpent herself. Yamada uses Eliot's anomie to retell Dante's story of exile from a position of strength. Yamada believes that she and others were imprisoned, in part, because it was expected "that the West Coast Japanese Americans would go without too much protest. . . . We were not perceived by our government as responsive Americans" ("Invisibility" 40). Like Dante, Yamada has returned from her desert sojourn, not hollowed like Eliot's despairing modernists, but enlightened and, like Dante, she has a message and a warning: "We need to raise our voices a little more. . . . To finally recognize our own invisibility is to finally be on the path toward visibility" ("Invisibility" 40). To be visible, she says, is to be less liable to injustice. So I am adding Yamada to the syllabus, not just because she wrote beautiful and important work but also because Dante wrote in the vernacular, because Wordsworth believed the world was too much with us, and because Lalla said you need more than salt to turn fresh water into the sea. These writers we teach and read and love are great because they remind us that we can be great, and the more we study and learn and share their work, the more we realize that the greatest thing we can aspire to be is kind.

NOTES

Thank you to my dear friends and colleagues Daniel Shaw and Julia Lisella and my two amazing editors for their incisive comments on drafts of this essay.

[1] For quotations from the *Inferno*, I use the Ciardi translation published in the Signet Classic edition, 2001.

[2] Though my class is called Great Works of Western Literature, I have had no trouble problematizing the idea of greatness; years ago I happily fought minor skirmishes getting women and people of color onto my syllabus. So why not problematize Westernness?

[3] My gratitude to my Monday reading group, which wanted to explore the literature of Japanese American incarceration in the wake of Trump's election and so allowed me to discover Yamada's poem. Thank you, Anita, Ann, Barbara, Michele, and Susan.

Teaching Dante to High School Seniors

Jessica Levenstein

It's the first day of the fall trimester. Fourteen high school seniors are sitting around an oval table, brand new copies of the *Inferno* in front of them, eyes expectant but apprehensive. To break the ice, I ask why they signed up for my Dante elective. "I read the Dan Brown book," says a girl toward the back of the room. "My mom's Italian," says the boy to my right. The rest are silent. It's clear to me that most of them did not seek out this class; they're in the room because this English elective fit their schedules. Without choosing to, they are about to read a poem about the consequences of sin, originally written in a language they don't know, reflecting a culture with which they are largely unfamiliar. I'm not worried, though. After years of close reading around other oval tables at the school, they are attentive to figurative language, form, and genre. More important, they are high school seniors in the twenty-first century. They live on social media, so they are intensely attuned to the art of self-presentation; they are on the verge of leaving home, so they are negotiating the difficulty of gaining independence from their parents; and they are in the process of forming their ethical identities, so they are invested in questions of fairness and responsibility. Dante's narrative will resonate for them in ways they can't anticipate.

I teach at a selective, secular, independent school in New York City. The students who are admitted to the school are bright, hardworking, and ambitious. At seventeen, they are juggling five academic classes; one or two arts classes; time-consuming athletic, service, and extracurricular commitments; standardized tests; and the college admissions process. The grade they earn in my class feels significant to them: in many cases, it represents their last opportunity to demonstrate their skills to the colleges they want to attend. They are anxious about their futures and ambivalent about beginning their last year of high school. In a typical class a few students may know the *Aeneid* and the Bible, but few will know them well. I need to provide them with tools to make sense of a poem steeped in references that will be lost to them, without overwhelming them with all they don't know. I need to allow them to gain an individual purchase on Dante's work without watering down the difficulty of the text. If things go well, students leave the class with both the skills they need to approach a profoundly unfamiliar fictional world and an understanding of the relevance of a narrative about facing failure and embracing change. Above all, studying the poem should give them a sense of the pleasures afforded by the *Commedia* and an interest in experiencing those pleasures still more deeply.

To accomplish these goals, I help the class understand the poem as crafted by a human hand, as informed by the poet's personal struggle, grievances, and passions. I draw attention to his stance as God's scribe, his effort to surpass his literary models, and his anxieties about the power of language. If the students can see the poet behind the veil of medieval history, religion, and culture, they can get to the heart of the poem's concerns.

To that end, I introduce several themes in the first few days that end up structuring much of the trimester's conversation: I mention the fluidity of the relationship between the pilgrim's humility and the poet's pride, the truth claim supporting the entire work, and Dante's conflicted relationship with Virgil. Three moments in *Inferno* 2 provide the foundation for these themes and shape subsequent discussions. The first is Dante's effort to mark his connection to others who have traveled to the afterworld, "Ma io, perché venirvi? o chi 'l concede? / Io non Enëa, io non Paulo sono;" ("But why should I go there? who allows it? / I am not Aeneas, nor am I Paul"; *Inf.* 2.31–32).[1] Students immediately perceive that Dante alone brings Paul's name into the poem; he's responsible for any association between the pilgrim and the apostle. The students' antennae for Dante's false humility allow them to see the poet as a human being they can recognize; he's seven hundred years too early for *Twitter*, but he's a master of the humblebrag. When we look at the second moment, the poet's first invocation, the students begin to appreciate how tenaciously Dante insists on the existence of a lived experience outside of the manuscript on which he transcribes the poem: "O muse, o alto ingegno, or m'aiutate; / o mente che scrivesti ciò ch'io vidi" ("O Muses, O lofty genius, aid me now! / O memory, that set down what I saw"; *Inf.* 2.7–8). This insistence on the actuality of the events Dante describes, combined with his acknowledgement that he is actually engaging in an act of writing, attune my students to the interplay between truth and fiction in the poem and cast Dante's work as one constructed by a human intelligence.[2] Finally, the third moment, Beatrice's limiting praise of Virgil's fame, introduces Dante's contradictory position toward his literary idol and hints at the scope of Dante's own ambition: "O anima cortese mantoana, / di cui la fama ancor nel mondo dura, / e durerà quanto 'l mondo lontana" ("O courteous Mantuan spirit, / whose fame continues in the world / and shall continue while the world endures"; *Inf.* 2.58–60). Moreover, the students inevitably appreciate the elegance of Beatrice's gibe. Just as they enjoy perceiving the boast inside the deprecation of "Io non Enëa, io non Paulo sono," they relish observing the insult concealed behind the compliment of "durerà quanto 'l mondo lontana."

We meet four times a week for forty-five minutes, and we use the Robert Hollander and Jean Hollander translation of the poem and its accompanying commentary. Students are assigned one or two cantos for each class, and one pair of students each night is responsible for the notes for that assignment. By the end of the eleven weeks, the students have read all of *Inferno*, *Purgatorio* 1 and 27 through 33, and *Paradiso* 33. In addition to the assigned reading, the students have access to maps, film clips, and interesting links on our course Web page. The core of the class, however, is the group discussion. Although I clarify confusion and provide guidance, my goal is to speak as little as possible.

The students responsible for the commentary can answer questions for their classmates, and I often ask students to work in pairs on identifying the most fruitful passages in that day's reading. Before discussing any passage, however, I'll ask one of the less vocal students or the student who seems most distracted to read the passage aloud. Inevitably, the student who has read aloud ends up contributing actively to the subsequent conversation. My own interventions tend to be textual; that is, because I'm familiar with the Italian text of the poem and the students are not, I'll point out textual evidence to support a student's observation. For example, after Dante faints at the end of *Inferno* 5, a student might suggest that his reaction could indicate the pilgrim's own issues with lust. I'd draw the student's attention to line 72, when the poet describes his state of mind just before he meets Francesca, using the same adjective as he does in the first terzina to describe his spiritual despair: "fui quasi smarrito" ("I almost lost my senses"; *Inf.* 5.72). In time, however, even without Italian, the students learn to look for the commentary's help in making such connections.

Our class discussion can touch on many ideas in a short span, but the students seem to become most animated when they find relevance in Dante's story for their own lives. Perhaps because social media—aided by *Photoshop*, beautifying filters, and the careful editing of posts and pictures—amplifies adolescent unease about self-presentation, the tension between truth and fiction in the *Commedia* attracts the most student interest. Students are very focused on credulity: how do we know what we can believe? When Beatrice flatters Virgil for his "parola ornata" ("polished words"; *Inf.* 2.67), and Virgil then describes Jason as deceiving Hypsipyle with his own "parole ornate" (*Inf.* 18.91), is Dante condemning ornate speech altogether? Is Beatrice herself not polishing her language to persuade Virgil to serve as the pilgrim's guide? Is the poet himself not coaxing his readers onto the straight path by means of poetic language? Perhaps no canto generates as exciting a discussion as *Inferno* 20, with its explicit examination of the relative value of truth and fiction and its consideration of the implications of such an appraisal for the *Commedia* itself. This past year, an otherwise fairly quiet student began thinking aloud about the techniques astrologers use. Astrologers begin with very general statements, she observed, such as "you care about your friends and family," so the listener responds, "Yes! That's me!" That way, when the astrologer predicts something more specific, the listener is already inclined to believe it; the general statement earned the listener's trust. Similarly, this student continued, Dante makes us believe the more outlandish claims in his poem by earning our trust with the verisimilitude of his narrative elsewhere. The rest of the class was quick to pick up the thread of the argument: if Dante himself makes use of the strategies of the fortune-tellers punished in the fourth bolgia, and if, moreover, by placing known figures in specific places in the underworld he is telling the afterlife "fortune" of every character in the poem, then no wonder the pilgrim weeps when he sees the contorted bodies of these punished souls. He knows he is practicing the same sinful art as the twisted soothsayers before him. And it is equally evident that the occasion of considering divination causes Dante to put the constructedness of his poem on display when he begins the canto with "Di nova pena mi conven far versi / e dar matera al ventesimo canto / de la prima canzon" ("Of strange new pain I now must make my verse / giving matter to the canto numbered twenty / of this first *canzone*"; *Inf.* 20.1–3).[3] The truth, or the falsity, of his poem is at stake.

The perils of fiction making connect also to another topic of particular interest to high school seniors: Dante's relationship with his guide and parental figure, Virgil. The scenes in the poem when Dante distinguishes between the fictive *Aeneid* and the truthful *Commedia* (e.g., *Inf.* 13.46–49, *Inf.* 20.97–99), are of enormous interest to adolescents, both preoccupied by the veracity of their own self-presentation and enmeshed in an ongoing recalibration of their relationship with their parents. As the students in my classroom are studying Dante's poem, they are also putting their final touches on their college applications and beginning to imagine a life outside the family home. The position of the pilgrim toward his "maestro e . . . autore" ("teacher and . . . author"; *Inf.* 1.85)—admiring, grateful, and loving—is not unlike their positions toward their parents. But Dante's effort to mark the difference between his narrative and Virgil's, by insisting on the falseness of Virgil's poem and the truthfulness of his own, also mirrors the necessary act of filial separation my students are enacting as they arrange for the next steps in their trajectory toward adulthood. The contradiction in Dante's relationship with his "dolce padre" ("gentle father"; *Inf.* 8.110) connects most closely to my students' own familial drama as we begin reading of Dante's journey through the Earthly Paradise. Virgil bids the pilgrim farewell, telling his charge:

> Tratto t'ho qui con ingegno e con arte;
> lo tuo piacere omai prendi per duce;
> . . . .
> Non aspettar mio dir più né mio cenno;
> libero, dritto e sano è tuo arbitrio.
>
> I have brought you here with intellect and skill.
> From now on take your pleasure as your guide.
> . . . .
> No longer wait for word or sign from me.
> Your will is free, upright, and sound.
>   (*Purg.* 27.130–31, 139–40)

Students, as they prepare for a similar scene at the gates of places that seem in their imaginations like their own paradises, can't help but be moved by Virgil's words. Dante makes the subtext of parental loss agonizingly explicit two cantos later:

volsimi a la sinistra col respitto
col quale il fantolin corre a la mamma
quando ha paura o quando elli è afflitto

. . . .

Ma Virgilio n'avea lasciati scemi
di sé, Virgilio dolcissimo patre.

I turned to my left with the confidence
a child has running to his *mamma*
when he is afraid or in distress

. . . .

But Virgil had departed, leaving us bereft
Virgil, sweetest of fathers.
(*Purg.* 30.43–45, 49–50)

These lines take on a profound and painful meaning for the students in the room. In the same way, the pilgrim's parallel aboard Geryon, to Phaeton, tragically ill-equipped to manage his father's team, and to Icarus, too tempted by the pleasures of flight to heed his father's warning, strike a chord for adolescents testing the limits of their independence from their parents. By the same token, perhaps Dante's entire journey can be cast as an effort to recapture the safety of childhood. After all, the pilgrim tells his teacher Brunetto Latini, "mi smarri' . . . / . . . / e reducemi a ca per questo calle" ("I lost my way . . . / . . . / and now along this road he leads me home"; *Inf.* 15.50, 54).

As Dante finds his way back home to the straight path, he confronts the question of moral accountability again and again, particularly as he hears and responds to the narratives of the damned souls he encounters on his journey through Hell. The sinners' varying ability to accept the blame for their own sins provides rich material for classroom discussion. Reading Francesca's own account of her adulterous affair with Paolo, my students seize on her verbal sleights of hand: her use of the passive voice to shift responsibility to Love; her insistence on the culpability of the Lancelot story rather than the actions that interrupted the lovers' reading. Reading the tale of Pier delle Vigne, they home in on Pier's defensive assertion that he stayed faithful to his "segnor" ("lord"; *Inf.* 13.75), without understanding which lord in fact deserved his faith. Teenagers, masters of the casuistic argument in their own negotiations with parents and teachers, easily recognize a fellow practitioner. Often sharing their homes, or even bedrooms, with siblings, they are also on perpetual alert for inequities. Why, they ask, is Virgil condemned for living "nel tempo de li dèi falsi e bugiardi" ("in an age of false and lying gods"; *Inf.* 1.72), but Capaneus is condemned for blaspheming those same false gods? Why bother putting Brunetto Latini in Hell at all, only to praise him effusively? The students' passionate interrogation of the structure of Hell, and Dante's choice to people it as he does, reflects their personal investment in fairness as a principle to live by.

Every other course I teach culminates in analytical writing assignments, but in the case of the Dante elective, I take a different approach: students are quizzed on about ten cantos at a time and tested twice in the trimester. Quizzes are meant to demonstrate mastery of the layout of Inferno: How is Hell structured? Which sins are punished where? What are the punishments for each sin? Quizzes invite students to enter the world of the poem and understand it on its own terms. Rather than shrinking back from the unfamiliar, students become masters of Dante's hellscape, and those who prepare for the quiz can easily achieve a perfect score. Tests, on the other hand, ask students to delve into the themes and ideas of their reading, focusing on Dante's language and imagery. Each test asks students to identify ten passages (Who is speaking? to whom? where?) and discuss the significance of the five passages most interesting among those ten. Most students do not confront much difficulty identifying passages, and many produce elegant, succinct readings of individual passages, demonstrating both an impressive un- derstanding of the ideas we have discussed and an ability to make connections and offer insights that we have not considered as a group. The most meaningful assessment of the course, however, is the final project, which the students work toward at home in the last two weeks of the trimester, while we read the desig- nated cantos in *Purgatorio* and *Paradiso* in class. For this final assignment, they engage with the poem in a project they design, using their own interests (in art, music, technology, literature, or even food) as a springboard for an exploration of the ideas of the poem.

Most recently, one student narrated a charming and accurate version of Dante's biography and voyage through Hell using a popular *YouTube* genre known as "Draw My Life"—a fast-motion video featuring changing illustrations on a whiteboard accompanied by a voiceover describing a life story. Another student explored the passage in *Inferno* 15 describing Dante's voyage home by composing a piece for the *cajón*, a box-shaped Peruvian percussion instrument. A third student came up with a "Fashion Inferno," condemning bad dressers to Hell for fashion sins ranging from wearing white after Labor Day to pairing socks and sandals, and assigning appropriate punishments to the various of- fenders (the sinners who wore too many brand names simultaneously are liter- ally branded, over and over again). A few years ago a student even submitted a *Twitter* page for Dante. The student had Dante post exactly thirty-four tweets, such as "Just passed by the noble @Jason. He was suffering for his exploits with Hypsipyle and Medea. Guess I'd better be careful with those #polished words" and "Just had a great conversation with @Homer, @Horace, @Ovid, @Lucan and @MantuanSpirit12. Those guys are truly the loftiest of poets. #WhatAn- Honor." Replicating a real *Twitter* page, the student listed how many accounts Dante himself was following: one. Although sometimes lighthearted, these projects in fact elicit a deep, sustained engagement with Dante's work. Because the students choose the angle from which they approach the poem, their pas- sions outside the class are reflected in their projects, and their work tends to go far beyond the requirements of the assignment. Indeed, when they present their projects to each other they revel in pointing out or noticing the unnecessary particulars of each project, such as the *Twitter* account's use of the word "honor" when tweeting *Inferno* 4, as if these details were inside jokes, shared by their classmates. Students who may have struggled to make sense of Dante's narrative now display a sense of ownership over the poem and leave the class satisfied by the sense of having met an intellectual challenge.

In the second trimester, students move on to a course that might be totally unrelated to Dante: a poetry-writing elective, or a trimester-long study of *Anna Karenina*, for example. In college, they sometimes continue their study of Dante, and often they do not. They have learned something, however, about the rewards of confronting a work or idea that is profoundly alien to them. They have learned to manage the discomfort caused by the unfamiliar, and to use resources to make sense of what they don't understand; they have learned to approach a literary work from its point of intersection with what they do know or care about. Moreover, in reading Dante in high school, my students surprise themselves by finding in the story of the spiritual journey of a medieval Italian exile an analogue to some of their own ventures in the modern world. The gaps in language, religion, location, and historical context fall away until all they are left with is the human experience, the ongoing quest to find their voices, to find their paths, and to find a meaning larger than themselves.

NOTES

[1] For quotations from the *Commedia*, I use Petrocchi's Italian text of the poem and the Hollander translation.

[2] Passages in the poem that draw attention to the act of writing itself are useful in helping students recognize that there is a human being behind the masterpiece they are encountering. Examples include *Inferno* 4.145–47 and 20.1–3.

[3] My own reading of this canto is deeply indebted to Barolini, *Dante's Poets* 214–22.

Teaching Dante in Prison

Ronald Herzman

My experience teaching Dante in a maximum-security correctional facility has dramatically shaped pedagogical strategies in all of my experiences teaching the *Commedia* since that time. My friend and colleague Bill Cook and I taught the entire *Commedia* in a college credit-bearing course twice in the early 1980s at Attica Correctional Facility in New York State, and reflecting on our experience from that time until the present has been invaluable for me in trying to figure out what it is we are supposed to do in any classroom when we are dealing with a magisterial text that puts so many different kinds of demands on its readers. In short, what was forced on us because of the unusual circumstances of Attica prison has taken on new life in other circumstances and might be helpful for others who must present a poem so vast and complex to their own students, of whatever stripe. In focusing on some issues we had to deal with that separated this course from our more usual teaching in a college classroom, I have come to realize what a formative experience it was—and what a fortunate one.

Perhaps it shouldn't have, but it came as a surprise to us once we got there to learn that our inmate students had never so much as heard of Dante before. It was up to us to make a case for him from scratch. Fortunately, our students came with no preconceptions. They were not programmed by half-formed as-sumptions that needed to be unlearned. They also did not come with an exag-gerated reverence for the author they were about to encounter. To be clear, reverence for Dante is not a bad thing. He has earned it. And by the end of the semester our students had it. But it has to be real. Reverence before it is earned is a great obstacle to the actual down and dirty work of engagement with the text, since there is an implicit assumption that in the very act of obeisance a goal has been achieved, and that the homage we are paying to a figure such as Dante is the only price of admission we need to join an important club, one which doesn't require a real engagement with the text for membership.

How should one introduce the *Commedia* under these circumstances? How does one introduce the big issues behind the issues, and behind the basic facts of Dante's life to folks who have never heard of him before? Quickly! We needed to explain why Dante matters at the outset of the course, a good thing to do under any circumstances, but especially necessary because we intuited right from the get-go that our job, and Dante's, was to earn our students' trust. What was at stake for Dante in writing the poem? An extended disquisition on the fine points of the Guelf-Ghibelline struggle might not be the best way to go about it. Teaching Dante always involves making hard choices, because there is never enough time to cover everything, so introductory material needs to be kept short to get on with the business of reading the poem. What really matters? That is the question to ask and try to answer as a run-up to text crawling. Teaching in Attica taught me to learn to do Dante without footnotes, and to cut to the chase about what is really fundamental.

Getting our students to trust Dante was a very tricky business for another reason as well. The default assumption of our inmate students was that everything they hear from anyone in authority is a lie. So why should literary authorities be any different? Why should they trust Dante? Convincing them to take Dante seriously as a truth teller rather than just another brand of liar was a key part of our work together. Dante made it easy for us by the basic contours of his life. His exile and their incarceration intersect at more than enough points that they were willing to give him (and us as teachers) the benefit of the doubt once we showed them how his exile and poem intertwined. That also gave us the advantage of convincing them early in the course that this poem had something to say directly to them. Locking Dante out was not all that different from locking them in.

One way they were ahead of the game is that in *Inferno* the characters that the pilgrim encounters *are* liars; our students' lie-detecting radar was good enough to read the dramatic encounters in the text with great acuity. They caught on to Francesca, for example, without our having to say anything. "She is putting the blame on someone else." Pause. "That's what I did." Pause. "That's why I'm here." But a very interesting takeaway from that experience demonstrates one way the inmates became our teachers, even though I didn't immediately perceive it at the time. The inmates were right in their larger intuition. So much of what we hear, even those of us who have the good fortune not to be in a maximum security prison, is in fact a lie: advertising, politics, media, you name it. We are constantly being lied to. Though I present the case obliquely as my classes work their way through the poem, the *Commedia* can provide a healthy inoculation against gullibility. Dante's poem is an exercise in learning to read carefully, to look beneath surfaces, to exercise judgment. Dante's infernal liars are sophisticated and subtle. Many if not most make impressive cases for themselves. The *Inferno* is an extended exercise in learning how to see what Dante's characters leave out of their story. We spent a lot of time with Farinata and Ulysses. Because our students saw this, we did not have to do too much to get them to have a good working understanding of the distinction between Dante poet and Dante pilgrim, a task that can sometimes prove frustratingly difficult when teaching the poem to beginners: they could identify with the pilgrim in their mutual search to see past the lies. They got irony.

Before diversity became a watchword, we had a pretty diverse group in our classroom: a former New York City police sergeant, a pimp, Muslims who knew the Bible cold ("Isn't that from Second Maccabees?"), various shades of murderers, inmates who would be there for the rest of their lives or close to it, inmates caught for minor-league drug trafficking who would be getting out soon, the young, and the old. Put them all together and what you get is a nuclear core of street smarts. Our students had stunning insights into the text and articulated them in class powerfully, insights they often came to on their own, with no prompting from us. Classroom sessions were always interesting and often electric. At the beginning of *Purgatory*, for example, when we were looking at the late-repentant and the excommunicated, one of our students expressed his skepticism about the possibility of deathbed conversions: "I've seen lots of people die. I don't buy it." That led to an interesting discussion, one to which the professors had little to contribute.

Street smarts differ from academic smarts, however. Dante mattered to these students in a way I have never seen before or since. Life, as it turns out, especially life at the bottom of the food chain, is good preparation for Dante. But they had a much more difficult time writing, both in essay exams and papers. Our students needed a high school diploma before they could take the course, but sometimes that diploma was earned long ago and far away, in other cases earned as part of the GED program inside the prison, and in most cases earned under conditions far from ideal. The majority of our students were from New York City, but they had not gone to Stuyvesant or Bronx Science. Essay exams and papers were part of the course. We tried to replicate, as much as the sometimes-exasperating conditions of a maximum-security prison allowed, the Dante course that we team-taught at State University of New York, Geneseo. But how should we negotiate the gap between spoken and written word? Not to put too fine an edge on it, where should we put the emphasis when it came time to figure out a grade at the end of the semester? No question we took this disparity into consideration, and students who did well in class participation did well in their final grade. Were we letting them off the hook, giving them a break we would not give to their unincarcerated colleagues? Or, to flip the question around, do we overprivilege the written word in our so-called normal classes? This remains for me a very open question in my teaching up to the present.

A real problem at every college or university in the country is that students have very different degrees and kinds of preparation. And it is also clear that bringing the writing skills of less well prepared students up to speed is one of the most important things that we as teachers can do to try to level the playing field. (In Attica, we tried to address this issue by putting together an impromptu writing center, bringing in several colleagues to help us do some serious one-on-one tutoring in preparation for their papers.) But along with that necessary goal there should be recognition that those whose writing skills are not at a level with the best of our students may nevertheless have all kinds of things to teach the rest of us and other ways of articulating what they know. We too often take the papers our students write as the final arbiter of their measured (i.e., graded) success in class, and perhaps even worse, the arbiter of how they have engaged the poem. I carried back from Attica a new sensitivity to this issue. Though it may seem counterintuitive, our inmate students also suffered from greater test anxiety than any other group I have taught. I learned something when I discovered that inmates who could bench press a small SUV were nervous wrecks before the final exam. I listen more carefully now to the needs of my nonincarcerated students.

Our inmate students were well enough acquainted with the world described in the *Inferno*, and, as we were looking at the text, their prison experience allowed them to reach insights before their teachers did. They intuited similarities between the stratified, rigid, controlled world of the *Inferno* and their own experiences with the hierarchies and controls that to a huge extent defined their lives. But it would be wrong to think their insights or their enthusiasm were limited to places where their infernal prison experiences guided their reading. The *Inferno* was not their favorite part of the poem. Their favorite part of the poem was *Purgatorio*. They wanted from Dante what is given in its most concentrated form in the *Purgatorio*: a detailed blueprint for moral improvement. What they were after was meaning. The eternal battle between those who see education as job craft and those who see it as soul craft came into high relief in Attica, and teaching there has given me a platform to argue for the latter in a world where more emphasis is being placed on the former.

I was called onto the carpet once, or more accurately, called into the stairwell, in a bit of comic relief that illustrates my point. The only time a guard ever came into the sacred space of our classroom during the two years we taught there was to escort me to a lieutenant waiting in the stairwell, who said in the most solemn and serious tone, "We don't take off our shoes in class. It sets a bad example for the men." Really? In an institution where seventy percent have committed a violent crime and thirty percent have taken a life, the rehabilitation process will grind to a halt at the sight of my socks? A lot of scarcely suppressed giggles when I came back to the classroom. Our students knew what was going on. But one of the veterans gave me something to ponder when he assured me that this was not simply another example among the many we had experienced of the guardians reminding us all who was in charge. (Another thing that gave us street cred with our students is that every so often we were subject to petty but annoying harassment from the guards.) The lieutenant in question, he assured us, was one of a minority of correction officers at Attica who actually was in favor of the inmate education program. But for the lieutenant, it seemed that one of the major purposes of the program was to instill order and discipline. Students were there to learn practical skills that would help them, whether for those who would return to the outside world or for those who would remain at Attica for a very long time. The notion that one could better approach the text in a laid-back classroom never crossed his mind. That we read Dante so that Dante can read us, that Dante was forcing us to engage in soul craft, and that this was what our students desperately wanted and just as desperately needed—these were not on his radar screen, I am pretty sure.

The biggest takeaway, the most important thing I learned teaching Dante in Attica, is so obvious that it is easy to miss: Dante is for everyone. Before we walked through the sixteen sets of locked gates to get to our first class, as nervous as we have ever been in our lives, we wondered whether this seeming unlikely marriage could possibly work. Now, it seems like the most natural thing in the world. Since teaching Dante in Attica, I have become even more of a missionary than I was before. One way I have put this zeal to use is that I have had the good fortune to direct fifteen Summer Seminars for School Teachers on the *Commedia* through the National Endowment for the Humanities and have consequently been able to watch with great pleasure a lot of what goes on in presecondary education: A large cross selection of the participants in these seminars now teach Dante regularly in their schools, and I have joined them virtually and in person in their classrooms across the country. This includes elite schools of various stripes and, happily, classrooms in the most ordinary and subordinary schools as well. Dante makes his mark in the most unlikely places. He allows you to meet him where you are. So often the grandest monuments of high culture are used as shorthand to establish a hierarchy, to reinforce distinctions between us and them. "Ah, Bach," as both William F. Buckley, Jr., and Radar O'Reilly have memorably put it. Regardless of whether the love for and deep understanding of Bach is genuine, when I hear these words they sound suspiciously like "I've got Bach . . . and you don't."

What teaching Dante in Attica taught me is there is no "you," at least as far as Dante is concerned. I don't know how Bach would go over in the slammer, but I do know that Dante possesses the great gift (as does Shakespeare, among other important examples) of hitting you wherever you are. Just do it. That an awful lot of Dante's subtlety and precision was lost in translation on our Attica students has continued to be something to ponder, no question. We did not have the time or the skills to discuss Dante's poetic artistry in any adequately detailed way, given the time at our disposal. Nor is it clear how our students would have responded. Were our students getting Dante lite? I have been re-playing this question in my mind for many years. I think that the best way to answer it is by way of a sliding scale. Many years ago, a student, a Vietnamese refugee who had mastered English with frightening rapidity, came into my of-fice beaming. "I have just read *Hamlet* three times," she said. "I think I under-stand fifty percent of it." Reflexively, I answered: "Good. I have been teaching *Hamlet* for about thirty years, and I think I am up to about sixty percent." Were we giving them watered-down Dante? Of course we were. But all the rest of us are likewise encountering watered-down Dante. The reason we teach Dante is that he is smarter than we are, and our own attempts to catch up to him in our reading, teaching, and scholarship should give us the humility to understand that the differences between us and our slammer students, or any other stu-dents, from eighth graders on up, matter far less than the similarities: we are all fellow pilgrims here. There is no magic threshold that one passes through. You get your membership card when you crack open the text and engage.

Beatrice in the Tag Cloud

Carol Chiodo

Anyone hoping to tackle Dante's *Divine Comedy* in a semester-long undergraduate course today faces two problems, both of scale.[1] The first is the poem itself—assigning all 14,233 verses during a semester is not for the faint of heart. Some instructors dodge the problem entirely, dividing the *Inferno* and the remaining canticles over the course of a year, whereas others apportion cantos from all three canticles with hopes for an abridged, yet complete, pilgrimage. This problem, however, doesn't lend itself to an easily generalized approach to teaching the *Comedy* in the undergraduate classroom. Far easier to tackle, at least in this setting, is the problem posed by the sheer number of resources at our students' fingertips.

Centuries of commentaries, studies, translations, adaptations, and more are available at the click of a mouse. In 2012, typing "dante's divine comedy" into a Google search box yielded almost instantly 2.5 million results. Five years later, if a student attempted a similar search, it could yield over forty times that amount. It is easy to see how a student might be overwhelmed by the prospect of a five- to eight-page essay on Dante's understanding of the concept of love, particularly if a search box is just a click away.

This search box problem has been described by media theorist Clay Shirky as "filter failure."[2] Shirky points out that information overload is not a new problem, but our diminishing capacity to filter for quality is unique to our information age. Yet, teaching students to manage this volume of information flow is analogous to the explicit aims of Dante's encyclopedic approach to knowledge in the *Comedy*. And developing the ability to filter, discern, and refine significant information is the crux of humanities coursework, requiring students to develop their skills in both inquiry and analysis.[3] Here, inquiry may be understood as the exploration of issues or works through the collection and analysis of evidence that results in informed conclusions, whereas analysis is the process of breaking complex topics into parts or, to use Shirky's term, "filtering" in order to gain a better understanding of them.

Of course the complexity of writing tasks associated with inquiry and analysis is determined by how much information or guidance is provided to the student and how much is left to the student to construct independently.[4] In this particular course, Dante in Translation, a weekly section provided an hour's worth of guided discussion, and two seventy-five minute lectures placed Dante's work in the intellectual and social context of the late Middle Ages. Students also had access to thirty additional hours of recorded lectures from a similar course on Dante, made freely available online by Yale Open Courses.[5] In addition to a final exam, students would write a final paper on a topic of their choice of approximately three thousand words that would draw on, presumably, their reading of the entirety of the *Comedy*, their notes from thirty (or even sixty) hours of lectures, the print and online resources placed on hold for the course in the library, and the flotsam and jetsam churned up by commercial search engines. Could this final writing task be scaffolded so that students could focus and support their written work with the substance of the poem through sustained, guided practice?

Leading students through the process of preliminary exploration of the *Comedy* with low-stakes writing assignments allows them to collect, reflect, and share their perspectives over the course of a semester. *WordPress*, a free and open-source content management system, facilitated the publication and collection of these assignments over the course of a semester.[6] In its role as an asynchronous online venue for discussion, the blog also extended and enhanced classroom discussion, creating a space for intellectual digression and creativity, as well as ongoing instruction.

Initially, students posted questions or comments on a specific theme or verses each week before arriving in class. Initial writing assignments were simply first-order expectations for learning, such as pick a passage you enjoyed and explain why; or summarize an encounter between the pilgrim and a soul in Hell. Soon, the prompts developed into second-order expectations, such as synthesis and evaluation, associated with successive milestones in the VALUE (Valid Assessment of Learning in Undergraduate Education) rubric. How does the pilgrim view the sins of the damned? What did you find perplexing? These would allow them to thread material from the lecture into their responses, drawing connections, probing questions, and suggesting the direction of our discussion.

As they entered the classroom, the most recent posts were projected for everyone to see. Late or missing comments were noted and rarely recurred; small conversations broke out among those puzzling over similar questions. The posts provided the class with collectively selected points for discussion. Sixty minutes later, these discussions would spill back into our online venue and more than a few would stay after class to "get something up on the blog" while it was on their mind. These posts were frequently collaborative, and went above and beyond those required for the course. From the very beginning, the students grasped the blog as a resource for them to plumb later on, a digital book of memory.

One prompt that captured the attention of several students was on sensory perception in the *Inferno*. Sights, sounds, smells, and the sense (or absence) of touch among the souls of the damned provided a rich vein a number of students would continue to explore throughout the course. The following is an example of an early post from a physics major:

> Throughout *Inferno*, of all the senses, Dante references sight the most. While this is understandable in that sight is the sense we depend most on, Dante seems to place much more emphasis on the eyes than necessary. Does Dante view them as a window through which souls can see and understand one another? In 1.10.131 (p. 139),[7] Dante refers to Beatrice as

the one "whose fair eyes see all." When Cavalcanti asks if his son has died or not, he asks if the light "strikes not the sweet light on his eyes." In Canto 13, Dante describes the eyes of a harlot as shameless (vv. 64–65). Even later still, in Canto 15 when Dante and Brunetto recognize each other, Dante speaks of fixing his eyes on him.

Once students completed a post such as this one, they were also asked to use *WordPress*'s tagging feature. When used thoughtfully, tagging is particularly apt for filtering large amounts of information while building momentum for a collective consensus. Indicated by the pound sign (#) on several social networks and microblogging services, it is a form of metadata. These, known in *Word-Press* as tags, make it easier for users to find posts with a specific themes or content, and it allows students to index small portions of writing (even a 140-character tweet) by whatever they deem valuable. Unlike other forms of metadata, however, tags can be subjective and even idiosyncratic. They can be descriptive or denotative, playful or sardonic. In social media, a hashtag archive is collected into a single stream under the same hashtag. An index would list alphabetically subjects and the location of their citation in the text (e.g., Acquasparta, Cardinal Matthew—*Par.* 12.124), but in *WordPress*, our tag archive is linked to the students' commentary on the blog. The archive is graphically displayed as a word cloud; the more frequently posts are tagged with a key word, the larger the word's appearance in the cloud.

The post above was tagged by the student as "sight," "Inferno," "eyes," and "senses." These tags allowed another student who, on reading Beatrice's words to the pilgrim in *Purgatory* 32, "al carro tieni or li occhi, e quel che vedi, / ritornato di là, fa che tu scrive" ("hold thine eyes now on the car and what thou seest do thou write when thou hast returned yonder"; 104–05), was prompted to return to his classmate's comments on sight and add his own reflections on bearing witness through the *Comedy.*

As the students' online discussions proliferated, and so much of their interests were reflected in the blog, they soon realized they were creating their own index for our class discussions, an index that would prove extremely valuable to them as they began formulating arguments for their final papers. Each word linked to posts on that topic, regardless of who wrote the post. It allowed students to dig through the blog and read comments across cantos, for example, or posts that examine Dante's relationship to the classical tradition. At our last meeting, the students remarked on how Beatrice seemed to dominate our tag cloud. Her arrival at the end of *Purgatory* coincided with their realization that tagging was a useful tool, and a number of reflections on our discussions on *Vita nova* at the beginning of the semester prompted the students to go back to their posts and retag them.

The blog posts are an example of sustained, guided practice where students have ample opportunities to write and receive feedback from both instructor and peers. By guiding students through systematically more complex pieces of writing—from description to synthesis, like the examples above—the blog helped students consolidate and transfer skills from one occasion to the next. And, in receiving formative assessments such as comments, encouragement, or critiques, students also are asked to make their thinking processes visible and to give grounds for them. We saw earlier the preliminary stages of formulating a paper topic, and how on the blog such a topic would be subjected to peer review. Choosing a topic, crafting an argument, harnessing textual support, and prewriting were all subject to peer scrutiny online and in class, and although students were reluctant to comment on others' work online, the classroom discussions shaped the final results.

We see this play out in the paper written by the physics major interested in the interaction between the gazes of Dante the pilgrim and the souls he encounters on his journey. The same student returns to this theme in a post a few weeks later, expanding and exploring his ideas in greater detail, adding:

> Overall, Dante seems to refer back to the eyes when Dante meets a new character and begins to understand or recognize who they are. . . . How Dante meets or has his gaze met by other characters becomes significant. Except for a few key moments in the *Inferno*, Dante does not meet [a] character's gaze but instead merely describes them, from the "burning coal" of Charon and the red-eyed ferocious Cerberus to the "slow-moving eyes" of the denizens of Limbo, some of which he does look up to and uplift himself with. He actively avoids one's view with the temptation of the gorgon's stare (which represents both physical and spiritual petrifaction) and the sinners in the final circle of Hell. Shortly after entering Purgatory, Dante meets up with Manfred, and the two share a mutual gaze, symbolically placing Dante on the same level as the other hopeful penitents as he prepares to climb the mountain. Partly through the journey, after being tempted by lust in the siren's dream, he awakes and immediately searches for Virgil's eyes and finds them.

The final paper would focus on the dynamics of the gaze in *Purgatory*, where "characters are present in a time-oriented environment and can thus be dynamically described through contrasts in aspects of vision. Within the canticle of atonement and spiritual development, Dante catalogs this spiritual progress of the Pilgrim as well as that of the penitent through changes in a character's ability to meet another's eyes." The student continues, "Specifically, Dante's progress as a penitent is described through how Dante views and is viewed by the other characters, with a reciprocal meeting of the eyes symbolizing equality between characters and a one-sided gaze symbolizing dominance on the part of the viewed."

This student essay draws exclusively from the blog, using the online lectures and notes from classroom lectures as secondary resources. As one student remarked, "With the blog, I didn't really need to go anywhere else." In addition to the blog posts providing students with ample opportunities to practice their writing skills in both analysis and inquiry, the associated tags create an expedient filter that allows students to focus on progressively expanding existing abilities with sequential writing tasks while not losing sight of the far more complex task that will complete their first journey as a reader through the *Comedy*.

NOTES

[1] It is a daunting task to introduce beginners to a field of study that has historically generated an infinitude of research. My thanks to Giuseppe Mazzotta and the students of Dante in Translation for their enthusiasm and sense of purpose in this endeavor.

[2] Shirky writes, "What we're dealing with now is not the problem of information overload, because we're always dealing (and always have been dealing) with information overload. . . . Thinking about information overload isn't accurately describing the problem; thinking about filter failure is."

[3] Inquiry and analysis are included among the essential learning outcomes as outlined in the report from the National Leadership Council, *College Learning for the New Global Century* (3).

[4] See the most recent report of the Association of American Colleges and Universities, *On Solid Ground: Value Report 2017*, which discusses the current landscape of key learning outcomes in undergraduate education according to the VALUE (Valid Assessment of Learning in Undergraduate Education) initiative. These rubrics, grounded in research and best practices derived from educational psychology, cognitive psychology, student development theory, and instructional design, generate data or qualitative and quantitative methodological assessment. The rubrics outline the intentional progression from benchmark (1), to milestone (2), milestone (3) and capstone (4) and in doing so provide valuable insight into student progression from first-order expectations for learning (for example, the memorization and description associated with the benchmark level) to second-order expectations for learning, such as synthesis and evaluation, associated with the successive milestones.

[5] The course is available online (Mazzotta, Dante in Translation). The same lectures are also available through Apple's online platform *iTunes U*.

[6] Although this particular instance of *WordPress* was installed on a local server and not publicly available, a public site would entail a number of other requirements, including a detailed classroom discussion of campus policies regarding student privacy and the possibility of students posting under a pseudonym, to mention just a few. For more on student privacy issues and helpful information about blogs in the classroom, see Sample's discussion.

[7] References are to the text assigned in the course, a reprint of Sinclair's 1939 prose translation for John Lane and Elkin Matthews at The Bodley Head.

NOTES ON CONTRIBUTORS

Nicolino Applauso is visiting assistant professor of Italian at Loyola University Maryland and lecturer of Italian, Latin, and Spanish at Morgan State University. His main research interests pertain to Dante studies, comic poetry, political satire, the Duecento, pedagogy, modern Italian and Italian American history, creative writing, and medieval European literature in its manifestations in history, music, ethics, and politics. His research has been published in the United States, Italy, England, Germany, and the Netherlands. He is completing three books: one on Dante and medieval political invective in Italy, a coedited volume on Dante and satire, and a monograph on the history of Italians in Baltimore and Maryland from the colonial era to the present.

Aida Audeh, professor of art history at Hamline University, is an expert on nineteenth-century European artists' use of Dante and his writing as source and inspiration. She is the author of several essays in books and journals, including *Dante Studies* and *Nineteenth-Century Contexts*. Her book, *Dante in the Long Nineteenth Century: Nationality, Identity, and Appropriation*, coedited with Nick Havely, appeared in 2012. Her groundbreaking articles on Vincent van Gogh's interest in Dante appear in two volumes of *Studies in Medievalism* (2018 and 2019).

Teodolinda Barolini, Lorenzo Da Ponte Professor of Italian at Columbia University, is author of *Dante's Poets, The Undivine Comedy: Detheologizing Dante, Dante and the Origins of Italian Literary Culture*, and numerous essays on Dante, Petrarch, and Boccaccio. Her commentary on Dante's lyric poetry, *Rime giovanili e della* Vita Nuova, was issued in English as *Dante's Lyric Poetry: Poems of Youth and of the* Vita Nuova. Editor of Columbia's *Digital Dante* Web site, Barolini has written the first digital canto-by-canto commentary to the *Commedia*, the *Commento Baroliniano*. She was elected to the Accademia Nazionale dei Lincei in 2018 and is a fellow of the American Academy of Arts and Sciences, the American Philosophical Society, and the Medieval Academy of America. Barolini served as the fifteenth president of the Dante Society of America.

Gary Cestaro teaches Italian and LGBTQ studies at DePaul University in Chicago. He is interested in the intersections among patriarchy, pedagogy, and pederasty in texts ancient, medieval, and modern. He has published articles on queer themes in Dante and is currently investigating Dante's reception of the ancient heroic couple for a forthcoming essay. He is author of *Dante and the Grammar of the Nursing Body* and editor of *Queer Italia: Same-Sex Desire in Italian Literature and Film*.

Carol Chiodo is librarian for collections and digital scholarship at Harvard University. She was formerly the inaugural postdoctoral research associate at the *Digital Humanities Lab* at Yale University. A scholar of medieval and early modern literature, book history, and digital humanities, she has taught at Southern Connecticut State University, Yale University, Princeton University, and the University of Leipzig.

Francesco Ciabattoni is professor of Italian at Georgetown University. He has published on Dante, Petrarch, Boccaccio, Valla, Berto, Pasolini, and Primo Levi. His monograph *Dante's Journey to Polyphony* is a comprehensive study of the role of music in Dante's *Commedia*. With Pier Massimo Forni, he edited *The* Decameron *Third Day in*

264 NOTES ON CONTRIBUTORS

Perspective, vol. 3 of *Lectura Boccaccii*. His main research focus is the interplay of music and literature. His book *La citazione è sintomo d'amore* is a study of the intertextual practice of literary allusion in Italian songwriters.

Elizabeth Coggeshall is assistant professor of Italian in the Modern Languages and Linguistics Department at Florida State University. She specializes in thirteenth- and fourteenth-century literature, history, and culture, with a particular interest in the intersections of poetry and ethics. She is the coeditor, with Arielle Saiber, of the Web site *Dante Today: Citings and Sightings of Dante's Works in Contemporary Culture*, a curated, crowd-sourced digital archive that showcases Dante's sustained presence in contemporary culture. She was the recipient of a 2018–19 university teaching award from Florida State University.

Paul J. Contino has been teaching Dante in the Great Books Colloquium at Pepperdine University since 2002. He previously taught at Christ College, the interdisciplinary honors college of Valparaiso University. He wrote the introduction to Burton Raffel's translation of *The Divine Comedy* and has published essays on an array of writers: Zhuangzi, Jane Austen, Mikhail Bakhtin, Arthur Miller, Czeslaw Milosz, Geoffrey Hill, Andre Dubus, and Alice McDermott. His primary scholarly focus is on the Christological dimension of Fyodor Dostoevsky's *Brothers Karamazov*.

George Dameron is professor and former chair of the Department of History at Saint Michael's College. He is the author of two books on the medieval Florentine church and several essays and articles on a wide variety of topics, including church property, purgatory, the historiography of medieval Florence, the black death, theoretical approaches to the study of the medieval economy, and magnates in northern Italy. His current work focuses on the political economy of grain in Tuscan cities from circa 1150 to 1350. He is a former president of the New England Historical Association.

Joanna Drell is professor and chair of history at the University of Richmond. She specializes in the history of medieval southern Italy and Sicily with a focus on the Normans and cultural intersection in the Regno. She is the author of *Kinship and Conquest: Family Strategies in the Principality of Salerno during the Norman Period*, and coeditor of *Medieval Italy: Texts in Translation*. Her present research focuses on memory and perception of the southern Italian kingdom.

Martin Eisner is associate professor of Italian studies at Duke University. He is the author of *Boccaccio and the Invention of Italian Literature: Dante, Petrarch, Cavalcanti, and the Authority of the Vernacular* (2013) and the forthcoming *Dante's New Life of the Book*.

Brandon K. Essary is associate professor and coordinator of Italian studies at Elon University. He has published on parody and matrimony in the *Decameron*, the Petrarch persona and shame in the *Canzoniere*, and improving students' intercultural competency in Italian-language courses. He is interested in innovative approaches to teaching Italian language and literature and has taught Italian language through paleography activities and calligraphy. He teaches language, literature, and history with video games.

Elsa Filosa is assistant professor of Italian at Vanderbilt University. Her research focuses on fourteenth-century Italian literature, with particular emphasis on Boccaccio. She has published *Tre studi sul De mulieribus claris*, as well as several articles in American and Italian journals, and she has coedited the proceedings of the American Boccaccio Association conferences of 2010 and 2013. As a recipient of the Villa I Tatti Fellowship for 2015–16, she researched her book *The Florentine Conspiracy of 1360: Political Turmoil in Boccaccio's Life and Work.*

Susan Gorman has taught in the Clemente Program for the Humanities for ten years. Earlier, she taught in the English and women's studies departments of Tufts University. Most of her written work is on American modernist women writers, which has led her to explore a connection between Dawn Powell (1896–1965) and Dante.

Suzanne Hagedorn is associate professor of English and has served as director of the program in medieval and Renaissance studies at the College of William and Mary, where she has taught since 1997. She has studied at the Università degli Studi di Firenze on a Rotary Foundation Ambassadorial Fellowship. She is the author of *Abandoned Women: Rewriting the Classics in Dante, Boccaccio, and Chaucer.*

Nick Havely is emeritus professor in the Department of English and Related Literature at the University of York, where he taught courses on English and Italian literature from 1971 to 2011. His recent work on Dante includes the Blackwell *Guide* to the poet, two edited collections of essays on Dante's reception in the nineteenth century, and a book for which he received a Leverhulme Research Fellowship: *Dante's British Public: Readers and Texts, from the Fourteenth Century to the Present.* A member of the Oxford Dante Society since 2012, he was recently made an honorary member of the Dante Society of America.

Peter S. Hawkins is professor of religion and literature at Yale Divinity School. His work has long centered on Dante, including *Dante's Testaments: Essays in Scriptural Imagination; The Poets' Dante: Twentieth-Century Reflections,* coedited with Rachel Jacoff; *Dante, A Brief History;* and *Undiscovered Country: Imagining the World to Come.* His most recent book, with Lesleigh Cushing, is *The Bible and the American Short Story.*

Katherine V. Haynes, associate professor of English, has taught medieval and Renaissance literature, including Dante and Shakespeare, at Aquinas College since 2006. Recent publications and presentations include book reviews for *Sixteenth Century Journal,* conference papers on the poetry of George Herbert and on Middle English Marian lyric, and a lecture on the significance of the First Folio to commemorate the Folger Shakespeare Library's exhibit on the four-hundredth anniversary of Shakespeare's death.

Ronald Herzman is distinguished teaching professor emeritus of English at State University of New York, Geneseo. He also is director of education and outreach for the Dante Society of America. He has directed eighteen seminars for school teachers for the National Endowment for the Humanities, fifteen of them on Dante. He is the recipient of the first Centers and Regional Associations Award for Excellence in Teaching Medieval Studies from the Medieval Academy of America. His introduction to the Middle Ages, *The Medieval World View* (with William R. Cook) has remained in print since 1983. Current research and writing center on Dante and the visual arts and on Dante and the Franciscans.

Christopher Kleinhenz, Carol Mason Kirk Professor Emeritus of Italian, taught Dante and Italian literature of the Duecento and Trecento at the University of Wisconsin,

Madison (1968–2007). Among his books are *The Early Italian Sonnet*; *Medieval Italy: An Encyclopedia*; *Approaches to the Teaching of Petrarch's* Canzoniere *and the Petrarchan Tradition*; and *Dante intertestuale e interdisciplinare: Saggi sulla* Commedia. He is a past president of the American Association of Teachers of Italian, the American Boccaccio Association, and the Medieval Association of the Midwest, and from 1988 to 2002 he edited *Dante Studies*. Recent honors include the Chancellor's Award for Excellence in Teaching, the ADFL Distinguished Service Award, *Fiorino d'oro* (Società Dantesca Italiana), fellow of the Medieval Academy of America, Mellon emeritus fellowship, and the Dante Society of America Distinguished Service Award.

Jessica Levenstein is head of the upper division at Horace Mann School in New York City, where she teaches in the English Department. Her scholarly work focuses on the classical tradition in the Italian Middle Ages and Renaissance, with particular emphasis on Dante's use of Ovid. She has published her work in collections of essays on Dante and intertextuality, as well as in *Dante Studies*, *Italica*, and *The Chronicle of Higher Education*.

Isabella Magni is the Mellon postdoctoral fellow in Italian Paleography at the Newberry Library in Chicago (2017–19), where she is working on the preparation of an online handbook for Italian paleography. She is associate editor of the Petrarchive project (with H. Wayne Storey and James A. Walsh), the new, rich-text digital edition of Petrarch's *Rerum vulgarium fragmenta*, and she has published essays on textual, philological, and editorial issues in the digital context. She is currently preparing a monograph on digital approaches to the representation of texts.

Simone Marchesi is associate professor of French and Italian at Princeton University. His main research area is the dialogue with classical and late antique texts engaged by medieval Italian writers, especially Dante, Petrarch, and Boccaccio. Published work on medieval authors includes two monographs, *Stratigrafie decameroniane* and *Dante and Augustine: Linguistics, Poetics, Hermeneutics*, and several articles and chapters in collections. He is the editor of *Dante Notes*, formerly the *Electronic Bulletin of the Dante Society of America*. He has recently edited and translated into Italian Robert Hollander's commentary to Dante's *Comedy*. Currently, he is working on *The Tower and the Garden*, a study on the image of Eden constructed in late-medieval vernacular fictions.

Ronald L. Martinez is professor of Italian studies at Brown University. In collaboration with Robert M. Durling, he published a monograph on Dante's *rime petrose* and an edition of Dante's *Divine Comedy* with English translation and commentary. Recent publications include essays on Boccaccio, Petrarch's Latin poetry, Renaissance spectacle, Ariosto's *Lena*, and Dante. His current research focuses on Dante's poetic valorization of early modern technologies.

Kristina Olson is associate professor of Italian in the Department of Modern and Classical Languages at George Mason University. Her research investigates the intersection of history and literature in the works of medieval and early modern Italian authors, paying particular attention to matters of language, gender, and reception. She is author of *Courtesy Lost: Dante, Boccaccio and the Literature of History*; coeditor of *Boccaccio 1313–2013*; and author of several articles on Dante, Boccaccio, and Petrarch. She served on the council (2015–18) and as vice president (2016–18) of the Dante Society of America and as vice president of the American Boccaccio Association (2017–20).

F. Regina Psaki is professor emerita of Romance languages at the University of Oregon. She has published on Dante, Boccaccio, medieval French and Italian romance, translation studies, and medieval feminist scholarship. She has taught Dante in English and Italian since 1989, and was awarded the Thomas F. Herman Faculty Achievement Award for Distinguished Teaching at the University of Oregon in 2006.

Suzanne Manizza Roszak teaches writing and literature at California State University, San Bernardino, and the University of California, Riverside. She specializes in multiethnic and transnational American literature. Her articles have appeared in *Studies in the Novel, Arizona Quarterly,* and *Children's Literature.*

Sherry Roush is professor of Italian at Penn State University, University Park, and the recipient of two teaching awards: a college-level award in 2004 and the statewide campuses Alumni Teaching Fellow prize in 2009. She is author of *Speaking Spirits: Ventriloquizing the Dead in Renaissance Italy* and *Hermes' Lyre: Italian Poetic Self-Commentary from Dante to Tommaso Campanella.* She is also coeditor of *The Medieval Marriage Scene* and the editor-translator of the facing-page edition of Tommaso Campanella's *Selected Philosophical Poems* in two volumes.

Brenda Deen Schildgen is distinguished professor emerita of comparative literature at the University of California, Davis; 2008 recipient of the UC Davis Prize for Undergraduate Teaching and Scholarly Achievement; and a recipient of National Endowment for the Humanities, Pew, and National Center for the Humanities fellowships. Author of more than fifty articles, she has published in *Dante Studies, Modern Philology, Journal of Comparative Literature, Religion and Literature,* and *New Literary History.* Her books include *Divine Providence, A History: Bible, Virgil, Orosius, Augustine, and Dante; Other Renaissances: A New Approach to World Literature,* translated into Arabic; *Dante and the Orient,* translated into Italian and Arabic; *Power and Prejudice: The Reception of the Gospel of Mark.*

Madison U. Sowell is provost and vice president of academic affairs at Tusculum University. Previously he served as provost at Southern Virginia University. For three decades he taught Italian and comparative literature at Brigham Young University, where he chaired the department of French and Italian and was a Karl G. Maeser General Education Professor, the Scheuber and Veinz Professor of Humanities and Languages, director of the honors program, and associate dean of undergraduate education. He is the author, coauthor, or editor of eight books, including *Dante and Ovid: Essays in Intertextuality,* and he has written over one hundred and thirty articles and reviews for journals, Festschriften, and encyclopedias.

H. Wayne Storey is professor emeritus of Italian at Indiana University, Bloomington, and president of the Society for Textual Scholarship (2019–2020). He served eight years as editor in chief of the society's journal, *Textual Cultures.* Storey studies and publishes on medieval manuscripts and early printed books in the Italian, Old Occitan, and Latin traditions. He is one of the principal proponents of material philology, and author, coauthor, or editor of seven volumes, including *Transcription and Visual Poetics in the Early Italian Lyric, Petrarch and the Textual Origins of Interpretation,* and the two-volume facsimile edition, with commentary, of Petrarch's autograph copy of the *Rerum vulgarium fragmenta* (VL3195). His ongoing digital edition and commentary of Petrarch's *Fragmenta* can be found at petrarchive.org.

Heather Webb is reader in medieval Italian literature and culture at the University of Cambridge and fellow in Italian at Selwyn College, Cambridge. She is the author of *Dante's Persons: An Ethics of the Transhuman* and *The Medieval Heart*. With George Corbett, she is coeditor of the three-volume *Vertical Readings in Dante's* Comedy.

SURVEY RESPONDENTS

Catherine Adoyo, *Georgetown University*
Jason Aleksander, *Saint Xavier University*
Nicolino Applauso, *Loyola University Maryland*
Beatrice Arduini, *University of Washington*
Guyda Armstrong, *University of Manchester*
William Askins, *Community College of Philadelphia*
Aida Audeh, *Hamline University*
Anne Babson, *The University of Mississippi*
Arthur Bahr, *Massachusetts Institute of Technology*
Steve Baker, *Columbia University*
Ruth Caldwell, *Luther College*
Roberta Capelli, *Università di Trento*
Mary Ann Carolan, *Fairfield University*
Santa Casciani, *John Carroll University*
Jo Ann Cavallo, *Columbia University*
Francesco Ciabattoni, *Georgetown University*
K. P. Clarke, *University of York*
Marc Cogan, *Wayne State University*
Jay Cole, *West Virginia University*
Chris Constas, *Boston College*
Paul J. Contino, *Pepperdine University*
Marsha Daigle-Williamson, *Spring Arbor University*
Carlos Delgado, *University of Southern California*
Sara Díaz, *Fairfield University*
Andrea Dini, *Montclair State University*
Joanna Drell, *University of Richmond*
Martin Eisner, *Duke University*
Brandon K. Essary, *Elon University*
Valerio Ferme, *University of Colorado, Boulder*
George Ferzoco, *University of Bristol*
Andrew Fleck, *San Jose State University*
Carmelo A. Galati, *Temple University*
Carlos Gatti-Murriel, *Universidad del Pacífico*
Paul Giordano, *University of Central Florida*
R. James Goldstein, *Auburn University*
Susan Gorman, *Clemente Program in the Humanities*
Karen Gross, *Lewis and Clark College*
Susanne Hafner, *Fordham University*
Suzanne Hagedorn, *College of William and Mary*
Carol E. Harding, *Western Oregon University*
Katherine V. Haynes, *Aquinas College*
Ron Herzman, *State University of New York, Geneseo*
Julia Bolton Holloway, *University of Colorado, Boulder*

Laurence Hooper, *Dartmouth College*
Jim Kerbaugh, *Illinois College*
Ilona Klein, *Brigham Young University*
Alison Langdon, *Western Kentucky University*
Suzanne Magnanini, *University of Colorado, Boulder*
Simone Marchesi, *Princeton University*
Marshall Marvelli, *Paisley IB Magnet School*
Leslie Zarker Morgan, *Loyola University Maryland*
Molly Morrison, *Ohio University*
Sarah-Jane Murray, *Baylor University*
Sheila J. Nayar, *Greensboro College*
Brian O'Connor, *Boston College*
Margherita Pampinella-Cropper, *Towson University*
Michael Papio, *University of Massachusetts, Amherst*
Deborah Parker, *University of Virginia*
Bernardo Piciché, *Virginia Commonwealth University*
Mark Rasmussen, *Centre College*
Joshua Reid, *East Tennessee State University*
Roberta Ricci, *Bryn Mawr College*
Paul Rockwell, *Amherst College*
Claudia Rossignoli, *University of St Andrews*
Sherry Roush, *Penn State University, University Park*
James Rushing, *Rutgers University, Camden*
Arielle Saiber, *Bowdoin College*
Brenda Deen Schildgen, *University of California, Davis*
Debora Schwartz, *California Polytechnic State University, San Luis Obispo*
Michael Sherberg, *Washington University in St. Louis*
Dennis Patrick Slattery, *Pacifica Graduate Institute*
Marie Smart, *Baylor University*
Madison U. Sowell, *Southern Virginia University*
Kirilka Stavreva, *Cornell College*
Glenn A. Steinberg, *The College of New Jersey*
Gregory B. Stone, *Louisiana State University*
Kristen Swann, *University of New Hampshire*
Dean Swinford, *Fayetteville State University*
Claudia Teinert, *Concordia University Texas*
Vincenzo Traversa, *California State University, East Bay*
Tonia Bernardi Triggiano, *Dominican University*
Elizabeth Walsh, *University of San Diego*
Stephen Westergan, *St. Norbert College*

WORKS CITED

Works by Dante

The Banquet. Translated by Christopher Ryan, Anma Libri, 1989.

Comedia. Edited by Federico Sanguineti, Sismel Edizioni del Galluzzo, 2001.

The Comedy *of Dante Alighieri the Florentine: I:* Hell; *II:* Purgatory. Translated with an introduction by Dorothy L. Sayers, Penguin Books, 1971.

The Comedy *of Dante Alighieri the Florentine: Cantica III:* Paradise. Translated by Dorothy L. Sayers and Barbara Reynolds, Penguin Books, 1962.

La commedia. Edited by Robert Hollander and Simone Marchesi, Loescher, 2016.

Commedia: *A Digital Edition*. Edited by Prue Shaw, Scholarly Digital Editions / Edizioni del Galluzzo, 2010.

Commedia: Inferno. Edited by Anna Maria Chiavacci Leonardi, Arnoldo Mondadori, 1991.

Commedia: Inferno. Edited by Emilio Pasquini and Antonio Enzo Quaglio, Garzanti, 1988.

Commedia: *Nuovo testo critico secondo i più antichi manoscritti fiorentini*. Edited by Antonio Lanza, De Rubeis, 1995.

Commedia: Paradiso. Edited by Anna Maria Chiavacci Leonardi, Arnoldo Mondadori, 1997.

Commedia: Paradiso. Edited by Emilio Pasquini and Antonio Enzo Quaglio, Garzanti, 1988.

Commedia: Purgatorio. Edited by Anna Maria Chiavacci Leonardi, Arnoldo Mondadori, 1994.

Commedia: Purgatorio. Edited by Emilio Pasquini and Antonio Enzo Quaglio, Garzanti, 1988.

La Commedia *secondo l'antica vulgata*. Edited by Giorgio Petrocchi, Mondadori, 1966–67. 4 vols.

Convivio. Edited by Cesare Vasoli, *Opere Minori*, vol. 1, pt. 2, Ricciardi, 1979, pp. 3–885.

Convivio. Translated by Andrew Frisardi, Cambridge UP, 2018.

The Convivio *of Dante*. Translated by Richard Lansing. 1990. *Digital Dante*, Columbia University Libraries, digitaldante.columbia.edu/library/dantes-works/the-convivio/.

Il Convivio (The Banquet). Translated by Richard Lansing, Garland, 1990.

Dante Alighieri: Four Political Letters. Translated by Claire Honess, Modern Humanities Research Association, 2007.

Dante's Inferno. Adapted by Sandow Birk and Marcus Sanders, illustrated by Birk, Chronicle Books, 2004.

Dante's Inferno: *The First Part of* The Divine Comedy *of Dante Alighieri*. Translated and illustrated by Tom Phillips, Thames and Hudson, 1985.

Dante's Lyric Poetry. Translated by Kenelm Foster and Patrick Boyde. Oxford UP, 1967. 2 vols.

Dante's Lyric Poetry: Poems of Youth and of the Vita Nuova *(1283–1292).* Edited by Teodolinda Barolini, translated by Richard Lansing, U of Toronto P, 2014.

Dante's Monarchia. Translated by Richard Kay, Pontifical Institute of Mediaeval Studies, 1998.

Dante's Paradise. Translated by Mark Musa, Indiana UP, 1984.

Dante's Paradiso. Adapted by Sandow Birk and Marcus Sanders, illustrated by Birk, Chronicle Books, 2005.

Dante's Purgatorio. Adapted by Sandow Birk and Marcus Sanders, illustrated by Birk, Chronicle Books, 2005.

Dante's Vita Nuova. Translated by Mark Musa, Indiana UP, 1973.

Dantis Alagherii Epistolae: The Letters of Dante. Translated by Paget Toynbee, 2nd ed., Oxford UP, 1966.

De vulgari eloquentia. Edited and translated by Steven Botterill, Cambridge UP, 1996.

De Vulgari Eloquentia: Dante's Book of Exile. Translated by Marianne Shapiro, U of Nebraska P, 1990.

La divina commedia. Edited by Umberto Bosco and Giovanni Reggio, Le Monnier, 1979. 3 vols.

La divina commedia. Edited by Nicola Fosca, Aracne, 2018.

La divina commedia. Edited by Stefano Jacomuzzi, Società Editrice Internazionale, 2008.

La divina commedia. Edited by Natalino Sapegno, La Nuova Italia, 1985. 3 vols.

Divina commedia: Testi letterari, strumenti didattici, percorsi interdisciplinari, prospettive multiculturali. Edited by Cristina Savettieri and Raffaele Donnarumma, Palumbo, 2007.

The Divine Comedy. Translated by Laurence Binyon. 1943. *The Portable Dante,* edited by Paolo Milano, Viking Press, 1947, pp. 1–544.

The Divine Comedy. Translated by Clive James, Picador, 2012.

The Divine Comedy. Translated with commentary by Charles S. Singleton, Princeton UP, 1970–75. 3 vols. in 6 parts. Includes the Italian text edited by Giorgio Petrocchi.

The Divine Comedy: Inferno. Translated by Robert M. Durling, edited by Durling and Ronald L. Martinez, Oxford UP, 1996.

The Divine Comedy *of Dante Alighieri.* Translated by Henry Wadsworth Longfellow, Boston, Ticknor and Fields, 1867. 3 vols.

The Divine Comedy *of Dante Alighieri.* Translated by John D. Sinclair. 1939. Oxford UP, 1978. 3 vols.

The Divine Comedy *of Dante Alighieri:* Inferno. Translated by Allen Mandelbaum, Bantam, 1982.

The Divine Comedy *of Dante Alighieri:* Paradiso. Translated by Allen Mandelbaum, Bantam, 1984.

The Divine Comedy *of Dante Alighieri:* Purgatorio. Translated by Allen Mandelbaum, Bantam, 1984.

The Divine Comedy: Paradiso. Translated by Robert M. Durling, edited by Durling and Ronald L. Martinez, Oxford UP, 2011.

The Divine Comedy: Purgatorio. Translated by Robert M. Durling, edited by Durling and Ronald L. Martinez, Oxford UP, 2003.

The Divine Comedy: Inferno. Translated by Mark Musa, Penguin Books, 1971.

The Inferno. Edited and translated by Robert Hollander and Jean Hollander, introduction and notes by R. Hollander, Doubleday, 2000.

The Inferno. Translated by John Ciardi. 1965. Signet Classic, 2001.

Inferno. Translated by Anthony Esolen, Modern Library, 2002.

Inferno. Translated by Robin Kirkpatrick, Penguin Books, 2006.

Inferno. Translated by Stanley Lombardo, introduction by Steven Botterill, notes by Anthony Oldcorn, Hackett, 2009.

Inferno. Translated by Mark Musa, Penguin Books, 1984.

Inferno. Translated with an introduction and notes by Mary Jo Bang, illustrated by Henrik Drescher, Graywolf Press, 2012.

The Inferno: *A Verse Rendering for the Modern Reader*. Translated by John Ciardi, New American Library, 1954.

Inferno: *Canti scelti*. Edited by Celestina Beneforti, Bonacci, 1996.

The Inferno *of Dante: A New Verse Translation*. Translated by Robert Pinsky, Farrar, Straus and Giroux, 1994.

Monarchy. Translated by Prue Shaw, Cambridge UP, 1995.

The New Life. Translated by Dante Gabriel Rossetti, New York Review of Books, 2002.

Paradise. Translated by Anthony Esolen, Modern Library, 2004.

Paradiso. Edited and translated by Robert Hollander and Jean Hollander, introduction and notes by R. Hollander, Doubleday, 2007.

Paradiso. Translated by Robin Kirkpatrick, Penguin Books, 2007.

Paradiso. Translated by Stanley Lombardo, introduction and notes by Alison Cornish, Hackett, 2017.

The Paradiso: *A Verse Rendering for the Modern Reader*. Translated by John Ciardi, New American Library, 1970.

Paradiso: *Canti scelti*. Edited by Celestina Beneforti, Bonacci, 1996.

The Portable Dante. Translated by Mark Musa, Penguin Books, 1995.

Purgatorio. Edited and translated by Robert Hollander and Jean Hollander, introduction and notes by R. Hollander, Doubleday, 2003.

Purgatorio. Translated by Robin Kirkpatrick, Penguin Books, 2007.

Purgatorio. Translated by Stanley Lombardo, introduction by Claire E. Honess and Matthew Treherne, notes by Ruth Chester, Hackett, 2016.

The Purgatorio: *A Verse Rendering for the Modern Reader*. Translated by John Ciardi, New American Library, 1961.

Purgatorio: *Canti scelti*. Edited by Celestina Beneforti, Bonacci, 1996.

Purgatory. Translated by Anthony Esolen, Modern Library, 2003.

Tutte le opere. Edited by Giovanni Fallani et al., Newton Compton, 2011.

Vita Nova. Translated by Andrew Frisardi, Northwestern UP, 2012.

Vita nova. Edited by Guglielmo Gorni, Einaudi, 1996.

La vita nuova. Edited by Michele Barbi, Hoepli, 1907.

Vita nuova. Edited and translated by Dino S. Cervigni and Edward Vasta, U of Notre Dame P, 1995.

Vita Nuova. Translated by Anthony Robert Mortimer, Oneworld Classics, 2011.

Vita Nuova. Translated by Mark Musa, Indiana UP, 1973.

Vita Nuova. Translated with an introduction and notes by Mark Musa, Oxford UP, 2008.

La Vita Nuova. Translated by David R. Slavitt, Harvard UP, 2010.

La Vita Nuova: *Poems of Youth.* Translated by Barbara Reynolds, Penguin Books, 1969.

Critical Works

Abramov-van Rijk, Elena. *Singing Dante: The Literary Origins of Cinquecento Monody.* Ashgate, 2014.

Abulafia, David, editor. *Italy in the Central Middle Ages, 1000–1300.* Oxford UP, 2004.

Adams, Laurie Schneider. *The Methodologies of Art.* 2nd ed., Westview Press, 2010.

Agnus Dei. Graduale Romanum, 1961. Recorded by the Alfred Deller Consort. *YouTube,* uploaded by Stephan George, 1 Jan. 2011, www.youtube.com/watch?v =dsFOxPa-r_4.

Alain of Lille. *The Plaint of Nature.* Translated by James J. Sheridan, Pontifical Institute of Mediaeval Studies, 1980.

Alessio, Gian Carlo, and Robert Hollander, editors. *Studi americani su Dante.* Introduction by Dante Della Terza, Franco Angeli, 1989.

Alexander, Jonathan J. G. *Medieval Illuminators and Their Methods of Work.* Yale UP, 1992.

Alfie, Fabian. *Dante's "Tenzone" with Forese Donati: The Reprehension of Vice.* U of Toronto P, 2011.

Alfie, Fabian, and Andrea Dini, editors. *"Accessus ad Auctores": Studies in Honor of Christopher Kleinhenz.* Arizona Center for Medeival and Renaissance Studies, 2011.

Alpatoff, Michael. "The Parallelism of Giotto's Paduan Frescos." *The Art Bulletin,* vol. 29, no. 3, 1947, pp. 149–54.

Aquilecchia, Giovanni. "Dante and the Florentine Chroniclers." *Bulletin of the John Rylands Library,* vol. 48, 1965, pp. 3–55.

Aquinas, Thomas. *The Summa Theologica of St. Thomas Aquinas.* Second and revised edition, 1920, translated by Fathers of the English Dominican Province. *New Advent,* online edition, produced by Kevin Knight, 2017, www.newadvent.org/summa/.

Ardizzone, Maria Luisa, and Teodolinda Barolini, editors. *Dante and Heterodoxy: The Temptations of Thirteenth-Century Radical Thought.* Cambridge Scholars Publishing, 2014.

Arduini, Beatrice. "Assigning the 'Pieces' of Dante's *Convivio*: The Compiler's Notes in the Earliest Extant Copy." *Textual Cultures: Texts, Contexts, Interpretation*, vol. 3, no. 2, 2008, pp. 17–29.

———. "Il ruolo di Boccaccio e di Marsilio Ficino nella tradizione del *Convivio* di Dante." *Boccaccio in America: Proceedings of the 2010 International Boccaccio Conference at the University of Massachusetts, Amherst*, edited by Michael Papio and Elsa Filosa, Longo, 2012, pp. 95–103.

Armour, Peter. "The *Comedy* as a 'Text for Performance.'" Braida and Calè, pp. 17–22.

———. *Dante's Griffin and the History of the World: A Study of the Earthly Paradise* (Purgatorio *Cantos XXIX–XXXIII*). Oxford UP, 1989.

———. *The Door of Purgatory: A Study of Multiple Symbolism in Dante's* Purgatorio. Oxford UP, 1983.

———. "Purgatory." Lansing, *Dante Encyclopedia*, pp. 728–31.

Ascoli, Albert Russell. *Dante and the Making of a Modern Author*. Cambridge UP, 2008.

Ash, Sarah L., and Patti H. Clayton. "Generating, Deepening, and Documenting Learning: The Power of Critical Reflection in Applied Learning." *Journal of Applied Learning in Higher Education*, vol. 1, 2009, pp. 25–48.

Associated Press. "Gloria Naylor, Who Wrote *The Women of Brewster Place*, Dies." *Associated Press News*, 3 Oct. 2016, www.apnews.com/f277adee81e7487591461f 21e62dcda5. Accessed 17 Apr. 2019.

Astin, Alexander W., et al. *Cultivation of the Spirit: How College Can Enhance Students' Inner Lives*. Jossey-Bass, 2011.

Aubrey, Elizabeth. *The Music of the Troubadours*. Indiana UP, 1996.

Audeh, Aida. "Dante in the Nineteenth Century: Visual Arts and National Identity." *Dante in France*, edited by Russell Goulbourne et al. Special issue of *La Parola del Testo*, vol. 17, nos. 1–2, 2013, pp. 85–100.

———. "Dante's Ugolino and the School of Jacques-Louis David: English Art and Innovation." *Nineteenth-Century Contexts*, vol. 35, 2013, pp. 399–417.

———. "Dufau's *La Mort d'Ugolin*: Dante, Nationalism, and French Art, ca. 1800." Audeh and Havely, pp. 141–63.

———. "Gustave Doré's Illustrations for Dante's *Divine Comedy*: Innovation, Influence, and Reception." *Studies in Medievalism*, vol. 18, 2010, pp. 125–64.

———. "Images of Dante's Exile in Nineteenth-Century France." *Annali d'Italianistica*, vol. 20, 2002, pp. 235–58.

———. "Rodin's *Gates of Hell* and Aubé's *Monument to Dante*: Romantic Tribute to the Image of the Poet in Nineteenth-Century France." *The Journal of the Iris and B. Gerald Cantor Center for Visual Arts at Stanford University*, vol. 1, 1998–99, pp. 33–46.

———. "Rodin's *Gates of Hell* and Dante's *Divine Comedy*: The Literal and Allegorical in the Paolo and Francesca Episode of *Inferno* 5." Havely, *Dante in the Nineteenth Century*, pp. 181–98.

———. "Rodin's *Gates of Hell* and Dante's *Inferno* 7: Fortune, the Avaricious and Prodigal, and the Question of Salvation." *Studies in Medievalism*, vol. 22, 2013, pp. 115–52.

———. "Rodin's *Gates of Hell*: Sculptural Illustration of Dante's *Divine Comedy*." *Rodin: A Magnificent Obsession*, edited by Iain Ross and Anthea Snow, Merrell Holberton Publishers, 2001, pp. 93–126.

———. "Rodin's *Three Shades* and their Origin in Medieval Illustrations of Dante's *Inferno* XV and XVI." *Dante Studies*, vol. 117, 1999, pp. 133–69.

———. "Vincent van Gogh, Dante, and the Studio of the South." *Studies in Medievalism*, vol. 27, 2018, pp. 123–49.

———. "Vincent van Gogh, the *Tre Corone*, and the Studio of the South." *Studies in Medievalism*, vol. 28, 2019, pp. 177–205.

Audeh, Aida, and Nick Havely, editors. *Dante in the Long Nineteenth Century: Nationality, Identity, and Appropriation*. Oxford UP, 2012.

Auerbach, Erich. *Dante: Poet of the Secular World*. Translated by Ralph Manheim, U of Chicago P, 1961.

———. "Figura." *Scenes from the Drama of European Literature*, by Auerbach, translated by Ralph Manheim, Meridian Books, 1959, pp. 11–76.

———. *Mimesis: The Representation of Reality in Western Literature*. Translated by Willard Trask, Princeton UP, 1953.

Augé, Marc. *Non-places: An Introduction to Supermodernity*. Translated by John Howe, Verso, 2008.

Augustine. *Confessions*. Translated by Henry Chadwick, Oxford UP, 1991.

Aurobindo Ghose, Sri. *Savitri*. Sri Aurobindo Ashram, 2009.

Austenfeld, Thomas. "How to Begin a New World: Dante in Walcott's *Omeros*." *South Atlantic Review*, vol. 71, no. 3, 2006, pp. 15–28.

Balfour, Mark. "The Place of the Poet: Dante in Walcott's Narrative Poetry." Havely, *Dante's Modern Afterlife*, pp. 223–41.

Balthasar, Hans Urs von. *Dare We Hope: "That All Men Be Saved"?* Translated by David Kipp and Lothar Krauth, Ignatius Press, 1988.

———. *The Glory of the Lord: A Theological Aesthetics: Studies in Theological Styles: Lay Styles*. Translated by Andrew Louth et al., edited by John Riches, vol. 2, Ignatius Press, 1986.

Baraka, Amiri. *The System of Dante's Hell*. Grove Press, 1965.

Barański, Zygmunt G., editor. *International Dante Seminar*. Le Lettere 1997.

———, editor. *"Libri Poetarum in Quattuor Species Dividuntur"*: Essays on Dante and Genre. The Italianist, vol. 15, Supplement, 1995.

———. "Magister Satiricus: Preliminary Notes on Dante, Horace and the Middle Ages." *Language and Style in Dante*, edited by John C. Barnes and Michelangelo Zaccarello, Four Courts, 2013, pp. 13–61.

Barański, Zygmunt G., and Theodore J. Cachey, Jr., editors. *Petrarch and Dante: Anti-Dantism, Metaphysics, Tradition*. U of Notre Dame P, 2009.

Barański, Zygmunt G., and Martin L. McLaughlin, editors. *Dante the Lyric and Ethical Poet*. Modern Humanities Research Association / Maney Publishing, 2010.

Barański, Zygmunt G., and Lino Pertile, editors. *Dante in Context*. Cambridge UP, 2015.

Barbarese, J. T. "Four Translations of Dante's *Inferno*." *Sewanee Review*, vol. 117, 2009, pp. 647–55.

Barlow, Henry Clark. *The Sixth Centenary Festivals of Dante Alleghieri in Florence and Ravenna by a Representative*. Williams and Norgate / Hermann Loescher, 1866.

Barnes, John C. "Vestiges of the Liturgy in Dante's Verse." *Dante and the Middle Ages: Literary and Historical Essays*, edited by John C. Barnes and Cormac Ó Cuilleanáin, Irish Academic P, 1995, pp. 231–69.

Barolini, Teodolinda. "Beyond (Courtly) Dualism: Thinking about Gender in Dante's Lyrics." Barolini and Storey, pp. 65–89.

———. "Commento Baroliniano." *Digital Dante*, Columbia University Libraries, digitaldante.columbia.edu/commento-baroliniano/.

———. Conclusion. Ardizzone and Barolini, pp. 259–75.

———. "Dante Alighieri." *Women and Gender in Medieval Europe: An Encyclopedia*, edited by Margaret Schaus, Routledge, 2006, pp. 190–92.

———. "Dante and Francesca da Rimini: Realpolitik, Romance, Gender." *Speculum*, vol. 75, 2000, pp. 1–28.

———. "Dante and the Lyric Past." Jacoff, *Cambridge Companion*, 2nd ed., pp. 14–34.

———. *Dante and the Origins of Italian Literary Culture*. Fordham UP, 2006.

———. "Dante and the Troubadours: An Overview." *Tenso*, vol. 5, no. 1, 1989, pp. 3–10.

———. *Dante's Poets: Textuality and the Truth in the* Comedy. Princeton UP, 1984.

———. "Dante's Sympathy for the Other or the Non-Stereotyping Imagination: Sexual and Racialized Others in the *Commedia*." *Critica del Testo*, vol. 14, no. 1, 2011, pp. 9–39.

———. "An Ivy League Professor Weighs in: Expert View." *Entertainment Weekly*, 26 Feb. 2010.

———. "Medieval Multiculturalism and Dante's Theology of Hell." Barolini, *Dante and the Origins*, pp. 102–21.

———. "Notes toward a Gendered History of Italian Literature, with a Discussion of Dante's *Beatrix Loquax*." Barolini, *Dante and the Origins*, pp. 360–78.

———. "Re-presenting What God Presented: The Arachnean Art of Dante's Terrace of Pride." *Dante Studies*, vol. 105, 1987, pp. 43–62.

———. *The Undivine* Comedy*: Detheologizing Dante*. Princeton UP, 1992.

Barolini, Teodolinda, and H. Wayne Storey, editors. *Dante for the New Millennium*. Fordham UP, 2003.

Barricelli, Jean-Pierre. *Dante's Vision and the Artist: Four Modern Illustrators of the* Commedia. Peter Lang, 1992.

Barsella, Susanna. *In the Light of Angels: Angelology and Cosmology in Dante's Divina Commedia*. Olschki, 2010.

Bauerschmidt, Frederick C., and James J. Buckley. *Catholic Theology: An Introduction*. Wiley Blackwell, 2017.

Bell, Bernard W. *The Contemporary African American Novel: Its Folk Roots and Modern Literary Branches*. U of Massachusetts P, 2004.

Bell, Rob. *Love Wins*. Harper Collins, 2011.

Bembo, Pietro, editor. *Dante col sito, et forma dell'Inferno tratta dalla istessa descrittione del poeta*. Venice, Aldo Manuzio and Andrea Torresani di Asola, 1515.

——, editor. *Le terze rime di Dante*. Venice, Aldo Manuzio, 1502.

Bemrose, Stephen. *Dante's Angelic Intelligences: Their Importance in the Cosmos and in Pre-Christian Religion*. Edizioni di Storia e Letteratura, 1983.

——. *A New Life of Dante*. Revised ed., Exeter UP, 2014.

Benedict XVI (pope). "Deus Caritas Est." Encyclical Letter, 2005, w2.vatican.va/content/benedict-xvi/en/encyclicals/documents/hf_ben-xvi_enc_20051225_deus-caritas-est.html. Accessed 11 Apr. 2019.

Beneš, Carrie. *Urban Legends: Civic Identity and the Classical Past in Northern Italy, 1250–1350*. Pennsylvania State UP, 2011.

Benfell, V. Stanley. *The Biblical Dante*. U of Toronto P, 2011.

Bergin, Thomas. "Dante's Provençal Gallery." *Speculum*, vol. 40, 1965, pp. 15–30.

Bergvall, Caroline. *Fig*. Salt Publishing, 2005.

——. *Via*. *Penn Sound*, 2005, writing.upenn.edu/pennsound/x/Bergvall.php.

Bernardo, Aldo S., and Anthony L. Pellegrini, editors. *Dante, Petrarch, Boccaccio: Studies in the Italian Trecento in Honor of Charles S. Singleton*. Center for Medieval and Early Renaissance Studies / State U of New York P, 1983.

Bertelli, Sandro. *La* Commedia *all'antica*. La Mandragora, 2007.

Bertoni, Giulio. *Il canzoniere provenzale della Biblioteca Ambrosiana R. 71. sup.* Gesellschaft für romanische Literatur, 1912.

Bertran de Born. *The Poems of the Troubadour Bertran de Born*. Edited by William D. Paden et al., U of California P, 1985.

Bhabha, Homi K. *The Location of Culture*. Routledge, 2004.

Biblia sacra iuxta vulgatam versionem. Edited by Robert Weber et al., 5th ed., edited by Roger Gryson, Deutsche Bibelgesellschaft, 2007.

Bindman, David, et al. *Dante Rediscovered: From Blake to Rodin*. Wordsworth Trust, 2007.

Birge-Vitz, Evelyn. "The Liturgy and Vernacular Literature." *The Liturgy of the Medieval Church*, edited by Thomas J. Heffernan and E. Ann Matter, Medieval Institute Publications, 2001, pp. 551–618.

Birk, Sandow, creator. *Dante's* Inferno. Directed by Sean Meredith, produced by Paul Zaloom and Sandow Birk, art direction by Elyse Pignolet, Dante Film, 2007.

Bloom, Harold. *The Anxiety of Influence: A Theory of Poetry*. 2nd ed., Oxford UP, 1997.

——, editor. *Dante*. Chelsea House, 1986.

——, editor. *Dante Alighieri*. Chelsea House, 2003.

——, editor. *Dante Alighieri*. Chelsea House, 2004.

——, editor. *Dante's* Divine Comedy. Chelsea House, 1987.

Boccaccio, Giovanni. *Boccaccio's Expositions on Dante's* Comedy. Translated by Michael Papio, U of Toronto P, 2009.

———. *Esposizioni sopra la* Comedia *di Dante*. Edited by Giorgio Padoan. *Tutte le opere di Giovanni Boccaccio*, edited by Vittore Branca, vol. 6, Mondadori, 1965.

———. *The Life of Dante (Trattatello in Laude di Dante)*. Translated by Vincenzo Zin Bollettino, Garland, 1990.

Boethius. *Fundamentals of Music*. Translated by Calvin M. Bower, Yale UP, 1989.

Bolton, Brenda. "Papal Italy." Abulafia, pp. 82–103.

Bonwell, Charles C., and James A. Eison. *Active Learning: Creating Excitement in the Classroom: ASHE-ERIC Higher Education Report No. 1*. Jossey-Bass, 1991, pp. 1–21.

Boschi Rotiroti, Marisa. *Codicologia trecentesca della* Commedia. Viella, 2004.

Boswell, John. *Christianity, Social Tolerance, and Homosexuality: Gay People in Western Europe from the Beginning of the Christian Era to the Fourteenth Century*. U of Chicago P, 1980.

Botterill, Steven. *Dante and the Mystical Tradition: Bernard of Clairvaux in the* Commedia. Cambridge UP, 1994.

Bowles, Edmund A. "Were Musical Instruments Used in the Liturgical Service during the Middle Ages?" *The Galpin Society Journal*, vol. 10, 1957, pp. 40–56.

Boyde, Patrick. *Human Vices and Human Worth in Dante's* Comedy. Cambridge UP, 2000.

———. *Perception and Passion in Dante's* Comedy. Cambridge UP, 1993.

Braida, Antonella. *Dante and the Romantics*. Palgrave Macmillan, 2004.

Braida, Antonella, and Luisa Calè, editors. *Dante on View: The Reception of Dante in the Visual and Performing Arts*. Ashgate, 2007.

Bregni, Simone. "*Assassin's Creed* Taught Me Italian: Video Games and the Quest for Lifelong, Ubiquitous Learning." *Profession*, 22 March 2018, profession.mla.hcommons.org/2018/03/22/assassins-creed-taught-me-italian/. Accessed 28 May 2018.

Brieger, Peter, et al. *Illuminated Manuscripts of the* Divine Comedy. Princeton UP, 1969. 2 vols.

Briggs, Charles. *The Body Broken: Medieval Europe, 1300–1520*. Routledge, 2011.

Brown, Ashley ML. *Sexuality in Role-Playing Games*. Routledge, 2015.

Brown, Harry. *Video Games and Education*. M. E. Sharpe, 2008.

Brownlee, Kevin. "Dante and the Classical Poets." Jacoff, *Cambridge Companion*, 2nd ed., pp. 141–60.

Brucker, Gene A. *Florence: The Golden Age, 1138–1737*. U of California P, 1998.

———. *Renaissance Florence*. Wiley, 1969.

Burgess, Glyn S. *The Lais of Marie de France: Text and Context*. U of Georgia P, 1987.

Burr, David. "Heresy and Dissidence." Barański and Pertile, pp. 106–18.

———. *The Spiritual Franciscans*. U of Pennsylvania P, 2001.

Cachey, Theodore J., Jr., editor. *Dante Now: Current Trends in Dante Studies*. U of Notre Dame P, 1995.

Cadden, Joan. *Nothing Natural Is Shameful: Sodomy and Science in Late Medieval Europe*. U of Pennsylvania P, 2013.

Caesar, Michael, editor. *Dante: The Critical Heritage, 1314(?)–1870.* Routledge, 1989.

Caferro, William. "Empire, Italy, and Florence." Barański and Pertile, pp. 9–29.

Caillois, Roger. *Man, Play, and Games.* Translated by Meyer Barash, U of Illinois P, 2001.

Campbell, C. Jean. *The Commonwealth of Nature: Art and Poetic Community in the Age of Dante.* Pennsylvania State UP, 2008.

Canning, Joseph. *A History of Medieval Political Thought, 300–1450.* Routledge, 1996.

Cannon, Zander. *Heck.* Top Shelf Productions, 2013.

Canzoniere G. Thirteenth century. Biblioteca Ambrosiana, Milan, MS S.P.5 (*olim* R.71 sup.). www.filmod.unina.it/cdg/G.htm. Accessed 16 Apr. 2019.

Capellanus, Andreas. *The Art of Courtly Love.* Translated by John Jay Parry, W. W. Norton, 1969.

Capéran, Louis. *Le problème du salut des infidèles: Essai historique.* Grand Séminaire, 1934.

Carroll, James. *Constantine's Sword: The Church and the Jews: A History.* Houghton Mifflin, 2001.

Casciani, Santa, editor. *Dante and the Franciscans.* Brill, 2006.

Cassell, Anthony K. "Dante's Farinata and the Image of the *Arca.*" Lansing, *Critical Complex* vol. 1, pp. 197–232.

———. *Dante's Fearful Art of Justice.* U of Toronto P, 1984.

———. *Inferno I.* U of Pennsylvania P, 1989.

Castro, Américo. "The Presence of the Sultan Saladin in the Romance Literatures." *An Idea of History: Selected Essays of Américo Castro*, edited and translated by Stephen Gilman and Edmund L. King, Ohio State UP, 1977, pp. 241–69.

Cecchetti, Giovanni. "An Introduction to Dante's *Divine Comedy.*" Slade, pp. 38–54.

Cervigni, Dino S., editor. *Dante and Modern American Criticism. Annali d'Italianistica*, vol. 8, 1990.

———. *Dante's Poetry of Dreams.* Olschki, 1986.

Cestaro, Gary. *Dante and the Grammar of the Nursing Body.* U of Notre Dame P, 2003.

———. "Is Ulysses Queer? The Subject of Greek Love in *Inferno* 15 and 26." *Dante's Plurilingualism: Authority, Vulgarization, Subjectivity*, edited by Sara Fortuna et al., Maney, 2010, pp. 179–92.

———. "Pederastic Insemination, or Dante in the Grammar Classroom." *The Poetics of Masculinity in Early Modern Italy and Spain*, edited by Gerry Milligan and Jane Tylus, U of Toronto Centre for Reformation and Renaissance Studies, 2010, pp. 41–73.

———. "Queering Nature, Queering Gender: Dante and Sodomy." Barolini and Storey, pp. 90–103.

Cham, Jorge. *Dante's* Inferno: *Academic Edition. PhD Comics*, 13 July 2015, www.phdcomics.com/comics.php?f=1813. Accessed 23 July 2016.

Cherchi, Paolo, and Antonio C. Mastrobuono, editors. *Lectura Dantis Newberryana.* Northwestern UP, 1988. 2 vols.

Christensen, Thomas, editor. *The Cambridge History of Western Music Theory.* Cambridge UP, 2002.

Chwast, Seymour. *Dante's* Divine Comedy: *A Graphic Adaptation.* Bloomsbury, 2010.

Ciabattoni, Francesco. *Dante's Journey to Polyphony.* U of Toronto P, 2010.

———. "Musical Instruments in Dante's *Commedia*: A Visual and Acoustic Journey." *Digital Dante,* Columbia University Librairies, digitaldante.columbia.edu/sound/ciabattoni-instruments. Accessed 18 Apr. 2019.

———. "Musical Ways around Ineffability: *Paradiso* 10–15." *Dante Studies,* vol. 131, 2013, pp. 25–49.

———. Review of the conference Dante and Music, U of Pennsylvania, Philadelphia, 5–6 Nov. 2015. *Dante e l'arte,* vol. 2, 2015, pp. 289–96.

Ciavolella, Massimo, and Gianluca Rizzo, editors. *Like Doves Summoned by Desire: Dante's New Life in Twentieth-Century Literature and Cinema: Essays in Memory of Amilcare Iannucci.* Agincourt, 2012.

Cino da Pistoia. *Poesie di Messer Cino da Pistoja.* 3rd ed., Manfredini, 1838.

Clark, Kenneth. *The Drawings by Sandro Botticelli for Dante's Divine Comedy: After the Originals in the Berlin Museums and the Vatican.* Harper and Row, 1976.

Clarke, K. P. "Humility and the (P)Arts of Art." Corbett and Webb, vol. 1, pp. 203–21.

Clarke, Paula. "The Villani Chronicles." *Chronicling History,* edited by Sharon Dale et al., Pennsylvania State UP, 2007, pp. 113–43.

Cogan, Marc. *The Design in the Wax: The Structure of the* Divine Comedy *and Its Meaning.* U of Notre Dame P, 1999.

Coleman, Edward. "Cities and Communes." Abulafia, pp. 27–57.

———. "The Italian Communes: Recent Work and Current Trends." *Journal of Medieval History,* vol. 24, no. 4, 1999, pp. 373–97.

Colish, Marcia L. *Medieval Foundations of the Western Intellectual Tradition, 400–1400.* Yale UP, 1997.

Compagni, Dino. *Dino Compagni's* Chronicle of Florence. Translated by Daniel E. Bornstein, U of Pennsylvania P, 1986.

Contino, Paul J. Introduction. *Dante: The* Divine Comedy. Translated by Burton Raffel, Northwestern UP, 2010, pp. xix–xxxii.

Cook-Sather, Alison, et al. *Engaging Students as Partners in Learning and Teaching: A Guide for Faculty.* Jossey-Bass, 2014.

Cooper, Donal. "Preaching amidst Pictures: Visual Contexts for Sermons in Late Medieval Tuscany." *Optics, Ethics, and Art in the Thirteenth and Fourteenth Centuries: Looking into Peter of Limoges's* Moral Treatise on the Eye, edited by Herbert L. Kessler and Richard G. Newhauser, Pontifical Institute of Mediaeval Studies, 2018, pp. 29–46.

Cooper, Donal, and Janet Robson. *The Making of Assisi: The Pope, the Franciscans and the Painting of the Basilica.* Yale UP, 2013.

Copeland, Rita, and Ineke Sluiter. *Medieval Grammar and Rhetoric: Language Arts and Literary Theory, AD 300–1475.* Oxford UP, 2009.

Corbett, George, and Heather Webb, editors. *Vertical Readings in Dante's* Comedy. Open Book Publishers, 2015–17. 3 vols.

Corley, Corin, translator. *Lancelot du lac / Lancelot of the Lake.* Introduction by Elspeth Kennedy, Oxford UP, 1989.

Cornish, Alison. *Reading Dante's Stars.* Yale UP, 2000.

Crescimbeni, Giovanni Mario. *Dell'istoria della volgar poesia.* Venice: Lorenzo Basegio, 1730. 6 vols.

Cunningham, Gilbert F. *The* Divine Comedy *in English: A Critical Bibliography, 1782–1900.* Oliver and Boyd, 1965. Vol. 1.

———. *The* Divine Comedy *in English: A Critical Bibliography, 1901–1966.* Oliver and Boyd, vol. 2, 1966.

Dameron, George W. "Angels, Monsters, and Hybridity in the *Divine Comedy*: Ancient Greek Cultural Legacies and Dante's Critique of the Church." Ziolkowski, *Greeks*, pp. 247–64.

———. "Church and Orthodoxy." Barański and Pertile, pp. 83–105.

———. "Florence." *Oxford Bibliographies in Medieval Studies*, 25 Feb. 2016, doi:10.1093/OBO/9780195396584-0168.

———. *Florence and Its Church in the Age of Dante.* U of Pennsylvania P, 2005.

Damrosch, David. "World Literature in a Postliterary Age." *Modern Language Quarterly*, vol. 74, no. 2, 2013, pp. 151–70.

Dante's Inferno. Electronic Arts / Visceral Games, 2010.

Dartmouth Dante Project. Dartmouth College, 2018, dante.dartmouth.edu. Accessed 16 Apr. 2019.

Davis, Charles T. *Dante's Italy and Other Essays.* U of Pennsylvania P, 1984.

———. "Poverty and Eschatology in the *Commedia*." Davis, *Dante's Italy*, pp. 42–70.

Davis, Gregson. "'With No Homeric Shadow': The Disavowal of Epic in Derek Walcott's *Omeros*." *The South Atlantic Quarterly*, vol. 96, no. 2, 1997, pp. 321–33.

Day, William R., Jr. "Economy." Barański and Pertile, pp. 30–46.

Dean, Trevor. "The Rise of the Signori." Abulafia, pp. 104–24.

———. *The Towns of Italy in the Later Middle Ages.* Manchester UP, 2000.

De Gennaro, Angelo A. *The Reader's Companion to Dante's* Divine Comedy. Philosophical Library, 1986.

De Rooy, Ronald. "A Cardboard Dante: Hell's Metropolis Revisited." Gragnolati et al., *Metamorphosing Dante*, pp. 355–65.

———. *Divine Comedies for the New Millennium: Recent Dante Translations in America and the Netherlands.* Amsterdam UP, 2003. E-book, 17 Oct. 2016.

De Sua, William J. *Dante into English: A Study of the Translation of the* Divine Comedy *in Britain and America.* U of North Carolina P, 1964.

Deusen, Nancy van. *The Cultural Context of Medieval Music.* Praeger, 2011.

Dimock, Wai Chee. "Literature for the Planet." *PMLA*, vol. 116, no. 1, 2001, pp. 173–88.

Di Scipio, Giuseppe, and Aldo Scaglione, editors. *The* Divine Comedy *and the Encyclopedia of Arts and Sciences.* John Benjamins, 1988.

Divine Comedy *Image Archive*. Cornell U, divinecomedy.library.cornell.edu/index .html. Accessed 16 Apr. 2019.

Doherty, Cathal, SJ. *Maurice Blondel on the Supernatural in Human Action: Sacrament and Superstition*. Brill, 2017.

The Doré Illustrations for Dante's Divine Comedy: *136 Plates by Gustave Doré*. Dover, 1976.

Dreher, Rod. *How Dante Can Save Your Life: The Life-Changing Wisdom of History's Greatest Poem*. Regan Arts, 2015.

———. "The Ultimate Self-Help Book: Dante's *Divine Comedy*." *The Wall Street Journal*, 18 Apr. 2014, www.wsj.com/articles/SB10001424052702303663604579 503700159096702. Accessed 25 July 2016.

Drell, Joanna H. "Using Dante to Teach the Middle Ages: Examples from Medieval Southern Italian History." Stavreva, pp. 59–65.

Dronke, Peter. *Dante and Medieval Latin Traditions*. Cambridge UP, 1986.

Drouin, Jennifer. "Diana's Band: Safe Spaces, Publics, and Early Modern Lesbianism." *Queer Renaissance Historiography: Backward Gaze*, edited by Vin Nardizzi et al., Ashgate, 2009, pp. 85–110.

Duggan, Maeve. "Gaming and Gamers." *Pew Research Center*, Dec. 2015, www .pewinternet.org/2015/12/15/gaming-and-gamers/. Accessed 28 May 2018.

Dulles, Avery. "Who Can Be Saved?" *First Things*, Feb. 2008, www.firstthings.com/ article/2008/02/001-who-can-be-saved-8. Accessed 28 May 2018.

Durling, Robert M. "Canto X: Farinata and Cavalcante." Mandelbaum et al., *Lectura Dantis:* Inferno, pp. 136–49.

———. "'Mio figlio ov'è?' (*Inferno* X, 60)." Picone, *Dante*, pp. 303–29.

Eisner, Martin. "The Word Made Flesh in *Inferno* 5: Francesca Reading and the Figure of the Annunciation." *Dante Studies*, vol. 131, 2013, pp. 51–72.

Eliot, T. S. *Dante*. Faber and Faber, 1966.

———. *The Poems of T. S. Eliot: Collected and Uncollected Poems*. Edited by Christopher Ricks and Jim McCue, Faber and Faber, 2015.

———. "Tradition and the Individual Talent." *The Sacred Wood: Essays on Poetry and Criticism*, Methuen, 1920, pp. 42–53.

———. "What Dante Means to Me." 1950. Hawkins and Jacoff, pp. 28–39.

Ellis, Adam. "Twenty-Three Circles of Hell That Should Exist for the Modern Age." *BuzzFeed*, 27 May 2014, www.buzzfeed.com/adamellis/circles-of-hell-that -should-exist-for-the-modern-age. Accessed 23 July 2016.

Ellis, Steve. *Dante and English Poetry: Shelley to T. S. Eliot*. Cambridge UP, 1983.

Emerson, Hunt, with Kevin Jackson. *Dante's Inferno*. Knockabout Comics, 2012.

Enciclopedia Dantesca. Istituto della Enciclopedia Italiana, 2nd ed., 1984.

Esposito, Enzo. *Bibliografia analitica degli scritti su Dante, 1950–1970*. Olschki, 1990. 4 vols.

———. *L'opera di Dante nel mondo: Edizioni e traduzioni nel Novecento*. Longo, 1992.

Essary, Brandon K. Syllabus and related materials for Dante's *Inferno*: From Poetry to Video Games. Elon U, Spring 2017, bessary.wordpress.com/cor-463-dantes-inferno.

Euripides. *Medea*. Translated by Diana Arnson Svarlien, Hackett, 2008.

Fabbri, Paolo, editor. *Il nono libro de madrigali a cinque voci (1599)*. Edizioni Suvini Zerboni, 1999.

Fallani, Giovanni. *Dante e la cultura figurativa medievale*, Minerva Italica, 1971.

Fassler, Margot, and Peter Jeffrey. "Christian Liturgical Music from the Bible to the Renaissance." *Sacred Sound and Social Change: Liturgical Music in Jewish and Christian Experience*, edited by Lawrence A. Hoffman and Janet R. Walton, U of Notre Dame P, 1992, pp. 84–123.

Faust, Jennifer L., and Donald R. Paulson. "Active Learning in the College Classroom." *Journal on Excellence in College Teaching*, vol. 9, 1998, pp. 3–24.

Ferguson, George. *Signs and Symbols in Christian Art*. Oxford UP, 1954.

Fergusson, Francis. *Dante's Drama of the Mind: A Modern Reading of the* Purgatorio. Princeton UP, 1953.

Ferrante, Joan M. "The Bible as Thesaurus for Secular Literature." *The Bible in the Middle Ages: Its Influence on Literature and Art*, edited by Bernard S. Levy, Medieval and Renaissance Texts and Studies, 1992, pp. 23–50.

———. *Dante's Beatrice: Priest of an Androgynous God*. State U of New York P, 1992.

———. *The Political Vision of the* Divine Comedy. Princeton UP, 1984.

———. Review of *Woman Earthly and Divine in the* Comedy *of Dante*, by Marianne Shapiro. *Italica*, vol. 54, no. 2, 1977, pp. 321–23.

———. *Woman as Image in Medieval Literature from the Twelfth Century to Dante*. Columbia UP, 1975.

Fitzgerald, Robert. "Mirroring the *Commedia*: An Appreciation of Laurence Binyon's Version." Hawkins and Jacoff, pp. 144–70.

Flaxman, John. *The Illustrations for Dante's* Divine Comedy. Edited by Francesca Salvadori, Royal Academy of Arts, 2005.

Fosca, Nicola. "Beatitudini e processo di purgazione." *Electronic Bulletin of the Dante Society of America*, 5 Feb. 2002, www.princeton.edu/~dante/ebdsa/fosca020502 .html. Accessed 28 May 2018.

Foster, Kenelm. "The Son's Eagle: *Paradiso* XIX." *The Two Dantes and Other Studies*, by Foster, U of California P, 1977, pp. 137–55.

Foucault, Michel. *The History of Sexuality: An Introduction*. Translated by Robert Hurley, Vintage Books / Random House, 1980. Vol. 1 of *The History of Sexuality*.

Franco, Charles, and Leslie Morgan, editors. *Dante: Summa Medievalis*. Forum Italicum, 1995.

Franke, William. *Dante's Interpretive Journey*. U of Chicago P, 1996.

Freccero, John. "Casella's Song: *Purgatorio* II, 112." Freccero, *Dante*, pp. 186–94.

———. "The Dance of the Stars: *Paradiso* X." Freccero, *Dante*, pp. 221–44.

———. *Dante: The Poetics of Conversion*. Edited by Rachel Jacoff, Harvard UP, 1986.

———. *In Dante's Wake: Reading from Medieval to Modern in the Augustinian Tradition*. Edited by Danielle Callegari and Melissa Swain, Fordham UP, 2015.

Fredericks, Jim L. *Faith among Faiths: Christian Theology and Non-Christian Religions*. Paulist Press, 1999.

Friederich, Werner P. *Dante's Fame Abroad*. U of North Carolina Studies in Comparative Literature, 1950.

Fubini, Mario. "Catone l'Uticense." *Enciclopedia dantesca*, vol. 1, pp. 876–82.

Fugelso, Karl. "Robert Rauschenberg's *Inferno* Illuminations." *Studies in Medievalism*, vol. 13, 2004, pp. 4–66.

Fumagalli, Maria Cristina. *The Flight of the Vernacular: Seamus Heaney, Walcott and the Impress of Dante*. Rodopi, 2001.

Gallagher, Joseph. *To Hell and Back with Dante: A Modern Reader's Guide to the Divine Comedy*. Triumph Books, 1996.

Gardiner, Eileen, editor. *Visions of Heaven and Hell before Dante*. Italica Press, 1989.

Gee, James Paul. *Good Video Games and Good Learning: Collected Essays on Video Games, Learning and Literacy*. Peter Lang, 2013.

———. *What Video Games Have to Teach Us about Learning and Literacy*. Palgrave Macmillan, 2007.

Gérard Zuchetto chante les Troubadours des XIIᵉ et XIIIᵉ siècles. Gallo CD 529, 1988. Vol. 1.

Gerbert, Martin. *Scriptores ecclesiastici de musica sacra potissimum*. 1784. Reprint ed., Olms, 1963. 3 vols.

Giamatti, A. Bartlett, editor. *Dante in America: The First Two Centuries*. Center for Medieval and Renaissance Studies / Dante Society of America, 1983.

Ginsberg, Warren. *Dante's Aesthetics of Being*, U of Michigan P, 1999.

Giovannetti, Luciana. *Dante in America: Bibliografia 1965–1980*. Longo, 1987.

Giuriceo, Marie. "A Comparative Approach to Teaching the *Divine Comedy*." *Slade*, pp. 94–100.

Goldin, Frederick, translator. *German and Italian Lyrics of the Middle Ages: An Anthology and a History*. Anchor Press / Doubleday, 1973.

———. *Lyrics of the Troubadours and Trouvères: An Anthology and a History*. Anchor Press / Doubleday, 1973.

Gracyk, Theodore, and Andrew Kania, editors. *The Routledge Companion to Philosophy and Music*. Routledge, 2011.

Graduale Romanum. Kyriale, Extracted from the Graduale Romanum 1961. Church Music Association of America, 2007, media.musicasacra.com/pdf/kyriale-solesmes.pdf. Accessed 12 Apr. 2019.

Gragnolati, Manuele. *Experiencing the Afterlife: Soul and Body in Dante and Medieval Culture*, U of Notre Dame P, 2005.

Gragnolati, Manuele, et al., editors. *Desire in Dante and the Middle Ages*. Legenda, 2012.

Gragnolati, Manuele, et al., editors. *Metamorphosing Dante: Appropriations, Manipulations, and Rewritings in the Twentieth and Twenty-First Centuries*. Turia and Kant, 2011.

Greeley, Andrew. *The Catholic Imagination*. U of California P, 2000.

Green, Louis. *Chronicle into History: An Essay on the Interpretation of History in Florentine Fourteenth-Century Chronicles*. Cambridge UP, 1972.

Greenaway, Peter, and Tom Phillips, directors. *A TV Dante*. British Broadcasting Corporation, 1990.

Gregory the Great. *S. Gregorii Magni Registrum epistularum*. Edited by Dag Norberg, Brepols, 1982.

Griffiths, Eric, and Matthew Reynolds, editors. *Dante in English*. Penguin, 2005.

Griffiths, Paul. *The Vice of Curiosity: An Essay on Intellectual Appetite*. Carnegie Mellon UP, 2006.

Guzzardo, John J. *Dante: Numerological Studies*. Peter Lang, 1987.

Hall, James. *Dictionary of Subjects and Symbols in Art*. Harper and Row, 1974.

Halperin, David M. *How to Do the History of Homosexuality*. U of Chicago P, 2002.

Harrison, Robert Pogue. *The Body of Beatrice*. Johns Hopkins UP, 1988.

Harvey, Allison. *Gender, Age, and Digital Games in the Domestic Context*. Routledge, 2015.

Havely, Nick. *Dante*. Blackwell Publishing, 2007.

———. *Dante and the Franciscans: Poverty and the Papacy in the* Commedia. Cambridge UP, 2004.

———, editor. *Dante in the Nineteenth Century: Reception, Canonicity, Popularization*. Peter Lang, 2011.

———. *Dante's British Public: Readers and Texts, from the Fourteenth Century to the Present*. Oxford UP, 2014.

———, editor. *Dante's Modern Afterlife: Reception and Response from Blake to Heaney*. St. Martin's Press, 1998.

Hawkins, Peter S. "All Smiles: Poetry and Theology in Dante's *Commedia*." Montemaggi and Treherne, pp. 36–59. Originally published in *PMLA*, vol. 121, 2006, pp. 371–87.

———. *Dante: A Brief History*. Blackwell Publishing, 2006.

———. "Dante and the Bible." Jacoff, *Cambridge Companion*, 2nd ed., pp. 125–40.

———. "Dante's Beatrice." Hawkins, *Dante: A Brief History*, pp. 71–97.

———. *Dante's Testaments: Essays in Scriptural Imagination*. Stanford UP, 1999.

———. "Moderno Uso." *Arion*, vol. 13, no. 1, 2005, pp. 161–84.

Hawkins, Peter S., and Rachel Jacoff, editors. *The Poets' Dante: Twentieth-Century Responses*. Farrar, Straus and Giroux, 2001.

Heaney, Seamus. "A Dream of Solstice." *Irish Times*, 18 January 2000, p. 1.

———. "Envies and Identifications: Dante and the Modern Poet." *Finders Keepers: Selected Prose 1971–2001*, by Heaney, Farrar, Straus and Giroux, 2002, pp. 184–96.

Hirsch, Rudolf. *Printing, Selling and Reading, 1450–1550*. Harrassowitz, 1967.

Holbrook, Richard T. *Portraits of Dante from Giotto to Raffael: A Critical Study*. Philip Lee Warner, 1921.

Hollander, Robert. *Dante: A Life in Works*. Yale UP, 2001.

———. "Dante's Cato Again." Kilgour and Lombardi, pp. 66–124.

———. *Dante's* Epistle to Can Grande. U of Michigan P, 1993.

———. "Teaching Dante to Undergraduates at Princeton." Slade, pp. 148–52.

Holmes, George. *Florence, Rome and the Origins of the Renaissance.* Oxford UP, 1986.

Holmes, Olivia. *Dante's Two Beloveds: Ethics and Erotics in the* Divine Comedy. Yale UP, 2008.

Holsinger, Bruce W. *Music, Body, and Desire in Medieval Culture: Hildegard of Bingen to Chaucer.* Stanford UP, 2001.

———. "Sodomy and Resurrection: The Homoerotic Subject of the *Divine Comedy.*" *Premodern Sexualities,* edited by Louise Fradenburg and Carla Freccero, Routledge, 1996, pp. 243–74.

The Holy Bible: Translated from the Latin Vulgate. Douay-Rheims Version. Tan Books, 1971.

Honess, Claire E. *From Florence to the Heavenly City: The Poetry of Citizenship in Dante.* Legenda, 2006.

Honess, Claire E., and Matthew Treherne, editors. *"Se mai continga . . .": Exile, Politics and Theology in Dante.* Longo, 2013.

Huizinga, Johan. *Homo Ludens: a Study of the Play-Element in Culture.* Beacon Press, 1955.

Iannucci, Amilcare A., editor. *Dante, Cinema, and Television.* U of Toronto P, 2004.

———, editor. *Dante: Contemporary Perspectives.* U of Toronto P, 1997.

———, editor. *Dante e la "bella scola" della poesia: Autorità e sfida poetica.* Longo, 1993.

———, editor. *Dante Today.* Special issue of *Quaderni d'italianistica,* vol. 10, nos. 1–2, 1989.

Inferno. Milano Films, 1911. Recall DVD —SDVD513: *L'Inferno.* Music by Tangerine Dream, 2006. *YouTube,* www.youtube.com/watch?v=shC-8LgcFf8. Accessed 19 Sept. 2019.

Italicus MS 1. The Divine Comedy. By Dante. Fourteenth century, Eötvös Loránd U Library and Archive, Budapest. *Dante Alighieri, Commedia: Biblioteca Universitaria di Budapest codex italicus 1: riproduzione fotografica (vol. 1); Studi e ricerche (vol. 2),* edited by Gian Paolo Marchi and József Pál, facsimile ed., Grafiche SiZ, 2006.

Jacobsen, Douglas, and Rhonda Hustedt Jacobsen. *No Longer Invisible: Religion in University Education.* Oxford UP, 2012.

Jacoff, Rachel, editor. *The Cambridge Companion to Dante.* Cambridge UP, 1993.

———, editor. *The Cambridge Companion to Dante.* 2nd ed., Cambridge UP, 2007.

———. "The *Divine Comedy*: Text and Contexts." Slade, pp. 79–86.

———. "Introduction to *Paradiso.*" Jacoff, *Cambridge Companion,* 2nd ed., pp. 107–24.

———. "Transgression and Transcendence: Figures of Female Desire in Dante's *Commedia.*" *Romanic Review,* vol. 79, 1988, pp. 129–42.

Jacoff, Rachel, and Jeffrey T. Schnapp, editors. *The Poetry of Allusion: Virgil and Ovid in Dante's* Commedia. Stanford UP, 1991.

Jacoff, Rachel, and William A. Stephany. Inferno II. U of Pennsylvania P, 1989.

Jansen, Katherine L., et al., editors. *Medieval Italy: Texts in Translation.* U of Pennsylvania P, 2009.

Jeffrey, David Lyle. "Dante and Chaucer." *The Sermon on the Mount through the Centuries: From the Early Church to John Paul II,* edited by Jeffrey P. Greenman et al., Brazos Press, 2007.

Jensen, Frede, editor and translator. *The Poetry of the Sicilian School.* Garland, 1986.

———, editor and translator. *Tuscan Poetry of the Duecento: An Anthology.* Garland, 1994.

John of Salisbury. *The* Metalogicon: *A Twelfth-Century Defense of the Verbal and Logical Arts of the Trivium.* Translated by Daniel McGarry, U of California P, 1955.

John Paul II (pope). *Address of His Holiness Pope John Paul II to the Diplomatic Corps,* Monday, 13 Jan. 2003, w2.vatican.va/content/john-paul-ii/en/speeches/2003/january/documents/hf_jp-ii_spe_20030113_diplomatic-corps. Accessed 12 Apr. 2019.

Jones, Steve. "Let the Games Begin: Gaming, Technology, and College Students." *Pew Research Center,* 6 July 2003, www.pewinternet.org/2003/07/06/let-the-games-begin-gaming-technology-and-college-students/. Accessed 28 May 2018.

Joyce, James. *Ulysses.* Penguin, 1960.

Kafai, Yasmin, editor. *Beyond Barbie and Mortal Kombat: New Perspectives on Gender and Gaming.* MIT P, 2008.

Kantorowicz, Ernst H. "The King's Advent and the Enigmatic Panels in the Doors of Santa Sabina." *Art Bulletin,* vol. 26, 1944, pp. 207–31.

Karras, Ruth Mazo. *Sexuality in Medieval Europe: Doing unto Others.* Routledge, 2012.

Kastanis, Angeliki, et al. "LGBT Data and Demographics." *UCLA School of Law Williams Institute,* 2019, williamsinstitute.law.ucla.edu/visualization/lgbt-stats/.

Kay, Richard. *Dante's Christian Astrology.* U of Pennsylvania P, 1994.

———. *Dante's Enigmas: Medieval Scholasticism and Beyond.* Ashgate, 2006.

Keen, Catherine. *Dante and the City.* Tempus, 2003.

Kilgour, Maggie, and Elena Lombardi, editors. *Dantean Dialogues: Engaging with the Legacy of Amilcare Iannucci.* U of Toronto P, 2013.

Kinder, John J., and Diana Glenn, editors. *"Legato con Amore in un Volume": Essays in Honour of John A. Scott.* Olschki, 2013.

The King James Bible Virtual Exhibit: The Medieval Bible. Curated by Eric J. Johnson, Ohio State University Library, library.osu.edu/innovation-projects/omeka/exhibits/show/the-king-james-bible/sections/the-medieval-bible. Accessed 29 May 2018.

Kinsey, Alfred, et al. *Sexual Behavior in the Human Female.* W. B. Saunders, 1953.

Kinsey, Alfred, et al. *Sexual Behavior in the Human Male.* W. B. Saunders, 1948.

Kirkham, Victoria. "A Canon of Women in Dante's *Commedia.*" *Annali d'Italianistica,* vol. 7, 1989, pp. 16–41.

Kirkpatrick, Robin. *Dante's* Inferno: *Difficulty and Dead Poetry.* 2nd ed., Cambridge UP, 1987.

———. *Dante: The* Divine Comedy. Cambridge UP, 2004.

Kleiner, John. *Mismapping the Underworld: Daring and Error in Dante's Comedy.* Stanford UP, 1994.

Kleinhenz, Christopher. "Biblical Citation in Dante's *Divine Comedy.*" Cervigni, *Dante,* pp. 346–59.

———. "Dante and the Bible: Intertextual Approaches to the *Divine Comedy.*" *Italica,* vol. 63, 1986, pp. 225–36.

————. *Dante intertestuale e interdisciplinare: Saggi sulla* Commedia. Aracne, 2015.

————, editor. *Medieval Italy: An Encyclopedia*. Routledge, 2004. 2 vols.

————. "On Dante and the Visual Arts." Barolini and Storey, pp. 274–92.

Klonsky, Milton. *Blake's Dante: The Complete Illustrations to the* Divine Comedy. Harmony Books, 1980.

Kren, Claudia. "Astronomy." Wagner, *Seven*, pp. 218–47.

Kuon, Peter. *Lo mio maestro e 'l mio autore: Die produktive Rezeption der* Divina Commedia *in der Erzählliteratur der Moderne*. Klostermann, 1993.

La Favia, Louis M. "'. . . Chè quivi per canti . . .' (*Purg.* XII, 113): Dante's Programmatic Use of Psalms and Hymns in the *Purgatorio*." *Studies in Iconography*, vol. 10, 1984–86, pp. 53–65.

Lal Ded. "Poem 44." *I, Lalla: The Poems of Lal Děd*, translated by Ranjit Hoskote, Penguin, 2013.

Lansing, Richard, editor. *The Dante Encyclopedia*. Garland, 2000.

————, editor. *Dante: The Critical Complex*. Routledge, 2003. 8 vols.

La Piana, Angelina. *Dante's American Pilgrimage: A Historical Survey of Dante Studies in the United States, 1800–1944*. Yale UP, 1948.

Latini, Brunetto. *Il Tesoretto (The Little Treasure)*. Edited and translated by Julia Bolton Holloway, Garland, 1981.

Laurenziano Pluteo MS 41.42. Old Occitan primer and anthology. Early fourteenth century, Biblioteca Medicea Laurenziana, Florence, teca.bmlonline.it/Image Viewer/servlet/ImageViewer?idr=TECA0000623982&keyworks=Plut.41.42#page/1/mode/1up. Accessed 16 Apr. 2016.

Laurenziano Rediano MS 9. Italian lyric poetry. Late thirteenth century, Biblioteca Medicea Laurenziana, Florence, archive.org/details/ilcanzionierelau00bibluoft. Accessed 16 Apr. 2019.

Le Goff, Jacques. *The Birth of Purgatory*. Translated by Arthur Goldhammer, U of Chicago P, 1984.

Le Normand-Romain, Antoinette. *Rodin: The Gates of Hell*. Translated by Allan Howard, Musée Rodin, 1999.

Levý, Jiří. *The Art of Translation*. Translated by Patrick Corness, edited by Zuzana Jettmarová, John Benjamins, 2011.

Lewis, C. S. *The Great Divorce*. Macmillan, 1963.

————. *Letters to Malcolm: Chiefly on Prayer*. Harcourt, Brace, Jovanovich, 1964.

Lewis, R. W. B. *Dante*. Lipper / Viking, 2001.

Liszt, Franz. *Dante Symphony. Franz Liszts Musikalische Werke*, vol. 7, I. *Für orchester Symphonien*, Nr. 1: *Eine Symphonie zu Dantes* Divina Commedia. Breitkopf and Härtel, 1920. *Partifi*, partifi.org/HfOZs/segment/.

Looney, Dennis. *Freedom Readers: The African American Reception of Dante Alighieri and the* Divine Comedy. U of Notre Dame P, 2011.

————. Syllabus for From Hell to Harlem: African American Responses to Dante's *Divine Comedy* from 1850 to Today. Department of Italian, U of Pittsburg, Spring 2001. *CORE*, dx.doi.org/10.17613/M6W37KV80.

Lucan. *The Civil War (Pharsalia)*. Edited and translated by J. D. Duff, Harvard UP, 1977.

Luzzi, Joseph. *In a Dark Wood: What Dante Taught Me about Grief, Healing, and the Mysteries of Love*. HarperCollins, 2015.

MacDougal, Stuart Y., editor. *Dante among the Moderns*. U of North Carolina P, 1985.

Mahrt, William Peter. "Dante's Musical Progress through the *Commedia*." *The Echo of Music: Essays in Honor of Marie Louise Göllner*, edited by Blair Sullivan, Harmonie Park Press, 2004, pp. 63–73.

Malato, Enrico, editor. *In ricordo di Charles S. Singleton*. Special issue of *Filologia e critica*, vol. 20, nos. 2–3, 1995.

Mandelbaum, Allen, et al., editors. *Lectura Dantis:* Inferno. U of California P, 1998.

———, editors. *Lectura Dantis:* Purgatorio. U of California P, 2008.

Mandonnet, Pierre, OP. *Siger de Brabant et l'averroïsme latin au XIIIme siècle*. Slatkine Reprints, 1976.

I manoscritti. Dante Online, www.danteonline.it/italiano/codici_indice.htm. Accessed 29 May 2018.

Marchesi, Simone. "Boccaccio's Vernacular Classicism: Intertextuality and Interdiscoursivity in the *Decameron*." *Heliotropia*, vol. 7, nos. 1–2, 2010, pp. 31–50.

———. *Dante and Augustine: Linguistics, Poetics, Hermeneutics*. U of Toronto P, 2011.

Marie de France. *Chevrefoil*. Bibliotèque national de France, Paris, Nouvelles Acquisitions Français MS 1104, fols. 32r–33r, gallica.bnf.fr/ark:/12148/btv1b105326322.r=1104.

———. *Chevrefoil*. British Library, London, Harley MS 978, fols. 150v–151v, www.bl.uk/manuscripts/FullDisplay.aspx?ref=Harley_MS_978.

———. "Lai du *Chevrefeuille* dans *Tristan et Iseult*." *Tristan and Iseult*. Performed by the Boston Camerata, 1989. Erato 98482. *YouTube*, uploaded by Massimo Onraed, 6 Apr. 2010, www.youtube.com/watch?v=e2uDdwUQLqU.

Marrone, Gaetana, editor. *Encyclopedia of Italian Literary Studies*. Routledge, 2007. 2 vols.

Marti, Mario. *Poeti del Dolce Stil Novo*. Le Monnier, 1969.

Martinez, Ronald L. "'L'Amoroso Canto': Liturgy and Vernacular Lyric in Dante's *Purgatorio*." *Dante Studies*, vol. 127, 2009, pp. 93–127.

———. "Cato of Utica." Lansing, *Dante Encyclopedia*, pp. 146–49.

———. *Cleansing the Temple: Dante, Defender of the Church*. Center for Medieval and Renaissance Studies / State U of New York P, 2017.

———. "Forese, the Book of Job, and the Office of the Dead: A Note to *Purgatorio* 23." *Dante Studies*, vol. 122, 2004, pp. 1–17.

———. "Mourning Beatrice: The Rhetoric of Threnody in the *Vita nuova*." *MLN*, vol. 113, no. 1, 1998, pp. 1–29.

Masciandaro, Franco. *Dante as Dramatist: The Myth of the Earthly Paradise and Tragic Vision in the* Divine Comedy. U of Pennsylvania P, 1991.

Mather, Frank J. *The Portraits of Dante Compared with the Measurements of His Skull and Reclassified*. Princeton UP, 1921.

Mathiesen, Thomas J. *Apollo's Lyre: Greek Music and Music Theory in Antiquity and the Middle Ages.* U of Nebraska P, 1999.

Mazzeo, Joseph Anthony. *Medieval Cultural Tradition in Dante's* Comedy. Cornell UP, 1960.

———. *Structure and Thought in the* Paradiso. Cornell UP, 1958.

Mazzotta, Giuseppe. "Alighieri, Dante." Lansing, *Dante Encyclopedia*, pp. 15–20.

———. "*Comedia*, ca. 1305–1321." Marrone, vol. 1, pp. 554–59.

———. "Commentaries." Marrone, vol. 1, pp. 559–61.

———. "*Convivio*, ca. 1304–1307." Marrone, vol. 1, pp. 561–62.

———, editor. *Critical Essays on Dante.* Hall, 1991.

———. "Dante Alighieri (1265–1321)." Marrone, vol. 1, pp. 547–54.

———. Dante in Translation. *Open Yale Courses,* Yale U, oyc.yale.edu/italian -language-and-literature/ital-310. Accessed 28 May 2018.

———. *Dante's Vision and the Circle of Knowledge.* Princeton UP, 1993.

———. "*De vulgari eloquentia*, ca. 1304–1305." Marrone, vol. 1, p. 563.

———. "Liberty and Grace." *Republicanism: A Theoretical and Historical Perspective,* edited by Fabrizio Ricciardelli and Marcello Fantoni, Brepols, forthcoming.

———. "Life of Dante." Jacoff, *Cambridge Companion,* 2nd ed., pp. 1–13.

———. "*Monarchia*, ca. 1317." Marrone, vol. 1, pp. 564–65.

———. "Opus restaurationis." *Dante, Poet of the Desert: History and Allegory in the Divina Commedia,* Princeton UP, 1979, pp. 14–65.

———. *Reading Dante.* Yale UP, 2014.

———. "*Vita nuova*, ca. 1294." Marrone, vol. 1, pp. 565–66.

McCracken, Andrew. "'In Omnibus Viis Tuis': Compline in the Valley of the Rulers (*Purg.* VII–VIII)." *Dante Studies,* vol. 111, 1993, pp. 119–29.

McGinn, Bernard. *Antichrist: Two Thousand Years of the Human Fascination with Evil.* Harper, 1994.

McGregor, James H., editor. *Approaches to Teaching Boccaccio's* Decameron. Modern Language Association, 2000.

McMahon, Robert. *Understanding Medieval Meditative Ascent: Augustine, Anselm, Boethius, and Dante.* Catholic U of America P, 2006.

Mediceo Palatino MS 75. By Luigi Alamanni, sixteenth century, Biblioteca Medicea Laurenziana, Florence.

Menzinger, Sara. "Dante, la Bibbia, il diritto: Sulle tracce di Uzzà nel pensiero giuridico-teologico medievale." *Dante Studies,* vol. 133, 2015, pp. 122–46.

Milano Trivulziano MS 1080. *The Divine Comedy.* By Dante, copied by Francesco di ser Nardo da Barberino, 1337, Archivio Storico Civico and Biblioteca Trivulziana, Milan, trivulziana.milanocastello.it/en/content/trivulziano-codex-1080 -and-text-known-'danti-del-cento'. Accessed 16 Apr. 2019.

Milbank, Alison. *Dante and the Victorians.* Manchester UP, 1998.

———. Message to Nick Havely. 13 Sept. 2016. E-mail.

Miller, James, editor. *Dante and the Unorthodox: The Aesthetics of Transfiguration.* Wilfrid Laurier UP, 2005.

Miller, Maureen. *Power and the Holy in the Age of the Investiture Conflict: A Brief History with Documents*. Bedford / St. Martins, 2005.

Mills Chiarenza, Marguerite. "Boethius." Lansing, *Dante Encyclopedia*, pp. 118–19.

———. *The Divine Comedy: Tracing God's Art*. Twayne, 1989.

"Ministry to Persons with a Homosexual Inclination." Pastoral Letter, United States Conference of Catholic Bishops, 14 Nov. 2006.

Minnis, Alastair J. *From Eden to Eternity: Creations of Paradise in the Later Middle Ages*. U of Pennsylvania P, 2015.

Minnis, Alastair J., and A. B. Scott. *Medieval Literary Theory and Criticism, 1100–1375: The Commentary-Tradition*. With the assistance of David Wallace, revised ed., Cambridge UP, 1991.

Mitchell, Helen R. "Fear and the Musical Avant-Garde in Games: Interviews with Jason Graves, Garry Schyman, Paul Gorman, and Michael Kamper." *Horror Studies*, vol. 5, no. 1, 2014, pp. 127–44.

Modesto, Filippa. *Dante's Idea of Friendship: The Transformation of a Classical Concept*. U of Toronto P, 2015.

Moevs, Christian. *The Metaphysics of Dante's Comedy*. Oxford UP, 2005.

Moleta, Vincent, editor. *"La Gloriosa Donna de la Mente": A Commentary on the* Vita Nuova. Olschki / Department of Italian, The University of Western Australia, 1994.

Mondia, Michele. Message to Nick Havely. 4 July 2016. E-mail.

Monneret de Villard, Ugo. *Lo Studio dell'Islām in Europa nel XII e nel XIII secolo*. Vatican City, 1944.

Montemaggi, Vittorio. *Reading Dante's* Commedia *as Theology: Divinity Realized in Human Encounter*. Oxford UP, 2016.

Montemaggi, Vittorio, and Matthew Treherne, editors. *Dante's* Commedia: *Theology as Poetry*. U of Notre Dame P, 2010.

Moore, Edward. *Studies in Dante*. Oxford UP, 1899.

Moraga, Cherríe. *The Hungry Woman*. West End Press, 2001.

Moreau, Dan. "The Nine Circles of Adjunct Hell." *McSweeney's Internet Tendency*. 27 May 2011, www.mcsweeneys.net/articles/the-nine-circles-of-adjunct-hell. Accessed 23 July 2016.

Morgan, Alison. *Dante and the Medieval Other World*. Cambridge UP, 1990.

Murakami, Haruki. *The Wind-up Bird Chronicle*. Translated by Jay Rubin, Vintage, 1997.

"Musical Settings of the *Commedia*, arranged by year of composition." Lansing, *Dante Encyclopedia*, pp. 905–12.

Najemy, John M. "Dante and Florence." Jacoff, *Cambridge Companion*, 2nd ed., pp. 236–56.

———. *A History of Florence, 1200–1575*. Blackwell Publishing, 2006.

Nandakumar, Prema. *Dante and Sri Aurobindo: A Comparative Study of the* Divine Comedy *and* Savitri. Affiliated East-West Press, 1981.

Narayan, R. K. *The* Ramayana: *A Shortened Modern Prose Version of the Indian Epic*. Penguin, 1972.

Nardi, Bruno. *La giovinezza di Virgilio*. Mondovì, 1927.

Nassar, Eugene Paul. *Illustrations to Dante's* Inferno. Associated University Presses, 1994.

Nasti, Paola, and Claudia Rossignoli, editors. *Interpreting Dante: Essays on the Traditions of Dante Commentary.* U. of Notre Dame P, 2013.

National Leadership Council for Liberal Education and America's Promise. *College Learning for the New Global Century.* Association of American Colleges and Universities, 2008.

Naylor, Gloria. *Linden Hills.* Penguin, 1985.

———. *The Women of Brewster Place.* Penguin, 1983.

Naylor, Gloria, and Toni Morrison. "Gloria Naylor and Toni Morrison: A Conversation." *Southern Review,* vol. 21, 1985, pp. 567–93.

Newcomb, Anthony. "Luzzaschi's Setting of Dante: 'Quivi sospiri, pianti, ed alti guai.'" *Early Music History,* vol. 28, 2009, pp. 97–138.

Newton, John. "Amazing Grace," *LyricFreaks,* www.lyricsfreak.com/y/yes/amazing+grace_20268854.html. Accessed 30 May 2018.

NPR Staff. "Sounds of Stars Fall in a Bavarian Forest." *Weekend Edition Saturday,* National Public Radio, 13 Aug. 2011, www.npr.org/2011/08/13/139600689/sounds-of-stars-fall-in-a-bavarian-forest. Transcript.

O'Connell Baur, Christine. *Dante's Hermeneutics of Salvation: Passages to Freedom in the* Divine Comedy. U of Toronto P, 2007.

O'Connor, Anne. *Florence: City and Memory in the Nineteenth Century.* Edizioni Città di Vita, 2008.

Olson, Kristina M. "Dante's Urban American Vernacular: Sandow Birk's *Comedy.*" *Dante Studies,* vol. 131, 2013, pp. 143–69.

———. "The Language of Women as Written by Men: Dante, Boccaccio, and Gendered Histories of the Vernacular." *Heliotropia,* vols. 8–9, 2011–12, pp. 51–78.

———. "Shoes, Gowns, and Turncoats: Reconsidering Cacciaguida's History of Florentine Fashion and Politics." *Dante Studies,* vol. 134, 2016, pp. 26–47.

———. "Uncovering the Historical Body of Florence: Dante, Boccaccio and Sumptuary Legislation." *Italian Culture,* vol. 33, no. 1, 2015, pp. 1–15.

On Solid Ground: Value Report 2017. Association of American Colleges and Universities, 2017.

Ovid. *Metamorphoses.* Translated by Frank Justus Miller, Harvard UP, 1977.

Paganini, Paganino, and Alessandro Paganini, printers. *Dante col sito, et forma dell'Inferno: Lo 'nferno e 'l Purgatorio e 'l Paradiso di Dante Alaghieri.* Toscolano Maderno: Paganini, 1527–33.

Paris, Gaston. *La Leggenda di Saladino.* Translated by Mario Menghini, Sansoni, 1896.

Parker, Deborah, and Mark Parker. *Inferno Revealed: From Dante to Dan Brown.* Palgrave Macmillan, 2013.

Pasquini, Laura. *Iconografie dantesche: Dalla luce del mosaico all'immagine profetica.* Longo, 2008.

Pelikan, Jaroslav. *Eternal Feminines: Three Theological Allegories in Dante's* Paradiso. Rutgers UP, 1990.

Pequigney, Joseph. "Sodomy in Dante's *Inferno* and *Purgatorio.*" *Representations*, no. 36, 1991, pp. 22–42.

Pertile, Lino. "Introduction to *Inferno.*" Jacoff, *Cambridge Companion*, 2nd ed., pp. 67–90.

———. "Life." Barański and Pertile, pp. 461–74.

———. "Works." Barański and Pertile, pp. 475–508.

Picchio Simonelli, Maria. *Inferno III*. U of Pennsylvania P, 1993.

Picone, Michelangelo, editor. *Dante: Da Firenze all'aldilà: Atti del terzo Seminario dantesco internazionale (Firenze, 9–11 giugno 2000)*. Franco Cesati, 2001.

———. "Giraut de Bornelh nella prospettiva di Dante." *Vox Romanica*, vol. 39, 1980, pp. 22–43.

———. "*Paradiso* IX: Dante, Folchetto e la diaspora trobadorica." *Medioevo Romanzo*, vol. 8, 1981–1983, pp. 47–89.

———. *Scritti danteschi*. Edited by Antonio Lanza, Longo, 2017.

———. "I trovatori di Dante: Bertran de Born." *Studi e problemi di critica testuale*, no. 19, 1979, pp. 71–94.

Picone, Michelangelo, and Tatiana Crivelli, editors. *Dante: Mito e poesia*. Franco Cesati, 1999.

Picone, Michelangelo, et al., editors. *Le culture di Dante: Studi in onore di Robert Hollander*. Franco Cesati, 2004.

Pieri, Marzia. "La *Commedia* in palcoscenico: Appunti su una ricerca da fare." *Dante e l'arte*, vol. 1, 2014, pp. 67–84.

Pietropaolo, Domenico, editor. *Dante and the Christian Imagination*. Legas, 2015.

Plato. *Symposium*. Translated by Christopher Gill, Penguin, 2003.

Pope-Hennessy, John. *Paradiso: The Illuminations to Dante's* Divine Comedy *by Giovanni di Paolo*. Random House, 1993.

Povoledo, Elisabetta. "Setting Dante's Journey to Eternity to Song." *New York Times*, 29 Nov. 2007, www.nytimes.com/2007/11/28/arts/28iht-dante.1.8514341.html?_r=0. Accessed 28 May 2018.

Prensky, Marc. "Listen to the Natives." *Educational Leadership*, vol. 63, no. 4, 2005–06, pp. 8–13.

Princeton Dante Project. Princeton U, 1999, etcweb.princeton.edu/dante/index.html.

Psaki, F. Regina. "The Sexual Body in Dante's Celestial Paradise." *Imagining Heaven in the Middle Ages*, edited by Jan S. Emerson and Hugh Feiss, Garland, 2000, pp. 47–61.

Putnam, Michael C. J. "Possessiveness, Sexuality, and Heroism in the *Aeneid.*" *Vergilius*, vol. 31, 1985, pp. 1–21.

Pyle, Eric. *William Blake's Illustrations for Dante's* Divine Comedy: *A Study of the Engravings, Pencil Sketches, and Watercolors*. McFarland, 2015.

Quinones, Ricardo J. *Dante Alighieri*. 1979. 2nd ed., Twayne, 1998.

Raffa, Guy P. *The Complete Danteworlds: A Reader's Guide to the* Divine Comedy. U of Chicago P, 2009.

———. *Danteworlds*. U of Texas, Austin, danteworlds.laits.utexas.edu.

————. *Divine Dialectic: Dante's Incarnational Poetry*. U of Toronto P, 2000.

"Recorded Musical Settings of the *Commedia*." Lansing, *Dante Encyclopedia*, pp. 913–14.

Reddy, William M. *The Making of Romantic Love: Longing and Sexuality in Europe, South Asia, and Japan, 900–1200 CE*. U of Chicago P, 2012.

Riccardiano MS 2909. Old Provençal troubadour lyrics. Biblioteca Riccardiana, Florence, archive.org/details/CanzoniereProvBertoni/page/n10. Accessed 16 Apr. 2019.

Rodinson, Maxime. *La fascination de l'Islam*. François Maspero, 1981.

Roglieri, Maria Ann. *Dante and Music: Musical Adaptations of the* Commedia *from the Sixteenth Century to the Present*. Ashgate, 2001.

————. "'La Dolce Sinfonia di Paradiso': Can Mere Mortals Compose It?" Braida and Calè, pp. 65–80.

————. "Music." Lansing, *Dante Encyclopedia*, pp. 631–34.

————. "Twentieth-Century Musical Interpretations of the 'Anti-music' of Dante's *Inferno*." *Italica*, vol. 79, 2002, pp. 149–67.

Rosenwein, Barbara. *A Short History of the Middle Ages*. 4th ed., U of Toronto P, 2014.

Rosser, Gervase. "Duccio and Dante on the Road to Emmaus." *Art History*, vol. 35, no. 3, 2012, pp. 474–97.

Rossini, Antonio. *Palinsesti danteschi: Riscrivere la* Commedia, *da Garibaldi all'era del digitale*. Carabba, 2017.

Rotimi, Ola. *The Gods Are Not to Blame*. Oxford UP, 1971.

Russell, Jeffrey Burton. *A History of Heaven: The Singing Silence*. Princeton UP, 1997.

Ruud, Jay, editor. *Critical Companion to Dante: A Literary Reference to His Life and Work*. Facts on File, 2008.

Ryan, Christopher. "The Theology of Dante." Jacoff, *Cambridge Companion*, 1st ed., pp. 136–52.

Saiber, Arielle, and Elizabeth Coggeshall. *Dante Today: Citings and Sightings of Dante's Works in Contemporary Culture*, Bowdoin College, research.bowdoin .edu/dante-today. Accessed 1 June 2018.

Salen, Katie, editor. *The Ecology of Games: Connecting Youth, Games, and Learning*. MIT P, 2008.

Saly, John. *Dante's* Paradiso: *The Flowering of the Self: An Interpretation of the Anagogical Meaning*. Pace UP, 1989.

Samek-Ludovici, Sergio, and Nino Ravenna, editors. *Illuminated Manuscripts: Dante's Divine Comedy Fifteenth-Century Manuscript*. Crescent Books, 1979.

Sample, Mark. "Pedagogy and the Class Blog." *Samplereality*, 14 Aug. 2009, www .samplereality.com/2009/08/14/pedagogy-and-the-class-blog/. Accessed 28 May 2018.

Sanguineti, Edoardo. *Dante reazionario*. Riuniti, 1992.

Santagata, Marco. *Dante: The Story of His Life*. Translated by Richard Dixon, Harvard UP, 2016.

Santangelo, Salvatore. *Dante e i trovatori provenzali*. Giannotta, 1921.

Savino, Giancarlo. "L'autografo virtuale della *Commedia*." *"Per correr miglior acque . . .": Bilanci e prospettive degli studi danteschi alle soglie del nuovo millennio: Atti del*

Convegno internazionale di Verona–Ravenna 25–29 ottobre 1999, edited by Lucia Battaglia Ricci, vol. 2, Salerno, 2001, pp. 1099–110.

Sayers, Dorothy L. Introduction. *The Comedy of Dante Alighieri the Florentine: I: Hell; II: Purgatory*, pp. 9–66.

Schaik, Martin van. *The Harp in the Middle Ages: The Symbolism of a Musical Instrument*. Rodopi, 1992.

Schildgen, Brenda Deen, editor. "Cluster on Teaching Dante's *Divine Comedy* Vertically." *Pedagogy*, vol. 17, no. 3, 2017, pp. 449–512.

———. "Dante and the Bengali Renaissance." Audeh and Havely, pp. 323–38.

———. *Dante and the Orient*. U of Illinois P, 2002.

———. "Dante in India: Sri Aurobindo and *Savitri*." *Dante Studies*, vol. 120, 2002, pp. 83–98.

———. Introduction. Schildgen, "Cluster," pp. 449–56.

———. "Philosophers, Theologians, and the Islamic Legacy in Dante: *Inferno* 4 versus *Paradiso* 4." Ziolkowski, *Islam*, pp. 95–113.

Schnapp, Jeffrey T. *The Transfiguration of History at the Center of Dante's Paradise*. Princeton UP, 1986.

Schultz, James A. *Courtly Love, the Love of Courtliness, and the History of Sexuality*. U of Chicago P, 2006.

Schulze Altcappenberg, Hein-Th. *Sandro Botticelli: The Drawings for Dante's Divine Comedy*. Royal Academy of Arts, 2000.

Scott, John A. *Dante's Political Purgatory*. U of Pennsylvania P, 1996.

———. *Understanding Dante*. U of Notre Dame P, 2004.

Sedgwick, Eve Kosofsky. *Epistemology of the Closet*. U of California P, 1990.

Sesini, Ugo. *Le melodie trobadoriche nel canzoniere provenzale della Biblioteca Ambrosiana (R.71 sup.)*. Chiantore, 1942.

Shakespeare, William. *The Tempest*. Edited by Peter Holland, Penguin, 1999.

Shapiro, Marianne. *Dante and the Knot of Body and Soul*, St. Martin's Press, 1998.

———. *Woman Earthly and Divine in the Comedy of Dante*. U of Kentucky P, 1975.

Shaw, Prue. *Reading Dante: From Here to Eternity*. Liveright, 2014.

Shelby, Lon R. "Geometry." Wagner, *Seven*, pp. 196–217.

Shirky, Clay. "It's Not Information Overload: It's Filter Failure." Web 2.0 Expo, New York, 18 Sept. 2008. *YouTube*, www.youtube.com/watch?v=LabqeJEOQyI. Accessed 1 June 2018.

Singleton, Charles S. *Dante Studies 1: Commedia: Elements of Structure*. Harvard UP, 1954.

———. *Dante Studies 2: Journey to Beatrice*. Harvard UP, 1958.

———. *An Essay on the Vita Nuova*. Harvard UP, 1949.

Slade, Carole, editor. *Approaches to Teaching Dante's Divine Comedy*. The Modern Language Association of America, 1982.

Smalley, Beryl. *The Study of the Bible in the Middle Ages*. 2nd ed., U of Notre Dame P, 1964.

Smith, Nathaniel B. "Arnaut Daniel in the *Purgatorio*: Dante's Ambivalence toward Provençal." *Dante Studies*, vol. 98, 1980, pp. 99–109.

Solnit, Rebecca. "Check Out the Parking Lot." Review of *Dante's* Inferno, by Sandow Birk and Marcus Sanders. *London Review of Books*, vol. 26, no. 13, 8 July 2004, pp. 32–33, www.lrb.co.uk/v26/n13/rebecca-solnit/check-out-the-parking-lot. Accessed 22 July 2016.

Sophocles. *The Three Theban Plays*. Translated by Robert Fagles, introduction and notes by Bernard Knox, Penguin, 1984.

Southern, R. W. *Western Views of Islam in the Middle Ages*. Harvard UP, 1962.

Sowell, Madison U., editor. *Dante and Ovid: Essays in Intertextuality*. Medieval and Renaissance Texts and Studies, 1991.

———. "'Quanto si convenia a tanto uccello' (*Inf.* 34.47): Dante's Satan as Winged Phallus." Alfie and Dini, pp. 169–81.

———. "'Substantial, Verbatim, (Un)Attributed, Misleading'? A Review Article on the Doubleday Dante (2007)." *Lingua Romana*, vol. 6, no. 1, Fall 2007, linguaromana .byu.edu/?s=Madison+U.+Sowell. Accessed 28 May 2018.

Squire, Kurt. *Video Games and Learning: Teaching and Participatory Culture in the Digital Age*. Teachers College Press, 2011.

Stagnino, Bernardino (Bernardino Giolito de' Ferrari da Trino), printer. *Opere del divino poeta Danthe con suoi comenti: Recorrecti et con ogni diligentia novamente in littera cursiva impresse*. Venice, 1512.

Stavreva, Kirilka, editor. "Cluster on Multidisciplinary Approaches to Teaching Dante's *Commedia*." *Pedagogy*, vol. 13, no. 1, 2013, pp. 43–144.

Steenberghen, Fernand van. *Maître Siger de Brabant*. Publications Universitaires, 1977. Philosophes médievaux 21.

Steinberg, Justin. *Dante and the Limits of the Law*. U of Chicago P, 2013.

Steinkuhler, Constance, et al., editors. *Games, Learning, and Society: Learning and Meaning in the Digital Age*. Cambridge UP, 2012.

Stephens, Walter, editor. *Tra Amici: Essays in Honor of Giuseppe Mazzotta*. MLN, vol. 127, no. 1, supplement, 2012.

Stewart, Dana E., and Alison Cornish, editors. *Sparks and Seeds: Medieval Literature and Its Aftermath: Essays in Honor of John Freccero*. Brepols, 2000.

Stone, Gregory B. *Dante's Pluralism and the Islamic Philosophy of Religion*. Palgrave Macmillan, 2006.

Storey, H. Wayne. "Method, History, and Theory in Material Philology." *Neo-Latin Philology: Old Tradition, New Approaches: Proceedings of a Conference held at the Radboud University, Nijmegen, 26–27 October 2010*, edited by Marc Van der Poel, Leuven UP, 2014, pp. 25–47.

———. "The Missing Picture in the Text of Escorial e. III. 23." *Italiana*, no. 1, 1988, pp. 59–75. Reprinted as "Guittone's Last Booklet: The Visual-Semantic Orientation of the *Trattato d'amore* in MS Escorial e. III. 23," *Transcription and Visual Poetics in the Early Italian Lyric*, by Storey, Garland, 1993, pp. 171–92.

Straet, Jan van der (Stradanus). *Discovery of America: Vespucci Landing in America*. 1587–89. The Metropolitan Museum of Art, New York, metmuseum.org/art/collection/search/343845. Accessed 16 Apr. 2019.

Straub, Julia. Syllabus for Dante in Victorian Literature. University of Basel, 2015.

———. A Victorian Muse: The Afterlife of Dante's Beatrice in Nineteenth-Century Literature. Continuum, 2009.

Strohm, Reinhard, and Bonnie J. Blackburn, editors. Music as Concept and Practice in the Late Middle Ages. Oxford UP, 2001.

Styron, William. Darkness Visible: A Memoir of Madness. Vintage Books, 1990.

Sullivan, Frank A., SJ. Salvation Outside the Church? Tracing the History of the Catholic Response. Paulist Press, 1992.

Swing, T. K. The Fragile Leaves of the Sibyl: Dante's Master Plan. Newman Press, 1962.

Takayama, Hiroshi. "Law and Monarchy in the South." Abulafia, pp. 58–81.

Taylor, Charles H., and Patricia Finley. Images of the Journey in Dante's Divine Comedy. Yale UP, 1997.

Tchaikovsky, Pyotr Ilyich. Francesca da Rimini. Op. 32, 1876. Musopen.org, musopen .org/sheetmusic/2176/pyotr-ilyich-tchaikovsky/francesca-da-rimini-op32/.

"Tenth Circle Added to Rapidly Expanding Hell." The Onion, 23 Sept. 1998, www .theonion.com/article/tenth-circle-added-to-rapidly-growing-hell-507. Accessed 23 July 2016.

Todorović, Jelena. Dante and the Dynamics of Textual Exchange: Authorship, Manuscript Culture, and the Making of the Vita nova. Fordham UP, 2016.

Took, John. Dante: Lyric Poet and Philosopher: An Introduction to the Minor Works. Oxford UP, 1990.

Torrens, James, SJ. Presenting Paradise: Dante's Paradise: Translation and Commentary. U of Scranton P, 1993.

Towsen, Nat. "The Nine NEW Levels of Hell." College Humor, 22 Apr. 2014, www .collegehumor.com/post/6966006/the-9-new-levels-of-hell. Accessed 23 July 2016.

Toynbee, Paget J. Dante in English Literature, from Chaucer to Cary (C. 1380–1844). Methuen, 1999. 2 vols.

———. A Dictionary of Proper Names and Notable Matters in the Works of Dante. 1898. Revised ed. by Charles S. Singleton, Oxford UP, 1968.

Traub, Valerie. The Renaissance of Lesbianism in Early Modern England. Cambridge UP, 2002.

Ullmann, W. "The Bible and Principles of Government in the Middle Ages." La Bibbia nell'Alto Medioevo, Atti della X settimana del CISAM, Spoleto, 26 aprile–2 maggio 1962. Presso la Sede del Centro, 1963, pp. 181–227.

Vatican Latino MS 3793. Italian lyric poetry. Biblioteca Apostolica Vaticana, digi .vatlib.it/view/MSS_Vat.lat.3793. Accessed 16 Apr. 2019.

Vatican Latino MS 5232. Old Provençal troubadour lyrics. Biblioteca Apostolica Vaticana, digi.vatlib.it/view/MSS_Vat.lat.5232. Accessed 16 Apr. 2019.

Vergilius Romanus. Vatican Latino MS 3867. Biblioteca Apostolica Vaticana, digi.vatlib .it/view/MSS_Vat.lat.3867. Accessed 16 Apr. 2019.

Villani, Giovanni. Nuova cronica. Edited by Giuseppe Porta, Guanda, 1990. 3 vols.

Virgil. Aeneid: Book IX. Edited by Philip Hardie, Cambridge UP, 1994.

———. Eclogues, Georgics, Aeneid: *Books 1–6*; Aeneid: *Books 7–12, Appendix Vergiliana*. Translated by H. Rushton Fairclough, Harvard UP, 1916–18. 2 vols.

Volkmann, Ludwig. *Iconografia Dantesca: The Pictorial Representations to Dante's Divine Comedy*. Grevel, 1899.

Vossler, Karl. *Mediaeval Culture: An Introduction to Dante and His Times*. Translated by William Cranston Lawton, Harcourt Brace, 1929. 2 vols.

Wagner, David L. "The Seven Liberal Arts and Classical Scholarship." Wagner, *Seven*, pp. 1–31.

———, editor. *The Seven Liberal Arts in the Middle Ages*. Indiana UP, 1983.

Walker, Paul. "On Identifying and Performing the Chants in Dante's *Divine Comedy*." *World of Dante*, www.worldofdante.org/comedy/dante/musicEssay. Accessed 1 June 2018.

Wallace, David, editor. *Beatrice Dolce Memoria, 1290–1990: Essays on the* Vita nuova *and the Beatrice-Dante Relationship*. Special issue of *Texas Studies in Language and Literature*, vol. 32, no. 1, 1990.

———. Course description for After Dante. Department of English, U of Pennsylvania, 2013, www.english.upenn.edu/courses/graduate/2013/spring/engl795.402.

———. "Dante in English." Jacoff, *Cambridge Companion*, 2nd ed., pp. 281–304.

Ward, Catherine C. "Gloria Naylor's *Linden Hills*: A Modern Inferno." *Contemporary Literature*, vol. 28, 1987, pp. 67–81.

Watkins, Mel. "The Circular Driveways of Hell." *The New York Times*, 3 Mar. 1985, nytimes.com/1985/03/03/books/the-circular-driveways-of-hell.html.

Watkins, S. Craig, and Anna Everett. "The Power of Play: The Portrayal and Performance of Race in Video Games." Salen, pp. 141–64.

Weaver, Jane. "College Students Are Avid Gamers." *NBCNews.com*, 6 July 2013, www.nbcnews.com/id/3078424/ns/technology_and_science-games/t/college-students-are-avid-gamers/. Accessed 1 June 2018.

Webb, Heather. *Dante's Persons: An Ethics of the Transhuman*. Oxford UP, 2016.

———. "Postures of Penitence in Dante's *Purgatorio*." *Dante Studies*, vol. 131, 2013, pp. 219–36.

Wetherbee, Winthrop. *The Ancient Flame: Dante and the Poets*. U of Notre Dame P, 2008.

Whalen, Brett Edward. *The Medieval Papacy*. Palgrave Macmillan, 2014.

Whitman, Walt. *Complete Poetry and Collected Prose*. Edited by Justin Kaplan, Viking, 1982.

Wickham, Chris. *Early Medieval Italy: Central Power and Local Authority*. U of Michigan P, 1989.

Wilhelm, James J. *Lyrics of the Middle Ages: An Anthology*. Garland, 1990.

Williams, A. N. "The Theology of the *Comedy*." Jacoff, *Cambridge Companion*, 2nd ed., pp. 201–17.

Williams, Charles. *The Figure of Beatrice: A Study in Dante*. Noonday Press, 1961.

Wlassics, Tibor, editor. *Dante's Divine Comedy: Introductory Readings: Inferno*. Lectura Dantis Virginiana, no. 6, Supplement, 1990.

————, editor. *Dante's* Divine Comedy: *Introductory Readings: Paradiso. Lectura Dantis Virginiana*, nos. 16–17, Supplement, 1995.

————, editor. *Dante's* Divine Comedy: *Introductory Readings: Purgatorio. Lectura Dantis Virginiana*, no. 12, Supplement, 1993.

Wood, David, et al. "The Role of Tutoring in Problem Solving." *Journal of Child Psychology and Psychiatry*, vol. 17, no. 2, 1976, pp. 89–100.

Woodhouse, John, editor. *Dante and Governance*. Oxford UP, 1997.

Wordsworth, William. "The World Is Too Much with Us." *The Seagull Reader: Poems*, edited by Joseph Kelly, 3rd ed., W. W. Norton, 2015, pp. 359–60.

World of Dante, The. U of Virginia, www.worldofdante.org/index.html.

Yamada, Mitsuye. "Desert Run." *Camp Notes and Other Writings*, Rutgers UP, 1998, pp. 1–5. Originally published in *Desert Run: Poems and Stories*, Kitchen Table: Women of Color Press, 1988.

————. "Invisibility Is an Unnatural Disaster: Reflections of an Asian American Woman." *This Bridge Called My Back: Writings by Radical Women of Color*, edited by Cherríe Moraga and Gloria Anzaldúa, Persephone Press, 1981, pp. 35–40.

Yamamoto, Traise. *Masking Selves, Making Subjects: Japanese American Women, Identity, and the Body*. U of California P, 1999.

Yousefzadeh, Mahnaz. *City and Nation in Italian Unification: National Festivals of Dante*. Palgrave Macmillan, 2011.

Zandonai, Riccardo. *Francesca da Rimini*. Op. 4, 1914. imslp.org/wiki/Francesca_da_Rimini,_Op.4_(Zandonai,_Riccardo).

Ziolkowski, Jan M., editor. *Dante and Islam*. Fordham UP, 2015. Originally published as an issue of *Dante Studies*, vol. 125, 2007.

————. *Dante and the Greeks*. Dumbarton Oaks, 2014.